James Hervey: Preacher of Righteousness

# James Hervey:

*Preacher of Righteousness*

**26 February 1714 - 25 December 1758**

George M. Ella

**Go** *publications*

Go Publications
The Cairn, Hill Top, Eggleston, Co. Durham, DL12 0AU, ENGLAND.


© Go Publications 1997
First Published 1997


British Library Cataloguing in Publication Data available


ISBN 0 9527 074 2 X

*Printed and bound in Great Britain by*
*Creative Print & Design Group (Wales), Ebbw Vale*

# Dedication

This book is dedicated to the pastors, teachers, administrators, employees and nigh two thousand members of Emmanuel Baptist Church, Enid, Oklahoma. My fellowship with this group of believers and the privilege of sitting under their pastor's ministry has proved beyond doubt to me that the Spirit still moves mightily where New Testament doctrines and preaching are upheld. I count it one of the greatest privileges of my life to have witnessed, as Bunyan, such a Palace Beautiful where Prudence, Piety and Charity are ever ready to refresh weary pilgrims.

My love to all the family and my deep gratitude goes out to you all for enabling me to present this, my own Christian testimony, to our readers.

# Table of Contents

# A Tribute to James Hervey

Mr. Hervey had great experience of God's love to him, and therefore his heart was full of love to God; and out of that abundance of his heart, his mouth spake. There was such a sweetness of heart-love upon his tongue that he used to speak of the love of the adorable Redeemer like one who had seen him face to face in the fulness of his glory. He would, with all the power of language, and dignity of sentiment, speak for a long time to-gether, in praise of the ever-blessed Saviour. But you might plainly see, though every body else was pleased, yet he was not satisfied with what he had said. He thought he had not said enough, and what he had said fell far below his Lord's merit. But still he would try again, and indeed was never weary. You could not hear him speak for any time upon this his favourite subject, without being convinced that he felt what he said; and if you had any love of God, when you went into his company, his conversation would enflame it. He had an excellency, which I never saw to so great a degree in any person. He never let an opportunity slip of speaking of the love of Christ. He would take occasion from the most common incident, and yet it would not appear forced: for he had a wonderful talent at spiritualizing and improving whatever happened about him; by which means, he hin-dered the conversation from turning upon trivial matters, and at the same time, kept it up with spirit and usefulness. Having set the Lord always before him, he saw the love of God in everything; and therefore it is not to be wondered that all objects and events should give him occasion to speak of it. In his last sickness, it continued still to be his favourite theme; for whenever my friend, who was much with him, came into the room, he would begin to talk of the love of Christ, and of the great things which Christ hath done for him, until his breath failed him; and as soon as he had recovered himself a little, he would proceed upon the same sweet subject:

so that he might have truly applied to himself the words of the prophet,
'My mouth shall be telling of thy righteousness and of thy salvation all the
day long; for I know no end thereof.'

William Romaine

# Foreword

It is both a privilege and a pleasure to accede to the author's request to contribute a foreword to this book.

Dr. Ella has provided us with an exhaustive treatment of his subject, the result of much research and patient labour. He covers a vast field revealing his wide reading and interests. Here the reader will find a mine of information apart from the main subject.

It was whilst a student for the ministry that I read Bishop Ryle's 'Christian Leaders' and was thus first introduced to James Hervey. I have always been grateful for that introduction to this humble servant of God who lived in obscurity yet exercised a powerful ministry. Apart form Ryle's essays, I have come across very little over the years relating to Hervey. This book then fulfils a real need and will serve to bring Hervey before the present generation. Sadly, he is little known even amongst professed evangelicals. A sense of history is something to be prized and appreciated yet possessed by comparatively few.

Hervey was one of God's special witnesses to the truths of the gospel in his day and a powerful advocate of the doctrines of grace. He spent most of his ministry in a quiet secluded parish yet living through quite stirring times. His frail state of health did not permit him to engage in itinerant work. He hardly stirred beyond the confines of his parish, yet the Lord greatly honoured and used his testimony.

The subject of this book was undoubtedly an eminent literary man who used his pen to advantage having great influence amongst the cultured classes. He was, as one writer states, 'able to translate his message into jargon of the genteel world.' Not a few were brought to saving faith and others were fully instructed in the Scriptures through his faithful ministry.

James Hervey's forthright views have sometimes been misunderstood but he was not a controversialist as such. Indeed, he wrote, 'Controversy

is what I naturally dislike, and what I have seldom found advantageous.'
His sole aim was to declare the whole counsel of God without fear or
favour. His great love for Christ and the souls of men is evident for all to
see in his writings. He was a man with a burning heart who fanned the
flames of devotion in others. At times, he reminds us of Samuel Rutherford
the Covenanting divine. Writing to one of his correspondents, Hervey says,
'I am glad that the beloved Traveller called at your home and gave you so
much of His company. Cold as the weather is, did not your heart burn
within you?' The reference here is to the Lord Jesus Christ and the journey to Emmaus on the day of the resurrection (Luke 24:32). Hervey's sole
aim in preaching and writing was 'to recommend his dear Redeemer.'
Even on the day of his death, although in great pain, he persisted in exhorting his doctor to attend to his eternal welfare — 'you tell me I have a
few moments to live. O let me spend them in adoring our great Redeemer.'
It has been rightly said that few lives have ever been more heavenly and
few deaths more triumphant.

    May this book reach a wide circle of readers and prove both stimulat-
ing and informative.

Maurice Handford
Editor of the *Gospel Magazine*

# Introduction:
# The Country Parson in the
# Eighteenth Century

**Passing rich with forty pounds a year**

One can hardly imagine a figure more isolated from his kind than that
of the country parson in the eighteenth century. His flock was small and
scattered and composed often of the landless poor. After the enclosures
system was introduced, these under-privileged swains had to work their
fingers to the bone for the far off Lord of the Manor who had bought up
most of the free-hold land, or serve the local yeoman or the Squire who
were still in a financial position to keep their inheritance. The poor parishioners were up at dawn to do the milking and employed during the day
with sowing, reaping or hay-making as the season demanded. There were
also chores such as hurdle-making, hedging, mucking-out, tool sharpen-
ing, threshing and the evening milking to keep them busy until well into
the dark night. In the few candle-lit hours they had to spare, they eked out
their humble livelihood by working at the loom or doing lace work for a
pittance. No matter how thrifty they were, they could not thrive and the
gap between the poor and the pauper was the price of a candle stump.

Socially speaking, the country parson was not part of this picture in
any way. He was usually one of the younger sons of a nobleman or gentleman who had invested his land and his money in his elder sons. The first
son invariably inherited the title and land, the second was given enough
money from his *pater* to pay for his public school education and find him
a place at the Inns of Court or in Government. The younger sons may or
may not have been sent to Westminster, Eton or Felstead and later the
Church was thought good enough for them. Daughters were married off to
the highest bidder and so were no problem at all. This meant that the
country parson could be no better off than his impoverished parishioners,
and this was often the case. Goldsmith's village preacher might have been

'passing rich with forty pounds a year' but there were many country and even town clergy that would have been thankful for half that amount.

## Relief systems for poor parsons

There were, however, several traditional institutions which came to the poor parson's assistance. These would provide him with a church, a vicarage, land and even financial aid. The first was the Vestry; a system of parish rates whereby moneys were levied for the upkeep of the church fabric and pews. Out of this fund the church warden, the parish beadle and the bell-ringers were paid and the parson was able to purchase his canonicals with the tax money. The parson's own pocket was eased by scot[1] money which was raised for the poor and for those who had served the Parish in any special way. If there was money to spare raised in this way, schools for both boys and girls were set up with the parish funds. The very poor of the parish did not need to pay such taxes and so they were said to 'get off scot free', which was the origin of the modern expression meaning not to be punished for a misdemeanour.

Another system of relief for country parsons was that of livings or patronages. A Bishop, a Lord or even the King would appoint certain clergymen to certain churches or glebelands which were financed by moneys donated and accrued for this purpose. Such livings in the early eighteenth century were 'worth' anything from £12 a year to several thousands. Other livings were financed by rich merchants, businessmen or bankers such as the Thorntons, Lord Dartmouth or Lord Carrington. Often the clergymen who were happy enough to take on such a 'living' found that they were but a slave of the man with the money and treated as such. John Newton fared well under the patronage of John Thornton but his young friend Thomas Jones[2] had a rough time working for Lord Peterborough's pay.

## Pluralism in plenty

The custom of granting livings and patronages was often misused so that bishops gave parishes to clergymen in their favour as sinecure posts to make sure that their income was raised. More than a few bishops also secured as many parishes as possible for themselves in order to supplement their own income. Often these livings were many miles away from one another and made it impossible for a clergyman to visit his flock. This gave rise to the notorious absentee vicars who sub-managed their parishes through low-paid curates. Thus Thomas Scott's vicar in Olney, Moses

---

[1]    From the Old Scandinavian 'skot' meaning 'tax' or 'treasure'. See also modern Swedish 'skat'.

[2]    Thomas Jones of Clifton, expelled from Oxford in 1768 for holding Methodist views. Not Hervey's friend, Thomas Jones of Southwark.

Brown[1], hardly ever visited the lace-making town but carried out his ministerial duties miles away as Chaplain to Morden College. He refused to give up Olney as he maintained that he would not otherwise receive enough income to look after his wife and thirteen children. Scott himself was only too aware of the financial perks available for 'pluralistic parsons' as they came to be known. In 1781 he bargained hard with his bishop, vicar and patron for the curacy of the Olney Church arguing that he should keep his former country curacies at Ravenstone and Weston because of the income involved. Perhaps the most famous, if not notorious, pluralistic country parson was Bishop Richard Watson (1737-1816) of Llandaff[2], one time Professor of Chemistry, Professor of Theology and Westmorland farmer. Besides the large income from his farm and books, the good bishop received sinecure salaries from two parishes in Shropshire, a further two in Leicestershire, two on the Isle of Ely, three in Huntingdonshire and no less than seven in Wales. It may come as a surprise to modern evangelicals that Brown, Scott and Watson were Evangelicals and contributed greatly in their various writings and preaching to the spread of the Gospel throughout the eighteenth century.

**Tithing or 'The Yearly Distress'**

Another custom during the eighteenth century was for clergymen of the Church of England such as Samuel Wesley, the father of John and Charles, to be part-time farmers. This was based on the age-old tradition of tithing which was looked upon as a law by both the ecclesiastical and secular authorities. Members of the parish had formerly been asked to donate a tenth of their income or produce to the service of the Church but after the tenth century this was regarded as a compulsion with stiff penalties for those who failed to pay. By the eighteenth century, protest against this practice was widespread and many clergymen found themselves burdened by lengthy court proceedings in their endeavours to obtain their supposed rights. Often parsons seemed to spend most of their time spying on their neighbours in order to work out what they could afford to pay. As most countrymen had little capital and bargained in kind, the tithes they paid their clergy were usually in the form of a sack of corn or a piglet or two. Whether they liked it or not, many clergymen were thus forced to be part-time farmers to look after the animals they received so that they could make some sort of a profit out of them and turn them into cash. Often the tithes were more or less the only source of food for the vicar, his large family and his livestock so at tithing time the clergyman's wife and any

---

[1]    Brown (often spelt Browne) was formally James Hervey's curate.

[2]    Not to be confused with Richard Watson (1781-1833) Secretary of the Wesleyan Missionary Society.

servants were kept very busy roasting malt, brewing beer and cider, baking bread, salting beans and curing bacon. The Vicar and his farmhands would stack the hay and straw for winter fodder and bedding for his animals.

The Vicar would give a dinner for his parishioners once a year, usually composed of roast beef, plum pudding and a pot of ale. The tenant farmers and country folk would then arrive one after the other with their tithes of money, animals or grain, often equipped with either lengthy excuses why they could not bring more or promises of what they would do providing future harvests were better. They would then make themselves comfortable around the Vicar's fire, toasting their toes and spinning yarns of days of yore.

One of the earliest poems of William Cowper, *The Yearly Distress*, was in support of his friend William Cawthorn Unwin (1744-1786), an evangelical pastor who never had difficulty in filling his house with farmers for the annual dinner but always had difficulty in extracting tithes from them because of their various excuses. Cowper, who was against this kind of payment, first describes the boorish manners of the guests at table and then describes the 'busy time' i.e. the business part of the evening:

At length the busy time begins,
Come neighbours we must wag—
The money chinks, down drop their chins
Each lugging out his bag.

One talks of mildew and of frost,
And one of storms of hail,
And one, of pigs that he has lost
By maggots at the tail.

Quoth one, a rarer man than you
In pulpit none shall hear,
But yet, methinks, to tell you true,
You sell it plaguy dear.

Oh why are farmers made so coarse.
Or clergy made so fine,
A kick that scarce would move a Horse,
May kill a sound divine.

Then let the Boobies stay at home,
'Twould cost him, I dare say,
Less trouble taking twice the sum,
Without the clowns that pay.

William Unwin was a pluralist who took great care of the two small parishes he served and could not be criticised for neglecting his sheep who loved him. Other clergymen fared less well. The records at Epworth in Lincolnshire show how Samuel Wesley's parishioners tried to cheat him out of his tithes by extreme means and how out of sheer jealousy, they hamstrung his cattle and were most likely guilty of setting the Vicarage on fire. As funds were not forthcoming from the traditional sources, Samuel Wesley had to experience the damp cold of a debtors' prison, forcing his wife Susannah and her nineteen children to fend for themselves. History shows that Susanna did not make a bad job of it owing to her self-discipline, the discipline that she meted out to her children, and their joint trust in God.

It was into this kind of country pastoral life that James Hervey was born. His father was a non-resident rector and pluralist, who served the parishes of Weston-Favell and Collingtree but lived in Hardingstone, not far from Northampton where he farmed a moderate-sized piece of land under his own patronage. However, he lived only two miles away from his rectorship on a total income of no more than £180 per annum from which he had to pay at least one curate and sometimes two. As he preached regularly in his churches to devoted congregations, we can conclude that he was more of the William Unwin kind than the fiery-tempered Samuel Wesley or the affluent, though bucolic, Bishop of Llandaff. Hervey took over the livings after his father's death and became a country parson with a difference, transforming the spiritual state of the countryside around Northampton as thoroughly as Baxter had transformed Kidderminster a century before.

Although the country parson has been highly caricaturised, Oliver Goldsmith's account of him in *The Deserted Village*, based on childhood memories from the time of James Hervey, shows that there were also fine men who filled such posts. Indeed Goldsmith's *Village Preacher* is a telling pen-portrait of the subject of our book:

Beside the bed where parting life was laid,
And sorrow, guilt and pain, by turns dismay'd,
The reverend champion stood. At his control.
Despair and Anguish fled the struggling soul;
Comfort came down the trembling wretch to raise,
And his last falt'ring accents whispered praise.

At church, with meek and unaffected grace,
His looks adorn'd the venerable place;
Truth from his lips prevail'd with double sway,
And fools, who came to scoff, remain'd to pray.

The service pass'd, around the pious man,
With steady zeal, each honest rustic ran;
Even children follow'd with endearing wile,
And pluck'd his gown, to share the good man's smile.

His ready smile a parent's warmth express'd,
Their welfare pleas'd him, and their cares distress'd;
To them his heart, his love, his griefs were given,
But all his serious thoughts had rest in Heaven.
As some tall cliff, that lifts its awful form,
Swells from the vale, and midway leaves the storm,
Though round its breast the rolling clouds are spread,
Eternal sunshine settles on its head.

# Chapter One:
# Hervey's Early Life and Education

## Horn book days

The subject of our biography was born in the country village of Hardingstone on February 26, 1713. We know very little of his family background apart from the fact that his mother was young James's private tutor until he reached seven years of age. Under his mother's care, Hervey learnt to read and write according to the usual methods of the early eighteenth century. This was by means of a so-called horn book, a sheet of paper with either the Lord's Prayer, a Bible story or one of Æsop's fables printed on it, covered with a sheet of transparent horn for protection. The method of teaching is known today as the 'story' method and its history is of great interest. The aim of educationalists in the early 1700s was to equip children to become God's stewards on earth and as such, they should know the Scriptures. They children were taught to read by spelling out and pronouncing Scriptural passages or morally suitable stories.

During the eighteenth century, evolutionary theories of language came into vogue through the writings of Blair and Beattie and the influence of Continental educationalists who followed the philosophy of the so-called Enlightenment. These theories radically changed the methods of teaching children. They maintained that 'primitive man' learnt to speak through first uttering grunts and groans—isolated noises with no definite semantic content, and then, over a period of millions of years, gradually formed these grunts and groans to make sentences or sense units. As a result of this, it was thought that children should be taught to read in the same stages that primitive man learnt to speak and write. From then on children were taught to reflect and imitate this evolution by first learning to read and pronounce basic senseless sounds rather than tackling stories that made sense from the start. The educationalist blandly forgot that children have not a supposed millions of years at their disposal to learn to read a language.

Nevertheless a great variety of teaching methods came into being during the following 200 years which made recognising and pronouncing either a morpheme, a syllable or a single letter the basis of learning to read. That this method was far from ideal is shown by the way these reading theories plagued generations of teachers who had to learn new reading methods every few years. Parents, too, suffered as they were not able to teach their children to read as new generations brought with them new theories of learning and different methods were prevalent in their children's schools to the ones they had learnt. Happily, towards the end of the twentieth century, pedagogues are now finding that the old ways were best, after all, and the story method is, once again, being used all over Europe. The stories, too, have a highly moral flavour, dealing with such topics as environmental protection and love to animals. Perhaps one day, by God's grace, the Scriptures will once again be used and we shall be back to the good old method that Christian mothers taught their children at the beginning of the eighteenth century.

## Marking time at grammar school

When James was seven years of age, his parents decided to send him to the Free Grammar School at Northampton where he was to be prepared for university entrance. The school may have been the best choice at the time, though John Ryland, Hervey's contemporary and biographer, says it was hardly better than a charity school. It was not a school that was capable of fitting out a child for life. The master, a Mr. Clarke, was vicar of St. Sepulchre's Church, Northampton, and knew much Latin and rather less Greek—but apparently little else. The boys were thus taught Latin and Greek conjugations, declensions and paradigms day by day from morn till eve with hardly a variation. John Cowper, William Cowper's younger brother, confessed on his death bed that he had been sent to schools for gentlemen (Dr. Pittman's Old Vicarage and Felstead) but, to his shame, he had only learnt Greek. The famous Dr. Johnson's boast that he learnt 'manly stuff' at school fails to impress us when we find out that apart from the Classics, he had learnt little else. This was all too usual for the education of the age. Trevelyan the historian quotes an adage of the eighteenth century that 'a girl which is educated at home with her mother is wiser at twelve than a boy at sixteen' who has been sent to school. John Wesley looked back with joy and thanksgiving to the early education he had received at the hand of Susannah, his mother but always complained about the limited education he had received at Charterhouses and the bullying that went on there.

Young James loved to learn and made excellent progress in grammar at his new school, soon wishing to go on and read the great classics. This was never to be, however. Mr. Clarke had a son who was the apple of his eye. He was also very dull and slow. His doting father thus decided that none of his pupils should be allowed to advance in learning beyond the stage that his own son had reached. Thus the bright pupils such as James were kept marking time until Clarke junior caught up. Whilst waiting for the slow coach, James found that he had plenty of time to learn games and other childhood pastimes and developed a keen interest in sports of all kinds. Above all, he loved to roam about the countryside, studying the flora and fauna which always awed him almost as much as observing the starry heavens, one of his greatest delights. When Ryland related the story of Hervey's childhood in 1791, shortly before his own home-call, one senses that he, as a teacher and Headmaster, was almost in angry tears at the poverty of Hervey's education. He thus says demonstratively, 'Only stand still, my reader, and consider for a few moments; here is a poor raw boy, kept at the grammar school for ten years, without any person to teach him one scrap of science, or so much as to lead him into the beauties of the classics, not suffered to hear Dr. Doddridge preach the Gospel, though he lived in the same town for several years.'[1] Ryland adds that Mr. Clarke did read the Greek New Testament to his pupils but Hervey told him that his teacher only once commented on the Scriptures read and that was to make a very foolish remark.

### Scholarship holder at Lincoln College

In 1731, when James was 17 years of age, his father realised that he could learn no more at the Grammar School and sent him off to Oxford to further his education. The fact that James had grown into a tall, lanky youth and stood head and shoulders over most of the other pupils, who seemed much younger and more immature than he was, must have helped his father come to a decision as James often told him how embarrassing this was. He thus became a student at Lincoln College and was placed under the tutorship of Richard Hutchins, a clergyman of the Church of England who took his doctorate a few years later and became rector for the years 1755-1781. Though the Herveys were far from poor[2], James' studies were made easier by his receiving a scholarship, or 'exhibition' as it was called at Oxford, of £20 a year, made possible through the kind attention of the Rector of Lincoln, Dr. Eusebius Isham who also showed kindness to Wesley and Whitefield. If, however, young Hervey had thought

---

[1]   *The Character of the Rev. James Hervey, A.M.*, p. 304.

[2]   Ryland always spoke of Hervey as being of most humble birth and just above the poverty line. Though not an affluent man, Hervey's father had a steady income and owned property including tenant houses. It seems that the fact that Hervey was given a grant-in-aid led Ryland to his conclusion. According to an anonymous article in the *Gentleman's Magazine* for Dec. 1760, p. 554, giving evidence provided by the rector of Little Billing who knew Hervey's family well, Hervey Sen. was prepared to keep his son at Oxford at his expense until he obtained his Master's degree.

that he would be given greater opportunities to learn at Oxford than at his old Northampton school, he was soon to be disappointed. It seemed that tutors were employed by the university merely to give the students some idea of the books they were to read and present them with a key to the college library which thus terminated their duties. Hutchins strove to be a little better than the average tutor and introduced Hervey to the Hebrew language besides assisting him to find suitable literature. John Ryland, never too eager to say anything good about Oxford, called James's tutor 'an Egyptian taskmaster' and said that the textbooks that James was given such as the *Westminster Hebrew Grammar* must have been invented by the devil to put people off learning the language of the Old Testament. Ryland, no mean Hebrew scholar himself, adds, however, in his biography of Hervey that his friend very quickly became one of Europe's leading experts in Biblical Hebrew. Nevertheless, on the whole, the learning situation at Oxford in the 1730s was so bad that many students, whose parents could afford it, went up to Oxford accompanied by their own private tutor so that they would be sure to learn something at university. Other, less industrious students, wasted their time spinning yarns like old seamen in the towns numerous taverns and wasted their money by backing cocks that were sure to lose at the numerous cockpits at the disposal of their pockets.

There is a great deal of doubt as to what Hervey actually studied at Oxford owing to the general chaos of studies there but also owing to Hervey's uncertainty as to his future calling. In 1760, a letter to Mr. Urban of the *Gentleman's Magazine*, commenting on a recently published biography of Hervey, argued that he had two thoughts in mind when entering Lincoln. He wished to take over the pluralist patronage of his father and wanted to study civil law. The author then states that after studying civil law for four years, Hervey was informed that should he wish to be ordained in the Church of England, he would have to take a degree in arts and not law, thus Hervey changed his faculty in his final year.[1]

## At Oxford during a time of turmoil

Politically Oxford was a seething pot of revolution though many of the students and most of the lower clergy who were supposed to teach them were conservative to the core. This is because it was the traditional revolutionary party of the Whigs who had ousted the Stuarts and many conservatives, non-jurors and clergy held the opinions of the exiled Francis Atterbury (1662-1732). This Anglican bishop taught that the true successor

---

[1]    See *Gentleman's Magazine*, 1760, vol. xxx, pp. 553-554. Hervey's earliest biographers state that Hervey spent seven years at Oxford but as he was ordained and started work as a curate in 1736, he spent five years in all at the university.

of Queen Anne was the Stuart Pretender James III and that he could be persuaded to take a middle stance between Popery and Latitudinarianism[1] if he were placed on his rightful throne. Thus, though the Stuarts had long been ousted and the Hanoverians were securely on the throne of England when Hervey went up to Oxford, the students' toasts were in honour of James and his clan and not George.

Many Arminian evangelicals still hoped that 'the King across the water' would return and take over the throne of England as they looked upon the politically powerful Whigs as too 'Calvinistic' by far. The story is well-known how Susannah Wesley refused to join in prayers with her husband for the King as she looked upon the Stuarts' successors as mere Regents until James III was enthroned. This may account for the fact that John Wesley, a fellow of Lincoln College whilst Hervey was there, always had a good word for the Stuarts and was full of admiration for Mary Queen of Scots whom he felt had been scandalously dealt with both by the English and Scottish Puritans. This did not mean that Wesley refused to support the Hanoverians. When Rowland Hill preached against British commitments in America, Wesley proved to be a most ardent supporter of the Hanoverian regime and condemned Hill openly. John Clayton, a close friend of Wesley's, was an out and out Jacobite and non-juror. The Whigs called all Jacobites in England 'Frenchmen' and in all their political campaigning stressed that those who opened their hearts to the Stuarts opened their doors to Popery. John Byrom, the Evangelical poet and Jacobite sympathiser, summed up the political confusion in the churches in verse, writing:

> God bless the King, God bless our faith's defender,
> God bless—no harm in blessing—the Pretender;
> But who Pretender is, and who is King,
> God bless us all! that's quite another thing.

Hervey could not have gone up to Oxford at a worse time, spiritually or academically. Though most of the tutors were clergymen, any student seen going to a church service became the laughing stock of the student body, many of whom were planning to become clergymen themselves after leaving university. George Whitefield went up to Oxford in 1732, a year after Hervey, and his biographer, John Gillies records the event by saying that Whitefield 'was exposed to the society of the wicked' there and adds one of his typical dour understatements by saying that 'Scriptural,

---

[1]  The teaching that reason must be appealed to as a source of revelation and authority alongside the Scriptures.

experimental religion was become quite unfashionable.'[1] Balleine opens his *History of the Evangelical Party* by stating that Oxford, intellectually speaking, was going through 'the darkest age in the University history.'

## Ryland on Hervey's education

Of Hervey's education at this time, John Ryland says, 'All the knowledge of this great and good man was carried on and attained by books. Truly speaking, he had no tutors: before he went to college he had none: while he was at college he had none. His nominal tutor taught him nothing, nor were regular lectures to be found in his college; consequently he was left to make his own way, and for a long time that was in the dark. . . . How exceeding defective and erroneous are our public and private schemes of education! or rather, we have no wise and good schemes at all. Every man who sets himself up as a tutor of youth, pursues the dictates of his own wild imagination, and the scholars fare accordingly. But the method of education at our public colleges are beyond description defective and bad. This is displayed in most lively and affecting colours, in the essays of the Rev. Vicesimus Knox.

If we survey our two universities, the beauty and grandeur of the buildings, the pleasantness of the gardens, the shady walks, the pleasant bowers, the public and private libraries, the instituted lectures upon all the liberal arts and sciences, the noble professorships, the large endowments and rich incomes of those colleges, with a thousand other advantages, which I cannot so much as name. Amidst all this profusion of advantages, Hervey had just as much help as though he had been born on the Coast of Guinea, or in the Sandwich Islands; and we have reason to think that thousands of our young men, who reside at the colleges, meet with the same fate. They go thither ignorant of science and divinity, and they come away ignorant as they went. What a most affecting consideration is this! that a young man of so fine a genius and capacity to receive all kinds of instruction, should be so vilely neglected!

I have as great an esteem and veneration for learned and good men at our public colleges, as most persons in the world: they must know that I do not write from a spirit of ill will and bitterness. If the concealing these errors and blemishes in public education would cure them, I would be the first man in the world to keep them secret, but the matter is impossible. The ignorance and insufficiency of our young nobility, and the great defects in the knowledge of divinity in the younger ministers of religion, is visible in every part of Great Britain, and cannot possibly be concealed from the common people in every parish.'[2]

---

[1]   *Memoirs of the Life of the Rev. George Whitefield, M.A.*, Falkirk, 1798, pp. 4-5

[2]   *The Character of the Rev. James Hervey*, pp. 302, 303.

Ryland did not complain in this way because he was a Baptist who had been denied access to the universities. He wrote as the founder of three colleges of national renown and the writer of a large number of school books, readers and primers which were enormously successful in educating young people. Many Anglicans sent their sons to Ryland's colleges at Warwick and Ealing or to the academy of his close friend Philip Doddridge, an Independent minister, at Northampton. They preferred such sound centres of learning for their sons rather than send them to Oxford or Cambridge because they wanted them to grow up to be men and not fops and coxcombs.

Be that as it may, it soon became obvious to Hervey and his fellow freshers that they were starting out on a system of theological education which gave them as little learning and spiritual life as possible and equipped them after doing little or nothing for a varied number of years, with a degree that was awarded without the requirement of a single examination. In fact the state of England's universities was more scandalous than Ryland suggested and degrees at England's two universities could be obtained on payment of a fee. This is why William Huntington, at the end of the century, when asked by mocking critics what degree he had, simply answered 'None because I could never afford to buy one'.

**Nature-study opens Hervey's eyes to book learning and a glimpse of the Creator**

By the grace of God, Hervey had no taste for a life of dissipation and, although he did little study in his first two years at university, he gradually redeveloped his old taste for learning and read more and more avidly. It was Hervey's interest in nature which God used to open his eyes to learning. He had been brought up in the country and was used to expressing himself in terms of country images and examples. Now he discovered Abbé la Pluche's book *Nature Displayed* and was thrilled with its language and subject matter. This caused him to obtain more books on nature and science and soon he was reading Dr. W. Derham's *Astro-Theology* and also his *Physico-Theology*. These works introduced Hervey to the Newtonian way of looking at the world with a synopsis of reason and revelation. They were not, strictly speaking, Biblical or evangelical works but they turned Hervey's mind to the Creator of Heaven and Earth and showed him that it was far from illogical to believe in God.

Subsequent to exploring the flora and fauna of this world in books and learning about the starry heavens which reflected God's glory, Hervey turned to the study of man in Keil's *Anatomy*. Years later John Ryland Sen. said that Hervey knew more about the structure of the human body than any other man he had ever met. The foundation for such a knowledge was laid at Oxford when Hervey found he would have to educate himself as there was no one else to teach him.

After learning as much as he could about the natural sciences and metaphysics, Hervey started to research into his own language. He thus became familiar with Pope and Addison and their efforts to reform language and please the ear as much as they informed the mind. He became especially fond of Spence's *Five Dialogues on Pope's Translation of Homer* as he could compare the original with the translation and the commentator's remarks and thus polish up his own knowledge of the Classics and poetry. After taking all these works into account, it is perhaps no wonder that when Hervey began to use his pen professionally in God's service, it was to preach Scriptural truths through the agency of nature in such a descriptive and musical language that he became widely known as the *prose poet*.

By 1733 Hervey was taking a more serious view of life and eager to reform his soul as well as his mind. In September of that year, the nineteen-year-old wrote to his sister in the expressive nature language for which he became famous, telling her of his feelings about his spiritual state:

> As I was the other day traversing the fields in quest of health, I observed the meads to have lost that profusion of fragrant odours which once perfumed the air—to be disrobed of that rich variety of curious dyes which surpassed even Solomon in all his glory. Not a single flower appears to gladden the sight, to bespangle the ground, or enamel the barren landscape. The clouds that ere long distilled the dews of honey, or poured themselves forth in showers of fatness, now combine in torrents to overflow the lifeless earth, to bury or sweep away all the faint footsteps of ancient beauty. The hills that were crowned with corn, the valleys that laughed and sung under loads of golden grain; in a word, the whole face of nature that so lately rejoiced for the abundance of her plenty, is become bare naked, and disconsolate. As I was continuing my walk, and musing on this joyless scene, methought the sudden chance exhibited a lively picture of our frail and transient state; methought every object that occurred seemed silent to forewarn me of my own future condition.

After confessing how vain life was to his sister, Hervey outlined to her his recently developed thoughts on religion. There was no word about his own unworthiness or sinfulness. He merely wrote in a grand display of self-confidence:

> To walk humbly with our God, dutifully with our parents, and charitably with all, will be an inexhaustible source of never-ceasing comforts ... What sweet complacency, what unspeakable satisfaction shall we reap from the contemplation of an uninterrupted series of spotless actions: No present uneasiness will prompt us impatiently

to wish for dissolution, nor anxious fears for futurity make us immoderately dread the impending stroke; all will be calm, easy, and serene; all will be soothed by this precious, this invaluable thought, that, by reason of the meekness, the innocence, the purity, and other Christian graces which adorned the several stages of our progress through the world, our names and our ashes will be embalmed, the chambers of our tomb consecrated into a paradise of rest, and our souls, white as our locks, by an easy transition, become angels of light.

These are serious thoughts indeed for one who was still in his teens and had yet experienced little of the world. But worldly thoughts they still are as young Hervey proudly believed that his immaculate character would earn him God's 'well done' and a home in Heaven as an 'angel of light'.

### A desire to be right with God engendered
From now on Hervey was to do his level best to prove that he was right with God. He began to take communion every Sunday and look around for fellow students who were tired of indolence and wished to live to more purpose. He did not have to search long and soon found friends both at Oxford and at Weston-Favell who were to assist him in radically changing his life and help him on his way to becoming a shining light in the cause of the Gospel. His new tutor and friend at Oxford was the Rev. John Wesley who, like Hervey, was still waiting for the shackles of sin to be removed so that he might become a new creature in Christ Jesus. Hervey's friend at Weston Favell, Risdon Darracott, proved to be a more immediate help as he had already found Christ through the ministry of Dr. Doddridge[1]. This young man soared up like a brilliant rocket in his early career for the Lord but burnt himself out in that work and died whilst still quite young. The first friend, however, to shake fundamentally Hervey's legal trust in his

---

[1]    Dr. Philip Doddridge (1702-1751), non-conformist leader who spent most of his short adult life in the Northampton area, training young ministers and working hard so that the 'dipped and sprinkled' in the Dissenting churches could live in peace. His most well-known writings are *The Rise and Progress of Religion in the Soul* and his biographical work on Col. James Gardiner. Doddridge is supposed to have pioneered a 'middle way' between Calvinism and Arminianism and has been accused of confused thinking in his doctrines, especially concerning the atonement and the Trinity. The confusion, however, was mostly in the theology of Doddridge's biographers who, in emphasising his liberality to others, have concluded that this was based on a liberal theology. Doddridge's friends such as George Whitefield, James Hervey and John Ryland, certainly felt one at heart and Christian commitment with Doddridge who broke with the leading men of his own denomination, such as Isaac Watts, to support friends of the Awakening. Though it has been pointed out in criticism that a number of Doddridge's students were Arians, it must also be stated that a number of the calibre of Risdon Darracott were pioneers of the Revival work.

own righteousness was not a university man by any means but an unlettered ploughman. Often free-churchmen sadly record that their churches stood by and watched as the Evangelical Awakening spread like a holy fire throughout the highways and bye-ways of Britain, fanned by such Anglican stalwarts as Hervey, Whitefield, Newton, Cowper, Toplady, Conyers, Romaine and Venn. If the church historian Balleine, however, is correct in declaring that James Hervey pastored the first Evangelical parish in the Midlands, it is only because an unnamed and unknown humble land-worker, a member of Dr. Doddridge's Dissenting church, pointed Hervey away from thoughts of his own righteousness so that he might find acceptance with God through the righteousness of Christ. That time was still to come. Meanwhile, Hervey was to wade through the slough of despond, seeking to find solid ground and save his own soul through his own righteous works. A most futile task!

# Chapter Two:
# The Holy Club

**Clubs galore!**

The eighteenth century was a time of 'republican organisations'. The word 'republican' used in this connection had really nothing to do with national politics but was used in the sense of 'democratic' or 'of the people'. Up to this period in history most organisations in England had been strictly hierarchical and were mostly of an ecclesiastical or political kind. Slowly but surely, social clubs of one kind or another came into existence uniting like-minded people in a common cause. Thus we find hunting clubs springing up, various sporting clubs and even drinking clubs. Evangelicals by no means stayed aloof to the more sensible of these organisations. William Cowper, the hymn-writer, could not imagine why a group of grown men could club together with the sole purpose of chasing a poor fox around the countryside in the name of sport, but he attended the meetings of the notorious Robin Hood Society and was the President of the Nonsense Club as an unconverted man, and a member of the Olney Archers for many years after conversion. Legh Richmond, well-known for his *Dairyman's Daughter* and other evangelical tracts organised friendly societies and insurance clubs for the poor and did a great reforming work in doing so. The famous Clapham Sect, with Wilberforce at its head, was a typical eighteenth century club as was Alexander Pope's Scriblerus Club. It was in the final years of the seventeenth century and throughout the whole of the eighteenth century that great clubs and institutions were founded such as the Society for Promoting Christian Knowledge, the Society for the Propagation of the Gospel in Foreign Parts, the Religious Tract Society, the Eclectic Society, the Society for the Abolition of Slavery, the Church Missionary Society and the Baptist Missionary Society. It is a great tribute to the outworking of the Evangelical Revival that most of these important societies were founded by evangelicals.

We can thus understand the social atmosphere which prevailed in early eighteenth century Oxford. What the university lacked in organised lectures and seminars, the students gained in organised institutions, paving the way for student unions and the welfare institutions of later years. There were, in fact, as many clubs at Oxford as the imagination allowed. The colleges themselves, of course, were clubs of a kind, based on the French pattern, and the students widened their functions by forming poetical societies, debating societies and clubs designed to promote the reading of Classical literature, to mention the more serious student organisations. For students of a less serious bent, there was the Amorous Club as well as the various drinking and sporting clubs. As organised sport had no place on the lean university curriculum, football and the newly developing game of cricket were practised in social clubs.

### The 'little company' of seriously minded men

Two or three years before Hervey went up to Oxford, three earnest young men had formed a club to suit their own desire to live a sober, scholarly life and be of permanent use to society at large. These men were Charles Wesley, William Morgan of Christ Church and Robert Kirkham of Merton College. A year later they were joined by John Wesley who was already a graduate of Oxford and, after two years as his father's curate, returned to Oxford as a Fellow and tutor.[1]

This newly formed fellowship was called simply 'our little company' at first but received several unflattering names from its critics. The name which stuck the most was 'the Holy Club' as many students felt that its members showed strong signs of religious snobbery. The members themselves gradually adopted this name feeling it best described their status and flattered their own opinion of themselves. The Holy Club was one of the most insignificant number-wise of all the clubs in the University, never boasting more than between five and fifteen members, including associates, at one time. Nor was the club particularly religious at first. The members met together simply to read the Classics during the week and a 'book of Divinity' on Sundays.[2] Hervey and Whitefield[3] joined the club some time in 1733.

---

[1]     In his *Short History of Methodism*, Wesley puts himself at the head of the list of founder members which he re-dates to the time of his return to Oxford. He has been considered *the* founder by most Wesleyans ever since. *Wesley's Works*, Conference Office, 1810, vol. VI, p. 402.

[2]     *Introductory Letter*, *The Works of the Rev. John Wesley, A.M.*, John Mason, 1829, vol. i

[3]     *Wesley's Works*, Conference Office, 1810, vol. VI, p. 402. Wesley states in his *Short History* that Whitefield did not join the Holy Club until 1735., i.e. the year the Wesleys left England for Georgia! This is quite contrary to the evidence which gives Whitefield a far greater role in the procedures of the Holy Club than John Wesley was at times ready to admit. See *George Whitefield*, Arnold Dallimore, Banner of Truth Trust, 1970 for a detailed account of Whitefield's actions at Oxford.

Perhaps more myths have been brooded, hatched and bred concerning the Holy Club than any other eighteenth century institution. Many a church historian has looked upon the club as fostering the Evangelical Revival in Britain and the Great Awakening in the American colonies and the new Republic.[1] Indeed J. S. Reynolds in his book *The Evangelicals at Oxford*, gives Oxford as the source of the Revival and 1735 as the date of its genesis. Actually these revivals had their roots in the previous century with the spread of evangelical awareness on the Continent of Europe, as also in Britain and the New World. Pioneers of the eighteenth century work such as Cotton Mather and the Tennents in North America, Theodor Untereyck and Theodor J. Frelinghuysen of Rhineland[2], Samuel Walker, George Thomson and William Romaine in England, the Erskines in Scotland and Griffith Jones, Daniel Rowland and Howell Harris of Wales had never anything to do with the Holy Club. Frelinghuysen, in particular, had evangelised throughout the Netherlands and Germany before going over to America and starting a work which Whitefield continued. Indeed both Walker and Romaine were contemporaries with Hervey and the Wesleys at Oxford and were soundly converted and served the Lord, nurtured by a completely different spiritual nursery. Thomson was an Oxford graduate but attended the university before the founding of the Holy Club. It must also be stressed that, few as the members of the Holy Club were, several never professed conversion of the evangelical kind and never shared the preaching aims of Romaine, Hervey, Whitefield and other men of the revival.[3] It was only when certain Holy Club members put their club days behind them and with them the self-righteous, self-imposed standards that they had drawn up that their search for righteousness became successful. Only when they had experienced Christ's righteousness imputed to them could they stand side by side with other revival saints and work for God. This is made clear by J. Wesley Bready in his book *England Before and After Wesley* who writes of the club, 'The Holy Club!—Very sincere had been that band of legal zealots, struggling, with monkish ardour

---

[1]   See, for instance, Skevington Wood's *The Inextinguishable Blaze*, p. 103. The author is not without criticism of the club's activities but grossly exaggerates their significance for the spread of the revival.

[2]   Not to be confused with J. A. Freylinghausen (1670-1739), himself a successful evangelist.

[3]   Reynolds lists the wider members as being John and Charles Wesley, George Whitefield, William Morgan, Robert Kirkham, Charles Kinchin, John Gambold, Benjamin Ingham, James Hervey, Christopher Atkinson, Miles Atkinson, Richard Hutchins, John Clayton and Thomas Broughton. Reynolds argues that Hutchins, Clayton and perhaps Broughton never adopted evangelical views. He also says that Ingham 'was led into ruinous heresy'. See H. M. Pickles' *Benjamin Ingham* for a more positive and sympathetic view of Ingham's conflict with Sandemanianism etc..

to hammer out their salvation by ascetic habits and rites!' Nevertheless, as Bready's title suggests, he sees the life of John Wesley as the hub of the wheel of the revival and the founder of evangelical faith. This draws the readers attention away from the true historical sources of the revival.[1] When Wesley was eventually converted, the eighteenth century work of the Spirit was well under way. Wesley cannot even be attributed with forming the first religious societies as the Welsh had a number of them and Darracott's society at Northampton had been founded during the Holy Club days and Hervey founded a religious society at Bideford on similar lines on May 21, 1739, Wesley's Foundry Society being founded over a year later.

### The Holy Club and the *Collegia Pietatis*

It has become customary for Christian writers dealing with the growth of the Evangelical Revival to compare the Holy Club with the *Collegia Pietatis* founded by Phillip Jakob Spener (1635-1705) of Halle University. Spener was supported by August Hermann Franke (1663-1727), famous for his work amongst orphans, and Johann Jacob Rambach (1693-1735) who did so much to reform the art of preaching. Spener, a Lutheran, was not, however, the first to establish such societies. He followed in the wake of the Calvinist Theodor Untereyck (1635-1693) of Mülheim/Ruhr who set up meetings for spiritual edification (Erbauungsversammlungen) all over North-Rhine-Westphalia and throughout the Lower-Rhine area. It was from amongst these early Reformed Calvinistic *Collegia* that Theodor J. Frelinghuysen was sent out to America in 1720 and was instrumental in the conversion of Gilbert Tennent who pre-dated Whitefield in the work of the great American revivals.

Actually any comparison with these societies in Germany is strictly superficial as the following facts serve to illustrate:

a. The first *Collegia Pietatis* were founded in the 1660s. The Holy Club came into being over 60 years later.

b. The *Collegia* were founded by men well grounded in Reformed doctrines, in particular concerning the righteousness of Christ, the sinfulness of man and the need for the new birth. The Holy Club was founded by unconverted men still groping in the dark as to the basics of Christian doctrine.

c. The German clubs were founded so that awakened pastors and their flocks could enter into a more intimate Christian fellowship with one another. The Holy Club members were all Fellows or students.

---

[1]    See also Stanford's description of the Holy Club in his biography of Philip Doddridge, pp. 88-89.

d. When the *Collegia* started members met around works of the British Puritans and Continental Reformers. This led them to study the Word of God more carefully for common edification and instruction. Emphasis was laid on a correct exegesis and didactic approach. The Holy Club members met to study the Classics and even after four years of meeting together they still only read Christian literature on Sundays. This literature was by no means Puritan or Reformed but consisted of books by the 'wrong Germans' i.e. works of mystics such as Johann Tauler (c.1300-1361) a Roman Catholic divine who became famous for his sermons to nuns. It is true that the Lutheran groups read Johann Arndt (1555-1621) who, some believe, had a bent for mysticism, but Arndt always insisted that right living can only be built on conversion and a sound knowledge of Christian doctrine.

e. The *Collegia* which were attached to the universities saw themselves as a reforming body within the Church whose task it was to rid it of all Romanist impurities, ritualism and faulty doctrines. They revitalised the doctrine of the priesthood of all believers and sought to abolish celebrations such as special saints days and fast days that had no Biblical basis. The Holy Club members were proud to follow the more popish Anglican traditions and rituals and made a special point of fasting on set days and taking communion often and at regular set times. Their early writings show that the degree of holiness shown by members was judged by the frequency with which they fasted and took communion.[1] Prayers for the dead became an essential part of the holiness teaching of the Holy Club, a practice which would have shocked members of the *Collegia Pietatis*.

f. At first members of the German societies met in one another's homes or in the university premises to share fellowship. By 1682 they became convinced that their work should be church based and thus met in their various churches as living members with an evangelistic calling to witness in their neighbourhoods. That this was a wise decision is shown by the German Protestant Church statistics for the eighteenth century. In 1700 a mere 5% of the population went to a Protestant church. By 1775 20% of the population were regular Protestant church-goers. In other words, the eighteenth century revival in Germany increased the Protestant community to a far, far greater extent than all the victories of Gustav Wasa during the Thirty Years War. On the other hand, the Holy Club was purely an inner university organisation and when societies were eventually formed by its members, the vast majority of these became separate organisations with their own form of government. Hervey, in fact, was the only member of the club who insisted on a church based ministry under an awakened

---

[1] See Introductory Letter, *Works*, vol. i, Mason, 1829.

pastor and did his best to persuade Whitefield and Wesley of the wisdom of this approach.[1]

By the grace of God the best fruits of both the German *Collegia* and the Holy Club were to join together in the great work of evangelising North America. Theodor J. Frelinghuysen, who was awakened through the teaching of Untereyck and the Calvinistic societies, sailed for New Jersey in 1720 and joined William Tennent who had been there since 1716. Frelinghuysen was instrumental in the conversion of William's son Gilbert Tennent (1703-1764). When George Whitefield visited America in 1738 as a born again man, he was able to reap where Frelinghuysen and the Tennents had ploughed, sown and watered.[2]

In point of fact, the Holy Club practised almost everything that the *Collegia Pietatis* sought to ban from their churches. Although most of the members eventually came to a saving knowledge of Christ, what they practised in the Holy Club was more akin to Roman Catholic asceticism and a popish display of righteousness according to works than Biblical Christianity.

## A sober assessment of the Holy Club's importance

It is extremely difficult to assess the spiritual importance of the Holy Club in the development of the succeeding Evangelical Revival. This is mainly due to John Wesley's completely contradictory accounts of the club recorded in his works over the years. It appears that, as time went on, the itinerant evangelist idealised his and his brother's role in the Holy Club and later attributed a spiritual maturity to its members which the facts openly deny. This idealised picture of the Holy Club is the standard view of many Arminian Methodists today. Thus we find Wesley writing in 1732 that the club members still only met several times during the week to deepen their knowledge of the Classics and on Sundays they met to read a theological book. Years later, however, in his *Short History of Methodism*[3], Wesley writes that the club's aim in meeting several times a week was to study the Greek New Testament. When the club was founded, John Wesley was at home in Epworth assisting his father as his curate. This, however, is

---

[1]    Samuel Walker of Truro agreed with Hervey about these matters and was severely criticised by John Wesley for this reason.

[2]    See *Geschichte der Evangelisation*, Paulus Scharpff, Brunnen-Verlag, 1964 and *Geschichte der evangelischen Weltmission*, Horst R. Flachsmeier, Brunnen-Verlag, 1963 for a detailed account of the eighteenth century revival in Germany and Dutch-German evangelistic activities in the American colonies. See also *Bible und Gemeinde*, 93 Jahrgang, Juli - September, 3/93 for a short pen-portrait of Johann Jacob Rambach and his work at Halle.

[3]    *Works*, vol. vi, p.402.

not the account John Wesley gives of the club's beginning. In his *Short History*, Wesley dates the foundation of the club from his return to Oxford and puts himself at the head of the list of founder members. Most Wesleyans have accepted John Wesley as *the* founder of the Holy Club and Methodism ever since.[1]

There are so many examples of such re-dating and re-assessing of John Wesley's position both by himself and his followers that J. H. Overton feels he must state dogmatically, 'John Wesley was the originator of scarcely anything that is specially connected with his name.'[2] In 1744, we even find Wesley writing that he and his brother Charles, whilst reading the Bible together in 1729, became the sole founders of the club, in fact the sole founders of the Methodists.[3] Such statements completely disregard the growth of the Calvinistic Methodists in Wales and the fact that their leaders were converted, doing evangelistic work and founding societies before the Wesleys had any idea of their calling. It also disregards the fact that fellow students of the Wesleys at Oxford such as Walker of Truro did pioneer work in the Evangelical Awakening though they never took part in the Holy Club's activities.[4] Wesley, indeed, often emphasises in his later works that the Holy Club members were already 'Bible Christians'.[5] Events show, however, that the major members of the club, the Wesleys, Whitefield and Hervey, were all converted several years after they left Oxford. Hervey's first major biographer, John Ryland, refers to the spiritual poverty of the Holy Club in his account of Hervey's membership there:

> The two first years were passed over in ignorance and indolence. He then fell into the hands of men that were ignorant of the method of acceptance with God. These men became his spiritual physicians; and foolish physicians they were: their religion consisted in a set of outward observances, and a punctilious regard to rules of their own devising—rising at stated hours—fasting several times in the week—giving the food they saved by fasting to the poor—saying prayers at certain hours—visiting the prisoners in the jails—frequent attendance upon the sacrament—binding themselves by vows and covenants, to certain virtues and practices. This was the sum total of their religion: they had no spiritual perception

---

[1]    *Wesley's Works*, Conference Office, 1810, vol. VI, p. 402.

[2]    See *John Wesley*, J. H. Overton, Methuen, p. 24.

[3]    See Minutes, *Works*, vol. vi, p. 336

[4]    See *Daniel Rowland*, Eifion Evans, Banner of Truth Trust for a detailed account of the growth of Calvinistic Methodism.

[5]    A Short History, *Works*, vol. vi, p. 402.

of the person of Christ: no understanding of his glorious righteousness for our justification: no acquaintance with the spirituality and
vast extent of God's law: no sense of the immaculate purity of God:
no conviction of the plague of their own hearts; no deep discernment of the power, deceit, and malignity of indwelling sin: no sight
of the absolute necessity of regeneration by God the Holy Spirit:
no knowledge of his divine person, and the infinite importance and
necessity of his operations in the scheme of our salvation: no experience of the pleasures of vital religion. In this dark, sad, joyless
state, he lived for eight years; that is to say, from the nineteenth
year of his age, till he was twenty-seven. All this time was spent in
reading improper books, trusting to his own virtue and righteousness for justification, and without the joys of God's salvation.[1]

Ryland goes on to say how Hervey's new friends—he can only mean
the Wesleys—poisoned his mind to the truths of the gospel and became a
great barrier to his becoming converted. The Holy Club members' practice of studying far into the night, Ryland believed, was the main reason
why Hervey, though once a strong athlete, ruined his health permanently
whilst at Lincoln College. Warning his readers about imitating this side of
Hervey, Ryland says, 'Before he attained his strength of mind and understanding, to enjoy his GOD and SAVIOUR in a free and full union of soul
with soul, he hurt his health by night studies, and broke his delicate constitution beyond the powers of recovery. Here it was that the great Toplady
mistook his way, and ruined his health; the great John Milton lost his eyes
by the same mistaken step. These three men were truly wise, and are now
eternally happy: but let us never make them patterns for our imitation in
that, which was the greatest blunder of their lives.'[2]
    Ryland also points out that Hervey was so ignorant of Bible truths
after his years at Oxford that he had no idea what or where Jerusalem was
and could not find Israel on a globe. It may be that Ryland is guilty of
some exaggeration in his grim picture of Oxford and the Holy Club. He
had no first hand knowledge of English university life himself. This was
chiefly because of the prejudices of English universities of the day against
non-conformists causing them to be banned from enrolling. Even Ryland
admits that the books mentioned above which Hervey studied carefully,
helped him in his education. Ryland, however, when referring to 'improper
books', is thinking more of the pseudo-religious and mystic books that
were read on Sundays by the Holy Club. Nevertheless, Ryland was one of

---

[1]   *The Character of the Rev. James Hervey, A.M.*, John Ryland, M.A., London, 1791,
p.148.
[2]   Ryland's *The Character of the Rev. James Hervey A. M.*, p. 78.

Hervey's most intimate friends over a period of twelve and a half years and it is obvious from both Hervey's and Ryland's works that the two shared their views on all matters openly. Ryland had thus every possible opportunity to sound Hervey out concerning his education. Furthermore, Hervey always bemoaned the fact that he had not read such authors as Marshall and Jenks whilst at university and had neglected his Bible. Ryland's dismal view of the Holy Club must be accepted as a statement of fact.

### Wesley's own earlier views of the Holy Club

Writing four years after the club was founded, Wesley outlined the purpose of the club to an angry father who accused the Wesleys of murdering his son. William Morgan, a founder member, had died as a result, it was alleged, of following the club's rules of fasting. The irate father's son had been the driving force in the practical application of the club's attempt at personal holiness. He had persuaded the other members to visit the sick, read to the illiterate and visit condemned prisoners. Mr. Morgan Sen., however, blamed the Wesleys for allowing religious fanaticism to come before health and life in their stubborn allegiance to rites and rituals. Wesley, in his defence, avoids going into too much detail concerning the extravagances of the club and states:

I. Whether it does not concern all men of all conditions to imitate Him, as much as they can, 'who went about doing good'?
Whether all Christians are not concerned in that command, 'While we have time let us do good to all men'?
Whether we shall not be more happy hereafter, the more good we do now?
Whether we can be happy at all hereafter, unless we have, according to our power, 'fed the hungry, clothed the naked, visited those that are sick, and in prison'; and made all these actions subservient to a higher purpose, even the saving of souls from death?
Whether it be not our bounden duty always to remember, that He did more for us than we can do for him, who assures us, 'Inasmuch as ye have done it unto one of the least of these my brethren, ye have done it unto me'?
II. Whether, upon these considerations, we may not try to do good to our acquaintance? Particularly, whether we may not try to convince them of the necessity of being Christians?
Whether of the consequent necessity of being scholars?
Whether of the necessity of method and industry, in order to either learning or virtue?
Whether we may not try to persuade them to confirm and increase their industry, by communicating as often as they can?
Whether we may not mention to them the authors whom we conceive to have wrote the best on those subjects?

Whether we may not assist them, as we are able, from time to time, to form resolutions upon what they read in those authors, and to execute them with steadiness and perseverance?

III. Whether, upon the considerations above-mentioned, we may not try to do good to those that are hungry, naked, or sick? In particular, whether, if we know any necessitous family, we may not give them a little food, clothes, or physic, as they want?

Whether we may not give them, if they can read, a Bible, Common-Prayer Book, or Whole Duty of Man?

Whether we may not, now and then, inquire how they have used them; explain what they do not understand, and enforce what they do?

Whether we may not enforce upon them, more especially, the necessity of private prayer, and of frequenting the church and sacrament?

Whether we may not contribute, what little we are able, toward having their children clothed and taught to read?

Whether we may not take care that they be taught their catechism, and short prayers for morning and evening?

IV. Lastly, Whether, upon the considerations above-mentioned, we may not try to do good to those that are in prison? In particular, Whether we may not release such well-disposed persons as remain in prison for small sums?

Whether we may not lend smaller sums to those that are of any trade, that they may procure themselves tools and materials to work with?

Whether we may not give to them who appear to want it most, a little money, or clothes, or physic?

Whether we may not supply as many as are serious enough to read, with a Bible, and Whole Duty of Man?

Whether we may not, as we have opportunity, explain and enforce these upon them, especially with respect to public and private prayer, and the blessed sacrament?[1]

## Man's whole duty

Wesley's two-fold emphasis on reading *The Whole Duty of Man* along-side the Bible shows how lacking in Christian knowledge and experience the Holy Club members were. This work was published anonymously in 1658 and became the mainstay of the ethically based doctrines of the non-Evangelical branch of the Church of England until far into the eighteenth century. It gave rise to a belief that good works and good manners were the backbone of Christianity. This, in turn, influenced the Neonomians, Amyraldians and Arminians in the development of their doctrines of duty-

---

[1]    Introductory Letter, *The Works of the Rev. John Wesley, A.M.*, John Mason, 1829, vol. i pp. 9-11

faith and righteousness by means of following the moral law. Hervey later saw how shallow the book's emphasis on human efforts was and compared it to Thomas Boston's *Human Nature in its Fourfold State*, saying, 'If another celebrated treatise is styled *The Whole Duty of Man*, I would call this *The Whole of Man* as it comprises what he *was* originally, what he *is* by transgression, what he *should be* by grace, and then what he *shall be* in glory'.[1] Writing against the wishy-washy views of man's ability to reform himself in the *Whole Duty of Man*, Henry Venn (1724-1797) posed the question in his rival book the *Complete Duty of Man*, 'How sin is expiated, and in what method are sinners restored to the favour of God and the hope of acceptance?' He argues in his *Preface* that there is no righteousness in the best efforts of man and the only righteousness which will stand blameless before the law is the righteousness of Christ, arguing, 'Dependence therefore upon that righteousness, as wrought out by him for believers and appointed of God for sinners to trust in, is the precious faith of the gospel by which the soul is justified before God. And as no other will reconcile the divine attributes, or answer the exigencies of mankind, concluded under sin, and always sinners; for nothing else must be the ground of our confidence towards God.' Sadly, Wesley delved too deeply into the moral fables of the *Whole Duty* and campaigned fiercely all his life against the doctrine so well described by Venn. To him it was not the doctrine of imputed righteousness but the doctrine of 'imputed nonsense'. Trusting in the righteousness of Christ was the greatest barrier between Hervey and salvation. Once Hervey was converted, he made Christ's righteousness and the atonement the theme of his major works, only to gain the enmity of the man who had once been his friend and tutor.

### The extent of Hervey's indebtedness to Wesley

Meanwhile Hervey was entering into the life of the Holy Club with heart and soul, full of thankfulness to John Wesley for taking him under his wing and assisting him in his Hebrew studies. This assistance given by Wesley to Hervey shows what a good teacher Wesley was in comparison to his colleagues. He taught Hervey how to analyse the grammatical structure of conjugations and declensions and find their correct syntactical position and opened up to him the complicated mystery of the Hebrew *modi*. From then on, Ryland tells us, Hervey 'went on like a race horse, or a giant: he entered into the simplicity, the energy, the imagery, and the majesty of the first language spoken upon earth; and to my certain knowledge, he was one of the first scholars in Europe for a familiar knowledge in the Hebrew Bible; and whilst the greatest part of the ministers of reli-

---

[1]  *Memoirs of the Life and Character of the Late Rev. James Hervey, A.M.*, John Brown, London 1822, Appendix, pp. 506.

gion hardly know the beginning from the end, or the top from the bottom of the sacred Scriptures of GOD, in their original language, this excellent man conversed with the Hebrew Scriptures with the critical knowledge of a Jewish Rabbi, and the devotional spirit of a lively Christian.'[1] John Brown records Hervey as saying to Wesley, 'I heartily thank you, as for all other favours, so especially for teaching me Hebrew. I have cultivated this study again, according to your advice. I can never forget that tender-hearted and generous Fellow of Lincoln, who condescended to take such compassionate notice of a poor under-graduate, whom almost everybody condemned, and no man cared for my soul.'[2] Under Wesley's dubious guidance, Hervey got up very early in the morning to commence studies and was still found at his books when most other students were returning from the taverns or sound asleep in bed. Hervey began to live as if food, personal care and health were of no importance whatsoever and gradually his bodily strength left him never to be recovered.

### Hervey's first close contact with a converted man

Whilst on holiday at Weston Favell with his parents, Hervey heard of a poor needy member of Doddridge's church who lived at nearby Hardingstone, so he decided to ride over and see if he could help in any way. Shortly after reaching the cottage, Hervey was joined by a young student of Doddridge's called Risdon Darracott who impressed Hervey greatly by the loving way in which he attended to the poor man. The name of Darracott is almost unknown to modern Christian readers[3] but George Whitefield saw Darracott as one of the great pioneers of the Awakening in England and wrote to Lady Huntingdon on February 25, 1750 to say, 'At Wellington I lay at the house of one Mr. Darracott, a flaming successful preacher of the gospel, and who may justly be called "The Star of the West."'[4] Soon Hervey had formed a deep friendship with Darracott who was endeavouring to set up a religious society amongst the students at Dr. Doddridge's Dissenting Academy at Northampton and discussed and corresponded with Hervey on the subject of the correct rules for the society's

---

[1]    *The Character of the Rev. James Hervey, A.M.*, pp. 146-147. Ryland, always very critical of Wesley, omits to mention Wesley's name as the fellow of Lincoln College who assisted Hervey in this way. Indeed there is some confusion as to the extent of Hutchin's and Wesley's influence on Hervey and often the one is attributed with doing what the other did. Ryland is most likely wrong in his estimate of Biblical Hebrew's antiquity as it shows linguistic signs of being developed from other known languages or at least being one dialect among many.

[2]    Ibid, p. 4.

[3]    See my article *The Poor Man's Preacher*, Evangelical Times, Vol. XXVIII No. 12, December 1994, p. 16.

[4]    Dr. Bennett used Whitefield's phrase for the title of his Darracott biography.

members. Darracott gave Hervey several books, amongst which was most likely Marshall on *Sanctification* which we know Hervey obtained at this time. This book was to be instrumental in Hervey's conversion but he left it unread for six years as he had quite different ideas of sanctification at the time. Darracott finished his studies under Dr. Doddridge in 1738 and pastored a work in Penzance for two years but could do little owing to very poor health which caused bleeding in his stomach. In 1741 he moved to Wellington in Somersetshire and took over a church with 28 communicants. He was shocked, however, to find that the communicants had not the faintest idea of the Christian religion. Darracott worked out a system of visitation which ensured that the neighbourhood received good Christian teaching, helped by the Bibles and books that he supplied them with. Part of this teaching was to catechise no less than a hundred children. Soon many of those whom Darracott had visited went to hear him preach at the meeting house, were converted and became church members. His fame, due to his faithful preaching spread and drew in many from the surrounding districts. Darracott's chapel proved to be too small and had to be enlarged several times. The faithful pastor, seeing that people were coming to hear him from all areas, took out preaching licences for the surrounding districts and took the gospel to them rather than compel them to come to him. Though conversions under his ministry were never few, during the last two years of his life, Darracott was blessed with seeing very many souls turn to Christ. The good man, never strong, worked himself literally to an early death at the age of forty-two. He thus followed in the steps of his own faithful father who had died in the ministry before reaching the age of forty. Darracott never forgot his responsibility to Christ's flock even on his death bed. As he realised his earthly pilgrimage was over, he said to those standing around him, 'I charge you see to it, that you meet me at the right hand of God at the great day.' Darracott's biography has been sympathetically outlined by Dr. Bennett (1815) and John Gillies has recorded Darracott's piety, faith and work in his *Historical Collections of Accounts of Revival* (1845).[1]

We find Harvey's confessions concerning his own lack of spirituality in a letter to Darracott dated June 3, 1736 in which he tells his friend:

> This cool morning, I took a walk with a design to consider the scheme which you are going to set on foot. My thoughts were all along attended with abasement and admiration to perceive you having recourse to and consulting me, when you daily converse

---

[1]    Banner of Truth Trust reprint, 1981. Gillies quotes numerous letters sent him by Darracott. See also my *The Poor Man's Preacher* (article on Risdon Darracott) ET, December, 1994.

with gentlemen who are far my superiors in wisdom and knowledge, but especially since you have the happiness of living under the same roof with the judicious and devout doctor (Doddridge). Yet, sir, I fear I am one of those who, as the inspired apostle says, are 'blind and cannot see afar off.'

Back at Lincoln College, Hervey tells Darracott how he is striving to lead a life honouring to the gospel and of his impending ordination:

> I employ every day an hour or more (which I think is as much time I can spare from my studies) with some well-inclined people of the poorer sort. We read Mr. Henry on the Holy Scriptures, and pray together. There is one set in one part of the city, and another in another. I meet at a neighbour's house. Oh that I could open my mouth as he did, so boldly and so powerfully! who will give me a little portion of that knowledge which he had in the mysteries of the gospel! that I may declare them to the people, clearly and convincingly. Above all, who will give me some of the humble zeal, that sacred and illustrious fervour which animated him who laboured more abundantly than all the apostles! I am preparing to enter into holy orders, and to take upon me the work of the ministry, that great, wonderful, and important work. So that I have the utmost reason to cry out as the distressed fisherman did to their partners, 'Come and help us.' Help me with your prayers to the Lord God my Saviour, that I 'may receive the Holy Ghost not many days hence,' by the laying on of hands; even 'the Spirit of wisdom and understanding, the Spirit of counsel and might, the Spirit of knowledge and fear of the Lord;' that He may be in me, rest upon me, and abide with me for ever, making me fit, every way qualified, and thoroughly furnished for this sacred function.[1]

After being at Oxford for five years, Hervey took his Bachelor degree and was ordained as a deacon of the Church of England on September 14, 1736, Dr. John Potter, the Bishop of Oxford performing the ceremony. Hervey was still not finished with his studies as he had not yet gained his A.M., which was his original aim. Now he believed he ought to conserve his energies for the pulpit and thus, against the advice of his father, he resigned from the university and relinquished his scholarship arguing that there were poorer students who would be in need of it.

---

[1]   Quoted by Charles Stanford from his private collection of Darracott's and Hervey's letters, in his biography of Philip Doddridge, pp. 87-88.

# Chapter Three:
# The Righteousness of Another

**Hervey discovers the hardest thing in religion**

Hervey started his life as a curate by assisting his father in his Weston
and Collingtree parishes.[1] He had become a minister of the Gospel, but a
minister who had no idea of the Gospel he was supposed to preach. John
Brown of Whitburn has painstakingly put together a list of the doctrines
which Hervey held on becoming a clergyman.[2] They are doctrines guaran-
teed to drive anyone away from the straight and narrow path leading to
salvation. Here we see Hervey boasting that his 'spotless actions' would
save him; his 'unshaken resolution' to do good would preserve him; the
terrors of the Law would always frighten him back to the path of duty
should he wander from it and Heaven's doors are open to all those who
'dress themselves with holiness' in this way. Hervey's years in the Holy
Club had changed him for the worse. He was now truly 'righteous overmuch' and a spiritual snob. But God had other things in store for James
Hervey and was already preparing the mind and heart of a humble ploughman in order to pull Hervey down more than a peg or two.

Owing to his poor health, the doctors had told Hervey that he ought to
follow the ploughman as he tills the soil and breathe in the freshly turned
earth. Fresh air and the odours of the land would work wonders for one
who has his nose in a book night and day. Hervey took this advice and
decided to follow a simple land worker about his daily chores. The man

---

[1]   After Hervey's first biography was published in 1760, an anonymous author wrote to
the *Gentleman's Magazine*, stating that Hervey did not become his father's curate but, on
being ordained, at once took up the curacy of Dummer in Hampshire. See GM, 1760, vol.
xxx, p. 554. No proof is offered for this assumption which contradicts the evidence given
by all other biographers and the information supplied in this work.

[2]   Appendix II, *Memoirs*, John Brown, London, 1822.

God had chosen for Hervey to accompany was another member of Dr. Doddridge's church a Mr. Clayton of Dallington. True, he was a man of no education, but he had a profound knowledge, backed with experience, of the doctrines of grace.

As Hervey trudged after the man across the newly turned soil, he thought he would enter into pious conversation with him and teach him a thing or two. 'What is the hardest thing in religion?' the newly-fledged clergyman asked him. The ploughman replied, 'I am a poor illiterate man, and you, Sir, are a minister. I beg leave to return the question.' Taking up the cue, Hervey said, 'I think the hardest thing is to deny sinful self.' He said this thinking of the Lord's words in Matthew 16:24 'If any man will come after me, let him deny himself, and take up his cross, and follow me.' Hervey then proceeded to lecture the man who was trying to plough a straight line, on needful human efforts to suppress sin and walk morally straight. The son of the soil soon realised what was lacking in Hervey's view of sanctification. 'There is another instance of self-denial,' he said patiently, 'to which the injunction extends, is of great moment, and is the hardest thing in religion, and that is, to deny righteous self.' The simple man had seen through the clergyman's false piety. Hervey's own righteous self, his own self-righteousness, was standing between him and a saving knowledge of Christ. Whilst Hervey was taking this in, it was the ploughman's turn to lecture to his clergyman friend. 'You know,' he continued, 'that I do not come to hear you preach, but go every Sabbath, with my family, to North-ampton, to hear Dr. Doddridge: We rise early in the morning, and have prayers before we set out, in which I find pleasure. Walking there and back I find pleasure; under the sermon I find pleasure; when at the Lord's table I find pleasure. We read a portion of the Scriptures and go to prayers in the evening, and we find pleasure; but to this moment, I find it the hardest thing to deny righteous self. I mean the instance of renouncing our own strength, and our own righteousness, not leaning on that for holiness, not relying on that for justification.'

'What an old fool! What a mixture of piety and oddity!', Hervey thought, and looked at the man as if he were mad. God was working in his heart, however, and suddenly Hervey found himself thinking of Christ's righteousness in comparison with his own. But Hervey was still bound by that Strong Man Satan and felt that he hated the righteousness of Christ as it stood in the way of an undisturbed trust in his own. In God's grace, Hervey could not forget this experience and was led to see that he had been the fool and the old ploughman had taught him solid sense and godly wisdom.

## A spiritual change becomes obvious

Hervey's letters to his sister and friends over the next five years show how slowly but surely a work of grace is taking place in the young minister's life. After 1734 we no longer find him boasting of the sweet satisfaction he will have in presenting himself before the Throne of Grace as a worthy child of God. On the contrary, writing to his sister from Oxford in May 1734 he says, 'Let us remember, and remembering, let us acknowledge, that we are nothing, and have nothing, and deserve nothing, but shame and contempt, but misery and punishment.' For the first time in his life, Hervey's eyes were on his own sinfulness and nothingness before God. Almost a year later, we find him, after visiting the assizes, saying, 'How melancholy a sight is it to see a poor criminal go up to the bar! All he has no longer his own; his very life is in the power of the magistrate, and he is in great danger of a speedy death. And if this be so dreadful, how infinitely more dreadful will it be to appear before a more strict and awful tribunal! The good Lord grant, that you and I may not be cast in that tremendous trial! A trial that will be undergone before angels and God: upon the issue of which our eternal life will depend. Was I to wish a wish for the dearest friend in the world, it should not be for gold, or jewels, or apparel: these things are fading, and the fashion of them passeth away; but it should be for a favourable sentence in that last and great day.'

Necessary as such an insight is before conversion can take place, Hervey was still unsure of his true state before God. Though he spoke of putting on the wedding garment and entering into the joy of his Lord, he still seemed to believe that this wedding garment could only be given if first the believer showed that he lived a humble and holy life, indeed, it would seem that he believed 'a humble and holy life' was the very wedding garment which would give him entrance into eternal life.

George Whitefield was the first of the Holy Club members to be converted and by the end of 1735 he was witnessing openly to Hervey. After his ordination by Bishop Benson on June 20, 1736 and his first sermon to his new flock at Gloucester, he wrote to Hervey to tell him how the Lord was blessing him:

My Dear friend,

Glory! glory! glory! be ascribed to an almighty triune God.— Last Sunday in the afternoon, I preached my first sermon in the church of St. Mary De Crypt, where I was baptised, and also first received the sacrament of the Lord's supper. Curiosity, as you may easily guess, drew a large congregation together upon the occasion. The sight at first a little awed me; but I was comforted with a heart-felt sense of the divine presence, and soon found the unspeakable advantage of having been accustomed to public speaking when a boy at school, and of exhorting and teaching the prisoners and poor people at their private houses, whilst at the university. By

these means I was kept from being daunted over much. As I proceeded, I perceived the fire kindled, till at last, though so young,
and amidst a crowd of those, who knew me in my infant childish
days, I trust, I was enabled to speak with some degree of gospel
authority. Some few mocked, but most for the present seemed struck;
and I have since heard, that a complaint had been made to the bishop,
that I drove fifteen mad the first sermon. The worthy prelate, as I
am informed, wished that the madness might not be forgotten before next Sunday. Before then, I hope, my sermon upon *He that is
in Christ, is a new creature*, will be completed. Blessed be God, I
now find freedom in writing. Glorious Jesus,

*Unloose my stamm'ring tongue to tell
Thy love immense, unsearchable.*

Being thus engaged, I must hasten to subscribe myself,
Yours &c.
G.W.

## Hervey replaces Whitefield at Dummer

A previous member of the Holy Club, Charles Kinchin, now asked
Whitefield to take over his church at Dummer in Hampshire as he had
been elected dean of Corpus Christi College, Oxford. Whitefield moved
over but had not been there long when the Wesleys wrote from Georgia,
challenging him to visit America. Whitefield responded to the call and it
was agreed that Hervey would take his place at Dummer. Hervey had hardly
left Collingtree when his flock there wrote to him, begging him to return
to them as their curate. Hervey was very much moved by this call but
realised that he was still not the man to walk in his father's footsteps and
lead such a devoted congregation. On June 29, 1737, he wrote a long and
loving letter to the Collingtree inhabitants who had set their signatures to
the written call, pointing out how good was their decision to have a true
man of God take over the cure of their souls, but he felt compelled to add,
'But I fear you make an over-favourable and mistaken judgement, when
you imagine me to be such a one, and pitch upon me for the purpose.' He
then goes on to outline in detail all that the Collingtree church should
require of a pastor. This excellent description of a man of God, carrying
out the calling of a shepherd, shows that Hervey knew the entire scope of
the gospel and the full catalogue of needs of both saints and sinners. He
also knew that he was still in need himself of being shepherded into the
arms of the Saviour.[1]

---

[1]    This description of the work of a pastor will be provided in an appendix.

Meanwhile Hervey had become fully convinced that if he were to become right with God, he must have a righteousness infinitely better than his own.[1] Whitefield, now in North America, wrote to him several times, showing him the way to Christ's righteousness but Hervey did not bother to reply. Giving up his old trust in himself was not easy. In a letter dated Philadelphia, Nov. 10, 1739, Whitefield points Hervey to the righteousness of Christ saying:

Dear Mr. H.

I received no answer to my last, yet I must write to you again. The many happy hours I spent with you when at Oxon, and the benefit I have received from your instructions and example, are yet fresh upon my memory. I long to have my dear friend come forth, and preach the truth as it is in JESUS. Not a righteousness or inward holiness of our own, whereby we may make ourselves meet, but a righteousness of another, even the LORD our righteousness; upon the imputation and apprehending of which by faith, we shall be made meet by his Holy Spirit to live with, and to enjoy GOD. Dear Mr. H. it is an excellent thing to be convinced of the freeness and riches of GOD's grace in CHRIST JESUS. It is sweet to know and preach, that CHRIST justifies the ungodly, and that all truly good works are not so much as partly the cause, but the *effect* of our justification before GOD. Till convinced of these truths, you must own free-will in man, which is directly contrary to the holy scriptures, and the articles of our church. Let me advise dear Mr. H. laying aside all prejudice, to read and pray over Saint Paul's epistles to the Romans and Galatians, and then let him tell me what he thinks of this doctrine. Most of our old friends are now happily enlightened. GOD sets his seal to such preaching in an extraordinary manner, and I am persuaded the gates of hell shall never be able to prevail against it. Oh that dear Mr. H. would also join with us! Oh that the LORD would open his eyes to behold aright this part of the mystery of godliness! How would it rejoice my heart! How would it comfort his own soul! He would then no longer groan under the spirit of bondage: No, he would be brought into the glorious liberty of the sons of GOD. I have wrote to dear Mr. O. as well as to you, out of the simplicity of my heart.

Ever yours in CHRIST,[2]

---

[1]   Letter 115, *Works*

[2]   *George Whitefield's Letters*, Banner of Truth Trust, p. 95

**Reading the right books**

It seems that Hervey was quite simply ashamed to write to Whitefield. He was realising that his theology up to now had been merely based on human endeavours yet he could not shake off the shackles and view Christ with Whitefield's eyes. He did, however, make a firm effort to understand his converted friend's point of view. Hervey had already Walter Marshall's *Gospel Mystery of Sanctification* in his possession and early in 1741 he supplemented this great work with Jenks on *Submission to Christ's Righteousness* and Rawlin on *Justification*. Jenks and Marshall were to stay with Hervey as the best of advisors for the rest of his life.

Jenks started off in his ministry convinced of the doctrines of Pelagius and scorned the articles of his own church which clearly refuted them. One day he was struck down with a realisation of his own sin and lack of righteousness and saw that the faith by which he had tried to live was merely a trust in his own holiness, or rather lack of it. Through reading Paul's epistles he realised that the sinner can only stand before God if clothed in Christ's righteousness and, pleading this righteousness, he found peace with God. Jenks subsequently wrote a book on submission to Christ's righteousness which first opened Hervey's eyes to the truths of the Gospel and gave him his main theme in his own preaching. Writing in his Preface to a new edition of Jenks' *Meditations*, Hervey referring to the four lepers in 2 Kings 7: says,

> Having found silver, and gold, and raiment, they could not forbear proclaiming the news, and communicating the spoil to their fellow-citizens. When I find a treasure incomparably more precious, when I find a teacher of wisdom, and a guide to glory, why should I hold my peace? Why should I enjoy these benefits myself alone? Why should I not, like those honest, though calamitous exiles, tell the glad tidings in the city, and invite my neighbours to partake of the blessing? These blessings, through the divine goodness, I have found in Jenks' *Meditations*.

Marshall (1628-80) was a Fellow of New College Oxford and was a minister at Hursely, Hampshire until the Act of Uniformity was passed in 1662. This act, forced through by Charles II at the Restoration, required all ministers to accept a revised form of the Prayer Book and swear allegiance to the new King. This was a formal repudiation of the National Covenant (1638) which fostered Presbyterianism. Many clergymen could not accept Episcopalianism and others, though true to the Church of England's articles, could not accept Charles II whom they saw as a tool of the Anti-Christ, Rome. Thus ensued the Great Ejection in which 2,000 ministers of the Gospel had to leave the Established Church and become Dissenting ministers or take up secular occupations. In 1689, 400 more followed them because of Jacobite preferences. These ministers became virtually a persecuted minority due to a series of laws called the Clarendon Code which restricted their activities. The fact that evangelicals on both sides continued to believe the same Reformed doctrines shows up the political nature of the 'Ejection' and the role church government plays in denomination-building rather than the doctrines of grace. Marshall's conscience, for instance, neither allowed him to serve under Charles II nor under a bishop so he joined the ejected. He went through a period of great spiritual distress but with the support of Dr. Thomas Goodwin was brought to a true assurance of faith which he described in his still famous book.[1]

Marshall has been seen as a great teacher throughout the succeeding centuries. Traill, the Erskines, John Ryland, Hervey, the Scottish Marrowmen, Cowper and Huntington were all soundly influenced by Marshall's book. William Cowper confessed that Marshall's doctrines were 'the very Life of my Soul, and the Soul of all my Happiness' and told an Evangelical cousin:

> I think Marshal one of the best writers and the most spiritual expositor of Scripture I ever read. I admire the strength of his argument and the clearness of his reasonings upon those parts of our most holy religion, which are generally least understood even by real Christians, as masterpieces of the kind. His section upon the union of the soul with Christ is an instance of what I mean, in which he has spoken of a most mysterious truth with admirable perspicuity, and with great good sense, making it all the while subservient to his main purpose of proving holiness to be the fruit and effect of faith.[2]

Hervey's references to Marshall in his works are legend and he never ceased to recommend him to new correspondents. Right at the beginning of his new born life, Hervey assured Whitefield that Marshall was one of the major means used by God to convert him. His views had still not changed towards the end of his life as shown by a letter to John Ryland Sen. in which he says: 'I really am more and more confirmed in my opinion, notwithstanding all the objections; or rather, I am more and more convinced, that Mr. Marshall's doctrine is the doctrine of the Gospel. To this my reason subscribes: this I think is taught in the Scriptures: this I am sure is approved and ratified by my own daily experience. When I depart

---

[1] Perhaps the most interesting and informative book on this subject from a Dissenting point of view is Thomas Coleman's *The Two Thousand Confessors of Sixteen Hundred and Sixty-Two*, John Snow, London, 1860.

[2] Letter to Mrs. Cowper dated 14 March, 1767.

from this precious truth, assurance by the direct act of faith, I fall into darkness and distress; but when, looking for no evidences in myself, I depend on the free promise of God in his word; when regarding myself only as a poor sinner, I confidently trust in Christ as my righteousness and salvation; then light beams forth, and comfort springs up.'[1]

### Awaiting the Royal Bridegroom

A week after turning down the call from the Collingtree church, we find Hervey writing to his sister, pleading with her to renounce her sin with him and be ever awake for the call 'Behold the Bridegroom cometh' that could now reach them at any time. It is very obvious that the Lord was trimming Hervey's and his sister's lamps for the great coming of Christ into their lives. Hervey tells his sister, 'our souls are sick of sin, sick of worldly-mindedness, sick of pride, sick of passion, and sundry other disorders, which, if not speedily healed, will bring us down, not only to the grave, but to the torments of hell.' Not long after Hervey was visited by two gentlemen who had come down from London. Their names are not given but they obviously came as messengers from God. Of the visit Hervey says, 'We talked of that infinitely condescending and gracious Friend of sinners, who came from heaven on purpose to be crucified for us, and is returned unto heaven on purpose to intercede for us.' He goes on to tell his correspondent that the fact of Christ's intercession was most important to him as he knew that it never ceases and always prevails. If these are not the wise words of a born again man, they show a proximity which is most encouraging indeed.

### The influence of Paul Orchard on Hervey

Though Marshall and Jenks were of great influence in bringing Hervey to the knowledge of the truth, God provided Hervey with a very good friend who was of great encouragement to him in his embracing of the gospel. This was Paul Orchard, a country gentleman who had been with Hervey at Oxford and was a fellow-member of the Holy Club. Like Whitefield, Hervey and the Wesleys, he became a man dedicated to God's Word, prayer and Christian charity. Though he did not enter the ministry, he was greatly used in encouraging the leaders of the Awakening in their endeavours for the Lord. Whitefield wrote to Orchard in 1739 to say:

> Was not my heart with your heart, when we rode by the way and talked to each other concerning the Scriptures? I thought our souls tallied together, and that we had both drank of the same spirit.

---

[1]      Letter XXXVII, p. 56 in A Series of Letters, Appendix to *The Character of the Rev. James Hervey, A.M.*

I have often, since that time, admired the grace of God in you, and even now feel my soul, whilst I am writing, intimately united with yours. What is all this, but the effect and fruit of God's everlasting love through Christ Jesus our Lord? What is it, but an instance of the sovereign will and good pleasure of God, who will have mercy on whom he will have mercy? OH how doth the free, the distinguishing grace of God excite the love of those, who are made partakers of it! What was there in you and me, dear Mr. Orchard, that should move God to chuse us before others? Was there any fitness foreseen in us, except a fitness for damnation? I believe not. No, God chose us from eternity, he called us in time, and I am persuaded will keep us from falling finally, till time shall be no more.[1]

After a year at Dummer, Hervey's health broke considerably and Orchard took his college friend under his wing at Stoke-Abbey, Devonshire, where Hervey stayed from 1738 to 1740. Both men became so close to each other in their common search for God's blessing that they entered into a solemn, written covenant with each other and the Lord to live a life in God's service. The covenant has been preserved and is quite unique as an expression of deep friendship and high spiritual zeal. On November 28, 1738 both friends signed the following statement:

We, the underwritten, whom God's providence has wonderfully brought acquainted with each other, for purposes, no doubt, of piety and everlasting salvation, sensible how blind and corrupt our nature is, how forward to fall into errors and iniquities, but how backward to discern or amend them; knowing also the great advantage of kind and affectionate, but, at the same time sincere and impartial reproof and admonition, do oblige ourselves to watch over each other's conduct, conversation and tempers; and whenever we perceive anything amiss therein; any duty ill done, or not done so well as it ought; anything omitted which might be for our spiritual good, or practised which will tend to our spiritual hurt; in fine, anything practised or neglected, which we shall wish to have been otherwise in a dying hour: All this we watch to observe, never fail to reprove, and earnestly endeavour to correct in each other, that so we may have nothing to upbraid one another with when we meet in the eternal state. We resolve to do all this with the utmost plainness, and all honest freedom; and, provided it be done with tenderness, with apparent good-will, and in private, we will esteem

---

[1] The full letter is found in *George Whitefield's Letters*, 1734 to 1742, BOTT, 1976. Also Letter XCV, p. 90, *Whitefield's Works*, Vol. I, Dilly, London, 1771.

it as the greatest kindness we can show, the truest interest of sincere friendship that we can exercise, and the only way of answering the gracious ends of Almighty wisdom in bringing us together. In witness and confirmation of which resolution, we here subscribe our names.[1]

## Whitefield's part in Hervey's conversion

Pious and praiseworthy as this statement is, there is still one thing lacking in its presentation. Still wanting is a personal confession of faith in the Lord Jesus Christ and an acknowledgement of His work in the heart. The major influence for the good on Hervey's life in this direction came through the testimony of George Whitefield. Hervey treasured his letters, though he was slow to respond to them, and read avidly anything that came from Whitefield's pen in the form of journals or sermons. Whitefield's sermon on 'What think ye of Christ?' was one of the final links in the divine process that brought Hervey to shed all trust in his own righteousness and take on Christ's imputed righteousness as Abraham and all born again saints before and after him. The sermon that so moved Hervey is on the subject of a sinner's justification through the obedience and death of Christ, received by faith. In the sermon Whitefield argues from Scripture in the same fundamental way that Paul, Calvin, Crisp, Gill and Toplady preached and which Hervey and Huntington later made their custom. A way which brought cries of 'Antinomianism' from Pharisees, Arminians, Neonomians and Grotians. Whitefield denounces any idea that the sinner's personal endeavours or works promote his salvation in any way, asking, 'What think you, then, if I tell you, that you are justified freely through faith in Jesus Christ, without any regard to any work or fitness foreseen in us at all? for salvation is the free gift of God. I know no fitness in man, but a fitness to be cast into the lake of fire and brimstone for ever. Our righteousnesses in God's sight are but as filthy rags. We cannot away with them. Our holiness, if we have any, is not the cause but the effect, of our justification in God's sight. "We love God, because he first loved us." We must not come to God as the proud Pharisee did, bringing in, as it were, a reckoning of our services. We must come in the temper and language of the poor publican, smiting upon our breasts, and saying God be merciful to me a sinner: For Jesus justifies us while we are ungodly. "He came not to call the righteous, but sinners, to repentance." The poor in Spirit only; they who are willing to go out of themselves, and rely wholly on the righteousness of another, are so blessed as to be members of his kingdom. The righteousness, the whole righteousness of Jesus Christ, is to be imputed to us instead of our own: "For we are not under the law, but

---

[1]    Taken from Brown's *Memoirs of Mr. Hervey,* p. 137.

under grace;" and "to as many as walk after this rule, peace be on them; for they, and they only, are the true Israel of God." In the great work of man's redemption, boasting is entirely excluded, which could not be, if only one of our works was to be joined with the merits of Christ.'

It was thus Whitefield's Christ-honouring sermon that finally opened Hervey's eyes and revealed to him that Jesus had indeed chosen him to become a bearer of a righteousness that was for ever acceptable to God. Now Hervey was truly converted and abandoned the filthy rags of his own righteousness to be clothed in Christ's righteousness. He made sure that Whitefield was one of the very first to hear the news. Hervey wrote joyfully:

> I now desire to work in my blessed Master's service, not *for*, but *from* salvation. I believe that Jesus Christ, the incarnate God, is my Saviour; that He has done all which I was bound to perform; and suffered all I was condemned to sustain; and so has procured a full, final and everlasting salvation for a poor damnable sinner. I would now fain *serve* Him who has *saved* me. I would glorify Him before *men*, who has justified me before *God*. I would study to please Him in holiness and righteousness all the days of my life. I seek this blessing, not as a *condition* but as a *part*—a choice and inestimable part—of that complete salvation, which Jesus has purchased for me.[1]

Here we see how Bible-based Hervey's new theology was. Up to now he had preached a universal atonement, applicable on condition that its receivers were both worthy of it and willing to accept it. There was thus no certain aim in Christ's atonement. The ordeal was gone through as a venture so that man might take up or leave salvation at will. The wherewithal was there, but it became effective only on reception. Now Hervey saw how Christ had not only *provided* a full atonement for him but also *procured* it, thus leaving nothing to chance. With this atonement came full justification and a will to be holy—and there were no 'ifs' and 'buts' about it. This is the mature Gospel that reforms man and it was now the full Gospel that Hervey was to preach and teach for the rest of his life. In believing that all salvation is of grace and not of the works of man, Hervey was to meet with great opposition. The Reformed doctrines of free-grace as opposed to free-will, were little held in Hervey's days and several of his closest friends, including John Wesley, were to condemn him for stressing the need for Christ's righteousness to the detriment, as they saw it, of the need for a righteousness of one's own. Hervey found in Whitefield a man

---

[1]    Evangelical Magazine, 1794, p. 503.

after his own heart and experience and he could confide in him how his once going the Wesleyan way was robbing the crown of righteousness from Christ's head. In one of his very first letters to Whitefield after his conversion, Hervey wrote:

Dear Mr. Whitefield,

Your favour struck me with an agreeable surprise: I verily thought my stubborn silence had razed me from your remembrance; but since you still have an affection for an ungrateful friend, I take this opportunity of returning my thankful acknowledgements.

I rejoice to hear the REDEEMER'S cause revives. Set up thyself, O incarnate God! Let disappointments attend the attempts of thy foes and the devices of hell: but let thy servants be prosperous, and their message crowned with success.

Dear Sir, I cannot boast of trophies erected here by the CAPTAIN of our salvation: I hope the arm of the LORD will be revealed more and more among us. I hope the triumphs of FREE GRACE will have wider spread and freer course, and prevail mightily over our unbelief. I own with shame and sorrow that I have been too long a BLIND LEADER of the BLIND: my tongue and my pen have perverted the good ways of GOD: they have darkened the glory of redeeming merit and sovereign grace. I have dared to invade the prerogatives of an all-sufficient SAVIOUR, and to pluck the crown off his head. My writings and discourses have derogated from the honours, the everlasting and incommunicable honours of JESUS. They presumed to give works a share in the redemption and recovery of a lost sinner: they have placed those filthy rags upon the throne of the LAMB, and by that means debased the SAVIOUR, and exalted the sinner.

But I trust the divine truth begins to dawn on my soul. O may it, like the rising sun, shine more and more, till the day break in all its brightness, and the shadows flee away. Now was I possessed of all the righteous acts that have made saints and martyrs famous in all generations: could they all be transferred to me, and might I call them all my own, I would renounce them all that I might win CHRIST. I would not dare to appear before the bright and burning EYE of GOD with such hay, straw and stubble. No, dear Sir, I would long to be clothed in a MEDIATOR's RIGHTEOUSNESS, and ascribe all my salvation to the most unmerited and freest grace.

I have just been giving an exhortation to my young brethren. I have warned them to remember their CREATOR in the days of their youth. My thoughts were led to the subject by an alarming PROVIDENCE, which snatched one of their fellows in the gaiety and bloom of life. May the hand of the ALMIGHTY set home the word of his ministers: may young persons come in the vigour of health, to the REDEEMER's feet, and devote their warm affections to his service. And O may the preacher himself both lead them in the way, and encourage them to follow. Dear Sir, cease not to pray for me: desist not to counsel me, since I perceive you cannot forbear to love me.

I am,

Yours affectionately,
JAMES HERVEY
Æt. 27 years.[1]

Hervey always showed great tolerance and love to those who opposed him from amongst his Christian brethren. He could behave so because he never forgot that it was a work of grace which had opened his own eyes at a time when he had believed exactly as his opponents. Writing to Lady F. Shirley he says:

There was a time when I would have most heartily joined opposition to gospel-doctrine, for then I thought to establish my own righteousness. I would fain have been something, and would have done something, to inherit eternal life, and could not brook a total submission to the righteousness of God; but repeated infirmities, repeated sins, repeated sorrows, have been the means, under the influence of the Spirit, to cure me of this arrogant temper. It is now the daily desire of my soul to see more and more the bitterness, the insufficiency of all that is called my own, but to delight myself in the unsearchable riches, and triumph in the transcendental excellencies, of Jesus Christ my Lord.[2]

**The thoughts of a changed man**

Once converted, Hervey went through a terrible period of bad-conscience. He was physically too ill to work for lengthy periods and now spiritual thoughts of his former life weighed him down, too. He could not forget the arrogance and self-righteousness which he had previously shown and though he rejoiced in God's grace, his own previous pride and vanity caused him great heart-ache. He became determined to have nothing to do with anything that might cause him to think highly of himself. Toplady relates how Hervey was talking to a man who began to flatter him because of his beautiful writings. Hervey put his hand on his breast and said, 'O,

---

[1]   Written from Bideford, 1741, Letter to Mr. Whitefield, Appendix, pp. i-ii, *The Character of the Rev. James Hervey, A.M.*

[2]   *Letters to Lady F. Shirley*, Letter XCVI

sir, you would not strike the sparks of applause, if you knew how much corrupt tinder I have within.'[1]

Hervey was a master of words and had written some beautiful poetry. Now, on reflection, he felt that writing poetry had been merely a self-titillation so he destroyed much of it. This is bad news indeed for those who are lovers of poetry as Hervey was a skilled workman in poetic crafts-manship. The snippets which have survived in Hervey's letters show how correct was his decision as the unconverted poet had merely revelled in the thought of receiving a crown of righteousness studded with the jewels of his own good works.

Referring to the self-praise in his former poetry Hervey states:

> These lines, in whatever hands they are lodged, and whatever else of a like kind may have dropt from my pen, I now publicly dis-claim; they are the very reverse of my present belief, in which I hope to persevere as long as I have any being. Far be it from me to suppose that any work of mine should, in order to create my peace, or cherish my confidence, be coupled with Christ's most holy acts. I speak the words of our church, and I speak the sense of the prophet, 'I will trust, and not be afraid;' wherefore? because I am inherently holy? rather because *God* is my salvation; God manifested in the flesh has finished my transgression, and made an end of my sin; and in this most magnificent work will I rejoice. I speak agreeably to the declaration of the Holy Ghost: 'Fear not, for thou shalt not be ashamed, neither shalt thou be confounded.' Why? because thy inherent goodness shall prevent thy confusion? No; but upon a foot-ing infinitely more solid, for a reason infinitely more satisfactory, because thy Maker is thy Husband; the consequence of which is, all thy debts and deficiencies are upon him, all his consummate righteousness is upon thee.[2]

Reading poetry had also been one of Hervey's chief delights. He loved Edmund Spencer and had spent many happy hours with his *Fairie Queen*. The poem so enraptured him, as it has enraptured thousands, so that he became fully absorbed in the sensuous delight of obtaining honey from the briars of contamination, as he put it. Hervey thus determined to read Spencer no more. Because of his eloquence in the pulpit and the charm of his letters, Hervey would reap praise upon praise from his admirers. This caused him to put aside any letter that flattered him and ignore any praise

---

[1]    Anecdotes, Incidents, and Historical Passages, *Works*, pp. 505-506.

[2]    Quoted by John Brown in his biography of Hervey, p. 16. The source is given as *Aspasio Vindicated* but I have been unable to find these lines in the work quoted.

that came his way so that his friends soon realised that they had better use plain speech when dealing with Hervey or they would obtain little response. It might be thought that Hervey went too far in guarding his eyes, ears, tongue and pen but he was determined not to know anything but Christ Jesus. Indeed, it may be supposed that Hervey's poetic skills encouraged several later hymn-writers to enlarge upon themes Hervey took up in poetry. Thus we find Hervey's earlier allusion to the Rock of Ages reflected in Augustus Toplady's later hymn of that name and Hervey's *Juvenal Imitated* contains themes which have been taken up verbatim by a number of later Christian poets, not the least being David Malet whose hymn bearing Hervey's last lines was published some time later.

Hervey's original composition bearing the well-known end-lines is:

Since all the downward track of time
God's watchful eye surveys;
O who so wise to choose our lot,
And regulate our ways?

Since none can doubt his equal love,
Immeasurably kind,
To his unerring gracious will
Be every wish resigned.

Good when he gives, supremely good!
Nor less when he denies,
E'en crosses from his sovereign hand
Are blessings in disguise.

# Chapter Four:
# The New Man in Christ Jesus

## The Bideford curacy

Hervey became curate at Bideford in 1740 under the rectorship of his friend Nichols who had been close to the Oxford Methodists. Now a converted man, Hervey did not hide his new found experience and faith under a bushel. Doctrinally, he was rapidly leaving Rationalism and Arminianism behind, overtaking Amyraldianism and Neonomianism and settling down to the Biblical doctrines of grace, often called Calvinism. He always, however, remained cautious on the topic of double predestination, fearing such teaching might discourage the faint and give the self-righteous a false assurance. His preaching, however, soon caused critics of Bible-based doctrine, including many former friends, to be startled at the change. This was particularly because of the way in which Hervey distinguished between law and gospel, rejecting any saving element in the former; a matter which earned for him the name of Antinomian from the theologically unsound. Hervey saw with true Biblical clarity that the law required a perfect obedience of the sinner to which he could never attain but the gospel taught a perfect vicarious substitution and perfect obedience worked out by Christ on our behalf and imputed to us as a surety thus removing all our guilt and punishment. It was a shock to Hervey to find that so many professing Christians rejected the doctrine of actual imputation, whether man's sins to Christ or Christ's righteous obedience to the elect. After conversion, he did not hesitate to condemn this denial as Socinian, pointing out Dr. Whitby, the darling of the Arminians, as one of the major purveyors of this heresy. Hervey's friends were quick to tell Hervey that his new faith had blinded his eyes to the value of the ecumenical theology of such as Richard Baxter (1615-1691) who wished to combine Calvinism with Arminianism, the Protestant faith with Popery and found a universal church in which peace reigned because doctrine was disavowed. Baxter, of course, denied that

God's demand for a perfect obedience was fulfilled by His Son, a doctrine which became the central part of Hervey's witness. Other friends advised Hervey to follow the teachings of Bishop Fowler who confused the doctrine of justification and imputed righteousness with man's own supposed, but non-existent, 'sincere righteousness'.[1] This smacked too much of the Neonomianism Hervey was only too happy to leave as he had experienced in his own soul the need for the righteousness of Another.

It would be wrong to think that Hervey was now becoming a haughty, controversial figure, raising the ire of his fellow men. Though once a man who seemed predestined to be an off-putting prig, always patting himself on the back for his holier-than-thou nature, there were now four new and transforming aspects in his nature which kept him humble and a man of peace. The first was Hervey's new view of himself. Speaking of the condescension of Christ to be his Shepherd, he wrote to his sister in 1741 to say, 'Unworthy, altogether unworthy of such an inestimable favour, I desire to lie at the feet of his free unmerited grace, seeking what he is ready to give, though I, alas! am most undeserving. And surely we have good reason to hope, and the very best encouragement to seek. For if he gave his life, and spilt his blood for us, will he not much rather give us pardon for our sins, and justification through his righteousness?' The second change, illustrated by this letter, was Hervey's commitment to positive gospel witness. His whole life was to become a testimony to others of Christ's righteous love and atoning sacrifice for His Church. He had no time for anything else. Wherever and whenever we find Hervey, whether in his church, breakfast room, study or at his pastoral walks, we find him witnessing to his Saviour's love. In his business letters as in his private letters, whether to the rich or the poor, we see Hervey as a shining testimony to the grace of God spending every breath in the service of the Master. The third reason why Hervey, by God's grace, was kept from becoming a public controversial figure was his broken health. Maintaining his flock sapped him of all the strength he had. As early as 1738, he confessed to his sister of 'a languor and faintness, a feebleness and inability for action'.

Hervey had to conserve and consolidate his energies for the 'one thing needed' to which the Lord had called him and he had become the last man on earth who could stand up in the heat of conflict and public debate and rant and rave over controversial issues. The fourth reason was that the Lord, in His kindness, gave Hervey a life of peace with a flock who adored him. Though he was criticised from many quarters, it was usually by men who either respected him highly or who were simply too far away to do him harm. The only harsh, fierce, unbending critic Hervey ever had was

---

[1]  *A Collection of Letters*, CXXVIII.

his own former tutor John Wesley who thundered against Hervey when that saint lay dying. But gentle Hervey's thoughts were too much in Heaven at that time to be troubled by a man who denied the righteousness that saves, thus living in opposition to his own preaching. But Wesley's controversy was more with himself and his highly conflicting conceptions of God's provisions and man's abilities inherent in his Arminianism. Hervey lived a life of faith outside of such realms and thus could not be affected by them.

Though a semi-invalid throughout all his ministry, Hervey still reached hundreds of thousands with his written ministry and thousands with his preaching. His numerous extant letters show how Hervey never hesitated, whether in writing to his own family, friends or strangers, to preach the whole counsel of God. Writing to a friend in 1741, Hervey tells him:

> If I had the righteousness of a saint, says one, O how happy I should be: If I had the righteousness of an angel, says another, I should fear no evil. But I am bold to say, that the poorest sinner that believes in Christ has a righteousness infinitely more excellent than either saints or angels. For if the law asks for sinless perfection, it is to be found in my divine Surety. If the law requires an obedience that may stand before the burning eye of God, behold it is in Jesus my Mediator. Should the strictest justice arraign me, and the purest holiness make its demands upon me, I remit them both to my dying and obedient Immanuel: with him the Father is always well pleased; in him the believer is complete. They who know Christ's power, will put their trust in him for sanctification of heart, and newness of life. Though sin is rooted in my soul, and riveted in my constitution, yet Christ can purge it out. Though it were twisted with every nerve of my flesh, yet he can make the rough tempers smooth, and the crooked dispositions straight: the vile affections, like legions of devils, he can root out, and fill every heart with the pure love of God. To which happy state of soul may both you and I be brought while here below; that we may be made meet to ascend to that habitation of God, where nothing unclean can enter.

One of the factors that helped shake Hervey into realising the folly of life without trusting in Christ as a surety was the severe illness of his father at this time. In April 1741. Hervey writes:

> My poor father lies languishing in a most deplorable and distressed condition. His case is uncommon: his pains are racking and extremely acute. Physicians have done their uttermost, and can

contribute no relief. Art stands baffled, medicines confess their impotence, and the disorder, sharp and inveterate, triumphs over all human applications. This may ere long be our case. O that we may be so wise as to make preparation for the worst! If we remember our Creator in the days of our health, he will not forget us when trouble and anguish take hold of us. Forget us! No, but will make all our bed in our sickness; will soften our agonizing pillow; will wipe off the dying sweat; will speak peace to our soul, when horrible dread overwhelmeth it, and will provide us an eternal building, when this earthly tabernacle totters, and sinks, and tumbles into dust. That the God of all consolation may do all this for my poor father now, and for you in the time of need, is the earnest prayer of, J. H.[1]

### An invalid's ministry to the sick and dying

Hervey's letters from Bideford show that he was missing his family very much, though he had good friends around him, and his thoughts were often at Hardingstone. In 1742, the small pox raged throughout Britain and Hervey saw how the disease could carry off one after another of his parishioners, whether rich or poor. He had hardly finished caring for one gentlewoman who was quickly released from her pains when he heard from his father that his two much-loved aunts had also been struck down. Hervey never quite knew where his father stood in spiritual matters and used every opportunity to speak of the gospel to him. Hervey now took the opportunity to encourage his father to be more open in his witness and to let Christ shine through him, remembering the message of Psalm 103:2, 'Bless the Lord, O my soul, and forget not all his benefits.' Speaking of how one quickly forgets the dead, Hervey likens this to how Christians (thinking of his own father) tend to forget the great work Christ has done for them. Thus Hervey gently admonishes his father to whom he always respectfully referred as 'Reverend and Honoured Sir' and says:

> Do we not unaccountably forget Jesus Christ, our almighty friend, and everlasting glory, our invaluable heritage? Where is the man that remembers his bleeding Saviour on his bed, and thinks upon him when he is waking? No; the Redeemer's inconceivable love, and the precious benefits of his passion, are buried in a deep oblivion. This world then of darkness, apparitions, and forgetfulness is the grand dormitory; flesh and blood the tomb of our immortal minds, *Nascentes morimur.*

---

[1]  Taken from Brown's *Memoirs of Mr. Hervey*, p. 372. Original source not given.

Hervey's ageing father now became ill again and his son was compelled to leave Bideford for a time to look after him. His sister, too, became very ill, an event which left Hervey greatly distressed as he loved her more than anything else in the world. He wrote to comfort her but also to show her that God carries out His own good plan even when we are stricken with illness, saying, 'Sickness and afflictions are God's call; they are divine admonitions, and warn us not to be fond of the world, but set our affections on things above. May the blessed Jesus make them effectual to our souls!' Hervey's sister recovered and though Hervey's father was able to carry on his work for another few years, his constitution was permanently ruined.

Witnessing to the sick and the dying is one of the most difficult tasks of the Christian and it is very difficult to name death by name and prepare a soul to meet his Maker. When writing or speaking to the sick and dying, Hervey never hesitated to draw spiritual truths from physical ailment. In the letter of October 12, 1742, Hervey told his ailing sister:

> The small pox is marking many, and carrying off some among us: it is a privilege of no small value to be past that infectious disorder: I have often thought that it is too lively an emblem of the condition of our souls, by corrupt nature and evil practice. So polluted, so loathsome is our better part in the eye of uncreated purity, till we are washed, till we are cleansed in redeeming blood. May we earnestly long to be washed in that fountain, opened in our Saviour's side, for sin and for uncleanness.

### Recanting his former life

George Whitefield was often invited by Hervey to preach in the neighbourhood and found Hervey's pulpit always open to him though pulpits in many other churches were closed. One of the greatest joys of his life was to see the man he so loved blossom into a true gospel preacher. Whitefield wrote to Hervey on December 23, 1742, encouraging him in the good work, saying:

> My Dear Brother Hervey,
>     I thank you for your kind and very agreeable letter. It was refreshing to my Soul, and stirred me to give thanks on your behalf. O my dear brother, I hope nothing will deter you from preaching the glad tidings of salvation to a world lying in the wicked one. I would not but be a poor despised minister of Jesus Christ for ten thousand worlds.
>
> For this let men revile my name,
> No cross I shun, I fear no shame:

All hail reproach, and welcome pain,
Only thy terrors, Lord, restrain.

The love of Christ doth him constrain,
To seek the wand'ring souls of men:
With cries, entreaties, tears, to save,
And snatch them from the gaping grave.

Go on, thou man of God; and may the Lord cause thy bow to abide in strength. I should be glad to come, and shoot some gospel arrows in Devonshire; but the cloud seems now to point towards America. Blessed be God for making any of my poor writings of use to you. If I did not proclaim free grace, the stones would cry out against me. Whilst I am writing, the fire kindles. This fire has been, of late, kindled in many hearts. Our large Society goes on well. We have many who walk in the comforts of the Holy Ghost. I hear of glorious things from various parts. I hope, ere long, we shall hear of persons going from post to post, and crying, 'Babylon is fallen, Babylon is fallen !' I trust you, my dear sir, will be made a happy instrument, in the Mediator's kingdom, of pulling down Satan's strongholds. Pray write me word, how the war is going on between Michael and the Dragon. For the present, adieu![1]

Though often writing in a reclining position as he was too weak to sit upright, Hervey wrote multi-paged letters to his old friends in the ministry who were hiding their lights, encouraging them to shine forth for Christ. He also saw it as a special ministry to any fellow-clergymen hitherto unknown to him to write to them if he had good grounds to fear that they were not preaching the true gospel. He told them that it would be unkind of him not to warn them of the error of their ways and a sign of unfaithfulness to his Master if he did not do so. Not a few ministers regularly received lengthy letters analysing their sermons point for point. These had been noted down by Hervey's expanding circle of friends and passed on to the evangelical pastor.

Hervey was now fervently preaching the evangelistic gospel of the doctrines of grace which are so anchored in the Scriptures but which are so foreign to the Arminian mind. Again, as in the case of the ploughman, God used the humble poor of his parish, as also a lady at whose house he boarded, to lead him into a deeper knowledge of the truth. The result of

---

[1]   *Whitefield's Works*, Vol. II, pp. 3,4, Tyerman's *The Life of the Reverend George Whitefield*, vol. ii, p. 47.

this break with all ideas of human agency, human ability and human righteousness gave rise to what are now called Hervey's *Recantation Sermons*
on Romans 5:19, which Augustus Toplady published in 1769. Now, though
far from strong, Hervey was conducting public worship every day and
preaching twice on Sundays and once on Tuesday and Friday respectively,
besides his house to house catechetical and visitation work. Through the
encouragement of Orchard, he set up a weekly evening prayer meeting
and founded an Assembly for Christian Improvement and a Religious
Society. The Assembly met in an inn on the first Tuesday of every month
from noon until seven in the summer and until four in the winter. It was
designed for people of leisure who could afford to dine together at one
shilling and sixpence a time and donate half a crown per meeting to the
poor. Those whose business prevented them from attending were expected
to pay both fees into the charity purse as if they had been present. As the
members met in a place frequented by the general public, prayers were to
be conducted before and after the meeting at the members own homes but
during the meeting much of the time was given over to Bible exposition
and discussion concerning the texts chosen for study. The religious society remained an evangelical stronghold in Bideford for over forty years.
One class was for men only, whereas the other class was for married cou-
ples and women into which no unmarried man was admitted. The classes
met alternately, once every two weeks. Their sole design was 'to promote
real holiness in heart and life, every member of it is to have this continually in view, trusting in the divine power and gracious conduct of the Holy
Spirit, through our Lord Jesus Christ, to excite, advance, and perfect all
good in us.'[1]

In his leisure time Hervey made copious notes on Scriptural topics and
corresponded with a large number of people. He formed a close friendship with the son of a parish clerk by the name of Donn, who was a brilliant mathematician and astronomer. Donn was able to deepen Hervey's
knowledge of the stars and planets but he died whilst Hervey was at
Bideford, though only twenty-four years of age. In the funeral service for
his young friend, Hervey used the knowledge of the departed to stir his
hearers up to prepare to meet their God themselves, saying:

> He that taught you to find your way through the trackless ocean,
> is himself passed into the invisible world, and landed on the eternal
> shores. He that taught you to speculate the skies, and observe the
> celestial bodies, is gone to a distance, vastly more remote and im-
> measurable than theirs. O that you would lay this his last remove to

---

[1]   Quoted from *Rules and Orders of a Religious Society*, Hervey's *Works*, p. 719.

heart, as diligently as you did his principles of navigation, in your memory. The same change must take place in you; and, in a little time, you must make your last voyage.[1]

### Hervey's fellowship with 'firebrand' Thomson

Only too conscious of his physical frailty which hindered his visiting and travelling greatly, Hervey now felt called to use the medium of writing as an avenue of service so that he could reach those whom he could otherwise not seek out. He thus started to work on his *Meditations among the Tombs*. This move was encouraged and facilitated by George Thomson (1704-82), minister of St. Ginny's[2] church, Stoke-Abbey, offering from time to time to take over Hervey's rather demanding new cure at Bideford, fourteen miles away, and thus allow Hervey to supply his charge at Stoke-Abbey and be looked after by Paul Orchard and his family. Orchard, however, died soon after Hervey moved to Bideford. Thomson was a brilliant scholar of independent means who, after graduating from Exeter College, Oxford, served as a chaplain on the *Tiger*, a man-of-war which took him to America. On inheriting his family estate and an annual income of £500, he settled down in Cornwall, becoming the Vicar of St. Ginny's. Thomson went through years of depression in his ministry caused by his own low spiritual state. Through reading Romans 3:26, 'To declare, I say, at this time his righteousness: that he might be just, and the justifier of him which believeth in Jesus' he was able to accept eternal security at Christ's hands and received peace with God at the age of thirty-five. He then became one of the very earliest Evangelicals of the Church of England, adding many souls to the Kingdom of God through his preaching, Thomas Haweis (1732-1820), chaplain to Lady Huntingdon, being one of his more notable converts. For his zeal, Thomson was called before the Bishop for acting in an 'unorthodox' manner and most of the neighbouring clergy shut their pulpits to him. Balleine calls Thomson 'a firebrand of the Berridge type' and when Bishop Lavington warned him that if he did not watch his steps, he would be defrocked, Thomson took off his gown and, folding it neatly, laid it at the Bishop's feet, saying he could preach just as well without it.[3]

Hervey had a more realistic view of his friend than that of the Bishop. He described Thomson as unfurling the gospel standard with a tongue touched from the heavenly altar, pleading with his people not to follow the wiles of Satan and lean on his broken reeds but to build their faith on the Rock of Ages. He preached to his flock as the ruined and undone sinners

---

[1]  Taken from Brown's *Memoirs of Mr. Hervey*, p. 142.

[2]  Also called St. Genny's.

[3]  *A History of the Evangelical Party*, p. 67.

they were, showing how God's mighty arm was still strong to save them from their plight. His message was always that 'They who know Christ's free goodness, will put their whole trust in him, and seek no other way to the Father of mercy but through his merit.'[1]

When Whitefield visited Bideford in 1743, just after Hervey left, he was amazed at the work Hervey had done there, telling friends that he had shepherded 'one of the best little flocks in all England.' He describes what he found in a letter dated November 11:

> The Rev. Mr. Thompson, Rector of St. Genny's, Cornwall, is here. God willing, I will go with him to-morrow. There is also another clergyman about eighty years of age, but not above one year old in the school of Christ. He lately preached three times and rode forty miles the same day. The Dissenting minister and his wife were very hearty; and, perhaps, here is one of the most settled female Christian Societies in the kingdom. I cannot well describe with what power the word was attended. Yesterday, in the afternoon and evening, it was just like as at Edinburgh. The old clergyman was much broken. A young Oxonian, who came with him, and many others, were most deeply affected. I suppose, there were upwards of two thousand, in the evening, in the meeting-house. Dear Mr. Hervey, one of our first Methodists at Oxford, and who was lately a curate here, had laid the blessed foundation.[2]

So fruitful was the work in Bideford that Whitefield decided to stay there for two weeks, preaching regularly in the neighbourhood. After the services at St. Ginny's, Whitefield and Thomson always found many weeping, convicted sinners who could not go home until they found peace with God. Thomson went from seat to seat to counsel the penitent and lead them to the Saviour.

## Troubles with the new rector

Hervey had hardly been a year at Bideford when Nichols, his Rector, died. There was no possibility that Hervey would be given the post as he was a mere curate and, besides, the living was a very lucrative one and Hervey knew all too well that it would be given to a person of influence and connections who was eager to climb higher in his clerical career. Writing to a friend on March 2, 1741, Hervey bemoaned the fact that spiritual abilities were seldom looked for in the race to the top which was only too

---

[1]    See Letter XIV, p. 748 ff. Hervey's *Works*.

[2]    Tyerman's, *The Life of the Reverend George Whitefield*. p. 78.

common in church matters. After a great delay, the new Rector was inaugurated and Hervey found that his worst fears were to be fulfilled. The new broom swept rigorously and looked upon Hervey as worse than cobwebs and did everything, by fair means or foul, to rid himself of his curate. The Rector who hardly showed his nose in the parish received the bulk of the revenues afforded by the living and expected his curate to do all his work for a small fraction of what he received himself. It is thought that at this time, Hervey had an income of no more than £15-20 per annum, including a small allowance from his father. Yet Hervey could not bear to have a penny in his pocket when others were in need and soon he was spending more on the parish poor than his very meagre salary permitted.

It soon became obvious that Hervey could find no common ground with his new superior nor any sympathy whatsoever. Hervey confided to a friend:

> Truly his usage bids fair to awaken a sharp resentment; but I think it moves me rather to pity; it grieves me to see one of his office act so mean, so equivocating, (I wish I could not say) so false and dishonest a part. My father and mother are amazed at his disingenuous and fraudulent tricks, though, for his credit's sake, I have not so much as mentioned to them the grand piece of injustice, that of receding from his promise, and withdrawing one-fifth of my stipulated allowance.[1]

The situation became worse as the Bideford congregation made it quite obvious that they regarded their beloved shepherd as the true pastor of the church and not the newcomer. Soon the Rector told the church that there was no money to be had at all for the luxury of a curate. The parishioners, however, knew that the only other pocket into which he intended to put the money thus saved was his own. The church rallied around Hervey and told the Rector that they would raise the money themselves for their curate's salary but their plan reached deaf ears. Though the Bideford congregation was large, the people were very poor and the effort would have meant a great sacrifice for them. A number of Hervey's gentlemen friends felt they must intervene and decided to set up a fund so that they could raise Hervey's income to at least £60 per annum, which was the average rate of pay for a curate at this time. This is the salary John Newton received on becoming curate at Olney, though it must not be forgotten that Hervey's contemporary William Romaine, great preacher and successful pastor as he was, received only £18 per annum. The £60 Hervey now received, however,

---

[1] Taken from Brown's *Memoirs of Mr. Hervey*, p. 375. Original source not given.

were not enough. As soon as Hervey received any money at all, he would give it to those whom he felt were in greater need. His friends had thus to hit upon a better idea of helping him than giving him money. They knew that he never said no to an 'honest' borrower so they used this fact to make sure Hervey always had at least a few pennies in his purse. Whenever Hervey was paid, his friends would go to him one by one and ask for a small loan which they invariably received. When they noticed that Hervey's pockets were empty, they would suddenly pretend to have come into money and pay back their loans. In this way they kept Hervey solvent. All these endeavours of the Bideford church and Hervey's friends seemed to antagonise the Rector all the more and he gave Hervey notice to leave.

### Further witness from Hervey's sick-bed

Hervey's dormant consumption again broke out and he was once more severely ill and retired to Bath to convalesce. Writing to a lady friend and her husband from there, he did not complain about his own state but used the topic of health to witness to the couple saying:

> I should rejoice to hear of you both being partakers of that which I wish you to enjoy; and none can be said to truly enjoy health, but those who improve it to the purpose: all others waste health, embezzle it, squander it away; all but those who use it as a precious opportunity of making their calling and election sure.[1]

Whilst at Bath in August, 1743, Hervey heard of a scandalous sermon an Anglican dignitary had preached in praise of wealth and his wealthy hearers. This fashionable clergyman received a lengthy letter from Hervey in no time, outlining in almost 19,000 words why he had 'dishonoured the divine Redeemer, and perverted his everlasting gospel,' advising the recipient 'to condemn that offensive sermon to the flames.' It seems that the preacher had complimented the Lords and Ladies and rich business people in his affluent congregation on their prosperity and taken their riches as a sign that they were right with God. Hervey outlines patiently the difference between worldly prosperity and spiritual prosperity, showing how much more difficult it is for the rich to gain the latter rather than the poor. Speaking of the clergyman's high-bred audience, Hervey tells him that he may address them as 'illustrious', 'worshipful' and 'right honourable' but without Christ they were miserable wretches. Hervey uses the example of godly Archbishop Usher who, as a young man, experienced great affluence, good health, a good reputation and what the world calls good luck

---

[1]    Letter XVIII, *Works.*

but he found all this gave him no joy as he was full of apprehensions that God had forsaken him and left him a reprobate.

After outlining the soul destroying symptoms of the lust for riches and the pride that so easily comes with prosperity, Hervey portrays the riches of Christ which provide a joy unspeakable and full of glory. To be reconciled to God, the Father, to have an interest in Christ the Son and to be renewed by the Holy Spirit are the prosperous riches of the believer. Then Hervey goes on painstakingly to outline the gospel concerning the Father's, Son's and Holy Spirit's work in redemption which was earned not with silver and gold but with the precious blood of the Prince of Peace. The preacher had been basing his 'eat, drink and be merry because you have the money to afford it' sermon on the wedding at Caanan. Hervey points out patiently how the scene of the marriage ceremony especially chosen by Christ to work his first miracle and probably chosen to show Christ coming for His Bride the Church and to show how the eternal joys of the gospel i.e. spiritual prosperity, can never come to those 'wedded by self-opinionativeness to their own righteousness.' Thus the miracles of our Lord are not there to pander to our lust for material profit but are 'so many living mirrors of his mediatorial mercies, in which we discern a most expressive figure of those spiritual good things which we extremely want, and may fully enjoy through Christ Jesus.'

There was another incident at Bath which did not come to the public's eye until years after it happened. Richard Nash Esq., commonly called Beau Nash and former Master of the Ceremonies at Bath, was perhaps the most talked of gentleman of his age, a playboy without rival and the centre of much eighteenth century gossip if not scandal. When he died, his papers were examined by his family to see what was worth preserving. Knowing what kind of a reputation Nash had, one would think that whatever he left behind him would be unimportant from a Christian point of view. This is not the case. Amongst his papers, there was a letter from Hervey warning the wanton rake of the wrath to come and the salvation which is freely given to repentant sinners. In the letter, Hervey uses the example of a deathbed scene he had witnessed in which a former society beau is convicted of the follies of his ways, realises that judgement is imminent, confesses that it is too late for him to repent—and meets death in indescribable agony and fear. The letter was wisely preserved by Nash's executors and appears in full in chapter five on Hervey's earlier works. It serves as a permanent and nigh perfect example of gospel application.

### Absent in body but present in spirit

After his dismissal from Bideford, the next few years were very difficult for Hervey. His elderly father was only too pleased to have him back as his curate at Collingtree but he was almost heart-broken to leave his town church and once again become a country parson. He kept up an intensive correspondence with his old flock and George Thomson used his influence to obtain permission from the Rector to preach once a month at Bideford. Hervey, however, was full of misgivings, blaming himself for not giving a better testimony to his former Rector, telling friends that his head was hanging down like a bulrush because of the anguish of his mind. This anguish became the greater when he heard that the Bideford Rector was playing the part of an hireling and striving to tempt his own sheep away from the Good Shepherd. Hervey wasted no time in addressing his Bideford correspondents, comforting them by explaining how the Lord stands round His people for ever as the hills surround Jerusalem and He will not permit them to fall. Of the renegade rector, he says:

> Whoever attempts the ruin of a soul that is staid on Jesus, must wrench the sovereignty from the hand of Omnipotence, and cause unshaken faithfulness to fail. So long as all things in heaven and earth, and under the earth, do bow, and obey the Lamb that was slain; so long as Christ is a God unchangeable and faithful, that cannot lie, so long shall a poor feeble worm, that trusts in him, be secure from apostasy and perdition.[1]

Hervey had made sure that all his former flock had been equipped with Bibles. Now, in order to keep the minds of his Bideford friends on their Lord and on the gospel, Hervey had a number of labels printed with gospel promises to be stuck into the blank pages at the beginning and end of their Bibles. The first label carried the words,

God hath given us exceeding great and precious promises, that by these we might be partakers of the divine nature. 2 Peter 1:4.

**Divine Teaching**
Isaiah 29:18 The eyes of the blind shall see out of obscurity.
Jeremiah 31:34 They shall all know me, from the least of them unto the greatest of them.
John 14:26 The Holy Ghost shall teach you all things.
Isaiah 58:11 The Lord shall guide thee continually.

**Pardon**
Isaiah 43:25 I am he that blotteth out thy transgressions.
Isaiah 1:18 Sins as scarlet, shall be as white as snow.
1 Peter 2:24 Who his own self bare our sins in his own body on the tree.
1 John 1:7 The blood of Jesus Christ cleanseth from all sin.

---

[1]    Letter XX, *Works*, p. 760.

## Justification
Romans 8:33, 34 It is God that justifieth.
Romans 3:21-24 Justified freely by his grace.
Isaiah 45:24, 25 In the Lord have I righteousness.
2 Corinthians 5:21 We are made the righteousness of God in him.

## Sanctification
Ezekiel 11:19, 20 I will put a new spirit within you.
Titus 2:14 Christ gave himself for us, that he might redeem us from all iniquity.
Hebrews 8:10-12 I will put my laws into their mind, and write them in their hearts.
1 Thessalonians 5:23 The God of peace sanctify your whole spirit, and soul and body.

On the label for the end of the Bible, he put:

## Temporal Blessings
1 Timothy 4:8 Godliness hath the promise of the life that now is.
Psalm 37:3 Verily thou shalt be fed.
Matthew 6:33 Seek first the kingdom of God, and all things shall be added.
1 Timothy 6:17 Who giveth us all things richly to enjoy.

## Temptation
1 Corinthians 10:13 God will not suffer you to be tempted above that ye are able.
2 Corinthians 12:9 My grace is sufficient for thee.
Romans 6:14 Sin shall not have dominion over you.
Luke 22:32 I have prayed for thee, that thy faith fail not.

## Afflictions
Job 5:17 Happy is the man whom God correcteth.
Lamentations 3:32 Though he cause grief, yet will he have compassion.
Psalm 50:15 Call upon me in trouble; I will deliver thee.
Revelation 3:19 As many as I love, I rebuke and chasten.

## Death
1 Corinthians 15:55-57 God giveth us the victory through our Lord Jesus Christ.
2 Corinthians 5:1 If our earthly house is dissolved, we have a building of God.
John 3:16 Whosoever believeth shall have everlasting life.
Psalm 23:4 Though I pass through death, I will fear no evil.

## Conclusion
God, willing more abundantly to show unto the heirs of promise the immutability of his counsel, confirmed it by an oath. Hebrews 6:17.

**Soliciting friends criticism of his writings**
A further anxiety Hervey had was that he had sent off his first literary efforts under the title *Meditations and Reflections* to Samuel Richardson for publication but had not heard how things were developing for months. Fearing that his printer was doing nothing, Hervey took the opportunity to add a dedication and a preface, urging competent people to whom he sent the manuscript to read 'with a file in their hands', performing the combined duties of severe critics and a kind friends. To one such solicited critic Hervey says:

> I hope, sir, my end in venturing to publish is an hearty desire to serve, in some little degree, the interests of Christianity by endeavouring to set some of its most important truths in a light that may both entertain and edify. As I profess this view, I am certain your affectionate regard for the most excellent religion imaginable will incline you to be concerned for the issue of such an attempt, and therefore to contribute to its success, both by bestowing your animadversions upon these small parts, and by speaking of the whole (when it shall come abroad) with all that candour which is natural to the Christian, and will be so greatly needed by this new adventurer in letters.[1]

**Hervey defends the Trinity**
There had long been a discussion in the churches concerning the Trinity and the Athanasian Creed. John Gale (1680-1722), William Whiston (1667-1752), Samuel Chandler (1693-1766) and Daniel Whitby (1638-1726), representing the major denominations had begun to decry the Athanasian view of the relationship between the Son, the Father and the Spirit in favour of more Sabellian, Socinian and Arian views. Indeed, these scholars preached that those whom they viewed as Hyper-Trinitarians hindered true ecumenical fellowship between the churches. Thus we see former Anglicans such as Whiston working closely with Baptists Gale and Foster to form a rather high ritualistic view of the church based on low views of doctrine and the oddities of the more bizarre Early Church Fathers. We also see Presbyterian Chandler developing Arian sympathies with high Anglican office bearers, and having the Dutch and Scottish universities, not forgetting the Royal Family, shower honours upon him for his endeavours. It had become fashionable to find unity in accepting diversity and place mutual tolerance before faith and order. Thus ministers of the gospel who stood firm on the Biblical doctrines of grace and the orthodox

---

[1]    Letter XXI, *Works*, p. 760.

teaching of the Church concerning the Godhead such as John Gill, Robert Hawker (1753-1827) and Hervey were actually accused of being unevangelical in doctrine and unevangelistic in practice.

Towards the end of 1745, we find Hervey defending the Thirty-Nine Articles against the criticisms of learned correspondents. Replying to one critic who found difficulty with Articles I, XIII and XVIII, Hervey shows how gently he dealt with those who were weak in the faith. His defence of the so-called Athanasian nature of the Trinity is quite novel. He tells his friend that if he cannot understand the doctrine of the equality of the Father and the Son, and no one can reduce the Divine Nature into human logic, he has no logical grounds for doubting it. All the more reason why he should give the Scriptures a hearing on the subject. He then shows how Scripture claims that all honours due to the Father are also given the Son and that Old Testament texts such as Numbers 21:6 referring to God are used by the New Testament writers to refer to Christ as Paul in 1 Corinthians 10:9. Hervey's friend accepted Article XX, so he was obviously a man who believed that the Bible was the Word of God and contained everything necessary for salvation. Other eighteenth century orthodox scholars such as Dr. Robert Hawker had a more difficult time as the Presbyterians who challenged them on the Trinity believed that the New Testament writers had completely misunderstood Christ's claims for Himself. Answering his correspondent who puts forward the theory that everyone will be saved who does his best, Hervey shows how those meet for salvation are the very ones who realise that they have most certainly not done their best, but usually their worst and without the promised righteousness of Christ and His atonement, they realise they are lost. Knowledge does not save but faith.

The correspondent had difficulties with the Anglican teaching that works done before the saving grace of God enters into a man are not acceptable to God. So he asked Hervey if he believed that God had made man incapable of doing good works. Hervey explains that he in no way believes that man was created with a natural incapacity to do righteous acts, 'Men were not made by their Creator with this incapacity, but they have brought it upon themselves by their own fault.' 'A corrupt tree' Hervey explains, 'must bring forth corrupt fruit.' Only by being engrafted into the true Vine, Jesus Christ, can a person hope to produce righteous fruit. Hervey points out that God says of Christ, 'This is my beloved Son, *in whom* I am well pleased.' He does not say, 'with whom' but 'in whom'. Hervey takes this to mean that God's pleasure is found in those who are in Christ their representative and He has no pleasure in those who still have their representation in Adam. Hervey ends his letter by affirming that faith is of God and not man, in other words, it is built on what the Scriptures say and not

on the decisions of a church. He also urges his correspondent to believe
that man can know nothing of God unless God gives him that knowledge.

As Hervey's friend seems to believe that the Thirty-Nine Articles are
rather too strict and precise in places, Hervey says:

> Your own meditations, I persuade myself, will discern, much
> more clearly than I can represent, that the compilers of our Articles
> are no other than the echo of St. Paul; or rather, that they only set
> their seal to the doctrines of Christ which he taught; and approve
> that verdict of heaven which he has brought in. This consideration
> will acquit them from the charge of harshness of expression, or
> uncharitableness of sentiment.

It seems that the correspondent not only accepted Hervey's teaching
but urged his friend to champion the cause and 'enter the lists against the
adversaries of the Trinity'. Hervey, writing on January 10, 1745 (O.S.)
declined the offer but went into great detail for his friend's sake concerning the deity of the Holy Spirit against which a Mr. Tomkins was objecting
at the time. Hervey finds evidence of the personality and deity of the Spirit
in the apostolic benediction of 2 Corinthians 13:14, 'The grace of the
Lord Jesus Christ, and the love of God, and the communion of the Holy
Ghost, be with you all.' Christ's command concerning the evangelistic
and teaching duties of the church and the Trinitarian administration of
Christian baptism recorded in Matthew 28:19 is proof enough for Hervey
that the Holy Spirit is a person and divine. Hervey also includes 1 John
5:7 concerning the Three who bear record, rejecting the textual criticism
which looks on this as a later gloss because it is not in the Alexandrine
manuscript. He questions the logic of those who find an omission in one
text and then assume that all occurrences of the passage in other texts must
be errors or forgeries. He questions why we should not take the universal
testimony of the majority of editions rather than the omissions of one as
our guide. Hervey then adds Romans 15:16 (the sanctifying of the Holy
Spirit), and John 16:13-15 (the Spirit as a guide to all truth) and goes on to
discuss the many Scriptural references to the various qualities and characteristics of the Holy Spirit which present Him as a divine person. Hervey
confesses, however, that those who say they are only prepared to believe
what they fully understand will, of course, have a difficult time compre-
hending anything. He is prepared to admit that in many things we see
through a glass darkly but he is also prepared to believe the Scriptures
which admit this human impediment but promise that we shall one day
know as we are known.

Tomkins' *Calm Enquiry* seems to have sown seeds of doubt into the
correspondents mind and we find Hervey writing a third letter, a month
later, discussing the topic of Christ's subjecting Himself to the Father,

whereas there is no mention in the Bible of the Father ever humbling Himself before the Son. Hervey points out how it was the particular office of the Son to humble Himself and be made in all things like us, sin excepted. This assumed nature is not Christ's full nature but is nevertheless the nature Christ voluntarily put on, making Himself lower than the angels, emptying Himself for the task He had set out to fulfil and, in so doing, save His people. Hervey's friend had put forward John 14:28 as a stumbling block to the equality of Christ with the Father. Again, Hervey points out that Christ claims that the Father is greater than He as He is speaking from the point of view of His human nature as Redeemer, sent to redeem by the joint decision of the Holy Trinity. Christ's throne, however, as Hebrews 1:8,9 shows, is divine and eternal but Christ was designated to put that throne aside during His passive and active obedience to the claims of the law for the elect's sake. Nevertheless, Hervey argues, the first chapter of Colossians makes it clear that Christ is the Creator and Head of the universe, the Alpha and Omega of all things and in Him dwells all the fullness of the Godhead.

Hervey admits that 1 Corinthians 15:28, 'And when all things shall be subdued unto him, then shall the Son also himself be subject unto him that put all things under him, that God may be all in all' is not an easy text to expound. He sees this as referring to the finished work of Christ and argues:

> The apostle affirms, that at the consummation of terrestrial things, when the state of human probation ends, and the number of the elect is completed, then shall the Son also himself be subject unto him that put all things under him, that God may be all in all: i.e. according to my judgement, the Son at the commencement of that grand revolution, will entirely resign the administration of his mediatorial kingdom; he will no longer act as an advocate or intercessor, because the reason on which this office is founded, will cease for ever; he will no longer, as a high-priest, plead his atoning blood on behalf of sinners, nor, as a king, dispense the succours of his sanctifying grace, because all guilt will be done away, and the actings of corruption be at an end: he will no longer be the medium of his people's access to the knowledge and enjoyment of the Father, because then they will stand perpetually in the beatific presence, and see face to face, know even as they are known. I may probably mistake the meaning of the words, but whatever shall appear to be their precise signification, this, I think, is so clear as not to admit of any doubt, that it relates to an incarnate person; relates to him who died for our sins, was buried and rose again, 1 Cor. 15:3,4. And can the surrender of all authority made by man Jesus Christ, be any bar to his unlimited equality as God?

This was not the end of Hervey's correspondence with his friend on the Trinity. A few weeks later we find Hervey writing at great length[1] on the deity and person of the Holy Ghost, showing how He is worthy of full worship, helping us in prayer, subduing our iniquities, mortifying the body, shedding abroad the love of God in our hearts, sanctifying us in all our faculties, transforming us into the divine image and sealing us until the day of redemption as the surety of our inheritance.[2] Author friends of Hervey's warned him that he ought to be more subtle in his writings concerning the deity, otherwise he would put people off. He should not name the Names of the Trinity but use circumlocutions suitable to refined taste. Hervey took up the challenge saying:

> I am willing to put the matter to trial, and myself to practice the advice I gave (to the above-mentioned critic). So far from secreting the amiable and majestic names of JESUS and the adorable TRINITY, that I have printed them in grand and conspicuous capitals; that all the world may see I look upon it as my highest honour to acknowledge, to venerate, to magnify my God and Saviour.[3]

Thus, when Hervey published his greatest work, *Theron and Aspasio*, the persons of the Trinity, as the Trinity Himself, were honoured with capitals throughout, which did not stop the work from going into edition after edition.

**The question of whether nature can bring a man to Christ or not**
One of Hervey's correspondents was so enraptured with his nature prose, apparently not grasping his Christian teaching in it, that he wrote to him asking if he thought man could gain direct access to God through nature. A contemplative walk at night with glow-worms glimmering, owls shrieking, the full moon rising and perhaps fear of a ghost haunting, Hervey explains lightly, will never bring a man to Christ. Though the starry heavens may display to some the attributes of God, 'They teach nothing of redemption; this the peculiar prerogative of revelation. Christ the day-star from on high, that points out and makes clear the way of salvation.'[4] In answer to the writer's question concerning Hervey's previous love for the classics and whether they do not furnish him with sufficient imagery, the man of God says:

---

[1]   Over 23 columns on 13 pages of tiny print in my Nelson, 1837 edition of Hervey's *Works*.

[2]   Rom. 8:26; Rom. 8:13; Rom. 5:5; 1 Thess. 5:23; 2 Cor. 3:18; Eph. 4:30; Eph. 1:14.

[3]   *Letters to Lady Shirley*, Letter XC.

[4]   Letter XXXI, *Works*.

Away, my Homer; I have no more need of being entertained by you, since Job and the Prophets furnish me with images much more magnificent, and lessons infinitely more important. Away, my Horace; nor shall I suffer any loss by your absence, while the sweet singer of Israel tunes his lyre, and charms me with the finest flights of fancy, and inspires me with the noblest strains of devotion. And even my prime favourite, my Virgil, may withdraw; since in Isaiah I enjoy all his majesty of sentiment, all his correctness of judgement, all his beautiful propriety of diction.

## Comforting the dying and the bereaved

In 1746, Hervey's youngest brother, Thomas who lived in Basinghall Street, London became seriously ill and as Hervey's father was too weak to make the journey, he asked his son, James, who was just recovering from a severe cold, to visit his brother. The two-day journey was a terrible strain on Hervey's physical resources and he arrived in London to find his brother, in a fierce fever, attended by doctors who could neither cure the sickness nor offer words of Christian comfort. Hervey's brother, who had recently married, had always been the most healthy in a family of sickly constitution. Now God called away the most robust and left the invalid at his bedside. Hervey returned home with a very heavy heart only to find on arrival that Mrs. Stonehouse, his doctor's wife and a good friend, had suddenly died at the age of 25, a few days after giving birth to a daughter. Dr. Stonehouse begged Hervey to stay with him for comfort and spiritual help, so Hervey found himself leaving a young widow to comfort a young widower and his new-born child. Hervey looked after Stonehouse's correspondence and business matters which had arisen from Mrs. Stonehouse's death but was also enabled to lead his doctor, a recent convert, into a deeper faith and love for Christ assisted by Dr. Doddridge. Indeed, it seems that Stonehouse had only recently heard the gospel preached for the first time due to a remarkable act of providence. A former patient had left Stonehouse a legacy with the condition that he should attend her funeral service and hear Doddridge preach. Stonehouse went to Castle Hill Church to gain an earthly inheritance and, at the same time, gained insight into how to obtain a heavenly one. Writing to one of Stonehouse's correspondents who was awaiting a letter, Hervey explains what has happened and says:

Your tender and sensible heart will naturally conclude Dr. Stonehouse is so oppressed with sorrow, as not to be capable, at present, of answering his most valued correspondents:
*Curæ leves loquuntur, ingentes stupent.*
But he intends, when time has somewhat alleviated his grief, and religion has more reconciled him to the awful dispensation, to

make a particular reply to the whole of your epistolary favour. You will, I do not question, recommend our distressed friend to the Father of mercies, and the God of all comfort. May we all lay this awakening stroke of Providence to heart, and give all diligence to have our sins pardoned through redeeming blood, our souls renewed by sanctifying grace; that whether we live, we may live unto the Lord; or whether we die, we may die unto the Lord; so that living or dying we may be the Lord's.[1]

**Whitefield, Stonehouse, Doddridge and Hervey**

Dr. James Stonehouse was a most remarkable character. As a young adult he had used his great talents to oppose revealed religion and published an anti-Christian work which ran into several editions. Philip Doddridge called him 'a most abandoned rake and an audacious deist.'[2] Through reading Doddridge's *Rise and Progress of Religion in the Soul* and conversations with Hervey, he was gradually led to see the folly of his ways and trust in Christ. Stonehouse was closely in touch with Whitefield who at first thought he might have a restraining influence on Hervey. It seems that Whitefield was so sure of the higher calling to the itinerant ministry that he felt all who were called to preach, including Stonehouse and Hervey, should be taking to the highways and bye-ways. Whitefield's letters show that he also interpreted Stonehouse's doubts about entering the ministry as a sign that he was ashamed to own himself a 'Methodist', which was indeed the case. Perhaps, however, Whitefield was guilty of wanting Stonehouse to run before he had learnt to walk. In Hervey's case, Whitefield did not seem to realise how weak his friend was, not having seen him for several years, nor did he realise how strongly he felt called to pastoral work. Writing to Hervey in 1749 about these problems, Whitefield says:

> Rev. and Very Dear Sir,—Perhaps I have heard from what corner your cross comes. It is a very near one indeed. A saying of Mr. B— has often comforted me: 'I would often have nestled, but God always put a thorn in my nest.' Is not this suffered, my dear brother, to prick you out, and to compel you to appear for the Lord Jesus Christ? Preaching is my grand catholicon, under all domestic, as well as other trials. I fear Dr. Stonehouse has done you hurt, and kept you in shackles too long. For Christ's sake, my dear Mr. Hervey, exhort him, now that he has taken the gown, to play the man, and let the world see, that, not worldly motives, but God's glory and a

---

[1]    Letter XLIV, *Works*, Dec. 5, 1747.

[2]    Taken from Malcolm Deacon's *Philip Doddridge of Northampton*, p. 105.

love for souls, have sent him into the ministry. I hope he will turn
out a flamer at last. O when shall this once be! Who would lose a
moment? Amazing that the followers of a crucified Redeemer should
be afraid of contempt. Rise, Hervey, rise, and see thy Jesus reaching out a crown with this motto, *Vincenti dabo*. Excuse this freedom. I write out of the fullness of my heart, not to draw you over to
me, or to a party, but to excite you to appear openly for God.[1]

Whitefield's contact with Stonehouse finally grew into a deep friend-
ship and the latter was one of a team of three (Stonehouse, Doddridge and
Hervey) to whom Whitefield committed his journals and letters to be revised for publication. Stonehouse was also one of the men along with
Doddridge, Hervey and Hartley, whom Whitefield called together at the
Countess of Huntingdon's Ashby-de-la-Zouch residence in 1751 to plan
the building of the New Tabernacle. Perhaps when writing to Hervey,
Whitefield had also forgotten that Stonehouse, along with Hervey and
Doddridge, had supported Whitefield in 1748 when opinion in Britain
was at its highest against him. Both Doddridge and Hervey opened their
pulpits to Whitefield and Stonehouse his own home at this time, a deed
which caused them much criticism from 'evangelicals', some of the harsh-
est coming from Isaac Watts.[2] After a long period of heart-search,
Stonehouse became an Anglican minister and was called to the lecture-
ship of All Saints, Bristol where he carried out a fine ministry and published a number of evangelical works. He inherited the title of Baronet in
1791, four years before his death. Though timorous at first, Stonehouse
entered more and more into the work of the awakening, now being remembered as one of its noblest supporters. His teaching, however, never
reached the profundity of his friends' and even after his conversion, he
remained unsure of the doctrines of faith and reconciliation. Perhaps the
main reason was that Stonehouse wrote a book soon after conversion which
went into seven editions in a couple of years, though its theology was all
milk with little meat. As the book sold so well, Stonehouse took this to
mean that it was of spiritual benefit so refused to alter its teaching, though
Hervey and other friends told Stonehouse that it displayed too low a view
of Scripture and too high a view of man. Hervey maintained that reconciliation is a blessing which God gives to his enemies, according to Romans
5:10. This reconciliation is fully procured through the atoning death of
Christ. Christ died for those who could not atone for themselves. Stonehouse

---

[1]    Tyerman's *Life of Whitefield*, p. 233.
[2]    Watts accused Doddridge of 'sinking the character of a minister, and especially of a
tutor' for preaching at Whitefield's Tabernacle. See full letter in Tyerman's *The Life of
Whitefield*, vol. ii, pp. 72, 73. Doddridge also reaped criticism from Daniel Neal.

maintained that reconciliation comes when sin is renounced, i.e. when what he called 'religious duties' were performed. Hervey maintained that it was impossible for a fallen man to perform religious duties such as loving the Lord our God with all our hearts because man's heart was totally at enmity with God. Before man can perform such a duty, he must be reconciled to God and freely justified. He must have a new life in Christ before he can perform religious duties which appertain to salvation. Stonehouse made the mistake of believing that the results of salvation were the causes of salvation. As those who are reconciled to God show concern and grief at their sin, Stonehouse believed that the latter had produced the former. Hervey argued that reconciliation was not a reward for right thinking and feeling but a removal of offence and a restoration to favour.[1]

At the beginning of 1747, we find Hervey wondering why Richardson has not yet brought out his second edition of *Meditations* with *Contemplations* and making plans to add his alterations for a third edition to it. We also read that Hervey is in close touch with his 'certain valuable and esteemed friend at Northampton', alias Philip Doddridge, and combining a visit to the infirmary with an hour's chat with his friend. Hervey sent Doddridge a copy of his *Contemplations* of which the Independent minister told a correspondent:

> I have just been writing to my good friend, Mr. Hervey; whose manuscript on the Stars, I have reviewed with pleasure. I hope it will be means of raising the hearts of many *above* the stars; and of fixing them on Him, who is, so much more than anything material, 'The bright and Morning Star'. I see, in Mr. Hervey, an example of diligence, humility, candour, and universal goodness, which I am sure ought to keep *me* humble, and, I hope, in some measure, does so.[2]

### Correspondence with 'quality' and convicts
Hervey's letters to his 'polite' friends of 'quality', to use Hervey's words for the gentry of his day, continue to be open and to the point. One friend is rebuked for passing on Crebillon's *La Sopha* to another friend. Hervey, commenting on the sordid contents of the book, asks his friend why he recommends arsenic in book form to others and advises him to throw his own copy into the fire. The gentleman also receives a rebuke for treating a passage of Scripture quoted by someone with a contemptuous

---

[1]    See Letter CIII, *Works*. The full letter will be found in Appendix II *Further Gems from Hervey's Literary Treasury.*

[2]    Written July 6, 1747, *Gospel Magazine*, 1771, p. 179.

laugh. Hervey presses on his friend the need to follow Christ in all things and ends his letter by writing:

> Dear sir, bestow a thought on these things. If the remonstrances are wrong, I willingly retract them; if right, you will not pronounce me impertinent. Love and friendship dictate what I write; and the only end I have in view, is the holiness, the usefulness, the happiness, the final salvation of my much esteemed friend. It is for this, this only, I have now taken my pen in hand, and for this I shall often bend my knees before God.

Hervey developed a concern for prisoners' welfare whilst a member of the Holy Club and continued to care for the souls of criminals and those treated as such because of circumstances which were beyond their powers. Writing in August 1747, to a friend, Hervey tells him of a visit to Northampton jail:

> I visited the poor condemned malefactor; found him an ignorant person; aimed chiefly at these two grand points, to convince him of the heinousness of his sin, and shew him the all-sufficiency of the Saviour to obtain pardon even for the very vilest of offenders. To preach and teach Jesus Christ, is our office; to make the doctrine effectual, God's great prerogative.

### Hervey's faith at its strongest when faced with death

Dr. Stonehouse increased his care for Hervey's bodily health which seemed to be on the decline. Hervey was in no pain and his understanding was not in the least impaired, yet his bodily strength was so weak that it took quite an effort to sit and stand. Hervey now told his friends that he believed he was a dying man and had reached the position in life where he wished to sit with greater assiduity at his divine Master's feet and to know nothing but Christ and Him crucified. Acts 6:4 was his heart's desire, 'But we will give ourselves continually to prayer, and to the ministry of the word.' It was at times such as this that Hervey gave the clearest testimony to his faith. Answering the question what hope had he regarding his future and immortal state, Hervey answers:

> Truly my hope, my whole hope, is even in the Lord Redeemer. Should the king of terrors threaten—I fly to the wounds of the slaughtered Lamb, as the trembling dove to the clefts of the rock. Should Satan accuse—I plead the Surety of the covenant, who took my guilt upon himself and bore my sins in his own body on the tree. Should the law denounce a curse—I appeal to him who hung on the accursed tree, on purpose that all the nations of the earth

might be blessed. Should hell open its jaws, and demand its prey—
I look up to the gracious Being who says, Deliver him from going
down into the pit, for I have found a ransom. Should it be said, No
unclean thing can enter into heaven; my answer is,—The blood of
Christ cleanseth from all sin: though my sins be as scarlet, through
his blood they shall be as white as snow. Should it be added, None
can sit down at the supper of the Lamb without a wedding-gar-
ment, and your righteousness, what are they before the pure law
and piercing eye of God, but filthy rags? These I renounce, and
seek to be found in Christ Jesus, who is the Lord, my righteousness. It is written in the word that he is to judge the world at the last
day, By his obedience shall many be made righteous.

So that Jesus, the dear and adorable Jesus, is all my trust. His
merits are my staff, when I pass through the valley of the shadow
of death. His merits are my anchor, when I launch into the boundless ocean of eternity. His merits are the only riches which my poor
soul, when stripped of its body, desires to carry into the invisible
world. If the God of glory pleases to take notice of any mean endeavours to honour his holy name, it will be infinite condescension
and grace; but his Son, his righteous and suffering Son, is all my
hope, and all my salvation. Dear sir, pray for me, that the weaker I
grow in body, the stronger I may become in this precious faith.[1]

By 1749, Hervey's friends were growing very concerned about his
health as he had been almost house-bound for months, only leaving his
home to take his church services. His friends consulted numerous doctors
in search of a remedy for Hervey's consumption but the bulk of advice
received was far from Hervey's natural leanings. Discussing the matter by
letter with Dr. Stonehouse who had become seriously ill himself, Hervey
explains how one doctor prescribes travelling, another light diversions,
another cheerful entertainment, yet another worldly pleasures, whilst most
of them warn against excess study and time spent in prayer. 'All these,'
claimed Hervey, 'might beguile away the time and take one's mind off
one's complaint for a while but they are far from being equal to the life he
pursued in the service of God which was more able to give a person lasting peace in his heart and hope for the future. If the doctors feel that cheerful conversation is a harmless diversion, what must they think of cheerful
conversation with God in prayer and profitable time spent in reading the
Scriptures, God's treasury of comfort? Surely such occupations cannot be
less healing in their powers and are certainly, therefore, a profitable 'di-

[1]   Letter XL, *Works*, Aug. 8, 1747.

version!' Rejecting the majority of advice for strong, sound reasons, Hervey concludes:

> Trifling company, and worldly pleasures, will serve only to aggravate the misery, and make us inwardly mourn, that while others are in the elevation of mirth, we are pressed with a weight of calamity; whereas, by means of those sovereign consolations, afflictions may be improved to the health of the mind, and become a most salutary expedient for furthering our spiritual happiness.[1]

## Criticisms of Hervey's literary work

Just as Hervey was feeling at his worst health-wise, criticisms of his writings came in. He had referred to the armed opposition to Charles I as 'rebels' which upset staunch critics of the King and he had been suspected of teaching baptismal regeneration. Hervey's answers show that he was no coward in presenting his views but could give a sound reason for the faith that was within him. Nor was he frightened of taking the bull by the horns and using Scriptural passages that many a commentator has skirted for reasons of theological diplomacy. Taking up these criticisms in an undated letter, Hervey says:

> With regard to my calling those persons who took up arms against King Charles I. rebels; you know it is the avowed tenet of the Church of England, and the declared sense of our legislators. If I was to alter that expression, especially since it has stood so long, it might probably disgust readers who are in a contrary way of thinking; at least it would give occasion for speculation, and stir up the embers of mutual animosity, which, I hope, are now sleeping, and upon the point of being extinguished. For my part, I look upon King Charles as one of the best men that ever filled a throne; and esteem the Puritans as some of the most zealous Christians that ever appeared in our land. Instead of inveighing against either, I would lament the misfortune of both; that, through some deplorable mismanagement, they knew one another no better, and valued one another no more. Otherwise, how happy might they have been! they, in so devout a sovereign; he, in such conscientious subjects.
>
> Washing away sins by baptism is a scriptural expression: 'And now, says Ananias to the converted persecutor, 'why tarriest thou? Arise, and be baptized, and wash away thy sins.' Where, I suppose, washing with water, which is the sign, is put for the application of

---

[1]   *Works*, Letter LVI.

the Lamb's blood, which is the blessing signified. This, I apprehend, extends to native impurity, as well as committed iniquity, since they both render us children of wrath. Not that it implies an extirpation of original corruption, but refers to its condemning power; which is done away when the atoning merits of Christ's death are applied and sealed to the soul. Upon the whole, I think the expression is justifiable. Yet if Mr. —'s remonstrance had come sooner, it would have been more explicit in its meaning, and more guarded from possibility of mistake: And was I called upon, to explain my sentiments, I should take leave to borrow Mr. —'s. words.[1]

Few could take criticism as well as Hervey and he asked his correspondent to give his 'most affectionate compliments' to the critic and tell him how much he was obliged to him and that he would be even more obliged if the critic would remember him in his effectual fervent prayers. On the other hand, Hervey hated to be complimented in any way and asked his friend in the same letter not to praise him so that he would become puffed up with vain conceit regarding himself and his writings. All his own efforts were earth and ashes, guilt and sin, he explained, adding, 'May the Lord of glory rebuke this arrogant spirit, and teach my soul to be humble, to be evermore dependent on his aid as a weaned child.'

**Happy in Christ though ill in body**
1750 was to be a turning point in the life of Hervey, marking off the young curate with still-developing doctrines from the mature rector of Collingtree who stood four-square in the doctrines of grace and was to write his major work on the imputed righteousness of Christ. Though bodily an invalid to be pitied, Hervey's trust in the Lord showed through his frailty and gave others strength. When one reads his joyful letter to his sister as spring returned, one realises that Hervey felt himself to be the happiest man on earth:

Dear Sister,- The country is now in its perfection. Every bush a nosegay, all the ground a piece of embroidery; on each tree the voice of melody, in every grove a concert of warbling music. The air is enriched with native perfumes, and the whole creation seems to smile. Such a pleasing improving change has taken place; because, as the Psalmist expresses it, God has sent forth his Spirit, and renewed the face of the earth. Such a refining change takes place in mankind, when God is pleased to send his Holy Spirit into

---

[1]    *Works*, Letter LXI.

the heart. Let us therefore humbly and earnestly seek the influences of this divine Spirit. All our sufficiency is from this divine
Spirit dwelling in our hearts, and working in us both to will and to
do. Without his aids, we are nothing, we have nothing, we can do
nothing; Would we believe in Christ to the saving of our souls? we
must receive power from on high, and be enabled by this divine
Spirit; for no man can say, that Jesus is the Lord, or exercise true
faith on his merits, but by the Holy Ghost. Would we be made like
unto Christ? It can be done only by this divine Spirit. We are transformed into the same image, says the apostle, not by any ability of
our own, but by the Spirit of the Lord. Would we be set on the right
hand of our Judge at the last day? This is the mark that will distinguish us from the reprobates, and number us with his faithful people. For unless a man, unless a woman, have the Spirit of Christ,
they are none of his. But, since we infinitely need this enlightening
and sanctifying Spirit, is the God of heaven equally willing to give
it? He is; indeed he is. To obtain this gift for us sinners, his own
Son bled to death on the cross. That we may be made partakers of
this gift, he intercedeth at the right hand of his father; and he has
passed his word, he has given us a solemn promise, that if we ask,
we shall receive it. See, remember and often plead in prayer, Luke
11:13. From your affectionate brother, &c[1]

### Kidnapped for health's sake

Hervey's friends, led by Dr. Stonehouse and Thomas Hartley, did not
fully sympathise with his faithful optimism in his own security, based on
his deep trust in his heavenly father. They did not want to lose a precious
friend through death but feared that Hervey would soon be with them no
more if he neglected his own health as they felt he was doing. Stonehouse
confessed that he knew of no remedy for Hervey's condition at present
and he must try a change of air. Thus, unknown to Hervey, they secretly
corresponded with their London friends including Hervey's brother William
at Miles End, George Whitefield,[2] the Countess of Huntingdon, William
Romaine and possibly with John Gill and, with their co-operation, they
conspired to abduct Hervey by gentle force and carry him off to London,
where they felt he could be looked after more professionally and so have
a better chance of recovery. Under the pretence of going for a short ride
with Hervey, his friends collected him at Weston Favell and proceeded to
take him to London. It was some time before Hervey realised what was

---

[1]  *Works*, Letter LXV.

[2]  It has been suggested that George Whitefield was the chief conspirator behind this
plot. See *Life of James Hervey, Gentleman's Magazine*, 1760, xxx, p. 378.

happening though his protests were loud and long when he found out, but his friends remained immune to his pleas to return. The group spent the night at St. Albans but Hervey was too shocked and dispirited, as he explained later, to receive his friend Nathaniel Cotton who had planned to visit him at the inn where he spent a night's break in the journey. Hervey arrived at Whitefield's house in Tottenham at three o'clock on the following afternoon for what would be a two years stay. He had no luggage whatsoever with him and had to send back home for a change of clothing. However, before we look into what happened in London and subsequent events, we must turn the clock back to examine in more detail the works which Hervey authored in the formative period covered by this chapter and the kind of books the author read to educate himself in the faith.

# Chapter Five:
# Hervey's Earlier Literary Works

**Toplady's opinion of Hervey as a writer**

On July 8, 1769, Augustus Montague Toplady (1740-1778) published a number of Hervey's sermons which he was certain Hervey himself intended to publish had his early death not intervened. Toplady had recently been made Vicar of Broad Hembury, Devonshire and wished to make it very clear to his first flock by his own preaching, writings and public testimony where he stood doctrinally and empirically. He thus edited and published works of Hervey to show that he followed that able exponent of Christ's righteousness in his view of the gospel. What Toplady said of his other great mentor, John Gill (1697-1771),[1] he echoes in his words of recommendation concerning Hervey's works, saying:

> Whoever reads them, will know who wrote them. 'Celebrated writers,' as this excellent author observes elsewhere, 'have a style peculiar to themselves.' This was eminently true of himself. His performance (some of his letters excepted, written in the youngest part of life) are indeed *as apples of gold in pictures of silver*: transmitting the most precious truths, through the channel of the most elegant, correct expression; and adoring the doctrines of God our Saviour, with all the heightening graces of exquisite composition. When Hervey's pencil gives the drapery, Truth is sure never to suffer, by appearing in ill dress. His prose is, in general, more lovely and harmonious, more chastely refined, and more delicately beautiful, than half the real poems in the world.—With Hervey in their hands, his delighted readers well nigh find themselves at a loss,

---

[1] See Rippon's *Memoir* and my *John Gill and the Cause of God and Truth* for similar utterances of Toplady's concerning Gill.

which they shall most admire; the sublimity and sweetness of the blessed truths he conveys, or the charming felicity of their conveyance.—There is, if the term may be allowed, a sort of *family-likeness*, discernible in all this author's pieces. You discover the lively signatures of the parent, in every one of his offspring. They not only carry the superscription of his name, but likewise bear the image of his genius, and are himself at second hand.

Toplady had to suffer greatly at the hands, tongues and pens of Arminian enthusiasts as they saw in this up and coming young man a defender of the doctrines of grace that made their arguments for human righteousness look insipid and lifeless. After their leader, John Wesley had spread the evil rumour that Hervey had died cursing him,[1] Hervey was on the black list of all Arminians. When thus Toplady proposed to print hitherto unpublished works of Hervey, the opposition's rage was great and immediately a further rumour was spread that Toplady only wished to enrich his own pocket by publishing works which thousands would be sure to buy and read. Thus, at the end of his *Preface*, Toplady wrote:

> I shall not detain the evangelical reader from this feast any longer, than just to assure him, that neither my excellent friend, who communicated the copy to me; nor myself, who communicated it to the world; propose to ourselves any sort of pecuniary advantage from this publication; nor will we accept of any, should the sale be ever so great.
> Respect for the memory of that holy man of God who preached these sermons, and in the hope of their being made useful to such as read them, were the motives which induced us to send them abroad.—One would wish to *gather up the very fragments that remain* of so distinguished a writer; and *that nothing* so apparently calculated for general benefit, might *be lost*.[2]

### Hervey's reasons for writing

It is quite obvious why Hervey began to write. The sole reason was to extend his evangelical work into the homes of the rich and well-educated who were, on the whole, the very people whose absence from church services was most conspicuous. Once asked why he did not spend more time in upper-class circles, Hervey replied that he hardly knew a 'polite family' in his area where the conversation turned on the things of God and where

---

[1]    Wesley's *Works*, vol. XIII, *A Letter to Dr. Erskine*, p. 123.

[2]    Preface to *Many Made Righteous by the Obedience of ONE, The Works of the Late Reverend James Hervey, A. M.*, vol. v, London, 1771, pp. 126, 127

any such interest were shown at all. Telling one of the few 'polite' ladies Hervey knew about his calling to write, he says: 'I shall have a very endearing obligation to bless his infinite goodness, if he is pleased to make the weak productions of my pen, acceptable to your Ladyship's taste, and beneficial to your best interests. To get wealth by one's writings, is a perishing acquisition. To win fame, is a splendid delusion. But, to further the comfort and salvation of a fellow creature, of a friend (here Lady Shirley), an honoured, and highly-esteemed friend, this is gain indeed.'

### Urging 'Beau' Nash to seek the Lord while he may be found

Hervey's first major onslaught into the citadels of the decadent rich was not meant for publication and was a very private matter indeed. This was his letter to Richard Nash in 1743 whilst Hervey was convalescing at Bath where Nash was Master of the Ceremonies. The letter is, literally speaking, a gem in its use of words and construction of argument. Evangelically speaking, it is a sound and courageous application of the gospel which comes as a savour of life unto life to some and death unto death for others. The letter must obviously have spoken to the playboy's heart as he kept it safely all his life. That life does not seem to have been affected by the letter but we may presume that the fact that Nash treasured it, indicates that it preserved him from an even worse pattern of life. The letter is recorded here in full as a comprehensive illustration of Hervey's language, style and evangelical fervour. To have summarised it in other words would have been to rob it of its impact.

### A most melancholy spectacle

Hervey begins his letter to Nash by quoting Isaiah 55:6, 'Seek the Lord while he may be found, call upon him while he is near.' He then goes on to write:

> Sir,—This comes from your sincere friend, and one that has your best interest deeply at heart; it comes on a design altogether important, and of no less consequence than your everlasting happiness, so that it may justly challenge your careful regard, It is not to upbraid or reproach, much less to triumph and insult over your misconduct; no, it is pure benevolence it is disinterested good-will prompts me to write; so that I hope I will not raise your resentment. However, be the issue what it will, I cannot bear to see you walk in the paths that lead to death, without warning you of your danger, without sounding in your ears the awful admonition, 'Return and live; for why will you die?' I beg of you to consider whether you do not, in some measure, resemble those accursed children of Eli; whom, though they were famous in their generation, and men of renown, yet vengeance suffered not to live. For my part, I may

safely use the expostulation of the old priest; 'why do you such
things? For I hear of your evil dealings by all this people: nay, my
brother, for it is no good report I hear,—you make the Lord's people to transgress.' I have long observed and pitied you; and a most
melancholy spectacle I lately beheld, made me resolve to caution
you, lest you also come into the same condemnation.

### Refusing the call of God

I was, not long since, called to visit a poor gentleman, erewhile
of the most robust body and gayest temper I ever knew; but when I
visited him, oh! how was the glory departed from him! I found him
no more that sprightly and vivacious son of joy which he used to
be, but languishing, pining away, and withering under the chastis-
ing hand of God! his limbs feeble and trembling, his countenance
forlorn and ghastly, and the little breath he had left sobbed out in
sorrowful sighs! his body hastening apace to the dust, to lodge in
the silent grave, the land of darkness and desolation; his soul just
going to God who gave it, preparing itself to wing away to its long
home, to enter upon an unchangeable and eternal state. When I
was come up into his chamber, and had seated myself on his bed,
he first cast a most wishful look upon me, and then began, as well
as he was able, to speak. 'O that I had been wise, that I had known
this; that I had considered my latter end! Ah! Mr. Hervey, death is
knocking at my doors; in a few hours more I shall draw my last
gasp, and then judgment, the tremendous judgment! How shall I
appear, unprepared as I am, before the all-knowing and Omnipotent God! how shall I endure the day of his coming!' When I mentioned, among many other things, that strict holiness which he had
formerly so lightly esteemed, he replied with a hasty eagerness,
'Oh! that holiness is the only thing I now long for: I have not words
to tell you how highly I value it. I would gladly part with all my
estate, large as it is, or a world, to obtain it. Now my benighted
eyes are enlightened, I clearly discern the things that are excellent.
What is there in the place whither I am going but God? or what is
there to be desired on earth but religion?'

But if this God should restore you to health, said I, think you
that you would alter your former course? 'I call heaven and earth
to witness,' said he, 'I would labour for holiness as I shall soon
labour for life. As for riches and pleasures, and the applauses of
men, I count them as dross and dung; no more to my happiness
than the feathers that lie on the floor. Oh! if the righteous Judge
would try me once more; if he would but reprieve and spare me a
little longer, in what a spirit would I spend the remainder of my

days! I would know no other business, aim at no other end, than perfecting myself in holiness: whatever contributed to that, every means of grace, every opportunity of spiritual improvement, should be dearer to me than thousands of gold and silver. But, alas ! why do I amuse myself with fond imaginations? The best resolutions are now insignificant, because they are too late : the day in which I should have worked is over and gone; and I see a sad horrible night approaching bringing with it the blackness of darkness for ever. Heretofore, (woe is me!) when God called, I refused; when he invited, I was one of them that made excuse: Now, therefore, I receive the reward of my deeds; fearfulness and trembling are come upon me; I smart, I am in sore anguish already, and yet this is but the beginning of sorrows! It doth not yet appear what I shall be; but sure I shall be ruined undone, and destroyed with an everlasting destruction!'

This sad scene I saw with my eyes; these words, and many more equally affecting, I heard with my ears; and soon after attended the unhappy gentleman to his tomb. The poor breathless skeleton spoke in such an accent, and with so much earnestness, that I could not easily forget him or his words; and as I was musing upon this sorrowful subject, I remembered Mr. Nash — I remembered you, sir, for I discerned too near an agreement and correspondence between yourself and the deceased. They are alike, said I, in their ways and what shall hinder them from being alike in their end? The course of their actions was equally full of sin and folly, and why should not the period of them be equally full of horror and distress? I am grievously afraid for the survivor, lest as he lives the life, so he should die the death of this wretched man, and his latter end should he like his.

## Heaping up wrath against the day of wrath

For this cause, therefore, I take my pen, to advise, to admonish, nay, to request of you to repent while you have opportunity if happily you may find grace and forgiveness. Yet a moment, and you may die; yet a little while, and you must die: And will you go down with infamy and despair to the grave, rather than depart in peace, and with hopes full of immortality?

But I must tell you plainly, sir, with the utmost freedom, that your present behaviour is not the way to reconcile yourself to God; you are so far from making atonement to offended justice, that you are aggravating the former account, and heaping an increase of wrath against the day of wrath. For what say the Scriptures — those books which, at the consummation of all things, the Ancient of Days shall open, and judge you by every jot and tittle therein—

what say these sacred volumes? Why, they testify and declare to every soul of man, 'That whosoever liveth in pleasure is dead while he liveth;' so that, so long as you roll on in a continued circle of sensual delights and vain entertainments, you are dead to all the purposes of piety and virtue; you are as odious to God as a corrupt carcass that lies putrefying in the churchyard; you are as far from doing your duty, or working out your salvation, or restoring yourself to the divine favour, as a heap of dry bones nailed up in a coffin is from vigour and activity. Think, sir, I conjure you, think upon this, if you have any inclination to escape the fire that never will be quenched. Would you be rescued from the fury and fierce anger of Almighty God? would you be delivered from weeping, and wailing, and incessant gnashing of teeth? Sure you would! Then I exhort you as a friend, I beseech you as a brother, I charge you as a messenger from the great God, in his own most solemn words, 'Cast away from you your transgressions; make you a new heart, and a new spirit, so iniquity shall not be your ruin.'

Perhaps you may be disposed to contemn this and its serious purport, or to recommend it to your companions as a fit subject for raillery; but let me tell you beforehand, that for this, as well as for other things, God will bring you into judgment. He sees me now write, he will observe you while you read; he notes down my words in his book, he will note down your consequent procedure; so that not upon me, but upon your own self, will the neglecting or despising of my sayings turn. 'If thou be wise, thou shalt be wise for thyself; if thou scornest, thou alone shalt bear it.'

Be not concerned, sir, to know my name; it is enough that you will know this hereafter. Tarry but a little, till the Lord, even the most mighty God, shall call the heaven from above, and the earth, that he may judge his people; and then you will see me face to face: there shall I be ready, at the dreadful tribunal, to joy and rejoice with you, if you regard my admonitions, and live; or to be—what God prevent, by inclining your heart to receive this friendly admonition.'

## Meditations among the tombs

The ideas for Hervey's first published work *Meditations among the Tombs* developed through conversations with his gentlemen Christian friends such as Thomson and Orchard and whilst having the freedom of their libraries. As these two fine men of God were Hervey's closest friends at this time, Hervey dedicated his first volume with several shorter works to Thomson's daughter and a succeeding work to Orchard's son. The actual scene of the writing, however, was in a large graveyard in Cornwall where Hervey sat amongst the tombs, reading the inscriptions to the memory of the dead. There he saw the graves of the new-born, young children, youths, newly-weds, soldiers in the prime of life and the old, drawing out Christian parallels from their various fates. Such melancholy musings hardly meet the taste of modern readers who immediately associate thoughts of death and the sad prospects of human life without God with depressions and psychological weakness. Christian poets and writers of the seventeenth and eighteenth centuries had no such inhibitions and believed that times of melancholy were God-given times of inner-searching and a coming to grips with one's own situation. Indeed, they wrote to encourage melancholy as a healthy thought-process, rather than play the part of a modern psychologist and ban such 'morbid' thinking. Thus we find John Milton, in his *Il Pensario*, praising 'divinest melancholy' as a true instrument of God and confessing that it brings 'all heaven before his eyes'. Edward Young, in his *Night Thoughts*, a truly neglected great poem, sees God's gift of melancholy as a step in God's conversion and transformation of sinful man. Yet later critics, no matter how sympathetic they are to Young's poetic genius, invariably judge *Night Thoughts* to be the work of a morbid, miserable man because they do not share Young's faith and are ignorant of a God who uses even melancholy to reveal Himself.[1] The same criticism is applied to the so-called *Graveyard poets*, including Blair and Cowper, who were often men with a great sense of humour. This humour, however, was not based on a godless mirth as Hervey makes plain when quoting Young to show that true peace of mind, comfort and joy are treasures from heaven:

——————————— Wouldst thou not laugh,
This counsel strange should I presume to give —
Retire and read thy Bible to be gay;
There truths abound of sovereign aid to peace.
But these, thou think'st, are gloomy paths to joy;
False Joys indeed are born from want of thought;
True joy from thought's full bent and energy:
And this demands a mind in equal poise,
Remote from gloomy grief and glaring joy.
Much joy not only speaks small happiness;
But happiness that shortly must expire
Can joy, unbottom'd in reflection, stand?
Can such a joy meet accidents unshock'd?
Or talk with threatening death, and not turn pale?

---

[1]    See, for instance, Harry H. Clark's *A Study of Melancholy in Edward Young*, Modern Language Notes, vol. xxxix, March 1923, pp. 129-202.

**Death need not be a morbid subject**

Hervey spoke often of death as he lived so close to it, but no one can accuse him of being morbid and depressive in his attitude to it. After a severe bout of weakness when death was uppermost in his mind, he could tell a friend,

> With regard to death, I humbly bless the divine goodness, I was under no terrifying apprehensions. It was desirable, rather than deprecated. A believing contemplation of GOD's infinitely rich mercy, of CHRIST's unspeakable meritorious atonement and right-eousness, enabled me to say with the apostle, *O death, where is thy sting! O grave, where is thy victory?*—How great then is the efficacy, and how precious should be the interests, of that holy religion; which could support the weakest of creatures, when all earthly succours failed: and could give courage to the most obnoxious of sinners, even when summoned to his final trial![1]

Hervey's *Meditations* was designed to make people aware of their own deaths and the prospects which faced them before God's judgement throne. It was a plea for sinners to make sure their houses were in order before setting off on the journey into eternal life as it might be a journey into eternal punishment. Such a book would hardly command a large reader-ship nowadays and one can hardly think of a Christian publishing house daring to produce a book written whilst the author was sitting amongst the tombstones. Divine Providence was very gracious to Hervey and his readers, however, and people of all walks of life, but mostly those who were termed in those days 'the quality' or 'polite people', i.e. the better off, bought edition after edition as the book spread throughout Britain, Europe and the American colonies. Indeed, Hervey was starting on a writing career which was to make him one of the most popular writers of the day.

**The poet of prose**

The specimens extant of Hervey's sermons show that he usually preached to the poor in a simple language that all could understand. Testimonies of Evangelical clergy who heard Hervey preach show that they were surprised and sometimes displeased at the earthliness of his language. Hervey's style in his books is quite different. His thoughts are expressed in an extremely cultured, polysyllabic, educated language. This language is at times such a portrayal of linguistic and poetic merit that it charmed many of the rakes of the day into reading what they would have scorned if it had come from the pen of another author. This is perhaps why people in the literary world still refer to James Hervey as the Poet of Prose.

---

[1]   Letter XIV to Lady Shirley, Sept. 23, 1751.

Speaking of the great stone edifices of the world, Hervey's thoughts would delight the heart of any architect, when suddenly we find the author speaking of God not disdaining to dwell in our souls by His Holy Spirit and making them His temple. Hervey goes on to discuss the plights of those lying under the grave stones, the young and old, rich and poor only to come time and time back to the word of God and find heavenly solutions to the sorrows, illnesses, accidents and age that drove the people to their various graves. The law comes heavy on Hervey's readers as he informs them of the sin that takes them to the grave. Crystal clear is the clarion call of the gospel as Hervey points to hope beyond. Though Hervey's language is flowery, his message is designed to cut to the quick in order to remove Satan's arrows. As the bells toll to lead the dead to the grave, Hervey reminds his readers that in the midst of life they are in death and they should be redeeming the time taking heed, watching and praying because the final summons might come at any time.

### Man's death as a forfeit and Christ's death as a security

As Hervey turns his gaze on the grave of a soldier who gave his life in defence of his King, we see him paving the way for the greater love of the Prince of Peace who gave his life as a ransom for many. Hervey tells us:

The one died being a mortal, and only yielded up a life which was long before forfeited to divine justice; which must soon have been surrendered as a debt to nature, if it had not fallen prey to war—But Christ took flesh and gave up the ghost, though he was the great I AM; the fountain of existence, who calls happiness and immortality all his own. He who thought it no robbery to be equal with God, he, whose outgoings were from everlasting; even he was made in the likeness of man, and cut off out of the land of the living. Wonder, O heavens! be astonished, O earth! He died the death, of whom it is witnessed, that he is 'the true God, and eternal life.' (1 John 5:20).

The one exposed himself to peril in the service of his sovereign and his country; which, though it was glorious to do, yet would have been ignominious, in such circumstances to have declined.— But Christ took the field, though he was the blessed and only potentate, the King of kings, and Lord of lords. Christ took the field, though he was sure to drop in the engagement; and put on the harness, though he knew beforehand that it must reek with his blood. That prince of heaven resigned his royal person, not barely to hazard but to the inevitable stroke; to death, certain in its approach, and armed with all its horrors.—And for whom? Not for those who were in any way deserving: but for his own disobedient creatures; for the pardon of condemned malefactors, for a band of rebels, a race of traitors, the most obnoxious and inexcusable of all crimi-

nals; whom he might have left to perish in their iniquities, without
the least impeachment of his goodness, and to the display of his
avenging justice.

### Christ paves the way from the grave to Zion

Hervey was not of the modern evangelical school which teaches that
our sins were not really imputed to Christ but God looked upon Christ's
willingness to suffer on our behalf as a metaphor for the real thing and
thus accepted it as if it were such. No, Hervey sees Christ as being made
sin for our sakes so that he could take on Himself the guilt and punishment
of our transgressions. The 'greater love' that Christ displayed on our behalf, seen from the perspective of the Bible, is that our Saviour was prepared to experience damnation and hell for our sakes and willingly and
lovingly took such a death upon himself, experiencing on our behalf the
turning away of His Father who could not look on and condone sin. Though
the warrior hero fell gallantly in battle, praised by all, of Christ's death,
Hervey says:

> But died not Christ as a fool dieth! Not on the bed of honour,
> with scars of glory on his breast; but like some execrable miscre-
> ant, on a gibbet! with lashes of the vile scourge on his back! Yes,
> the blessed Jesus bowed his expiring head on the accursed tree,
> suspended between heaven and earth, as an outcast from both, and
> unworthy of either.

Hervey now goes on to plea with his readers to look to Christ in faith,
to the only one who has trodden the paths of death and triumphed over the
grave providing us with a highway from Calvary to Zion which will lead
us to life eternal. Time and time again, as regular as the tolling funeral
bells, Hervey pounds into his readers minds, and we trust, their hearts,
that those who have set their hope in Jesus shall never die (John 11:26).
Whether the reader be old like Simeon or in the prime of life like persecut-
ing Paul, they can receive their marching orders from Christ, the Captain
of Salvation, become 'pioneers of hope' and be led by Him to the eternal
City. Then, on that glorious resurrection morn, when the Lord Jesus Christ
shall descend from heaven with the shout of the archangels and God's
clarion call shall awaken the dead, the dead in Christ shall be raised spotless and triumphant, sharing in the spotless, triumphant nature of Christ
who cleansed them from all sin to present them perfect before His Father.
On that great day they will hear their Redeemer's voice saying:

> I accept you, O my people! Ye are they that believed in my
> name. Ye are they that renounced yourselves, and are complete in
> me. I see no spot or blemish in you: for ye are washed in my blood,

and clothed with my righteousness. Renewed by my Spirit, ye have glorified me on earth, and have been faithful unto death. Come, then, ye servants of holiness, enter into the joy of your Lord. Come ye children of light, ye blessed of my father, receive the kingdom that shall never be removed; wear the crown which fadeth not away, and enjoy pleasures for evermore!

## Reflections on a flower garden

Whilst walking in the finely kept grounds of Thomson and Orchard, Hervey obtained the idea of writing his next work which he called *Reflections on a Flower Garden* (published in February 1745). Here Hervey developed his view of nature being the handmaid of the gospel which was to become one of the major themes in William Cowper's poetic witness. 'Consider the lillies of the field' was an exhortation which Hervey never forgot and always utilised in his service to nature's Creator. In this work, Hervey starts with the dawn chorus led by the lofty lark describing its heavenly flights in a language which again takes away all the novelty the later Romantic poets such as Wordsworth and Shelley claimed for themselves in verbalising the effects of nature's morning song. Struck with the beauties of dew-laden nature as he is, Hervey sees them as nothing but a foretaste of the beauties of Paradise restored for the eternal inhabitants of Christ's Kingdom. He does not hesitate to allow things seen to point out to him things unseen and to be yet enjoyed by the elect of God. Foremost of these future blessings will be, for Hervey, to behold the beauties of Christ of which nature at its height is only a dimmer reflection of the glories of its Creator, the Son of Righteousness. All that nature provides us with as human beings, Hervey reminds his readers, quoting Paul, glorious as they are, remain but dung in comparison to what God has in store for us.

## The difference between Hervey's works and those of other Christian nature poets

Here we see the great difference between the Christian nature poet of prose James Hervey and the Christian nature poets of paradise restored, John Milton and William Cowper. The two latter poets looked to the restoration of nature and man as a renovation of what Satanic influence had marred. Hervey, lover of nature as he was, yet believed that nature's greatest beauties would all prove transient and temporary, mere shadows of the glories to come when redeemed man will receive eyes to see a better and lasting creation that God has prepared for His loved ones. Thus it is wrong to look on Milton and Cowper as the greater poets with a greater message of things to come merely because of their great optimism concerning the future of the visible world and the restoration of what Satan has destroyed. Hervey had his gaze continually fixed beyond this, settled in eternals and absolutes which he knew from the revealed Word represented the character of God and His heavenly plans for His chosen ones. This is not to belittle the great Christian message couched in Miltonic and Cowperian poetry. These men viewed nature as pointing to God's blessings for mankind which is a thoroughly legitimate and correct point of view. Hervey, however, saw nature as pointing directly to Christ. Every time a new day dawned, he would think of the Son of Righteousness, every time his eyes were delighted by a beautiful flower, he was reminded of the beauties of Christ. An animal feeding its young, pointed him to a Saviour offering Himself for His people. This, too, is legitimate and correct but can obviously only be seen by eyes given such insight by God. Not that Hervey was platonic in any way. It was merely that he accepted the Bible teaching that the most beautiful lily of the field was nothing compared to the New Creation and that the most expressive picture of Christ in His Heavens which we have in Scripture is still seen by His people as through an ancient polished metal mirror, darkly, albeit a fore-view of seeing our Saviour face to face.

### The world given to the elect in stewardship

Just like Milton and Cowper, however, Hervey pointed out that God has given us the world as an exercise in stewardship and witness and we are to show forth God's glory in it as the culmination and most perfect part of God's creation, entailing our lordship over the rest. Hervey also sees, in the same way as the two other great Christian poets, that man lost his lordship through the fall and was only able to keep it by Christ's maintaining an elect people who lived in a state of propitiation which restored man to his correct function over nature and over reprobate man. This was not, however, because of his inborn abilities as Adam's offspring. He had lost those. It was only because of the Last Adam's intervention to maintain the world for His elects' sake. In other words, Christ's atoning death for His elect, vouchsafed before the world and time began, has a preserving function for the world and its inhabitants for all time, past, present and future. This is until He comes again in glory when this world will be folded up and put away as a thing of mere time, to be superseded by the eternal world. This present world, as Hervey points out, was made for man as his kindergarten. It was a man's infant world. The new world into which mature, elect man will be admitted is God's own world into which only those are welcomed who reflect God's own character as partakers of the righteousness of the Son, having the sanctifying activity of the Holy Spirit within them, thus making them fit to be adopted by the Father. This is something that systematic theologians tend to leave out of their teaching. They rarely have an answer to the question of how Christ's atonement benefited the visible world and reprobate man. Christian poets such as Milton, Hervey and Cowper were often used by God to teach in verse and poetic diction what was inexpressible in formal prose. In this, they were following in the inspired footsteps of the Biblical writers.

## Hervey as a systematic theologian

Having said this, it must not be thought that the Poet of Prose had no skills in systematic theology. In his reflections on the beauty of the flower garden, he delights in pausing to give the reader an analytical, systematic, compact prose account which simplifies the matter for those which are so carried away with Hervey's style and language that they miss the teaching. It is as if Hervey suspects this and thus continually brings the reader down to earth and more sober, logical thought. He never does this, however, without a didactic purpose, applying his teaching to the needs of his readers. Concerning the creation of life forms on earth and man's reasserted stewardship in nature in spite of his having fallen from this God-given position of honour, Hervey says:

1. Christ made them (life forms), when they were not.—He fetched them up from utter darkness, and gave them both their being and their beauty. He created the materials of which they are composed, and moulded them into this endless multiplicity of amiable forms, and useful substances. He arrayed the heavens with a vesture of the mildest blue, and clothed the earth in a livery of the gayest green; his pencil streaked, and his breath perfumed whatever is beautiful or fragrant in the universe. His strength set fast the mountains; his goodness garnished the vales; and the same touch which healed the leper wrought the whole visible system into this complete perfection.

2. Christ recovered them when they were forfeited.—By Adam's sin, we lost our right to the comforts of life, and fruits of the ground: his disobedience was the most impious and horrid treason against the King of kings. Consequently his whole patrimony became confiscated; as well the portion of temporal good things, settled upon the human race during their minority; as, that everlasting heritage reserved for their enjoyment when they should come to full age. But the 'seed of the woman,' instantly interposing, took off the attainder, and redeemed the alienated inheritance. The first Adam being disinherited, the second Adam was appointed heir of all things, visible as well as invisible; and we hold our possession of the former, we expect an instatement in the latter, purely by virtue of our alliance to him, and our union with him.

3. Christ upholds them, which would otherwise tumble into ruin.—By him says the oracle of inspiration, all things consist. His finger rolls the seasons round, and presides over all the celestial revolutions. His finger winds up the wheels, and impels every spring of vegetative nature. In a word, the whole weight of the creation rests upon his mighty arm, and receives the whole harmony of its mo-

tion from his unerring eye.—This habitable globe, with all its rich appendages, and fine machinery, could no more continue, than they could create themselves. Start they would into instant confusion, or drop into their primitive nothing, did not his power support, and his wisdom regulate them every moment. In conformity to his will, they subsist steadfast and invariable in their orders; and wait only for his sovereign nod, to 'fall away like water that runneth apace.'

4. Christ actuates them, which would otherwise be lifeless and insignificant.—Pensioners they are, constant pensioners on his bounty; and borrow their all from his fullness. He only has life; and whatever operates, operates by an emanation from his all sufficiency. Does the grape refresh you with its enlivening juices? It is by a warrant received, and virtue derived, from the Redeemer. Does bread strengthen your heart, and prove the staff of your life? Remember, that it is by the Saviour's appointment, and through the efficacy of his operation. You are charmed with his melody, when the 'time of the singing of birds is come, and the voice of the nightingale is heard in our land.' You taste his goodness in the luscious fig, the melting peach, and the mushy flavour of the apricot. You smell his sweetness in the opening honey-suckle, and every odoriferous shrub, Could these creatures speak for themselves they would, doubtless, disclaim all sufficiency of their own, and ascribe the whole honour to their Maker.—'We are servants,' would they say, 'of him who died for you, Cisterns only, dry cisterns in ourselves, we transmit to mortals no more than the un-created fountain transfuses unto us. Think not, that from any ability of our own, we furnish you with assistance, or administer to your comfort. It is the divine energy, the divine energy alone, that works in us, and does you good.—We serve you, O ye sons of men, that you may love him who placed you in these stations. O ! love the Lord, therefore, all ye who are supported by our ministry; or we shall groan with indignation and regret at your abuse of our services. (Rom. viii. 22.) Use us, and welcome; for we are yours, if ye are Christ's. Crop our choicest beauties; rifle all our treasures, accommodate yourselves with our most valuable qualities; only let us be incentives to gratitude, and motives to obedience.

### A descant upon creation
Hervey was so taken up by the theme of Christ holding the whole creation in the word of His power that he placed a footnote in his *Reflections* announcing that this would be the major theme of a work to follow by way of appendix. This Hervey promptly wrote under the title *A Descant upon Creation,* declaring:

Can any thing impart a stronger joy to the believer, or more effectually confirm his faith in the crucified Jesus, than to behold the heavens declaring his glory, and the firmament showing his handy-work? Surely it must be matter of inexpressible consolation to observe the honours of his Redeemer, written with sunbeams over all the face of the world.

## The Biblical doctrine of imputation

It is in his *Descant*, that Hervey takes up the highly controversial topic of man's sin imputed to Christ and Christ's righteousness imputed to man which earned for Hervey the intense criticism of John Wesley. Many an admiring biographer of Wesley and Wesleyan writers on Hervey have tried to gloss over Wesley's harsh criticism of his former pupil's doctrine of imputed righteousness[1] by striving to prove that the antagonism was really all on Hervey's side but was merely the result of the fevers of a dying man who did not really know what he was talking about. Others see in Hervey's final work on imputed righteousness, *Theron and Aspasio,* a personal attack on John Wesley,[2] whereas Hervey, in view of Wesley's former statements on the topics, thought Wesley would agree with him until Wesley showed that he had obviously changed his mind. Wesley, indeed, urged Hervey not to debate with him in public on imputation, which Hervey never liked to do, but Wesley took the liberty of going to the press twice against his former pupil on the subject whilst Hervey was terminally ill with consumption.

The prose poet did not take up his doctrine of imputed righteousness when in dying delirium with a mind twisted into doddering opposition to the Arminian leader. This doctrine had been Hervey's life-long theme from the time he met the Northamptonshire ploughman at the dawn of his salvation and it was the doctrine that still comforted him on his death-bed. Here in his *Descant* Hervey says:

Was not Christ (to use the language of his own blessed Spirit) a worm, and no man? (Psalm xxii. 6.) In appearance such, and treated

---

[1]  See *Mr. Wesley's Letter* in Hervey's *Works* and also Wesley's *Some Remarks on Mr. Hill's Review of all the Doctrines taught by Mr. John Wesley, Some Remarks on Mr. Hill's Farrago Double-distilled, A Letter to The Rev. Mr. Hervey* and *A Second Letter to the Rev. James Hervey* (vol. xv of the 1812 edition), *Remarks on Dr. Erskine's Defence of the Preface to the Edinburgh Edition of Aspasio vindicated* and *A Letter to Dr. Erskine* (vol. xiii).

[2]  See T. B. Shepherd's *Methodism and the Literature of the Eighteenth Century*, p. 174 and Frederick C. Gill's *The Romantic Movement and Methodism*, p. 79, for a surprising combination of these errors. Gill's maintaining that Wesley always spoke kindly of Hervey yet he mentions Wesley's ungrounded abuse of Hervey in the same breath, shows how even educated and scholarly sympathisers with Wesley are unable to view the Arminian Methodist founder critically and objectively.

as such—Did not he also bequeath the fine linen of his own most
perfect righteousness, to compose the marriage-garment for our
disarrayed and defiled souls? Did he not, before his flesh saw corruption, emerge triumphant from the grave; and not only mount the
lower firmament, but ascend the heaven of heavens; taking possession of those sublime abodes in our name, and as our forerunner.

**The marriage garment**
Hervey wished this point to go home to the hearts of his readers so he
appended a lengthy footnote to the word 'marriage-garment'. This was
against the false teaching prevalent in the churches that Christ's sufferings
passively fulfilled the law for sinful man but active obedience was to be
practised by the Christian to warrant his justification and sanctification.
Hervey linked the obedience of Christ to the full law as a demonstration of
His righteousness which is the only righteousness accepted by God as
such and which is imputed to the elect in the atonement as a covering
away of their sin. Thus at the eschatalogical and sotereological Marriage
Feast of the Lamb, all those will be able to partake who are clothed in
Christ's righteousness. Of these truths Hervey says:

> This, and several other hints, interspersed throughout this work,
> refer to the active and passive righteousness of Christ, imputed to
> believers for their justification. Which in the opinion of many great
> expositors, is the mystical and the most sublime meaning of the
> wedding garment, so emphatically and forcibly recommended by
> the teacher sent from God, (Matth. xxii. 11.) A doctrine which some
> of those who honour my *Meditations* with a perusal, probably may
> not receive with much, if any approbation. I hope the whole per-
> formance may not be cashiered for one difference of sentiment;
> and I beg that the sentiment itself may not hastily be rejected with-
> out a serious hearing. For I have the pleasure of being intimately
> acquainted with a gentleman of good learning and distinguished
> sense, who had once as strong prepossessions against this tenet, as
> can well be imagined. Yet now he not only admits it as a truth, but
> embraces it, as the joy of his heart, and cleaves to it as the rock of
> his hopes.
>   A clear and cogent, treatise, entitled *Submission to the Right-
> eousness of God,* was the instrument of removing his prejudices,
> and reducing him to a better judgment,—in which he has been hap-
> pily confirmed by the authority of the most illustrious names, and
> the works of the most eminent pens, that ever adorned our church
> and nation,—in this number, are Bishop Jewel, one of our great
> reformers; and the other venerable compilers of our homilies; Arch-
> bishop Usher, that oracle of universal learning; Bishop Hall, the

devout and sprightly orator of his age; the copious and fervent Bishop Hopkins; the singularly good and unaffected Bishop Beveridge; the everlasting honour of the bench of judicature, Lord Chief Justice Hales; the nervous, florid, and persuasive Dean Stanhope; the practical and perspicuous Mr. Burkitt; and to summon no other evidence, that matchless genius Milton, who in various parts of his divine poem, inculcates this comforting truth; and in one passage, represents it under the very same image, which is made use of above.[1]

Hervey is arguing against the charge that his doctrine of imputed righteousness based on the active obedience of Christ is a novelty and he goes on to explain how the book he mentioned, was written by Benjamin Jenks (1646-1724) and was going through its eleventh edition. Jenks' book, of course, was one of the major factors in bringing Hervey to a reformed view of the doctrines of grace and the gentleman he writes of who came to a new view of imputation through reading Jenks may well be Hervey himself.

Another major poet who did not hesitate to express his belief in the imputed righteousness of Christ, and had read Hervey as a new convert, was William Cowper (1731-1800) who wrote to his cousin Martin Madan concerning imputed righteousness:

I plead guilty to the doctrine of original corruption, derived to me from my great progenitor, for in my heart I feel the evidences of it that will not be disputed. I rejoice in the doctrine of imputed righteousness for without it how should I be justified? My own righteousness is a rag, a feeble defective attempt insufficient of itself to obtain the pardon of the least of my offences, much more my justification from them all. My dear Martin, 'tis pride that makes these truths unpalatable, but pride has no business in the heart of a Christian.[2]

## Contemplations on the Night

Hervey's next work, was completed in the summer of 1747 and entitled *Contemplations on the Night and the Starry Heavens with a Winter-Piece.* This work was dedicated to Paul Orchard's son of the same name. Orchard had died whilst his son was still in his early infancy and Hervey, who had promised to exercise a spiritual oversight over him at his bap-

---

[1]    See *Paradise Lost*, Book X, lines 214-223, beginning, 'Thenceforth the form of servant to assume.'

[2]    *Cowper's Works*, Ryskamp and King, vol.1. p.107

tism, took over the supervision of his spiritual care and education. Thus, in the dedicatory letter introducing the work, Hervey writes a short biography of Paul Orchard Sen. so that his son will grow to know what a fine man of God his father was.

## Science as a handmaid of the gospel

Hervey was a keen scientist and his library contained not only the books that he was continually lending or giving away but two microscopes, a telescope and an orrery. In a postscript to Lady Shirley, dated June 7, 1751, Hervey recommends scientific study and says:

> Would not a good microscope be a refined and improving companion for some of your Ladyship's rural hours? I bless the providence of GOD for that curious instrument which has discovered so much of his incomprehensible wisdom, his amazing power, his condescending and most profuse goodness, even in the minutest specks of the animalcula creation. This would render the fields and gardens, an inexhaustible fund of entertainment. This would shew you wonders of mechanism, of symmetry, and decoration, in what we usually disregard, as the refuse of nature. It would raise, I believe, the most venerating and truly amiable ideas of the almighty Creator; and help to tune the soul for that song of the four and twenty elders; Thou art worthy, O LORD to receive glory, and honour, and power: for thou hast created all things, and for thy pleasure they are, and were created.

Hervey, however, felt that natural science was a futile occupation if it left out experimental research into the ways of God with His world. He therefore prefixed his *Contemplations on the Night* with the words:

> While Galileo lifts his tube, and discovers the prodigious magnitude of those radiant orbs; while Newton measures their amazing distances, and unites the whole system in harmonious order by the subtle influence of attraction; I would only, like the herald before that illustrious Hebrew, (Gen. xli. 43.) proclaim at every turn, 'Bow the knee, and adore the Almighty Maker, magnify his eternal name, and make his praise like all his works, to be glorious.

## The forerunner and out-runner of the Romantic poets

Hervey's previous works had shown great expertise in descriptive writing but as the author had aimed at the nobility and university educated as his readers, much of what he wrote, unlike his sermons, was couched in a language that demanded a classical education to understand it. In *Contemplations on the Night*, this language approaches the linguistic background of a more general reader and is equally more understandable to the reader of today. Indeed, Hervey's language shows a marked development from the Augustan sesquipedalianism of the so-called golden-age of poetry in which the writer stood aloof from the events he described to the more empirical description of events as experienced personally by a soul and mind opened in empathy to the sounds and sights of nature. This, of course, is the language of Coleridge and Wordsworth, which has often been called the language of the heart and which Wordsworth claimed was an invention of his very own. Hervey, however, went further than Wordsworth who published over half a century after him. He was empirically and linguistically able to merge the best of all forms of verbal expression. The fact that he felt strongly that he was in God's creation and thus part of it, did not distract him from his gift of exact description. This gift was deepened by Hervey's ability to incorporate the feelings of all his senses into the descriptive act so that the reader is able to taste, see, touch, smell and hear the beauties of God's creation. All lovers of Romantic literature will have an ear open for the sound of the horn echoing over the hills which became the signature tune of Romantic writing. Here is Hervey writing not in the Wordsworthian nineteenth century when the Romantic movement had become a slave to its own fossilised system of neo-classical poetic diction and linguistic clichés but in the linguistic creativity of 1747 when these images were fresh from the senses, in the mind and on the lips of James Hervey. This is how he opens his book on the starry summer night:

> The business of the day dispatched, and the sultry heats abated, invited me to the recreation of a walk, a walk in one of the finest recesses of the country, and in one of the most pleasant evenings which the summer season produced.
> The limes and elms, uniting their branches over my head, formed a verdant canopy, and cast a most refreshing shade. Under my feet lay a carpet of nature's velvet; grass intermingled with moss, and embroidered with flowers. Jessamines, in conjunction with woodbines, twined around the trees; displaying their artless beauties to the eye and diffusing their delicious sweets through the air. On either side, the boughs, rounded into a set of regular arches, opened a view into the distant fields, and presented me with a prospect of the bending skies. The little birds, all joyous and grateful for the favours of the light, were paying their acknowledgments in a tribute of harmony, and soothing themselves to rest with songs, while a French horn from a neighbouring seat, sent its melodious accents, softened by the length of their passage, to complete the concert of the grove.

From this descriptive poetic prose, Hervey surprisingly leads the readers on to political thoughts and contemplates that this scene could not have been witnessed with such a peaceful eye if the recent plots, hatched at Rome, to put England once again under the rule of a Roman tyrant had not been thwarted by the grace of God shown in the 1745 bravery of the victors of Culloden. He also thinks of recent news he has heard in a 1746 pamphlet entitled *Popery Always the Same*, which outlined that all freedom of movement and worship has been denied the French Protestants in the southern parts of their country where they were undergoing persecution. Hervey is now deep in to the subject of liberty and we can imagine Hervey thinking in terms of Cowper's words written in a similar circumstance, 'England, with all thy faults, I love thee still!'

## The public reception of Hervey's works

The impact Hervey's earliest works had on Europe and the New World was amazing by any standards. On June 14, 1746, Richard Pearsall, who was to look upon Hervey as his great monitor, wrote to his friend Philip Doddridge to tell him:

> This week I have been surprised by a book which fell into my hands, entitled *Meditations on the Tombs and on a Flower Garden*, by James Hervey, A. B. I have been charmed with the lively images, striking expressions, and serious piety which I find there. I wondered much to see a young clergyman acquainted so much with the genius of the gospel, and animated with such a warm love to his Redeemer. Pray, dear Sir, do you know who and where he is? Not that I think the question will be needed to be asked long if he goes on to publish. Whoever he is, methinks I cannot but love and admire him.

Although Hervey published only 750 copies of his *Meditations* at first, soon thousands were echoing Pearsall's words that they could not help but love and admire Hervey. A second edition of many thousand copies was speedily printed and then yearly, and sometimes even twice to four times yearly, for the next 50 years editions after editions were printed, not taking into account the numerous pirate editions that saw the light of day.[1] After a year or two, the Welsh were reading Hervey in their mother tongue as were the Dutch and the Spanish. Hervey's work became a best-seller in its French translation and became equally popular in its German rendering.

---

[1]    In his abridged Ph. D. thesis, *Methodism and the Literature of the Eighteenth Century*, T. B. Shepherd states that during the eighteenth century 25 editions were published. This state, however, had already been reached in the 1780s and further editions were published regularly until well into the next century. The editions quoted from in this work are dated 1771, 1774, 1804 and 1837 respectively.

**The reasons for Hervey's popularity**

In the providence of God there were many reasons why Hervey's work became so popular. The English speaking world had become used to the debased language of the Restoration in which every vulgarism was allowed and the heroes of books were sots and Cassanovas and their heroines, though upper-class, were little better than harlots. Hervey wrote at a time when the reading public was longing for a language that decent people could read and use without shame. One of the pioneers of this clean-up in the language was Joseph Addison whose writings in the *Spectator* were highly influential in reforming the vocabulary of true gospel preachers of the time. Hervey was thrilled with the clean dignified yet informative language of this newspaper and wrote from Bideford to tell his sister about it in October, 1742 saying:

> See how our judgments and inclinations alter in process of time! I once thought I should make less use of the Spectators than you; but now I believe the reverse of this is true, for we read one or more of those elegant and instructive papers every morning at breakfast: they are served up with our tea, according to their original design. We reckon our repast imperfect without a little of Mr. Addison's or Mr. Steele's company.

Another major reason for Hervey's success was his wise choice of Samuel Richardson of Salisbury Court, Fleet Street as his publisher and printer. Richardson did not share Hervey's zeal for the gospel but he did believe that the English language had become impotent as a literary medium and as a medium for edifying the mind and morals of the public. He also believed that there was no realism in English literature as the amours of rakes and coxcombs described by the Restoration fops were even more fairy-tale-like than the Mother Goose Tales which were coming over from France. With his stories of *Pamela, Clarissa* and *Sir Charles Grandison*, Richardson depicted not only the kitchen sink reality of actual life but presented heroes to the public eye who were Christian in virtue and not far away from Christians in doctrine and who had a solution to social and moral problems rather than wallowing in them. The immediate reaction to Richardson's works by the critics was one of scorn and amusement and they invented for him the names 'Mr. Gravity' and 'Mr. Serious'. Honest literary critic Augustine Birrel (sometimes Birrell), summing up the criticism of the ages against Richardson, writes:

> The real truth I believe to be is this: we are annoyed by Richardson because he violates a tradition. The proper place for an eighteenth century novelist was either the pot or the sponging-house.

He ought to be either disguised in liquor or confined for debt. Richardson was neither the one nor the other.[1]

Such was also the criticism against Hervey whose language and thought has been called by superior literary experts 'mawkish', 'pinchbeck', 'impoverished' and 'common place'. One of Hervey's major faultfinders was none other than that king of critics, Dr. Johnson, who, to the embarrassment of his friend and biographer James Boswell, mercilessly denounced Hervey's *Meditations*. Boswell records of Johnson:

> He thought slightingly of this admired book. He treated it with ridicule, and would not allow even the scene of the dying husband and father to be pathetic. I am not an impartial judge; for Hervey's *Meditations* engaged my affections in my early years. He read a passage concerning the moon, ludicrously, and showed how easily he could, in the same style, make reflections on that planet, the very reverse of Hervey's, representing her as treacherous to mankind. He did this with much humour; but I have not preserved the particulars. He then indulged a playful fancy, in making a *Meditation on a Pudding*.[2]

Rather than being amused by Johnson's pudding which is of very low taste, any critical reader will at once see that the man who made authors tremble, dreading his reviews of their books, had completely missed Hervey's point. In writing of the moon, Hervey is keen to show God's providence in designing the earth and time to be the servants of man in subduing and exerting stewardship over creation as God's feoffee. Johnson cannot see that Hervey is using language for its original purpose, to commune with God and to make God's ways known on earth so that man will become wise in God's wisdom. Johnson looked on Hervey's language as a means of displaying art for art's sake. In his *Meditations on a Pudding*, Johnson does not show that he can use this art for its own sake, either, but he misuses a Herveyan-styled language on a subject which is no didactic use to anyone. Christian poets such as Milton, Young, Byrom, Hervey, Brown, Steele and Cowper always believed that if art were not a didactic instrument for the betterment of mankind, it would be an art to no useful purpose and thus not an art at all. Johnson displays a great technical command of language in his parody on a pudding, but it is a language completely borrowed from Hervey. The critic sadly shows himself entirely at a

---

[1]    *Res Judicatae*. See references to Richardson and a discussion of his literary influence in my *William Cowper: Poet of Paradise*.
[2]    *Boswell's Life of Johnson*, John Murray, 1876, p. 387.

loss to understand Hervey's art in depicting the beauties of Christ and His creation. As Laurence E. Porter says in his bicentenary appreciation of Hervey, 'The sparkle and wit, the indifference and rationalism of the Augustan age had nothing to say to the troubled soul . . . but it was the revival hymns and the tedious *Meditations* which in their own generations caused men to think of their latter end and led them into the knowledge of God's way of salvation.[1]

### Art for art's sake not the true poetry of the heart

Writing towards the end of the nineteenth century, church historians J. H. Overton and F. Relton ask 'Can we wonder that Johnson ridiculed Hervey in his parody, *A Meditation on a Pudding*?' Where Johnson ridiculed Hervey's nature language, the two High Churchmen believed 'the exaggeration is very marked' in Hervey's evangelical and reformed theology. In particular, they could not accept Hervey's highly Biblical language concerning the blackness of man's sin and the purity brought with Christ's salvation. Hervey had gained the wry smiles of the churchmen by commenting on Psalm 51 in the words:

> Though my conscience be more loathsome with adulterous impurity than the dunghill, though treachery and murder have rendered it even black as the gloom of hell, yet, washed in the fountain for sin and for uncleanness, I shall be, I say, not pure only—this were a disparagement to the efficacy of my Saviour's death-but I shall be fair as the lily, white as the snow. Nay, let me not derogate from the glorious object of my confidence; cleansed by this sovereign, sanctifying stream, I shall be fairer than the full-blown lily, whiter than the new-fallen snow.[2]

Anyone in anyway familiar with his own experience, the words of Isaiah or the words of Jesus Christ Himself, will find these sentiments true, soberly demonstrated and very much to the point. The art for art's sake theory was developed in the eighteenth century when intrinsic value and goodness was secularised from practical, moral and spiritual good. It was critics of the historical Christian faith such as Lessing in his *Laokoon* (1766) who pioneered this idea as proof that man was growing up and becoming 'enlightened' enough to stand on his own feet. All this has earned the oft-quoted quip, 'What is the use of goodness if it is good for nothing?'

---

[1]  *A Bicentenary Appreciation,* p. 13.

[2]  *The English Church from the Accession of George I to the End of the Eighteenth Century,* pp. 142, 143.

**From the human to the angelic**

Notwithstanding the critics, Hervey's works, like Richardson's, sold and sold, which can hardly be said for many of the works of their nose-in-the-air critics. Even Johnson had to have sponsors to keep him going, whereas neither Richardson nor Hervey ever had to rely on others for a penny. To sum up Richardson's works, we could use the words of the woman who told him, 'Ah, dear Mr. Richardson, in *Clarissa* you have shown us the good woman we all would be. Now show us the good man we all should love.' The latter request was fulfilled in Richardson's *Sir Charles Grandison* which prompted Cowper's first major Christian poem *Ode on Reading Mr. Richardson's History of Sir Charles Grandison* in 1754. To sum up Hervey's *Meditations* and *Contemplations*, however, we can say that Hervey showed man his true fallen state but showed what that man could become when united with Christ. Richardson pointed his readers eyes to man made good, whereas Hervey pointed his readers eyes to the Perfecter of man. It is a tragic display of the hypocrisy of many a worldling disguised in clerical gowns that both Richardson's and Hervey's major critics came from the Established and Dissenting churches. One dirty-minded clergyman, the Rev. Mr. Skelton, begged Richardson to write a sordid story of a bad woman who was lewd and a pub-crawler, saying, 'This is a fruitful and necessary subject which will strike and entertain to a miracle.' Richardson's German friends, however, told him that he had depicted human life to the full, all that was left for him to do now was to write about angels. Though Richardson was obviously first influenced by Hervey, it is easy to trace the latter's popularity on the Continent as following in the footsteps of Richardson's own Continental acceptance. Richardson wrote no more after Grandison, and it was as if the Continentals accepted in Hervey's works the angelic that they had wished from Richardson's pen.

**Hervey's works filled a great need in European literature**

A further reason for Hervey's success abroad was that Continental literature had nothing quite like it though there was a ready market for it. The French, always concerned with expressing the best possible ideals through the best possible language, immediately took to Hervey's works as an expression of their own literary aims, even arguing that the ideals in them were more French than British. French literary critics such as Daniel Mornet[1] stressed that Hervey's works, along with those of Young whom Hervey loved to quote, touched the longing for the romantic, tragic and meditative which was part of the French soul of that time. The Germans were enraptured by the sweet melancholy of Hervey's works. They were

---

[1]    Le Romantisme en France au XVIIIe siècle, Paris, 1932.

turning from a literature which had been for and about the nobility or would-be-noble, full of fossilised thought processes and stylistic structures and turning to the cultural, social and moral needs of the common man. Back to nature and natural man was rapidly becoming their all-embracing theme. Hervey, to them, was an author who allowed the heart to speak to the head, taught the imagination to roam freely, looked at the basic desires of man and taught the glories of nature. They were also thrilled by Hervey's strong religious emotion. Indeed, it was the religious writings of both Germany and England that were to form the basis of the Romantic Movement, which clung to a religious element throughout the works of major German Romantic writers such as Eichendorf and Novalis and though present in such writers as Coleridge, developed into something approaching Deism, or even Pantheism, in the later British Romantics led by Wordsworth.

### Richardson's business sense protects Hervey

Richardson's great business acumen was put to Hervey's service. The publisher paid Hervey well but was astonished at the way the kind-hearted author gave money to the poor at the same rate as he received it from his publisher. Thus Richardson insisted on keeping much of the money in trust, using it discretely, on consultation with Hervey, for charitable purposes. It was obvious that Richardson thought Hervey tended to squander money on the undeserving rather than use it where it was truly needed. This was not quite true as Hervey was careful to assist those whom he termed 'the deserving poor,' never giving more than an initial guinea to beggars or those professing to be in need whom he did not know. Richardson's caution, however, was quite justified as Hervey was continually sought out by complete strangers who were only too pleased to receive their guinea.

### Hervey praised by evangelical writers

Though the secular world applauded these earlier works of Hervey, their praise was nothing to the accolade given by fellow believers. Henry Venn, a best-selling author himself, sent a parcel of valuable books for study to a Miss Riland of Leicester, among them being a copy of *Meditations* of which Venn said:

> The *Meditations* and *Contemplations* which I send you are the fruit of Mr. Hervey's pen—the most extraordinary man I ever saw in my life! as much beyond most of the excellent, as the swan, for whiteness and a stately figure, is beyond the common fowl. These thoughts deserve your most serious regard. You may look upon them as you would upon Aaron's rod, by which such wonders were wrought: for these thoughts have been made the means of giving

sight to the blind; life to souls dead in trespasses and sin; and winning the young, the gay, the rich, to see greater charms in a Crucified Saviour, as your own dear parents do, than in all that glitters and dazzles vain minds. How happy shall I be to hear Miss Riland say, 'How tender, affecting, and irresistible, are the pleadings of Mr. Hervey, for his adored Immanuel![1]

[1]   *Henry Venn, Life and Letters,* John Hatchard, London, 1835, p. 332.

# Chapter Six:
# Hervey's Evangelical Library

## Hervey's attitude to books

Although Hervey inherited a substantial library of theological books from his grandfather[1] which he felt he was bound to keep for family reasons, he never extended it in any way because as fast as he read or bought new books, he gave them away to those whom he thought were more needy than himself. Friends who sent him books, knowing what they felt was Hervey's weakness, usually stressed that the books were meant for himself and not for others. Hervey would reply that his books were his own in the same way as the flowers in his garden belong to the bees. Just as the bees' industry in his garden rewarded them with honey, so, he hoped the milk and honey of the Word would become the reward of his parishioners on reading his books. Once the young John Ryland, eager to give Hervey a token of his gratitude for being his tutor so long, bought a beautifully bound edition of Baskerville's *Virgil* and proudly presented it to Hervey. The latter was overcome with gratitude at the kind gift but said to Ryland, 'My dear friend, if I intended to keep this book, I would accept it; but as I shall never read it, you must allow me to pay for it, for I shall surely give it away.' This was not because Hervey despised Virgil. He had been Hervey's favourite poet for many years, but Hervey had had various copies of the poet and knew very much of him off by heart. Ryland, on relating this incident, explains that Hervey's taste for holiness and his devotion to Christ had, in his final years when Ryland had fellowship with him, almost expelled his great love for Virgil out of his heart.

Hervey rarely gave a book away without writing some admonition, Christian wish or passages from Scripture to go with it. One person would be given an exposition on creation, another on the perseverance of the

---

[1]    See *Works*, Letter CXIII.

saints and yet another would receive a tract on redemption pasted into his gift. His most frequently quoted verses were those to do with pardon, justification, sanctification and those dealing with temptation, affliction and death. Hervey had also a one-page tract outlining the whole plan of salvation which he enclosed in many a Bible or book he distributed. Only two days before his death, when a debtor visited Hervey to balance his accounts, Hervey told him to use the money to make a list of all the promises of God which could be put onto a single page and have that placed in Bibles for distribution.

**Criticisms for spending money on books for distribution**
Hervey was an avid reader throughout his life and kept in touch with most developments in the theological world. During the months of illness which kept him at home and unable to write, he was still able to read and perhaps devoured more good literature at the end of his life than at the beginning of his Christian walk. Whenever Hervey heard of an important new book being published, he would send off for it at once, even if this meant applying abroad. Indeed Hervey read a very large number of foreign authors, this task being made easy by the fact that they wrote in the *lingua franca* of the age, Latin. Hervey came under fire for spending so much money on the books he distributed when, in the opinion of his critics, he should be a man of one book, the Bible, and not praise men's works or prescribe what people should read and he ought to use his money more profitably. Hervey met these criticisms in his usual gentle way by writing:

> When I consider the practice of recommending religious books, as implying some respectable regard to a man's own judgment, I undertake it with reluctance; but when I consider it as exercising an act of friendship to my fellow students in the school of Christ, I execute it with pleasure. Far from obtruding myself into the chair of Moses, far from presuming to dictate, to prescribe, or so much as direct, I would only imitate the four leprous men, at the entering of the gate of Samaria, having found gold and silver, and raiment, they could not forbear proclaiming the news, and communicating their spoil to their fellow citizens. When I find a treasure incomparably more precious, when I find a teacher of wisdom, and a guide to glory, why should I hold my peace? why should I enjoy these benefits alone? why should I not, like these honest but calamitous exiles, tell the glad tidings in the city, and invite my neighbours to partake of the blessing?[1]

---

[1]    Quoted without source by John Brown's appendix to his Hervey biography entitled *Mr. Hervey's Recommendation of Books*, p. 510.

The Christian world has just cause to be grateful for Hervey's generosity in spreading good Christian literature and recommending these books in his writings. By this means, he rescued many a book from oblivion and later Christian publishing houses have been drawn to the Christian classics of former years solely through the testimony left behind him by Hervey. Just two months before being called to glory, Hervey encouraged friends such as William Cudworth and John Ryland to organise an 'Evangelical Library' in the form of cheap editions of the best books. 'Methinks if a subscription to modernise valuable authors, and thus rescue them from the pit of oblivion, was properly set on foot by some men of eminence, and the proposals well drawn up, it would meet with due encouragement. I have often wondered that such an attempt has never yet been made. How many excellent books of the last century are now out of print, whilst such a number of useless and pernicious writings are continually published?'

### Herman Witsius (1636-1708)

It is most difficult to determine which books written by true men of God Hervey preferred to others. As soon as he recognised true Biblical treasures in a book, he would be so thrilled with the contents that he proclaimed their author as the very best. Thus Hervey's letters reveal the names of quite a number of authors who were, at the time of reading, each his favourite. One of Hervey's most loved foreign authors was the Dutchman Herman Witsius whose books Hervey ordered direct from Amsterdam or received through his friend, John Ryland. He was the one author, Hervey affirmed, that he ought to have read at university as it would have helped him greatly in his search for the truth.[1] On reading Witsius' *Animadversiones Irenicæ*, Hervey wrote, 'A choice little piece of polemical divinity, fairly stated, accurately discussed, and judiciously determined, with a perspicuity of sense and a solidity of reasoning, exceeded by nothing but the remarkable conciseness, and the still more remarkable candour of the sentiments.' The Dutchman's work on the covenants, *Economia Federum* was sent to Hervey as a present by Ryland in February, 1753 and Hervey wrote back, full of enthusiasm, saying, 'I received your obliging letter, and very valuable present of Witsius, which I shall thankfully keep as a monument of your friendship, and attentively study as a magazine of evangelical wisdom. May the Lord Jesus Christ transfer the precious truths from the writer's pen to the reader's heart!' Hervey had read Witsius some years previously but was not able to recognise his value. Now, he did indeed experience that transfer mentioned in his letter to Ryland and told another friend concerning the work, 'I wish, for my own sake, that you were somewhat acquainted with the author, because, if you should be in-

---

[1]   See *Works*, Letter LX.

clined to know the reason and foundation of my sentiments on any particular point, Witsius might be my spokesman; he would declare my mind
better than I could do myself.'[1] In his famous work *Theron and Aspasio*,
Hervey refers to Witsius work as, 'a body of divinity, in its method so well
digested; in its doctrines so truly evangelical; in its language so refined
and elegant; in its manner so affectionate and animating; that I would recommend it to every student of Divinity. I would not scruple *to risk all my
reputation* upon the merits of this performance: and I cannot but lament it,
as one of my greatest losses, that I was *no sooner* acquainted with this
most excellent author, all whose works have such a delicacy of composition, and such a sweet savour of holiness, that I know not any comparison
more proper to represent their true character, than *the golden pot which
had manna*; and was outwardly *bright* with burnished gold; inwardly *rich*
with heavenly food.'

Witsius wrote his *Economy of the Covenants between God and Man*[2]
as the English title runs, to combat Socinianism, Grotianism and
Arminianism which, he argued, were public adversaries of Biblical truths
and had 'defiled the doctrine of God's covenants' and thus it was 'absolutely necessary to oppose them.' On discovering how very fond of Witsius
Ryland was, Hervey wrote to his friends in Amsterdam and ordered a picture of the Dutchman to adorn Ryland's parlour. Ryland called one of his
sons Herman Witsius Ryland after his favourite author.

### Campegius Vitringa (1659-1722)

The Orientalist and commentator Campegius Vitringa, who followed
Witsius to Franeker and Leyden universities, was another Dutch favourite
of Hervey's. Of Vitringa's commentary on Isaiah, which Hervey read in
Latin, he says, 'Extensive learning, accurate criticism, and an unction of
pure evangelical holiness, runs through the whole of the book.' Hervey
was also full of praise for Johann Heinrich Alting (1583-1644), tutor to
the Prince of Palatine and later professor at Heidelberg and Groeningen.
Unlike most of his brethren of the same academic and spiritual abilities,
Alting published nothing in his life-time, his works, including his famous
*Exegesis Augustane Confesionis* and *Explicatio Catecheseos Palatine*,
being published posthumously by his son, Jacob Alting, no mean scholar
himself. Of Alting's *Works*, Hervey writes, 'They are, I think, an excellent
and concise system of didactic, practical, and polemic divinity, very proper

---

[1]    Letter CXIV in 1837 *Works*.

[2]    Thanks to Thomas K. Ascol and James I. Packer, the eighteenth century translation
published by John Gill and his circle has been recently made available (1990) in a two-
volumed, bound edition which will prove a God-send to all who feel called to witness for
God to their fellow men.

in my opinion for the study of a young Christian minister. In this book is a catechism, which pleases me better than any I ever perused.'

### Karl Heinrich von Bogatzky (1690-1774)

High up on his list of favourite German authors was Karl Heinrich von Bogatzky, August Hermann Franke's pupil and close friend. His *Golden Treasury of the Children of God, whose Treasure and Heart are in Heaven* published at Breslau in 1718 had reached 19 German editions by the fifties before being translated into English and becoming a best-seller both in Britain and the New World. Even today the work is highly treasured amongst evangelicals and often quoted in Christian literature. Many of Bogatzky's 411 hymns, full of evangelistic fervour, still find a place in Continental hymn books. Hervey says of his own copy of the *Golden Treasury*, 'It is pretty well-thumbed, for there is rarely a day passes that I do not make use of it; and particularly when I am so languid as to be incapable of attending to my usual studies. The author very properly calls it 'A Golden Treasury for the Children of God', who esteem the word of God more than gold, and much fine gold, and from which they may daily be supplied with proper advice and relief in all manner of spiritual necessities, as thousands have happily experienced already. The verses are elegant, and edifying on most of the subjects; and it was his earnest desire and prayer, that the Lord, in his infinite goodness, would please to bless his endeavours to the good of many souls, and to the glory of his holy name. Mr. Bogatzky observes judiciously, that it is not to be expected that a performance of this nature will suit the taste of those who unhappily mistake mere outward morality for true Christianity; but such as either have or desire to have a real experience of the kingdom of God in their soul, will find in it much to the awakening, comforting, and encouraging their hearts in the right way.'[1]

### Hermann August Franke (1663-1727)

Hervey also read the works of Bogatzky's former tutor Hermann August Franke, famous for his *Pietas Hallensis*, his orphanages and his work with Spener in the *Collegia Pietatis*. Referring to Professor Franke's *Short Introduction to the Christian Religion* and his *Nicodemus: Or a Treatise Against the Fear of Man* which had recently been translated by the Society for the Reformation of Manners, Hervey says, 'I think him one of the most eminent Christians, and most extraordinary men I ever heard of, as his *Pietas Hallensis*, which I read with admiration and deep humility, sufficiently demonstrates; and had I been a member of the society for the reformation of manners, when the dedication of his Nicodemus had been

---

[1]   Letter CLV in *Works*.

118  *James Hervey*

presented to them, I should have made a motion to have had an hundred
pounds expended in a proper distribution of that most important book, as
there can be no material reformation till the fear of man is removed; and as
nothing can be better calculated to extirpate such fear, and promote all the
other laudable ends of the society.'[1]

## Martin Chemnitz (1522-1586)

Another German author whom Hervey loved to read was Martin
Chemnitz. Of his *Harmonia Evangelica* Hervey wrote, 'This illustration
of our Lord's life is sweetly practical, as well as judiciously critical. The
author is a Lutheran: there seems to be abundance of the heavenly unction
diffused through his work; I often read it, and hope to receive considerable edification and comfort from it. It consists of a folio volume, pretty
bulky; it is indeed a truly valuable work, in which the learned reader will
find traces of lively devotion, many pieces of solid criticism, and many
fine views opened to see more clearly the wisdom, beauty, and transcendent excellency of our blessed Redeemer's life. This book is particularly
estimable, for displaying with great perspicuity, and enforcing with pro-
portionable zeal, that distinguishing article of Christianity, *justification
through the righteousness of Jesus Christ.*' Chemnitz, called 'the first theologian of the Reformation' obviously influenced Hervey greatly in his work
*Theron and Aspasio*, written to counteract the tendency in the preaching
of his day to emphasise that righteousness was a virtue to be achieved by
human effort.

## Johann Albrecht Bengel (1687-1751)

The works of Bengel with their maxim of 'put nothing into the Scriptures, but draw everything from them' became strong favourites amongst
the earlier preachers and teachers of the Evangelical Revival in Britain
and the Great Awakening in North America. In particular, Bengel's *Gnomen
Novi Testamenti* was of great use in combating the new wave of higher
criticism which was challenging orthodox Christianity at the time. Commenting on Bengel's annotations to the New Testament, Hervey says, 'They
present the reader with many refined observations on the elegancies of the
style, and sublimity of the doctrine. They are a pattern of the concise manner, and, which is perhaps the crowning excellency, they all along indicate
a heart glowing with a love of its subject.'

## Liborius Zimmermann

One of the tasks Hervey wished, but failed, to accomplish before his
early death was to bring out a new, enlarged edition of Liborius

---

[1]    Letter CLIV in *Works*.

Zimmermann's *De Eminentia Cognitionis Christi* in a paraphrased form
to be called *Excellency of the Knowledge of Christ* which was a commentary on a hymn of Luther of the same name. Moses Brown, his curate, had
translated part of Zimmermann and passed on his efforts to Hervey for
completion. Of the work, Hervey told Ryland, 'There are some charming
evangelical truths in it, most comfortable, encouraging, delightful! But it
seems to want order, and a proper arrangement. Here it should be pruned,
and there it should be grafted. If I should attempt to dispatch this business,
I must beg, not only your perusal of the piece, but your correction of the
translation, and especially your examination; your exact and rigorous examination of the doctrine.' Hervey found Zimmermann especially comforting in times of illness. From 1749 on, Hervey strove to write an introduction to Zimmermann's works but his own illness and early death intervened.

### The Scotch divines

Coming nearer home, Hervey showed a deep fondness for the Scottish
divines of the late seventeenth century and early eighteenth century and
their works were amongst the few from which Hervey never parted. It is
difficult to discover whom Hervey preferred amongst the Erskines, Traill,
Boston, Charnock, Brown and other staunch Scots Puritans and revival
preachers. Perhaps his favourite was Ralf Erskine who combined sound
theology with a beautiful, lyrical language. Hervey kept Erskine's Son-
nets, which became known as the *Beauties of Erskine*, on his desk and
constantly read them from his earliest longings for peace with God until
his death. In his last weeks, they were especially comforting to him. He
testified that, 'I have met with none more evangelical, more comfortable,
or more useful during this long interval of time. I would advise my dear
friends who possess it to read it frequently, and may the spirit of our gracious God write it on their hearts.' Hervey was rather more critical of
Erskine's other works because of their style but said of Ralf's joint collection of sermons with his brother Ebenezer that, 'was I to read (them) with
a single view to the edification of my heart in true faith, solid comfort, and
evangelical holiness, I would have recourse to Mr. Erskine and take his
volumes for my guide, my companion, and my own familiar friend.' This
highly positive statement must be compared with John Wesley's *Journal*
entry on reading these sermons on Friday October 20, 1751. Wesley says
'But how was I disappointed! I not only found many things odd and
unscriptural, but some that were dangerously false; and the leaven of
Antinomianism spread from end to end.'

### Thomas Boston (1676-1732) and the Marrow Men

Thomas Boston and the Marrow Men were favourites of Hervey as
they emphasised the Biblical nature of faith as being a gift of God and not

a virtue. This was in contrast to the Deists and Latitudinarians who believed that man's reason and his own abilities could teach him to attain faith through virtue. This philosophy of faith being a striving to do one's duty, thereby substituting grace for the moral law, was the sum total of teaching in the book *The Whole Duty of Man* which was almost rivalling the Bible at the time. Hervey's position was always, 'The moral law indeed spoke terror, and nothing but terror, to impotent man.'[1] Hervey wrote concerning Boston's *Human Nature in its Fourfold State*, 'This, in my opinion, is one of our best books for common readers. The sentences are short, the comparisons striking, the language is easy, and the doctrines evangelical; the method is proper, the plan comprehensive, the manner searching and yet consolatory. If another celebrated treatise is styled 'The Whole Duty of Man,' I would call this 'The Whole of Man,' as it comprises what he *was* originally, what he *is* by transgression, what he *should be* by grace, and then what he *shall be* in glory.' When Hervey read *The Marrow of Modern Divinity* with notes by Boston he wrote to William Hog, saying, 'I never read the "Marrow" with Mr. Boston's notes, till this present time, 1755; and I find, by not having read it I have sustained a considerable loss. It is a most valuable book; the doctrines it contains are the life of my soul, and the joy of my heart. Might my tongue or pen be made instrumental to recommend and illustrate, to support and propagate such precious truths, I should bless the day wherein I was born. Mr. Boston's notes on the "Marrow" are, in my opinion, some of the most judicious and valuable that ever were penned.'

The 'Marrow' was written by Edward Fisher in 1646, two years after writing his *An Appeal to the Conscience, as thou wilt answer it at the great and dreadful day of Jesus Christ.* In 1720, the Assembly of the Church of Scotland pronounced the work to be Antinomian but as it was supported by such saints as James Hog, Thomas Boston, Ebenezer and Ralf Erskine and Gabriel Watson, the Assembly's findings must be questioned. The fact that James Hervey came down on the side of the 'Marrow Men' helped relieve the Scotsmen from the accusation of heresy in their home country. The whole question centred around the relationship between law and grace, neither side having said the last word on the subject.

After Hervey had written his first three volumes of *Theron and Aspasio* on the imputed righteousness of Christ, he planned to write a fourth to show more specifically how the righteousness the believer possesses in Christ worked out in practice in his life. When Hervey read Boston's *View of the Covenant of Grace,* he wrote, 'This is an excellent treatise; it seems, in point of clear, comfortable, evangelical divinity, even to surpass his book on the four-fold state. I am desired, and indeed I am much inclined

---

[1]    Letter CXLIX, *Works.*

to write another volume, and to make Sanctification or Gospel-Holiness the subject. If Divine Providence enables me to execute this work, I shall reckon it my duty to bear my testimony to the distinguished worth of this piece.' Again, Hervey's untimely death put an end to this—and many other projects that Hervey had in mind.

## Robert Traill (1642-1716)

The works of Robert Traill were avidly read by Hervey. Traill, son of a learned Scottish minister who was banned for life to Holland because of allegedly holding a conventicle, followed so closely in the steps of his father that he, too, was obliged to seek refuge in Holland after which he ministered in London and Cranbrook. Usually, Hervey's letter to the Edinburgh bookseller and pastor John Traill is included in Hervey's works to show his reverence for Robert Traill and their very close interest in the same doctrines. John Traill had begun to re-published his famous uncle's works and sent Hervey a complimentary gift of the first two volumes in the summer of 1755. Hervey was thrilled with them and wrote back to tell Traill:

> I received your very valuable and no less acceptable present, some weeks ago, I should have acknowledged the favour sooner, but I chose to stay till I had tasted the dish you set before me, and indeed I find it to be very savoury meat, the true manna; food for the soul. Your worthy relative was a workman that need not be ashamed. He knew how clearly to state and solidly to establish the faith of God's elect and the doctrine according to godliness. Oh! that my heart, and the heart of every reader, may be opened by the eternal Spirit, to receive the precious truths! The letter at the end of the volume (*A Vindication of the Protestant Doctrine concerning Justification, and of its Preachers and Professors, from the unjust charge of Antinomianism.*) is a judicious performance. It rightly divides the word of truth, and lays the line, with a masterly hand, between the presumptuous legalist, and the licentious Antinomian. I am particularly pleased with the honourable testimony borne to those two excellent books, Dr. Owen's *Treatise on Justification*, and Mr. Marshall's *Gospel Mystery of Sanctification*; books fit to be recommended by so good a judge.

Hervey might well have praised Traill's defence against false charges of Antinomianism as the work referred to the very same charges which were brought against Owen, Marshall, Gill, Romaine and Toplady, besides Hervey himself, and after Hervey's death were pinned on Hawker, Huntington, Doudney, Kershaw, Philpot, Gadsby, in fact on any man who shared Owen's appreciation of the Scriptures.

## Moses Brown

Hervey had a very competent Christian writer on his very doorstep in the person of his own curate, Moses Brown. Hervey first came into contact with Brown in 1749 when he was a curate himself and did not hesitate to call Brown to assist him when he became Rector of Collingtree. Writing of one of Brown's earlier works, Hervey says:

> I hope the divine Providence will give his *Sunday Thoughts* an extensive spread, and make them an instrument of diffusing the savour of true religion. Seldom, if ever, have I seen a treatise that presents the reader with so full, yet concise a view; so agreeable, yet so striking a picture of true Christianity, in its most important articles, and most distinguishing peculiarities. Though I am utterly unacquainted with the author, I assure myself he is no novice in the sacred school, and has more than a speculative knowledge of the gospel; every page discovers traces of an excellent heart, that has itself experienced what the muse sings.[1]

Brown was equally enamoured of Hervey's work and when, in February 1749, he first read *Meditations*, he committed his praise to poetry, beginning his lengthy laudatory with the words:

> As some new *star* attracts th' admiring sight,
> His splendours pouring through the fields of light,
> Whole nights, delighted with th' unusual rays,
> On the fair heavenly *visitant* we gaze.
> So thy famed *volumes* sweet surprise impart;
> Mar'kd by all eyes, and felt in ev'ry heart.
> Nature inform'd by thee, new paths has trod,
> And rises *here*, a preacher for her God;
> By fancy's aids mysterious heights she tries,
> And lures us, by our senses, to the skies.
> To deck thy *stile* collected graces throng,
> Bold as the pencil's *tints*, but soft as song.
> In themes how rich thy vein! how pure thy choice!
> Transcripts of truth, own'd clear from Scripture's voice:
> Thy judgment these and piety attest,
> Transcripts—read only fairer in thy breast:
> *There*, what thy works would show, we best may see,
> And all *they* teach in doctrine, *lives* in thee.[2]

---

[1]   *Works*, Letter LVII.

[2]   The full poem can be found with further poems on the same subject by various author's in vol. i of *Meditations* and *Contemplations* (in two volumes), Galvin Alston, Edinburgh, 1774.

## Charles Chauncy (1592-1672)

One book Hervey was very loath to part with was Chauncy's *Neonomianism Unmasked*. It seems that a person had loaned the book to a friend of Hervey's who in turn, lent it to Hervey. After a while, the friend, who seemed to be unsure who the original owner was, asked Hervey to return the book, explaining his dilemma. Hervey replied, 'I return, though with reluctance, *Neonomianism Unmasked*. I thought it had been yours by purchase and mine by promise. I very much esteem it, because of its excellent evangelical doctrine; and more, because it is improved by several remarks from your pen. If it does not really belong to another person, I must still maintain my claim.'

## John Gill (1697-1771) and John Brine (1703-1765)

Besides John Ryland, Hervey had a number of friends amongst the Baptists whom he held in high esteem and he kept the Baptist bookseller, George Keith, John Gill's son-in-law, busy supplying him with books. Hervey's admiration for Gill was immense. This was based on personal gratitude to Gill for visiting him often on his sick-bed and also for the wisdom and spiritual wealth to be found in his works. Hervey found Gill's commentary on the Song of Solomon superb and when commenting himself on Song of Solomon 2:14 in his book *Theron and Aspasio*, he says:

Should the reader have an inclination to see this sacred, but mysterious book explained, I would refer him to Dr. Gill's *Exposition of the Canticles:* which has such a copious vein of sanctified invention running through it, and is interspersed with such a variety of delicate and brilliant images, as cannot but highly entertain a curious mind; which presents us also with such rich and charming displays of the glory of Christ's person, the freeness of his grace to sinners, and the tenderness of his love to the church, as cannot but administer the most exquisite delight to the believing soul. Considered in both these views, I think the work resembles the paradisaical garden described by Milton, in which:

Blossoms and fruits at once of golden hue,
Appear'd with gay enamell'd colours mix'd.[1]

Ryland wrote to Hervey early in 1753, recommending Gill's sermons to his friend and was pleased to find that Hervey knew Gill personally and already had a copy of the work Ryland had offered to send him. Although Hervey always called John Gill and John Brine master builders in Israel and he looked to them as his closest advisors along with Cudworth and Ryland, he still did not hesitate to differ with them on certain points, al-

---

[1] Hervey's *Works*, 1837, *Theron and Aspasio*, Letter IX, p. 380

though he made every effort to keep from his writings any suggestion that he opposed them. Writing in October, 1758, he told a friend, 'I have certainly a very great esteem for Dr. Gill, yet I never could assent to his notion of eternal justification. I am very much obliged to you for pointing out to me the passage in *Theron and Aspasio* which seems to favour, or proceeds upon such a tenet. It shall be altered in the next edition.' Whenever Brine was criticised in public such as in the pages of the *Northampton Mercury* or *Monthly Review*, Hervey wondered how he would fare in their hands as he shared Brine's doctrine in most points. Hervey seems to have responded negatively at first to Brine's writings on the assurance of faith.[1] Brine looked on faith as that gift of God which enables a sinner to pray, 'If thou willt, thou canst make me clean'. Hervey tended to understand faith more as a fixed conviction in the mind of the believer based on the subjective feeling of already having an interest in Christ. This may seem hair-splitting in its practical outworking but Brine wished to stress that faith was solely dependent on God's will, rather than human interpretations of their actions. The fact that Hervey informed those who were checking through his own manuscripts that they should be careful to preserve his view of the matter but not in such away that he appeared to oppose Brine's view shows that Hervey did not wish to make too much of the matter, especially as he had learnt to respect Brine's 'clear head and a warm heart' and believed Brine to be, with Gill, an expert at logical thinking.

### John Bunyan (1628-1688)

Whatever the denomination, there must have been very few saints who were not charmed and edified by that 'sweet dreamer' John Bunyan, another Baptist. Even years after Hervey had determined not to openly display his poetic skills, we find him delighting friends in private by his proficiency in verse. His thoughts concerning Bunyan, for instance, brought out once again the true poet in him and he wrote in the fly-leaf of Dr. Stonehouse's copy of the *Pilgrim's Progress*:

> Far o'er the arches of yon azure skies,
> Mansions of bliss, immortal structures rise;
> Of pearls the walls, of gold the shining floors,
> On crystal hinges turn the tuneful doors.
> There the brave troop of crimson Martyrs stands,
> Crowns on their heads, and sceptres in their hands.
> There Wisdom's sons, a long illustrious train,

---

[1]    See Hervey's letters to Ryland dated April 5, 1755, April 12, 1757, April 20, 1757 and May 13, 1758.

Each on his throne, to endless ages reign.
There too, with looks of love, in robes of light,
The Saviour shines, magnificently bright;
Would you my friend, of heavenly life possessed,
Sit with those saints in everlasting rest?
Would you, when earth's no more, survive above,
And 'midst the radiant files of angels move?
A guide, behold! this pilgrim works the way,
To those blest regions of eternal day.

### Daniel Defoe (1660-1731)

Another Dissenting writer whose books Hervey loved to read was Daniel Defoe. The generations succeeding Defoe have either stressed his literary endeavours, his political fortitude or his religious insight, each in separate studies. An evaluation of Defoe which successfully unites these elements has still to be written. Hervey never separated his view of Defoe as a writer from his view of the man as a professing Christian. Of Defoe's *Family Instructor* Hervey writes, 'If you love entertainment, my next shall recommend a book, that is as entertaining as a novel, yet edifying as a sermon.'

### Tobias Crisp (1600-1643)

Hervey used the edition of Crisp edited by John Gill and was full of praise for the great soul-winner, always confessing that it was Crisp who had taught him the value of good works which 'proceed from the SPIRIT of the LORD JESUS, dwelling in our Hearts; and then they will be truly good.'[1] Of Crisp's sermons, he wrote to Lady Francis:

> Do not harbour any fear, Madam, concerning the propriety of your sending Dr. Crisp's sermons to Mr. K-. They are, I think, the very discourses which he wants. Especially, if he is inclined to distress of conscience, on account of his spiritual state. I know not any treatises more proper, or more excellently calculated, to administer solid consolation. They are, under the divine influence, one of my first counsellors, and principle comforters. They often drop manna and balm upon my fainting and sickly graces. The LORD JESUS CHRIST grant that your Ladyship may experience the soul-cheering, conscience-healing, Heart-reviving Power of these precious Doctrines!
>
> The Doctor has, as you justly observe, some expressions, which seem to contradict positive commands or peremptory assertions of

---

[1] Letter LXXXIV to Lady Francis Shirley, p. 202.

Scripture. But these expressions, when examined and explained, will generally be found to coincide with the truth that is in JESUS. They are not contrary to the pure Word of the Gospel, but, to our pre-conceived ideas. We have not been accustomed to the joyful sound of grace and salvation—infinitely rich grace, and perfectly free salvation—therefore they are a *strange* language to our ears. O! that we may more frequently hear, and more diligently read, till, like the Colossian converts, We know the grace of GOD in truth!'[1]

Hervey was referring to the occasional depreciating mention of works of righteousness by Crisp where he is striving to keep his readers from believing that their good works are in any way meritorious. Later critics of Reformed theology have culled these few expressions from the entirety of Crisp's writings in order to label their author an Antinomian. Obviously sensitive to such criticisms of Crisp, Hervey wrote again to Lady Francis on the subject, saying:

I do not wonder, that people object to Dr. Crisp, and such divines as magnify the exalted SAVIOUR, who sits at GOD's right hand; but pour contempt upon the fallen creatures, who dwell in houses of clay: who would represent the divine REDEEMER, as the meridian sun, and all the race of Adam, as glow-worms of the night.—There was a time, when I should have joined, most heartily joined in the opposition. For then I fought to *establish my own righteousness*. I would fain *be* something; would fain *do* something to *inherit eternal life*; and could not brook a total *submission to the righteousness of GOD*. But repeated infirmities, repeated sins, and repeated sorrows, have been the means, under the influence of the SPIRIT, to cure me of this arrogant temper.—It is now the daily desire of my soul, to see more and more the littleness, the insufficiency, the meanness of all that is called my own. But to delight myself in the *unsearchable riches*, and triumph in the transcendent excellencies of CHRIST JESUS my LORD.—And, I do assure you, Madam, that when I wander from this path, I *stumble upon dark mountains*; I fall into briars and thorns; I lose my peace, my tranquillity, my hope.—If this be the case, as it really is, your Ladyship will allow, that I have reason, notwithstanding every contrary suggestion, to adhere inseparably to *this Way*.[2]

Though Hervey felt that Crisp was as sound as a bell, he did query his writings at times as when he wrote to Ryland at the beginning of 1755, to

[1]    Ibid, Letter XCIII, p. 221.
[2]    Ibid, Letter XCVI, p. 223.

tell him: 'Doctor Crisp says, 'There is no wrath to believers; Christ has bore it all; exhausted it wholly, and carried it—clean away.' This is a comfortable doctrine. But how will it consist with some Scriptures, that seem to speak the contrary sentiment; with that passage in Micah particularly; *I will bear the indignation of the Lord, because I have sinned against him.* This is evidently the voice of a believer—of a confirmed believer—of a believer in the very exercise of faith: for he calls God, My God, and the God of my salvation. He says, *The Lord will bring me forth to light: I shall behold his righteousness.*'[1]

### John Owen (1616-1683)

For Hervey, anyone with any resemblance of orthodoxy must, at some time or other, be found recommending Owen. This noble contender for the truth found God through a sermon preached on the words, 'Why are ye fearful, O ye of little faith?' From then onwards, he never hesitated to proclaim his faith and, through the providential hand of God, became Dean of Christ Church, Oxford and a preacher before Parliament and chaplain to Cromwell and in 1652 was elected Vice-Chancellor of Oxford. There is hardly a Christian topic which Owen does not comment on in depth in his works and whether he is writing on Arminianism, the divine origin of the Scriptures, the Holy Spirit, justification or preservation, he is pure bibline through and through and the fact that his works are still in print shows that his message has still not lost its power to appeal to Spirit-filled men. Hervey was no exception and wrote concerning Owen's *On Communion with God*, 'This presents us with the spirit and quintessence of the gospel; with the noblest privileges and strongest consolations of Christianity, animating us thereby to all the duties of holy obedience. There are pinks and roses in the path, marrow and fatness on the table, milk and honey in the cup. In many treatises the author has done worthily, but in this I think he excelleth all.' Hervey read closely Owen's *On Indwelling Sin in Believers*, admiring his stance between those who preach sinless-perfection and those who believe that being in Christ places them above and beyond the righteousness which they reflect. Hervey says, 'The author's pen is indeed a dissecting knife, goes deep into the subject, and lays open the plague of the heart: like a workman that needs not be ashamed, he demonstrates his point from the unerring word of God, and the acknowledged experiences of Christians; like a compassionate, as well as an able physician, he all along prescribes the proper antidote; nay, he shows how the poison may be so overruled by the divine grace, and so managed by the watchful patient, as to become medicinal, salutary, and conducive to the most benefi-

---

[1]    *The Character of the Rev. James Hervey, A.M.,* Appendix, A Series of Letters, pp.26, 27.

cial purpose.' On the whole, Hervey found Owen's works full of 'that unction from the Holy Spirit which tends to enlighten the eyes and cheer the heart, which sweetens the enjoyments of life, softens the horrors of death, and prepares for the fruitions of eternity.'

## Benjamin Jenks (1646-1724)

Jenks was an author who influenced Hervey more than any other with the exception of Marshall and we have already seen how Jenk's *Submission to the Righteousness of God* and Whitefield's sermons were means of bringing Hervey to a knowledge of the truth. Jenks' *Prayers and Offices of Devotion* never ceased to be a best-seller throughout the awakening. Written in 1697, it had reached its eleventh edition by the time of Hervey's youth and had reached 26 editions by the end of the century. George Simeon printed the twenty-seventh edition of the work in 1810 and it remained highly popular for almost another century. Of this book, Hervey said, 'It is truly admirable for the spirituality, sublimity, and propriety of the sentiments, as well as for the concise form and pathetic turn of the expression.' Jenks' work for young people on the *Victory of Chastity* was thought by Hervey to be the best book on the subject and he distributed it amongst his young people. Jenks' *Meditations* was Hervey's main source of doctrine and he found within the two volumes sound teaching on most issues and highly adapted to 'impress the conscience, and build up the soul in faith, holiness and comfort.'

A work that combined sound historical research and able exegesis was Rollin's *Ancient History*. This book was the staple fare of evangelicals of all denominations during the eighteenth century, praised not only by Hervey but by fellow Anglicans such as Toplady and Baptists such as John Gill and John Ryland. Toplady, who was most impressed by the learning, theology and lyrical style of the latter told him that he was a Rollin, a Witsius and a Watts all in one. Of this volume Hervey says, 'A work in which the most entertaining and instructive events of antiquity are regularly digested, elegantly related, and stripped of those minor incidents which make the story move slow, and are apt to fatigue the attention: concise but judicious observations are interspersed; many very distinguished predictions of Scripture are explained and confirmed by correspondent facts, from the most authentic memoirs of classical literature: Indeed, a perpetual regard to the elucidation and honour of the sacred oracles, runs through and ennobles the whole performance.'

## William Cudworth (Died 1763)

A contemporary author who worked very closely with Hervey and who became his chief friend and supporter and, one might say spokesman during Hervey's illness, was William Cudworth, one of Whitefield's preachers and friend of Cennick. John Wesley, who, with his preachers, succeeded Cudworth at the Norwich Tabernacle, took great offence at Cudworth for preaching 'Antinomianism', going to print against him in his *Two Dialogues between an Antinomian and his Friend.* Wesley gave up the work at the Tabernacle after complaining that he had taken over 'bullocks unaccustomed to the yoke.' This fact obviously helped to strengthen Wesley's low opinion of Cudworth against whom, according to Tyerman, he 'spoke with a severity which he seldom used.' Tyerman, ever on Wesley's side, feels that it was Hervey's friendship with Cudworth which alienated him from Wesley.[1] On the other hand, John Brown of Whitburn claims that Cudworth wrote one of the best vindications of the doctrines of grace ever, defending them against the unorthodox teaching of Sandeman and Bellamy. Cudworth became pastor of Margaret Street, Oxford Road, London until his death in 1763. Margaret Street then fell on evil days but the good work Cudworth commenced was revived for a short time by William Huntington's ministry at Margaret Street before Providence Chapel was built. Cudworth defended Hervey's theology in his *Defence of Theron and Aspasio* and published a simplified version of Marshall's *Gospel Mystery of Sanctification.*

## Walter Marshall (1628-80)

Undoubtedly Hervey's favourite of favourites when it came to Christian writing was Walter Marshall whose works played a leading role in directing Hervey along the paths of righteousness. Yet Marshall was by no means generally accepted by evangelicals as the Master in Israel Hervey believed he was. Usually the more Arminian or Grotian the reader's personal views, the less respect he will have for Marshall. John Wesley, for instance, could not accept Marshall's Pauline doctrine that 'in the flesh dwelleth no good thing.'[2] The very idea caused Wesley to say of the Christian in Marshall's teaching, 'What a wonderful communion is there between light and darkness! What strange fellowship between Christ and Belial!' Needless to say, the passage Wesley had just read in Marshall was speaking about the flesh *warring against* the Spirit and not sharing fellowship with Him. Nevertheless, Wesley feels he can say, 'What can we infer from hence, but that Mr. Marshall's book, containing so much poison mixed with food, is an exceedingly dangerous one, and not fit to be recommended to any but experienced Christians.'[3]

Yet even William Huntington, a Calvinist of the Calvinists, could not accept all that Marshall said. In the section entitled *Small Legacies* in his

---

[1]  See Tyerman's *The Life of Whitefield* and *The Oxford Methodists* for his view of the relationship between Cudworth and Wesley. Lady Huntingdon finally took over the work of the Norwich Tabernacle.

[2]  Romans 7:18.

[3]  Journal, entry for 20 November 1767.

*Last Will and Testament,* Huntington first bequeaths his best books i.e. the Bible, Elisha Cole on the *Sovereignty of God,* Bunyan's *Pilgrim's Progress* and *Come and Welcome to Jesus Christ,* Boston's *View of the Covenant of Grace* and Romaine's *Life and Walk of Faith* and then refers to, 'part of Mr. Marshall's *Gospel Mystery of Sanctification',* indicating that he cannot recommend all of the *Gospel Mystery* to his family and church members. The New Divinity School in North America led by Bellamy went to great length to criticise Hervey's attachment to Marshall and Boston as did Andrew Fuller in England. One writer, hiding behind the pious-sounding name of *Evangelicus* wrote in a 1760 issue of the *London Magazine,* 'The late Rev. James Hervey, in a prefatory discourse prefixed to a late edition of Marshall on *Sanctification,* has expressed himself in these re-markable terms:- 'Were I (said he) to be banished into some desolate is-land, possessed only of two books besides my Bible, this should be one of the two, perhaps the first that I would choose.' And yet the book which the ingenious recommender so extravagantly applauds, contains many things not only dark and unintelligible, but of very dangerous tendency; against which the renowned piety of these great men will be no antidote, but, on the contrary, make the poison work more powerfully by its being received in such a vehicle.' This highly negative view of Marshall and Hervey was not at all typical of the *London Magazine* which published a number of very positive reviews of Hervey's books and letters recommending the very doctrine of sanctification that Marshall and Hervey identified with true Christian holiness.[1] Hervey realised that the reason many professing Christians could not accept Marshall was that empirically they had no personal knowledge of the doctrines contained in his works. To see sanc-tification as a work of grace in the soul sponsored solely by the electing love of God in Christ and the inner-working of the Spirit is a doctrine few can accept as it emphasises man's acute inability to perform works of righteousness in his own strength. This conviction moved Hervey to add a footnote to Dialogue XVI in his *Theron and Aspasio,* saying:

> It is with great pleasure, and without any diffidence, that I refer my readers to Mr. Marshall's treatise on *Sanctification,* which I shall not recommend in the style of a critic, or like a person of taste, but with all the simplicity of the weakest Christian, I mean from my own experience. It has been one of the most useful books to my own heart; I scarce ever fail to receive spiritual consolation and strength from the perusal of it; (here follow the words quoted in the *London Magazine).* Should any person, hitherto a stranger to the work, purchase it on this recommendation, I must desire to

---

[1]    This book was recently published by Evangelical Press but it is now out of print.

suggest one caution: That he be not surprised if, in the beginning, he meets with something new and quite out of the common road; or if surprised, that he should not be offended, but calmly and attentively proceed. He will find the author's design opening itself by degrees: He will discern more and more the propriety of his method; and what might, at the first view, appear like a stumbling block, will prove to be a fair, compendious, and ample avenue to the palace of *truth*—to the temple of *holiness*—and to the bowers of *happiness*.

This book is not so much calculated for careless insensible sinners, as for those who are awakened to a solicitous attention to their everlasting interests, who are earnestly inquiring with the Philippian jailer, 'What shall I do to be saved?' or passionately crying, in the language of the apostle, 'O wretched man that I am! who shall deliver me from the body of this death?' If there be any such, as no doubt there are many in the Christian world, I would say with regard to them, 'O that such persons were acquainted with the doctrines, and influenced by the directions contained in this treatise! They would, under the divine blessing, recover them from their distress, and restore them to tranquillity; they would comfort their hearts, and thereby establish them in every good word and work.

Realising that his correspondent Lady Shirley would perhaps have difficulty delving into Marshall because of the low view of man and high view of Christ's righteousness that author had, Hervey was very careful how he introduced her to the book. He thus wrote:

> Has your Ladyship seen a book, entitled *The Gospel Mystery of Sanctification*, written by Mr. *Marshall*; now re-published, with a recommendatory letter by Mr. *Hervey*? It is a book, which has been and is singularly comforting, edifying, beneficial to my own heart; and from an earnest desire, that it may be made equally or more eminently so to yours, I would venture to recommend it to your Ladyship. The reading of the book, I have sometimes thought, is like the eating of olives. Which, on the first trial, are generally insipid, if not disgustful. But upon a repeated use, they become palatable, pleasing, and delicious.[1]

Ryland, who had spent a number of weeks a year for six years as a young man discussing literature with Hervey, laying the foundations for

---

[1]    Letter CIII, Lady Francis Shirley collection.

his own extremely wide reading, mentions a huge number of books that Hervey read, but which are not taken up in this chapter as Hervey's own testimony to the authors is lacking. Ryland, often used Hervey as an example to his own students, and stressed how important reading had been to Hervey's spiritual and moral development. In his own highly enthusiastic and rather exaggerated way, Ryland says of the virtue engendered through Hervey's reading:

> Praise and renown have always been the rewards of real virtue, and fire up a generous ambition to excel; to consider what patterns of virtue are gone to heaven before us; what prudence, justice, temperance, and fortitude, shone in the tempers and characters of the great and good men of the Old and New Testament. The great Basils, Chrysostoms, the Bradwardines; the great Bacons, the Boyles, the Miltons, the Polhills, the Owens, the Witsiuses, the Charnocks, the Bateses, the Howes, the Hurrions,[1] the Wattses,[2] the Doddridges, the Brines, the Gills, the Edwards, the Hallyburtons, the Fenelons, the Rollins; with millions of heroes more, all flashed their brightest virtues upon Hervey's understanding, imagination, and passions; and roused him to an unbounded ardor to excel in every virtue, and rise and shine in every Christian grace.[3]

---

[1]    Hervey had read, for instance, Hurrion's sermons on *Christ Crucified and Glorified*.

[2]    Hervey recommended Watts on the *Love of God, and its influence on all the passions*.

[3]    Ryland's *The Character of the Rev. James Hervey A. M.*, p. 171.

# Chapter Seven:
# The Rector of Collingtree

## Hervey in London

We must now return to the story of Hervey's abduction to London and consider the last eight years of his short life. Though the long journey had left him 'weary and dispirited', Hervey showed no anger towards his friends, whom he knew were zealous only because of their affection for him. The nearest he came to rebuking them was in a letter to Stonehouse who had obviously reproved Hervey for not feeling too happy at his sudden change of address. To this kidnapper for friendship's sake, he wrote, 'My Dear Friend,—If you chide, I must accuse. Pray where was your warrant, where your commission to impress me into this journey? However, as becomes a good Christian, I forgive you and your accomplice.'

The bulk of this letter is taken up with Hervey's praise of his host, Whitefield and his delight at receiving a visit from an old friend. Hervey's correspondent had obviously a clear call to the ministry which others could see better than himself. Hervey thus admonished his kidnapper to 'Preach the glorious gospel. Be an ambassador of the most high God. Devote yourself to this most important, most noble service, and your divine Master, I hope, will furnish you with employ, and open a door for your usefulness. The fruit of such labours will abide.'[1]

## An unsolicited portrait and unwelcome poetry

As much as Hervey's devoted London friends were anxious to prolong his life and stabilise, if not improve his health, they also encouraged him to write for the present and future generations and also persuaded him to have his portrait painted so that the world would gain some physical insight concerning the author of heavenly teaching who was becoming more

---

[1]  *Works*, Letter LXVI.

and more popular. The chief contender for the portrait, which was to be
painted by Williams, was George Whitefield but Hervey did not think
much of the latter idea at all and said of the project:

> I have been prevailed on to sit for my picture. If ever portrait
> was the shadow of a shadow, mine is such. O that I may be renewed
> after the amiable image of the blessed Jesus! and when I awake up
> after his likeness, I shall be satisfied with it.[1]

A month later, Hervey was really worried as his friends had ordered
his portrait to be mass-copied in mezzotint form and put up for general
sale. The print was to carry, as its caption, verses in Hervey's honour by a
Mr. Nixon whose enthusiasm for the cause was rather greater than his
poetic genius. The lines he proposed were:

> Williams! 'tis yours to bid the canvas wear,
> By art illusive, Hervey's form and air;
> Oh! with like happy labour, could I trace
> Each virtue, each exalted Christian grace,
> Each heavenly gift with which his soul is blest,
> And fix the bright assemblage in my breast;
> Then how transcendent far would be my plan,
> You paint his mimic shade: I'd live the man.

It needs no stretch of the imagination to realise that Hervey was horri-
fied at the prospect. However, Hervey's friends were doing this for the
very best of reasons. Hervey was giving money away to the needy as fast
as he received it and it was thought that the sale of the mezzotint and
verses would raise funds to assist Hervey in his social work. Indeed, a
number of friends were now regularly subscribing to Hervey's benevolent
schemes. Notwithstanding, when Hervey was told of the verses he wrote
at once to the author, telling him to postpone publishing them with the
picture because if they appeared at the same time sales might be encouraged, which was the last thing he wanted. Hervey just did not want to
become a public figure in any way as he knew how detrimental to personal
holiness fame could be. This was one wish that Hervey's friends were not
prepared to grant him and Mr. Nixon's lines were joined by much lengthier
poetical works by Dr. Nathaniel Cotton[2], Moses Brown, Thomas Gibbons,
John Duik, Peter Whalley and a large number of other poets hiding behind

---

[1]    *Works*, Letter LXVIII.
[2]    It was Cotton who introduced the poet William Cowper to Hervey's works.

pseudonyms but all proclaiming Hervey as the transformer of English literature because his writings transformed lives.

## Meeting all the friends of the revival

One great effect of Hervey's stay in London was that he was able to meet John and Charles Wesley again and hear a growing number of true evangelical preachers who were being encouraged and instructed by William Romaine and his circle. His enforced stay in London thus became a kind of sabbatical leave for him, a period in which he could be filled with new blessings from the preached word rather than solely filling others. In the same letter in which he spoke of his different opinion to his friends concerning having his portrait painted, Hervey closes with the information:

> On Sunday I heard the admired Mr. Romaine. His text was Rom. v.1.; his doctrine evangelical. The faith which purifies the heart, and works by love; the imputed righteousness of Christ, comprehending both his active and passive obedience; the operation of the blessed Spirit in producing this sound and lively faith, were the substance of his discourse.[1]

To another friend, Hervey writes explaining the strong meat he received from Romaine's words concerning Christ's vicarious suffering in the form of dying for sinners and being obedient on their behalf. Romaine, he explains, shows how our justification is based on the complete sufficiency of Christ's sacrifice in matters of our punishment and guilt. These words, together with Romaine's strong emphasis on the illumination and influence of the Holy Spirit were highly comforting to Hervey. They must have been a great comfort to many others as Hervey says Romaine preached to 'thronged auditories'.[2]

It was no wonder that Hervey was not too critical of his abductors when they had provided him with such a gospel feast. Whitefield was thrilled to have Hervey at hand whenever he returned to London and would have loved to have had him by his side on his journeys. Indeed, whenever he stayed anywhere for some weeks, he would write to Hervey asking his friend to join him. For instance, in March, 1751, Whitefield invited Hervey to stay with him at his brother's house in Bristol 'for a month or two' and just a month later, Whitefield confessed to Hervey that he would consider it a great favour if Hervey made Whitefield's Tabernacle House his per-

---

[1] *Works*, Letter LXVIII.

[2] Letters to Lady Francis Shirley, Letter XVII.

manent home. Hervey, however, was now feeling very homesick and he
was sad that he had not been given the opportunity to give his flock 'parting advice', though he made up for it in letter-form, using the example of
Barnabas who exhorted the disciples to cleave to the Lord. He was also
much in sorrow concerning the welfare of his mother, sister and ageing
father. Though invalid Hervey could not care for his own family, he soon
had another invalid on his hands. Whitefield was stricken down with the
fever and Hervey had a hard time trying to stop him preaching as he was
more fit for bed at the time than the pulpit. 'Desist for a while,' Hervey
told him, 'that you may persist for a long season.'

Both Whitefield's home and that of Hervey's brother William in Miles
Lane were always open to a stream of visitors. Thus Hervey was able to
meet many a new gospel friend. Lady Huntingdon played a prominent
part in introducing Hervey to Lady Gertrude Hotham, Lady Chesterfield
and the Countess Delitz. It was Whitefield, however, who introduced
Hervey to Lady Selina Huntingdon and her kinswoman Lady Francis
Shirley, both women from then on becoming Hervey's most faithful correspondents. Hervey committed most of Lady Francis' letters to the flames
at her request but the glimpses we have of her through Hervey's replies
show what a work of grace had begun in the life of this former reigning
belle of the Hanoverian court. William Cudworth popped in from time to
time and brought his good friend John Cennick. John Gill was a regular
visitor at Miles Lane. In March, 1753, when John Ryland informed Hervey
of Gill, Hervey could tell him, 'I have the pleasure of knowing the author,
and I hope the benefit of being interested in his prayers. When I was at
London, he was so friendly as to visit me at my brother's, (who lives not
far from the Doctor's) and always left me wiser; and I am sure it was not
owing to his incapacity or negligence, if I was not better.'[1]

## A deep testimony of faith sent by a humble country woman

William Cowper used to say that it was the prayers of the humble
cottager that God used in governing His creation rather than the plans and
intrigues of the worldly-wise. Hervey, whilst at William's house, was soon
to realise this, too, as a poor old lady, one of his hearers at Weston Favell,
now wrote him a triumphant letter of faith that could not have been bet-
tered by the pen of the best educated saint in the kingdom:

> Reverend Sir,—I humbly beg your pardon for presuming to
> write to you. Being one of your hearers, I was very much affected
> with your good sermons, having known and experienced the truth
> of them, viz. That persons must be convinced of their *undone* state

---

[1]    Letter IV, Ryland collection.

by NATURE, and brought into a state of *concern,* or *self-condemnation,* before they will seek and *earnestly* desire the knowledge of Christ crucified. To one who feels the condemning power of the Law, Christ is precious. Such have tasted the bitterness of sin; for till then they are *alive without the law,* as St. Paul saith, Rom. vii. 9, nor seeing that the LAW requires *perfect* obedience, and that THEIRS at the best is *very imperfect.* Hence the best of us in our carnal state are striving to be justified by our own *works*; yea, though we cannot but know that we often break the laws of God, Rom. iii. 20, 28.

But then we think, It is true I am a sinner, and there is none without sin. Thus we do presume upon our seeming obedience, not considering how great a CHANGE must be wrought upon our soul by repentance; and that we must be united to Christ by faith, and *partake of his likeness,* without which Christ, as to us, is dead in vain, Gal. ii. 21. And when the Holy Spirit has convinced us of our misery by sin, John xvi. 8, and need of Christ, then, usually, we are thinking TO DO something to purchase an interest in him; not considering we must be *humble supplicants* at his feet, waiting for *every thing* we want at the throne of grace—repentance, pardon, sanctification, redemption—as purchased by Him: Eternal life is the gift of God, Rom. vi. 23.

It is the *humbled* person who will accept of Christ in all his offices; not only as a priest to atone for sin, but also as a prophet to teach, and a king to rule over him, and subdue all his sins. The covenant of grace answers all our wants: there is not only *mercy* to *pardon,* but also *grace* to *sanctify,* and renew our nature. It is the humbled believer who can sincerely say, 'Christ is the power of God unto salvation,' Rom. i. 16.

And now I think nothing more needful than for clergymen to preach as *you* do; for though Christianity is generally professed among us, yet many seem as unconcerned about these things us if there were no such truths in the gospel. This is the way of preaching which has ever been most effectual to the converting of sinners; and may the blessed Spirit attend the word preached, 'purifying the hearts of your hearers by faith,' Acts xv. 9. That the righteousness of Christ, accepted and applied to themselves by a lively faith, may entitle them to heaven, Rom. v. 19; and that their *sincere,* though *imperfect* obedience may evidence their title to be true and real, is the hearty desire of, reverend sir, your most humble servant.[1]

---

[1]    Letter LXXXIII, *Works.*

This letter shows something of the strong influence for the good that Hervey had exercised during his curacy under his father. Hervey did his level best to make sure his flock was supplied with good preachers, telling them that the poor of his parish long for the milk of the Word. All the congregation honour a true preacher, he told those who were to supply for him, most of them will be attentive and many of them edified. Then, as he felt a twinge in his heart at being separated from his flock, he would add, 'It grieves me, it pains me at my very soul, that I am dismissed, or rather cut off from the honourable and delightful service of the ministry.'

## Hirelings neglect the flock in Hervey's absence

Hervey's father was not very careful about how the Collingtree pulpit was filled and he felt duty bound to keep it open for neighbouring ministers. Two of these used this freedom to denounce Hervey's doctrines from his own pulpit and sought to turn the Collingtree flock's hearts away from their curate. On February 23, 1751, Hervey told a friend:

> Sir, Mr.—and Mr.—may have tried, and may repeat their attempts, to alienate the affections of my Collingtree hearers. I am under no concern with regard to myself. *Fragile cupiens illidere dentem, offendet solido*, will, I believe, be the issue of their endeavours. I am only sorry, for the people's sake, that they should squander away their ministerial talents and ministerial labours to so poor a purpose. Let them be more incessant in warning every man, and teaching every man, that they may present every man perfect in Christ Jesus. Thus let them seek to win their affections, and I do rejoice, yea, and will rejoice, in their success. Dear sir, the way to secure the love of others is, to love them, to pray for them, and with a willing assiduity to set forward their true happiness. This, whenever I was amongst them, my people will confess, I did not cease to do. And the God of heaven knows I daily bear them on my heart, and often recommended them to the tenderest mercies of our everlasting Father. Never, therefore, be apprehensive of my losing either their esteem with regard to my conduct, or their affection with regard to my person. O that their precious souls were as firmly united to Christ, as their favourable opinion is secured to me! Well, should neighbours undermine us, and friends forsake us, the adorable and all-condescending God is faithful. He changeth not. His word of grace endureth for ever. He loves his people with an everlasting love. And O what worms, what dust, what mere nothings, are all men, are all creatures, before that infinitely blessed Author of all perfection! What a sense had the Psalmist of this weighty truth, when he poured forth that rapturous exclamation, 'Whom have I in heaven but thee? and there is none, upon earth,

that I desire in comparison of thee!' May this, my dear friend, be the continual language of your heart; and of his, who hopes to be, both in time and to eternity, affectionately yours,
&c.

## Whitefield introduces Hervey to Lady Francis Shirley

Towards the end of 1749, Whitefield suggested to Lady Francis Shirley that she should write to Hervey and discuss with him her spiritual fears and joys in her life of faith, assuring her that his friend would be only too willing to bear her up in prayer and advise her where he could. Whitefield also told her of Hervey's *Meditations* and *Contemplations*, assuring her that they would be of great assistance in her walk with God. This subject provided a good opening to the correspondence and Hervey soon provided her Ladyship with the books. The accompanying letter is so typical of Hervey's use of every opportunity to recommend his Saviour. After a few introductory words concerning Whitefield, he says:

And how happy shall I think the Author, if they may be a means of raising in your Ladyship's mind, a more frequent advertence to, and more amiable apprehensions of, the ever-present, the all-gracious GOD!—That GOD, whose transcendent perfections shine through universal nature; and are displayed, with infinitely superior lustre, in the redemption of mankind by JESUS CHRIST!—That ineffably excellent GOD, whom to know, is the only wisdom; whom to love, is the truest happiness; and whom to enjoy, in his own heavenly and everlasting kingdom, is such a felicity, as I cannot express, but shall most earnestly pray, that your Ladyship may possess.[1]

Hervey was not only delighted to correspond with her Ladyship for the sake of her own problems and delights in serving the Lord but also for the opportunities it gave him to hear of God's work in the world at large and to reach through Lady Shirley a number of Christian worthies whose fellowship would otherwise have been denied him because of the sedentary nature of his life. Even when Hervey was in London, he remained confined to his room, if not bed-bound, apart from the moves between his brother's at Miles End and Whitefield's at Twickenham. In an undated letter to Lady Shirley, written probably in the spring of 1752, Hervey confesses that he has put on his overcoat to go out only once all the winter and then caught a heavy cold which re-confined him to his bed.

---

[1]    *Letters to Lady Francis Shirley*, Letter II.

Happily, some 120 of Hervey's letters to Lady Shirley have been preserved in a separate volume whose early editors have been far less thorough in erasing names. Thus many a person who is merely an initial or a
dash in the official *Collection* of Hervey's letters now becomes a person
of flesh and blood with a background and name. Here we find Romaine,
Doddridge, Whitefield, Hales, the Bishop of Norwich and many others
mentioned by name which help to reconstruct events historically, which
are described in the larger collection. It is also more helpful to the reader
to be able to trace the development of a sincere friendship between two
people rather than to see hundreds of letters addressed to 'Dear Friend'
and not know which friends or how many friends this salutation covers.
Hervey's correspondence with Lady Shirley is also of great informative
value as they show us how Hervey utilised his time of invalidity to commence writing his greatest work, *Theron and Aspasio*, and how, through
her interest, Hervey took up literary tasks such as his work on Lord
Bolingbroke's critical theories, which otherwise might never have been
penned.

### A sample of Hervey's teaching sent to Lady Francis

From the start of his correspondence with Lady Shirley, we find Hervey
emphasising the unsearchable riches of Christ as the treasures both rich
and poor should strive after. These treasures, Hervey explains, consist of
pardon of sin, the imputed righteousness of Christ and the gift of the Holy
Spirit. In these letters, Hervey reveals his great skill in introducing one
doctrine after another and expounding them in succinct brevity, simplicity
and depth. As a New Year's greeting to his correspondent, Hervey opens
1752 with the words:

> I have the pleasure of presenting to your Ladyship, on the com-
> mencement of the New Year, one of the most distinguishing and
> noble privileges of Christianity, *The Intercession of CHRIST*. Which,
> in whatever light we view it, is a most comfortable doctrine: but,
> when considered in its full extent, is an inexhaustible source of
> consolation. To do this, will be the pleasing employ of your Lady-
> ship's own meditations. To hint a few of its leading properties, will
> be business enough for the present letter.
> *Who* is it, that intercedes?—JESUS CHRIST the RIGHTEOUS.
> In whose mouth there was no guile. Who did always those things,
> which were pleasing to his heavenly Father.—If men, that are en-
> compassed with infirmities, pray and prevail; how much more pre-
> vailing must *his* intercession be, who is 'holy, harmless, undefiled,
> and separate from sinners,' in his nature, in his heart, and in all his
> conversation.

*To whom* He prays.—To his own Father. Who declared by a voice from Heaven his entire and infinite Complacency in so glorious a Son. If the poor widow made suit to an unjust judge, and was heard: how assured may we conclude, that our blessed Advocate is heard, when he intercedes in our behalf, with his own Father, with our Father—with the Father of everlasting compassion?

*What* he pleads.—He pleads his own merits. His intercession is founded on his oblation. Therefore it is said, *his blood speaketh better things, than the blood of Abel.* Which text, at once points out the nature, and proves the efficacy, of CHRIST's intercession. He does not intercede by prostrating himself before the Throne or making any verbal supplication. As the blood of Abel had a voice, and cried aloud for vengeance on the murderer. So, the blood of JESUS has a voice in the ear of God, and cries more loudly for pardon, for grace, for every spiritual blessing, in behalf of his people. If the blood of one saint cried with such a forcible importunity: O! what un-paralleled, what unknown success must attend the cry of his blood, who is King of Saints, and the cause of sanctity!

*For what* he prays.—In his last solemn address to his almighty Father, he gives us a specimen of his intercession, and a sample (if I may use the expression) of the blessings he implores. He prays— That we may be *sanctified by the Truth*—That we may be *kept from evil*: the evil, that is in the world; and the evil, that is in our hearts—That we *may be one*: perfectly united to our divine Head, by a true faith; and to one another, by cordial love—That we *may be with him, where he is; and see his glory*, and rejoice in his joy.

*How often* he intercedes—Moses interceded for the Israelites, while they were in the valley, fighting with Amalek. But he could not continually carry on that important work. Whereas, our High-Priest ever liveth to make intercession for us. There's no intermission of his suit.—When some foreign ambassadors came, pretty early in the morning, to have an audience with Alexander; they were told, 'His majesty is not stirring.' Upon which, they expressed some surprise, that a potentate, who had so many, and such momentous affairs to manage, should sleep so long. The King, hearing of their observation, ordered them to be informed; That, though 'he slept, Parmenio waked.' And though we sleep, though we forget, too often forget ourselves, and our adored Redeemer : He, the great Keeper of Israel neither slumbers, nor sleeps ; never, never forgets either us, or our interests Nay, when We sin through the deplorable Infirmity of our Nature, He still appears In the presence of GOD for us.

*For whom* He intercedes.—This is an inquiry of the last importance. *I pray not for the world*, is his own declaration. For whom

142 *James Hervey*

then? How shall we know, whether you and I are in the happy number? Happy doubtless, they are, whom the great IMMANUEL remembers in his Kingdom. It would be a most desirable privilege, to be mentioned in the prayers of all the eminent saints in the world. But unspeakably more desirable, to have our names written on the palms of his hands, whom the Father heareth always. Permit me to mention one mark whereby we may determine this Doubt. Has the LORD shed abroad in our hearts a spirit of Grace and Supplication for ourselves? This is a fruit of CHRIST's intercession; and a sure sign, that he has undertaken our cause. We should never hear the reflected echo, if there was not first the direct sound. And we should never have these breathings after GOD and Glory,' if the blessed JESUS had not acted as our Advocate with the Father.

What use may we make of this Doctrine?—It should encourage us to pray: and to pray in faith, nothing doubting, '*Having a GREAT HIGH-PRIEST, that is passed into the Heavens, JESUS the Son of GOD, let us come boldly to the Throne of Grace, that we may obtain mercy, and find grace to help in time of need.*'

I THINK, my Lady, you have a note under my hand, for a few thoughts on the love of CHRIST. How glad am I to pay, as far as my ability will reach, all my obligations to your Ladyship! Especially when they are of a Nature so peculiarly pleasing. Shall we then consider

The *original* of his love? It is free; perfectly free; without any desert, or the least amiableness in us. We love our kind friends, and generous benefactors; those that are accomplished in themselves or serviceable to our interests. But CHRIST loved us, when we were sinners; when we were forgetful of him; nay, enemies to him by evil tempers, and wicked works He loved us (O sovereign, most un-merited kindness!) when we deserved nothing, but utter abhorrence, and eternal vengeance.

The *commencement* of his love. His love is not of yesterday. His love, like his outgoings is from everlasting. *I have loved thee*, says he to his Church *with an everlasting love*. We value the affections that is of long standing; has taken deep root ; and still continues unshaken. *How excellent then, is thy loving-kindness*, O blessed JESUS ! which, *before the mountains were brought forth or ever the earth and the world were made,* was fixed upon sinful dust! O! that we, my Lady, should be in the thoughts be upon the very heart, of GOD's adorable Son, even from the ages of eternity !

---

¹ *Letters to Lady Francis Shirley*, Letter XXII.

The *duration* of his love. It is invariable and eternal. *Having loved his own, He loveth them even unto the end.* It neither began with time, neither will it end with time. As no worthiness in us caused it; so neither will our failings extinguish it; no, nor our infirmities damp it. We change frequently; our holy frames fail; but our adored Redeemer is the same yesterday, to day, and for ever.

Fear not then, my honoured Lady; *neither life nor death nor things present nor things to come, nor any other creature, shall be able to separate us* from the ever tender, the ever constant, the ever triumphant love of GOD our Saviour.

The *effects* of his love. It brought him from the Heaven of Heavens, to dwell in clay, and be lodged in a manger. It brought him from those happy mansions where is the *fulness of joy*, and where are *pleasures for evermore*; to be *destitute, afflicted, tormented* in this Vale of Tears. O my Lady, it made him, who is heir of all things, not to have where to lay his head; till he was stretched on the racking cross, and laid in the gloom of the grave. Un-paralleled and stupendous! *Who can declare the noble acts of the* Redeemer's love, *or shew forth all his praise*?

The *fruits* of this love. To this is owing all the good, we possess, or expect; every spiritual and heavenly blessing. If our eyes are enlightened, in any degree, to see the things that belong to our peace: if our desires are awakened, to seek the *inheritance incorruptible, undefiled, and that fadeth not away*: for this we are indebted to the love and grace of CHRIST. If we are sanctified in part, and desirous to grow in true godliness: if we are perfectly justified before GOD, and adopted to be his sons and daughters: these also are streams, which issue from that in-exhaustible fountain, THE LOVE OF CHRIST. As it was stronger than death, in its actings and sufferings; it is richer than all worlds in its precious, precious fruits. All the inconceivable and everlasting joys of the glorified state, are its purchase and its gift.

JUSTLY, therefore, does the Scripture make use of all the endearing relations, that subsist among mankind, to represent the love of C H R I S T. Great is the love of a friend; greater the love of a brother; greater still the love of a parent; greatest of all the love of a bridegroom: but infinitely greater than any, than all; is the love of the ever blessed IMMANUEL to his people When all has been said, all has been imagined; it transcends every comparison; it exceeds all thought; or, as St. Paul speaks, *it passes knowledge.*— May your Ladyship have more and more exalted apprehensions of it; and live under a delightful sense of its richness and perpetuity!—May it be your sweet incitement to every duty, and your sov-

ereign cordial under all tribulation!—And when eternity, the vast
eternity opens, it shall be, in a sense that no heart can conceive,
your crown of rejoicing; your exceeding great Reward.—And, I
hope, you will sometimes pray, that it may be the present Comfort
and eternal Joy of,
My Lady, Your Ladyship's much obliged, and most dutiful humble
servant.[1]

## Hervey's appreciation of Doddridge

During this period, Hervey kept up a steady correspondence with his
friend Dr. Philip Doddridge to whom he was much indebted for a number
of reasons. Doddridge, with Hervey and Dr. Stonehouse, assisted by the
young John Ryland, provided a steady witness in the Northampton area
and did a great work amongst the sick. Stonehouse, supported initially by
Doddridge and later by Hervey founded a hospital in Northampton in 1744
and the trio also maintained a steady work for the Lord at Northampton
Jail. Hervey never forgot that it was one of Doddridge's converts who
helped him to understand the need for Christ's righteousness and it was a
pupil of Doddridge's, Darracott, who had deepened Hervey's trust in God
and introduced him to sound Christian literature. John Ryland used to be-
moan the fact that Hervey had not come under Doddridge's tutorship when
a youth but the mature Hervey seemed to be intent on making up for this
loss and counted Doddridge as one of his closest advisors. Doddridge was
one of the close circle of friends to whom Hervey sent his manuscripts for
correction and advice as the following letter illustrates:

Dear Sir,—Your observations are perfectly just, and Dr.
Doddridge's remarks are admirably judicious; his alterations are
indeed excellent and charming. Oh, may they be equally impres-
sive on me as I transcribe them, and on all that may hereafter read
them! Many most solid and valuable corrections has the Doctor
already made in my little piece, but, in my opinion, these are beyond them all. I cannot but wish he had leisure to have went through
the whole with his improving strokes; but, as the business of his
academy and ministry is so various, and so important I cannot prevail with myself to make such a request. I will try, and do the best
I can to proceed on the plan which he has formed, and to follow
(*magno licet intervallo*) the example he has set. Be so good as to
make my most grateful acknowledgments: Let your tongue speak,
for really my pen cannot write, how greatly I am obliged to him. I

[1]    *Letters to Lady Francis Shirley*, Letter XXIV.

will venture to turn, what was used formerly as an imprecation, into a wish and a blessing on this occasion, 'May God do so to him, and more also!'

Oh that our writings may be accompanied with the blessed Spirit; and that the spirit of our writings may be operative on our hearts, and apparent in our conversation. Ever yours, &c.[1]

When in November, 1751, Hervey heard through Dr. Stonehouse that Doddridge lay dying in Lisbon, he told Lady Francis, 'The departure of such valuable persons, should tend to wean us from the world, and endear Heaven to our Affections. Beza said, when he was told of Calvin's death; 'Now I have a fresh motive, to be as a stranger on earth, and to set my affections on things above.' Writing to one of his copy-readers in 1754, Hervey says, 'I now feel the loss of our valuable friend Dr. Doddridge, to whose judgement I ever paid the highest difference; but since he is gone, and we can have no more of his personal counsels, let us redouble our attention to his writings.'

## Pearsall approaches Hervey for advice

Another of Hervey's correspondents at this time was Richard Pearsall of Taunton who had been greatly encouraged in his own ministry and writing but was led, wisely or not, to mould his own works on Hervey's style so that they do appear to be imitations at times. Pearsall sent Hervey his manuscripts, to which Hervey replied:

Rev. and Dear Sir,—Give me leave to return my best thanks for your obliging letters and very valuable manuscripts: those, I mean, which you were so kind as to transmit for my use. I look upon them as a detachment of auxiliary forces, seconding and supporting a feeble attempt to oppose the enemies, and to spread the conquests, of Free Grace. I wish they had fallen into abler hands: for mine, weak, always weak by nature, are now enervated to the last degree by sickness. For several hours, I have been unable to take up my pen; and could only endeavour, by resting myself in some easy posture, to sustain a being, whose strength is become labour and sorrow.

I now return, after a long delay, your truly pleasing and profitable letters. I have read them with singular pleasure; and, I hope, with some improvement. Many parts I perused several times; and the warm piety, garnished by an elegant fancy, made them as de-

---

[1]   *Works*, Letter CX.

lightful as if they were new. I cannot pretend to the merit of doing your compositions any service; unless it be in this one circumstance, that, I have detained them from you for a considerable time; by which means, they will be, in a manner, new to your own eye: and you will be much more capable of judging maturely, concerning each sentiment, and every expression.

One thing, in general, let me remark: That, my worthy friend's genius is too rich; his invention quite luxuriant. He must use the pruning knife, and cut off several of the shoots. Yes, though they are perfectly beautiful, they must be sacrificed; that, the fruit may acquire the finer flavour. There is a certain prettiness in some periods, that betrays us all into an ill-judged redundancy; which, though its neatness should secure it from being tiresome, yet, weakens the force of the principal thought.

I wish you would introduce some suitable descriptions to beautify the last letters. As they all turn upon the same subject, and have no pieces of entertaining *scenery* to enliven them, I fear, they will read a little flat and heavy; especially when compared with the preceding ornamented pages.

A few alterations I have proposed, and only proposed. Admit, or reject them, as shall appear, on your own examination, most expedient. Don't, dear sir, be *hasty* in publication. Compositions, that would spread far and continue long, in an age of so much refinement, should be touched and re-touched.

I remain, dear sir, your obliged friend, and affectionate brother,

James Hervey.[1]

It was through Pearsall that William Cowper gained a liking for Hervey. He had read Hervey in his pre-conversion years and had not thought much of him at all, being put off by the flowery language. After his conversion, an Evangelical aunt on his father's side sent Cowper a copy of Pearsall's *Reliquia Sacrae: or Meditations on Select Passages of Scripture,* and *Sacred Dialogues between a Father and his Children* and the poet 'liked it much, especially the latter part.' As it was general knowledge that Pearsall had been influenced by Hervey, Cowper turned to the latter and was pleased to find him 'one of the most spiritual and truly Scriptural writers in the world,' stating that he could now not give Pearsall the preference.[2]

---

[1]    Tyerman's *The Oxford Methodists*, pp. 265, 266.

[2]    See references to Pearsall and Hervey in the Clarendon Press edition of Cowper's *Works*, edited by King and Ryskamp.

## Whitefield writes from Georgia

Whitefield set sail for Georgia in the September of 1751 and wrote on his arrival to Hervey expressing the warmest friendship but also confessing his greater love for the salvation of souls and his joy at how the Lord was using him:

> My Very Dear Friend, I long to write to you, and inform you, that, I love you in the bowels of Jesus Christ. This leaves unworthy me, endeavouring to do something for Him on this side the water. Glory be to His great name. He causes His work to prosper in my worthless hands. Follow me with your prayers; and who knows but we may meet once more on this side heaven. I find our dear Mr. Hervey is to be detained longer from thence. I think he will have to bury many stronger men. I wish Lisbon may be blessed to Dr. Doddridge. I hope you write to Lady Huntingdon, and see her frequently. I was rejoiced to hear, from my dear yoke-fellow, that, her Ladyship was bravely: this was joy indeed. It is a new year. God quicken my tardy pace, and help me to do much work in a little time! This is my highest ambition.[1]

## Delivered from a great fire

Whitefield had been one of the greatest factors, apart from his physical weakness, binding Hervey to London. Though Hervey did all that the doctors advised to regain the health which was always fleeing from him, he relapsed time and time again. At the beginning of 1752, his life was saved by a hair's breadth but not due to any success the doctors had in combating his consumption. His brother's house was part of a block of buildings which incorporated a sugar baker's shop. A fierce fire broke out in the shop, intensified by the huge amount of sugar. Within minutes, the block was ablaze and surrounded by a huge mob which hindered the firefighters from placing their fire-engines in strategic positions. The Herveys' house became full of smoke and had to be abandoned as three engines began to pour water on it. Hervey found himself standing outside the house, with his feet in water, almost smothered by the smoke. It was quite impossible to get to a safe place quickly as the great mob of spectators blocked their flight. Suddenly the skies grew even darker than the smoke had made them and the clouds broke into a deluge of rain on the house, drenching it for several hours until the last flame was extinguished. Referring to the great confusion and consternation in a letter to Lady Francis, Hervey, true to his way of drawing Biblical parallels with everything, wrote:

---

[1]  Tyerman's *The Oxford Methodists*, p. 268.

It put me in mind of that tremendous day, *when the heavens shall pass away with a great noise, when the elements will melt with fervent heat, and the earth with all the works that are therein shall be burnt up.* Then, when the possessions of the mighty shall be no more found; may your Ladyship have *a House not made with hands, eternal in the heavens*! When the wealth of the covetous shall come utterly to an end; may your Ladyship enjoy *an inheritance incorruptible, undefiled, and that fadeth not away.*

The Herveys, drenched to the skin and with lungs sore from the smoke, returned to their house to find it intact apart from the damp and the smells. Hervey caught a violent cold which turned into a burning fever but he refused to be accommodated by other friends.

### Called back to Weston-Flavell through the death of his father

Hervey's mother, whom he always addressed as 'Honoured Madam' wrote at the beginning of April, 1751 to tell her son that his father was seriously ill and that, if his strength allowed, he should be making plans to end his visit to London and return home. Though Hervey's father recovered somewhat, he remained extremely weak and spent most of his time in semi-sleep, apparently not realising what was going on and having no inclination to speak. Hervey did not know where his father stood spiritually and could merely say of his state to a friend, 'I hope his great work is done, his interest in Christ secured, and his soul sanctified by grace. For indeed, such a state of languishing is as unfit to work out salvation, and lay hold on eternal life, as to grind at the mill, or to run a race. Oh that we all may give diligent attention to the things which belong to our peace, before the inability of sickness, and the night of death approaches.'[1] A year later, Hervey Sen. died and his son who was still officially his father's curate, was compelled to return to Weston and take over the living, though he did not feel up to the task at all. He told Lady Francis, he was determined to make a try if he could 'bear the journey, and undergo the fatigue', saying, 'O! that I had strength of constitution, to watch over a flock, and feed them with the milk of the Word! But the will of the LORD is best. He employs whom He will employ and whom He will He lays aside. Wise and righteous are all his ways.'[2]

Though only 70 miles away, the journey to Weston took two days by coach but Hervey arrived back at his curacy after a smooth journey. The Hervey's house in Weston was two miles from Northampton and situated so well that one wonders why Dr. Stonehouse had made such efforts to

---

1     *Works*, Letter CVIII
2     *Letters to Lady Francis Shirley*, Letter XXIX.

transport Hervey to London for 'a change of air': The house was on top of a small hill overlooking meadows to the right, going down to the river and to the left a large garden backed by a field. As he told Lady Francis, 'We hear none of the tumultuous din of the world, and see nothing but the wonderful and charming works of the Creator.'

## Vicar of Weston and Rector of Collingtree

It seems that, because of the fee simple attached to the house, farm and church buildings at Hardingstone, Hervey was no longer regarded as curate, as he still was at Collingtree, but, on the death of his father, he was now Vicar of Weston. On the first Sunday after returning, Hervey climbed the steps of his pulpit for the first in this capacity, addressing his old flock as his 'new' parishioners. He preached with great weakness for half an hour on the words, 'Preach the gospel to every creature.' His outline was, a. What the gospel means. b. What blessings it comprehends. c. By whom these blessings were purchased, d. To whom they are offered. He then exhorted his flock to secure these unspeakable blessings and told them that the end of his preaching to them, the design of his conversation with them and the principle aim of his whole life would be to make them acquainted with this delightful doctrine and assist them in obtaining this great salvation.

Unknown to Hervey, many schemes were afoot to have him given more authority in church life and obtain for him not only the vicarship of Weston but also the rectorship of Collingtree which Hervey's father had left vacant. At first, Hervey would not consider the idea but suggested that Dr. Stonehouse should be given the living. Strong pressure, however, was put on Hervey to take on the post. In a letter dated May 19, 1752, shortly after returning to Weston, Hervey tells Lady Francis of another preferment which he had received through the recommendation of George Whitefield. He had been made a chaplain, probably to the Countess of Huntingdon whose chaplain Whitefield also was. Lady Francis was rather put out because Hervey had not asked her to procure the honour for him but Hervey replied that he had not asked for such a post and it came as a complete surprise. Meanwhile Hervey's mother and sister, backed by his friends were coming to an agreement with the Bishop of Peterborough and other high church officials to have Hervey made Rector of Collingtree. The situation could not have been more complicated. The living had been the freehold property of Hervey's father and in his patronage thus Hervey was the rightful heir. As far as the Church was concerned, however, Hervey was not eligible to receive the living as he had not even applied for his Master's degree after the appropriate time had elapsed after taking his bachelor degree at Oxford, yet the rectorship specified an M. A. from Cambridge. There was also a question of some £1,200 in stamp duties (£30 per document) which had to be paid to the Church and Lord Chancellor before Hervey could take up the post. It seems a strange way of promoting the spread of the gospel that church positions could be given at the recommendation of a friend, the death of a father, the gaining of a degree or the payment of a huge fee, but the majority of the Collingtree parishioners felt that it was all to the furtherance of the gospel if it helped them gain Hervey as pastor. Now Hervey felt honour-bound to follow his family's and friends' wish, go to Cambridge to receive his Master of Arts, then proceed to London to obtain a dispensation from the Archbishop, then seek out the Lord Chancellor to obtain the necessary seals then dash off to Peterborough to receive institution from Dr. Thomas, the Bishop there. Hervey was very apprehensive concerning his reception at Cambridge but his reputation at Oxford had gone before him and after performing a few exercises, he received his M. A. degree.

### More haste, less speed

During Hervey's round-trip to procure all the necessary documents and qualifications, Hervey's life was at great risk, not merely because of his weak constitution. He set off, for speed and comfort's sake as the sole passenger in a new 'machine' as he puts it, called *The Berlin*, which normally held four passengers and was drawn by two horses. The driver, eager to show off his new invention, soon espied a stage-coach in front of him and decided to overtake it. The stage-coach driver took exception to this new-fangled means of rival transport and whipped up his horses accordingly. Soon a great race was in progress with the two-horsed Berlin gaining on the four-horsed, though far heavier, stage-coach, both drivers lashing mercilessly at their horses. As they were neck and neck, their wheels entangled, Hervey's coach, being the lighter, immediately overturned and the coachman of the other vehicle flew through the air with the impact and landed bleeding on the ground. Hervey was bruised (he called it slight) and the skin was torn from his leg, though no bones were broken. Hervey's reaction was typical of him, 'Have I not abundant reason to adopt the Psalmist's Acknowledgement? *Thou hast delivered my life from death, mine eyes from tears, and my feet from falling.*—Have I not abundant reason, to make his grateful inquiry? *What shall I render unto the LORD for all his benefits towards me?*—And ought I not to add his holy resolution? *I will walk before the LORD in the land of the living.* So long as this life exists, which has been so wonderfully and mercifully preserved, it shall be devoted to the honour of my great Deliverer.'[1]

### Hervey becomes a pluralist

Hervey's visit to the Bishop of Peterborough in order to become a pluralist must have caused him some embarrassment and there are various versions recorded of the conversation Hervey had with the Bishop. Hervey's

---

[1]    *Letters to Lady Francis Shirley*, Letter XXXVII.

first biographer, writing a matter of months after his death records Hervey as telling the Bishop, 'I suppose your lordship will be surprised to see James Hervey come to desire your lordship to permit him to be a pluralist, but I assure you I do it to satisfy the repeated solicitations of my mother and my sister, and not to please myself.' This did not seem upright enough for a subsequent biographer who wrote in the *Gentleman's Magazine* for August, 1760, 'It must however be acknowledged by the friends of Mr. Hervey, that if it was wrong to become a pluralist to please himself, it was equally wrong to become a pluralist to please others; if it was right, an apology was impertinent, and if wrong, ridiculous.' After disagreeing with his subject on several issues, including Hervey's practice of learning texts off by heart so that they could be a comfort to him in times of affliction, this biographer sums Hervey's character up as displaying goodness rather than wisdom.

This version was too much for another anonymous writer who interviewed Hervey's friends on the matter and received the information that Hervey had only rejected pluralism because of his bad health, not because of any moral scruples. To him, such pluralism, it was alleged, was the law of the land and thus was an opportunity to be used responsibly. This writer gives Hervey's explanation to the Bishop as, 'When I waited on your lordship about two months ago, I had so much the appearance of a dead corpse, that you will be surprised to see me in the land of the living, and coming to take a second preferment; to which I am induced, not by an inordinate desire of wealth, but of subsisting my family comfortably, and of being as extensively useful as possible.'[1] All this gave rise to years of speculation concerning a conversation which, most likely, only the Bishop and Hervey witnessed, the majority concluding that Hervey was basically against pluralities but bowed to the advice of others.

Whatever Hervey told the Bishop, we soon find him telling Lady Francis with what warmth he was accepted at Collingtree when the news spread that he was to become their rector:

> It would have pleased your Ladyship to have observed how glad the honest folks were, to see their old curate. And why were they glad? For no other reason, that I can conceive, but because I used to converse with them in private, just as I spoke to them from the pulpit; and endeavoured, at every interview, to set forward their eternal salvation. This, I find, is the grand secret, to win the affections of a flock. And in this, as in every other part of true Christianity, our interest and our duty are connected. When we are bidden to

---

[1] *Gentleman's Magazine*, December, 1760, vol. xxx, p. 554.

obey the blessed JESUS, we are bidden to take the most effectual
way, of being happy in ourselves, and acceptable to others.[1]

Meditating on these truths, Hervey decided to preach on Ephesians
3:8 in his first sermon to the Collingtree flock as their rector in July, 1752,
'To me, who am less than the least of all saints, is this grace given, that I
should preach among the gentiles the unsearchable riches of Christ.' He
showed how the Christian is like a flourishing and stately tree as the deeper
his roots go into the humbling soil of the gospel, the higher he is raised up
and clothed with the foliage of every blessing that Christ's grace and glory
give. Though a Christian ought never to feel higher of himself than he is,
to covet the unsearchable riches of Christ for His service is no sordid or
ignoble passion but a generous and heavenly disposition.

### Correspondence on the subject of Lord Bolingbroke

Hervey had started on a new major work whilst in London which dealt
with the subject of imputed righteousness.[2] He was persuaded to put this
work aside for a year or so to concentrate on another topic at the request of
Lady Francis. She had read Lord Bolingbroke's published letters on the
study of history and found them to adopt such a critical attitude to the
historical veracity of the Old Testament that she begged Hervey to put
both his learning and Christian faith into a work refuting Bolingbroke's
theories of history and the Bible. Hervey did research on the subject and
tackled the problem in a series of letters to Lady Francis, not expecting, at
first to publish them, which, by degrees, Lady Francis persuaded him to
do. After much delay and small quibblings from the side of the publisher,
who, for instance, objected to Hervey addressing Lady Francis as 'My
Lady' and insisted he should correct such slips with the salutation 'Madam',
Hervey's work was published in November, 1752 under the title, *Remarks
on Lord Bolingbroke's Letters on the Study and Use of History*.

### Hervey's friendship with John Ryland

Whilst Hervey was putting the finishing touches to his work on
Bolingbroke, he received a letter from a young Baptist minister and educator, John Collet Ryland. The Baptist quickly won the Anglican's heart
and soon the two friends were corresponding on doctrines they held in
common and on writers whom they held in high esteem. Ryland found that
he and Hervey had common friends and acquaintances such as Doddridge,
Gill and George Keith, John Gill's son-in-law and book-seller, the Stennetts
and Benjamin Wallin. It is greatly edifying to read the sixty-five letters of

---

[1]    *Letters to Lady Francis Shirley*, Letter XXXIII.

[2]    *Theron and Aspasio.*

Hervey to Ryland which have been preserved and find out more about the lives of these two fine Christians and many a detail about Wallin, Hurrion, Mather, Witsius, Crisp, Gill, Brine, Wesley, Owen, Marshall, Witherspoon, Jenks and a number of other leading men of God. Soon the correspondence grew into a deep friendship with the result that Ryland and his wife often spent their holidays at Hervey's Weston home and for a time, the two lived only a few miles from each other. Ryland became Hervey's first major biographer and his own words concerning his qualifications to write such a biography show how deeply impressed he was by his friend's holy life and the privilege he had of knowing him so intimately, as he expressed in his Preface:

> As I had the advantage above any other man now living to contemplate this mirror of the divine perfections, and this miracle of redeeming mercy, who can blame me for standing still to feast mine eyes with such a charming spectacle, and to admire the grace of Christ, till my soul was lost in holy adoration and secret praise?[1]

**Work on *Theron and Aspasio***

It was not long before Hervey was sending Ryland copies of his ideas for his planned major work on imputed righteousness which he had now decided to call *Theron and Aspasio* and build up in dialogue and letter form with descriptive elements to fuse the various parts together. So far, Hervey envisaged the two main characters discussing Christ's active righteousness and supposed rational and Scriptural arguments against the teaching. The holiness of Christ displayed by His obedience to and fulfilment of a perfect law was to be examined as also the insufficiency of man's active obedience to justify him before God. He planned also, he told Ryland, to show how the end of the law is to convince of sin and bring the sinner to Christ. The whole theological set-up was to be given a literary form and held together by descriptions of rural scenes and scientific knowledge regarding the human body. Aspasio was to take on the role of a Christian, sound in gospel theory and practice, and Theron was to be the person who gradually came to see his own deficiencies and depravity and acknowledged the need for a better righteousness than his own. The work was to end with the death of Aspasio, confidently and triumphantly safe in the arms of Jesus. At the time of writing (February, 1753) Hervey had only a patch-work of details in his mind and he sent copies of the work already done to Ryland, Medley[2], Gill, Brine, Pearsall, Whitefield, Stonehouse,

---

[1]   *The Character of the Rev. James Hervey, A. M.*

[2]   There were a number of leading Baptists by the name of Medley at this time and though Hervey praises Medley's skilled help, he gives us no clues as to which Medley he is referring. He can hardly mean the most famous of the Medleys, educator, hymn-writer and pastor Samuel Medley (1738-99). Medley was converted as a naval officer under the ministry of Whitefield and Gifford and he was only 14 years of age when Hervey sent out his manuscripts.

Wesley and several other friends for advice and correction. The work of copying out these many hundreds of pages must have been a mammoth task indeed. At times, however, Hervey could only write out one corrected copy and sent this on its rounds through his friends' hands. Had the copy been lost on its way, Hervey had nothing to replace it and would have had to compose it again. Ryland was in possession of Hervey's *Aspasio Vindicated* whilst it was still in shorthand form, so Hervey obviously sent his manuscripts in shorthand to friends such as Doddridge and Ryland who were shorthand experts themselves and taught shorthand in their various academies. By 1754, however, when his *Theron and Aspasio* was nearing completion, Hervey began to use an amanuensis. Hervey received very positive support for the work from all of his friends except John Wesley who initially criticised Hervey for writing too openly on the question of election, particular redemption and predestination. This was strange criticism indeed as Hervey hardly touches on the subjects in *Theron and Aspasio*. Hervey was shocked at 'the startling and horrid things' Wesley said about particular redemption and began to fear that Wesley was, in reality, using the contemporary discussion about the scope of the atonement to prejudice people against Hervey's principle point, the imputed righteousness of Christ.[1] As Hervey told Lady Francis, if you put the wolf's skin on a sheep, the rest of the flock will shun him and the dogs will worry him. Hervey also complained that Wesley was introducing the topic of predestination as an argument against the perseverance of the saints.[2] This was also typical of Wesley as witnessed by his response to John Gill in 1752. Gill wrote his *The Doctrine of the Saints' Final Perseverance* which was answered by Wesley's *Predestination calmly considered*.

## Ryland's influence on Hervey

Ryland's brotherly influence on Hervey was not only in promoting his reading but also his preaching. Ryland had written some meditations on Galatians 6:14, 'God forbid that I should glory, save in the cross of our Lord Jesus Christ, by whom the world is crucified unto me, and I unto the world.' On reading the work, Hervey realised that the sentiments were so much his own that he could use them in his own witness. He thus wrote to Ryland, saying:

> When your sweet meditations upon Gal. vi. 14. came to my hand, I was considering about a proper text for a sermon to be preached before the clergy at our approaching visitation; and I can recollect none that pleases me so much as, 'God forbid,' &c. You will excuse me, if I take the liberty to enrich my discourse with

---

1   See Letter CXCVI, *Works*.

2   See Letter LXXIV, Lady Francis collection.

some of your hints; and pray for me, dear Sir, I beseech you, that I may open my mouth boldly, and declare the truth as it is in JESUS. Your heart is made for friendship. Though mine is much less warm and tender, it has, I assure you, a very warm and tender regard for Mr. Ryland: to hear from him, will always be esteemed a favour: to hear of his happiness, will always be enjoyed as a pleasure by, Dear Sir, Your truly affectionate brother in our LORD JESUS CHRIST, JAMES HERVEY.[1]

### Hervey's first printed sermon

Though he had a good text, Hervey set off for Northampton to deliver his sermon with real fear and trembling. He told Lady Francis, 'I know not how I shall speak, so as to be heard, in that very large and lofty church. May the LORD GOD omnipotent make his strength perfect, in my extreme weakness! . . . . O! for the eloquence of an Apollos, and the fervour of a Boanerges, to treat worthily of such a subject. I am quite ashamed of my poor, jejune, spiritless composition. And I am no less ashamed of my unbelief: that I dare not trust God for utterance; but, before an audience that is critical forsooth, must use my notes.'[2] This is typical of Hervey's own view of his preaching which led Romaine to dwell on this factor when preaching at Hervey's funeral, part of which sermon is placed at the beginning of this biography as a tribute to Hervey. Nevertheless, Hervey thought of having one hundred and fifty copies of his sermon printed under the title *The Cross of Christ the Christian's Glory* for distribution chiefly amongst the Anglican clergy as an attempt to demonstrate to them the doctrines which they ought to be preaching themselves. Then Hervey heard of a poor teenage youth who was both seriously ill and a physical cripple, so, after consulting his bookseller, he had an extra two thousand published, the sale of which was to go towards paying for the boy's medical treatment. As a second thought, because the bookseller seemed so convinced that the sermon would be eagerly read, Hervey had a further 200 copies printed for distribution amongst his own flock. The edition was quickly snapped up and a second edition, one of many reprints, was published a few months later. A friend of Hervey's, Dr. Hales who had no less than six royal patrons, made sure that each received a copy of the sermon. Through Lady Francis' connections, Lady Chesterfield and the Countess of Delits[3] also received copies. Hervey's comment on this success was to think of the invalid who profited from the sales and say, 'God has been pleased to pity the poor youth.'

---

[1]   Letter V, *The Character of the Rev. James Hervey, A. M.*

[2]   Letter LVI to Lady Francis.

[3]   Also spelt 'Delitz'.

**Hervey's thoughts on royalty**
      The fact that royalty was reading *The Cross of Christ the Christian's Glory*, caused Hervey to remark to Lady Francis in his unique way of using earthly things to point to the heavenly:

      I have been thinking—Should one of those Royal personages, who perhaps may honour my discourse with a perusal, vouch safe to call at my house, or make me a transient visit; I should be astonished at the favour—Should one of them submit to poverty, or go into voluntary exile, to do me good; I should be lost in wonder. It would create a painful delight—But, should any of them, open their bosom to the sword, or tinge the axe with their blood, in order to save me from ruin! My heart can hardly bear the thought. Surely, I should much rather bid death welcome, than obtain life at such a price.—Yet, my honoured Madam, did not HE, who is Prince of the Kings of the earth, leave his celestial throne for me? Did HE not stoop to the lowest humiliation, and had he where to lay his head for me? Was he not willing, nay, desirous to die ; to die, like the vilest slave, and in the severest torment, for me? These are his words ; I have a baptism to be baptised withal; and how am I straitened, till it be accomplished! He longed (all-gracious, ever-blessed Being!) He longed for the hour, when he should give us this amazing Demonstration of his Love. When He should speak it, in dying pangs; and write it, in his heart's blood.—Can I wish you, Madam, a greater blessing; than that you may be enabled to comprehend with all saints, what is the length and breadth, and height and depth of this love?—And pray, don't dishonour this adorable and boundless love, by entertaining hard or forbidding apprehensions of the altogether—lovely JESUS. Doubt not, but he has laid down his life, in divinely tender compassion to your precious soul: That He has bore all your sins, and fully expiated your guilt: That he has the same bowels of mercy for you now, as when he hung in agonies on the cursed Tree; will withhold from you no manner of thing that is good; and will never leave you, nor forsake you, till He brings you to his own blissful presence, and heavenly kingdom.[1]

**Many great preachers and pastors made their contributions to *Theron and Aspasio***
      Now reactions were coming in to the many copies of Hervey's first sketches of his *Theron and Aspasio* which he had distributed amongst his friends. Hervey was thrilled with John Brine's comments on his work and

---

[1]   Letter LVII to Lady Francis.

told Ryland of Brine's clear head and warm heart, confessing that he had received such sublime sentiments from him that he was determined to weave them into his *Theron and Aspasio* to adorn his work like beautiful flowers. Indeed, when one takes into account the number of eighteenth century stalwarts to whom Hervey turned for advice and the amount of such he gladly received and incorporated into his work, it is no wonder that Hervey's book became the mouthpiece of sound Biblical theology throughout the rest of the century and many years afterwards. Though the literary form and language were Hervey's, the cream of evangelical witness from all the major denominations had been put to use in it. Thus, when Hervey speaks, we hear not only his voice but that of Brine, Gill, Ryland, Pearsall, Whitefield and Doddridge in a clear united testimony to the doctrines of grace in the world-wide call of the gospel. Hervey made no secret of this collective side of his work and promised to share his profits with those who helped him. Hervey knew what he would do with his own share. The poor of Ryland's congregation, for instance, were fitted out with Bibles by Hervey as soon as royalties started coming in and it seems that every subsequent penny was put to similar usage.

### Opposition from unlikely quarters

James Hervey, like William Huntington who took up Hervey's mantle on the topic of Christ's active obedience and righteousness, had to experience opposition from a very unexpected quarter. Some members of Lady Huntingdon's circle were as little impressed by Hervey's teaching on the purpose of the law and on imputation as they were with Huntington's similar teaching thirty years later. One of this circle, by the name of Thomas Hartley (1709(?)-84), a close friend of Hervey's and Whitefield's, affirmed that he believed in the righteousness of Christ but could not accept that this righteousness could be imputed to man as a gift from God. When Hartley, now Rector of Winwick, heard that Hervey was to publish his views in his *Theron and Aspasio*, he campaigned at the Countess of Huntingdon's gatherings that the work ought to be suppressed. Hartley also complained of his fellow Christians who taught God's vindictive wrath against sinners. Perhaps this is one of the reasons why Thomas Haweis, just starting out on his ministry as 'one of Our Lady's men' as the Huntingdonians were playfully called, rode the fifty miles from Oxford to Weston to hear Hervey preach. Haweis was delightfully surprised at his reception. He must have recognised the same fine teaching he was used to from George Thomson of St. Ginny's. On meeting Hervey, he tells us:

> I found him tall, much emaciated; with serenity of countenance, and cordial welcome, he wished me to dine and spend the day with him, which I accepted with pleasure. His preaching was purely evangelical, and very similar to his writings, in beautiful comments

on the Scriptures he quoted; but his manner of delivery far from the elegance I expected in the tone of voice and action.

The latter comment probably refers to the fact that Hervey's congregation consisted mainly of the very poor and uneducated and Hervey made it a special point to speak to them in a manner they understood. That the lowly in Hervey's congregation were graduates in the School of Christ became obvious when Hervey's aged domestic brought out Haweis' horse from the stable and helped the young minister to mount. It was usual for a servant on such an occasion to doff his cap and open his hand for a gratuity. Instead of this, the old Christian opened his heart to God and with cap in hand asked the Lord's blessing and protection for Haweis on his home journey.

Hervey was of the same stamp as his servant. In spite of Hartley's criticisms, Hervey wished that his critic's publications would be accompanied by abundant blessings and bring much honour to our crucified Lord.[1] Sadly, after rejecting the doctrine of Christ's righteousness and questioning the wrath of God against all ungodliness, Hartley became infatuated with extra-scriptural revelation and collaborated with Emanuel Swedenborg (1688-1772)[2] influencing him negatively in his views of the Trinity and translating his works into English. Hartley's friendship with the Countess, Whitefield, Hervey and Dr. Stonehouse is often quoted to show how 'ecumenical' and even unorthodox these stalwarts were in theological matters. Hartley, however, did not take up Swedenborgianism until 1769. Hervey, for instance, had been dead eleven years by then.[3]

## Plans for the publication of *Theron and Aspasio*

Hervey had told his bookseller about his planned work on imputed righteousness and found him enthusiastic about the project. He informed Hervey that the work would fill three volumes and he thought of printing 5,000 copies in small octavo and 750 in large. Hervey thought this was an extremely risky proposal and thought it better to produce the work on a

---

[1]    Letter VI in *The Character of James Hervey, A. M.*

[2]    Swedenborg denied the doctrine of the Trinity and maintained that the original gospel as described in the Word of God had been lost. In 1757, he proclaimed a new messianic age. Swedenborg's work is still a puzzle to scholars and his influence is still present amongst some otherwise evangelical circles. *The Schaff-Herzog Encyclopædia of Religious Knowledge*, for instance, gives a lengthy and extremely positive account of Swedenborg's life and works, leaving out all that might appear negative to an orthodox Christian.

[3]    See, for instance, Deacon's *Philip Doddridge of Northampton*, p. 88 where, referring to a meeting between Doddridge, Hervey, Whitefield, Stonehouse and Hartley in 1750, the latter is referred to as a Swedenborgian which 'vividly displayed Doddridge's determination, tolerance and ecumenical spirit.' Hartley was not a Swedenborgian at the time but this only becomes clear in a note to this effect at the end of the book.

smaller scale, printing according to demand. Thus any errors found in the first printing could be speedily corrected. He also felt that publishing the work in three volumes would 'clog the sale'[1], but after completing the work, he found he could cut out nothing. In point of fact, the bookseller had his way but when *Theron and Aspasio* appeared, it turned out that both he and Hervey had underestimated the demand. It sold out in no time and went into three editions in the first year. At the same time, Hervey's earlier works were appearing in Dutch and Hervey found that his popularity was spreading on the Continent. His *Meditations* had received an even wider readership through their appearing in verse form, transcribed by the pen of a Mr. Newcomb of Hackney. Hervey found the versification, 'extremely well executed.'

During the summer of 1754, Hervey was able to spend six weeks working hard on his *Theron and Aspasio* manuscript, giving it the final polish before publication. One can tell that his appetite for sound theology was really being whetted as he read as much as he could on the great doctrines of the Bible to make sure that his views were defensible. His letters are now full of theological and linguistic comments on the works of other Christian writers and Hervey had never shown himself more critical of works which lacked a true Christian spirit.

### Hervey the theological critic

Typical of this period is Hervey's letter concerning Bishop Fowler whose *Design of Christianity* was widely proclaimed as an epitome of the soundest Christian doctrine but Hervey was shocked at the author's treatment of the doctrine of Christ's righteousness imputed to sinners, so, going against the tide of admirers, he wrote objectively:

> As to Bishop Fowler's *Design of Christianity*, he has, as far as I have read, good sense, clear language, and sometimes fine striking sentiments. But I most cordially embrace the proposition; viz. 'That faith justifieth only as it apprehendeth the merits and righteousness of Jesus Christ,' which he most peremptorily condemns; Please to cast your eye to the fifth line of the next paragraph—(the Bishop's words are, 'Imputation of Christ's righteousness consists in dealing with sincerely righteous persons as if they were perfectly so, for the sake of Jesus Christ;)—and compare his 'sincerely righteous persons' with St. Paul's declaration; Rom. iv. 5, that Christ justifieth the ungodly. When you have perused and considered Bishop Fowler's treatise thoroughly, please to let me have it again;

---

[1] Hervey's problems concerning publishing a three-volumed work can be found in Letter CXXII, *Works*.

especially as you and Mr. H-r apprehend he has given better directions for the attainment of true holiness than Mr. Marshall.[1]

Writing to the person who had sent him Fowler, Hervey tells him:

> St. Paul, I am apt to think, upon a perusal of the treatise, would
> say, the author has good sense, may be no bad moralist, but being
> 'ignorant of God's righteousness, and going about to establish his
> own righteousness, he has not submitted to the righteousness of
> God,' Rom. x.3. Lord, give us an understanding that we may know
> him that is true! Then we shall see Christ Jesus, the God-man, to be
> in the grand affair of salvation, like the meridian sun; and all other
> things like the stars at noon-day.[2]

Each true Biblical saint, guided by Scriptural light, has, nevertheless,
his own favourite doctrine which he sees as a personal touchstone of true
Christian testimony and looks for its evidence in others. Bunyan and Gill
spoke of the inner Spirit-inspired realisation that sensibilised a sinner to
see his own sinful state. Cowper and Huntington stressed the need for a
feeling of being vile and but a worm in God's sight. Hervey found little
work of God in a soul if that soul still spoke of his own sincere efforts to
reach the unattainable heights of righteousness which God demands of all
but finds only in those whom Christ has clothed in His righteousness.

It was not that Hervey was becoming so enamoured with his own works
that he questioned all and sundry who were competing with him in theological writing. His praise for Jenks and Marshall still knew no bounds
and he mentioned a large body of writers whom he thought expressed
Christian truths better than himself. For instance, since 1752 John Wesley
had been fighting a losing battle with John Gill on the doctrines of grace,
striving to 'prove' to the Baptist scholar that a Christian could be a child
of God today and a child of the devil tomorrow. So, about the same time as
he wrote of Bishop Fowler, Hervey says of John Gill:

> Dr. Gill shall tell you my sentiments, in relation to Wesley, on
> the perseverance of the saints. Both their pamphlets on this subject
> I send you. Whether his replies and interpretations in the first part
> are sound and satisfactory, judge you; the considerations suggested

---

[1]   Letter CXXVIII, *Works.*

[2]   Letter CXXXIV, *Works.* Ryland sent Hervey a copy of a book by an author named
Fowler of which both seemed to approved, though Hervey had not yet read the book. This
is, most likely, a different author to the Bishop as he is referred to as 'Mr. Fowler.' See
Hervey's letter to John Ryland dated April 21, 1753 (Letter V.).

in the latter part, I think, are full of weight, rich with consolation, and worthy of a place in our memories and in our heart. May our own meditation fix them in the one, and the Spirit of our God implant them in the other![1]

During this time of intensive reading and research, Hervey did not neglect his Bible. Writing in the same letter as he recommends Gill on the perseverance of the saints, he agrees with his friend of the jejune and irksome nature of trying to master the laws of Britain. This compels him to add:

> Not so the Scriptures! God has, in tender indulgence to our disposition, strewed them with flowers, dignified them with wonders; enriched them with all that may delight the man of genius, and make the man of God perfect. May we, as new born babes, desire the sincere milk of the word; and grow in love, in holiness, in every amiable and happy accomplishment. Do not you practise that excellent rule, of selecting for meditation each day a text of Scripture?

## Samuel Walker of Truro (1714-1761)

Around 1754, Hervey had a surprise visit from Walker of Truro one of the most enigmatic yet most successful ministers of the Gospel in the eighteenth century.[2] Walker had been a passionate dancer and card-player who followed an invitation in 1746 to take up a curacy in Truro solely because of the fashionable Assembly Rooms there. He was converted through the witness of George Conon, Headmaster of Truro Grammar School and told his congregation from the pulpit what had happened to him and how he would not rest until members of his congregation received the same saving experience. Walker was contemporary with Hervey at Oxford but obviously never met him, nor joined in the Holy Club's activities. Yet, nevertheless, he must be counted as one of the first Evangelicals and in the very front line of the Awakening. Walker remained all his life at Truro, working under the theoretical oversight of a Rector who never showed his face in the neighbourhood. The Rector, however, allowed Walker a free-hand,

---

[1]   Letter CXXX, *Works*. Hervey is referring to Gill's, *The Doctrine of the Saint's Final Perseverance* and *The Doctrine of Predestination, Stated and Set in the Scripture Light*. Wesley's denial of these doctrines is contained in his *Serious Thoughts upon the Perseverance of the Saints* and *Predestination calmly considered*. See my chapter *Laying the Axe to Popery's Roots*, in *John Gill and the Cause of God and Truth*. Needless to say, Tyerman in his biography of Hervey (p. 270) refers to Wesley's two works and says of them, 'It would not be rash to say, that, both were unanswerable, though Hervey thought differently.'

[2]   See Edwin Sydney's excellent biography *The Life and Ministry of The Rev. Samuel Walker, B. A.*, based on an earlier unpublished work of Rowland Hill's.

demanding only of him that he regularly forwarded half the income he received from pew-fees and offerings. Protests were numerous at the thought of a converted pastor preaching in the tiny town, famed for its gayness and frivolity and approaches were made to Walker's Bishop who was a sworn foe of Evangelicals. Walker, however, was a man of great learning, fine, polished manners and commanding personality, absolutely correct and blameless in all he did and loved by his flock. This left Bishop Lavington with no grounds for criticism whatsoever. The critics, fearing for the 'good reputation' of the gambling town, persuaded the Rector to dismiss Walker privately. The Rector promised to do so and went to visit his curate to ask for a return of the church keys. Walker received his superior with such an elegance and dignity of manner, coupled with such politeness and charm that the Rector could find no words of complaint and retired fully overwhelmed by Walker's personality. Now Walker's critics became the Rector's critics and they accused him of breaking his word and forced him to try again, this time with more strength of character. The Rector called a second time but was as unsuccessful as the first. When Walker's critics demanded that the Rector should try a third time, he replied, 'Do you go and dismiss him, if you can. I feel in his presence as if he were a being of superior order.'

Something of this awe is reflected in Hervey's account of his meeting with Walker, although this was spiced with Hervey's honest insight into the faith which really made Walker what he was:

> I was lately favoured at Weston with a visit from the Reverend Mr. Walker of Truro, who is indeed a most excellent man, much of a gentleman, and seems well to deserve the character he bears: there is something in him very engaging, yet very venerable. During our conversation, I felt a kind of reverential awe on my mind, blended with more than fraternal affection. How old is he? By his looks he appears to be past forty. What a reproach is it to our men in power, nay, to the nation itself, that so valuable a person should at this time of life be no more than a country curate? But he, good man! disregards the things of this world. That time which too many of his brethren spend, to the disgrace of their function, in worldly compliances, and hunting after church preferments, he employs as a faithful labourer in the vineyard of Christ; and pays all due obedience to the apostle's important injunction, 'Redeem time!' How would some of the primitive bishops have sought after a man of his exemplary piety, and have given him every mark of their real esteem! *Sed tempora mutantur, et nos mutamar in illis.*

> I am much pleased with the account of the religious society at Truro, of which Mr, Walker is the founder and present director, It is an admirable plan! I would have endeavoured (had my health

permitted my attendance) to have formed one of the same kind at Northampton. I heartily wish so useful an institution was more known, and well established in all the principal towns in this kingdom; as I am persuaded such a society must be productive of great good, and in some degree revive the drooping interest of Christianity, wherever it was prudently managed. We had in this neighbourhood a religious assembly, of which I myself was a member; but no one could be admitted who did not understand Greek, as the chief design of that meeting was to improve each other in scriptural knowledge, and consequently could be of little use comparatively with Mr. Walker's plan.[1]

## Helping the widow in need

Hervey still had an ear for others in distress. In 1753, he heard of a widow in need whose only asset was an unpublished work on the death of a number of stalwart Christians entitled *Burnham's Pious Memorials or the Power of Religion on the Mind in Sickness and in Death*. Hervey did not agree with all the sentiments expressed in the work such as the story of a man who was so filled with a longing to meet Christ that he refused to take medicine when he was declared terminally ill. Nevertheless, he approved of the work as a whole, but was more concerned with publishing the book with a view to obtaining a source of income for the destitute widow whose name he never seems to have known or quickly forgot. The widow had approached Hervey through a friend with a suggestion that he should write a preface to the work, and, feeling the cause was just, he complied. The book seems to have laid over a year at the printers but when it was eventually published, many readers thought Hervey was the author. This caused quite a few eye-brows to be raised amongst those who were used to rather a different style and piety from Hervey's pen. They were even more surprised when Hervey told them that he had no idea who the author was.

## Hervey's correspondence misused

Hervey's letters were now being circulated amongst his friends as the spiritual treasures they were. Sometimes this was not to Hervey's liking. One day he was surprised to find a substantial part of one of his letters quoted in a newspaper as authoritative evidence against a person with whom he had no quarrel. It was quoted in a most offensive way and, though the author had not received Hervey's permission, he had presented it as if Hervey himself had submitted the letter for such a publication. Hervey thought that this kind of misuse of his letters was most certainly not the

---

[1]    Letter CXXXII, *Works*.

purpose for which he wrote them and that such authors, no matter how well-meaning and pious they are, have more zeal than wisdom and forget that in their charge of duty, they should give no offence, neither to the Jew nor to the Greek, nor to the church of God. True to his habit of not being over critical of others, when he was all too conscious of his own failings, Hervey emphasised that his words were directed to himself as much as anyone else.

### Advising friends how to behave

The more letters Hervey wrote, the more people wrote to him for advice but also for the pleasure of corresponding with a famous man. At first, Hervey answered all the letters personally but after 1753 only replied to those which he found either edifying and enlightening to the soul and mind or which gave him a chance to genuinely assist others. Writing to one gentleman who seemed to be on the brink of faith, Hervey advises him on almsgiving and how to behave himself as a Christian in front of his servants. Of the former Hervey says:

> I think one guinea is full enough for giving away to a person whose character we are ignorant of. There are too many (dolet dictum!) to whom an alms in the way of money is only an administration of fuel to their lusts. Not that I presume to fix such a charge upon the present petitioner; yet this conviction makes me cautious, where I have no assurance of the person's sobriety. Had it not been for his father's worth, I should have almost thought it my duty to have shut my hand, till I received some satisfactory recommendation. We are stewards of our Master's goods, and discretion is requisite in the discharge of such an office, as well as fidelity.

Hervey believed firmly that it was every Christian's duty to give what he could to the needy but he distinguished between 'the industrious poor' or 'the deserving poor' and those who were poor because of their own idleness or love of strong drink. He was not prepared to finance laziness and scrounging for its own sake in any way. After giving the gentleman advice about giving to the poor, however, Hervey had a gentle rebuke for him concerning how he treated his servants. He told the gentleman:

> I fancy, my dear friend, you did not take notice of an unbecoming expression which dropt from your lips while I sat at your table. You were a little chagrined at the carelessness of your servant, and said to him with some warmth, 'What in the name of God, do you mean?' Such expressions from your lips will be much observed, and long remembered. I need say no more; you yourself will perceive, by a moments reflection, how faulty they are to themselves,

and how pernicious they may be to others. May the good Lord pardon and deliver you from evil! and may both of us more frequently meditate on this important text, 'Set a watch before our mouths, and keep the door of our lips!'[1]

## Hervey solicits further criticism of his *Theron and Aspasio*

As Hervey's popularity grew, people wrote to him requesting a picture which they wished to frame and adorn their walls. Hervey was frightened at the very thought and told those who wished for his likeness that it was not worth framing and he did not like giving away what savours more of vanity than benevolence. If Hervey's correspondent persisted, he would receive a picture but also the obligation to read *Theron and Aspasio* through with a view to making suggestions for betterment. He was told, 'Retrench where I am redundant; clear up, where I am obscure; polish what is uncouth.'[2] Hervey, who always said that it was better for him to have his errors corrected than his praise trumpeted about, was re-writing a quarter of the work as new ideas came in and as his own skill in mature expression developed. To one whose book he corrected and sent back, he requested that the author should apply a leaden pencil to his own works and mark in the margin passages which were clumsy or did not express the truth clearly. As his friend was smarting under severe criticism from a 'popular gentleman from Durham' because of his otherwise acceptable work, Hervey comforted his friend and then went on to mention his own works, saying:

> Never fear, my friend; our writings, as well as our lives, are in the hand of God Almighty: if he will spread, what shall obstruct them? if he will work by them, who shall disannul his design? O may we cry to him, cleave to him, and live by faith on him! for 'not by might, nor by power,' nor by eloquence of composition, nor by interest of patrons, 'but by my Spirit, saith the Lord.'
> Pray, take a little pains with my Theron and Aspasio; you can scarcely imagine what enquiries are made after it, and what a demand there is for it, even before publication. It makes me rejoice with trembling. All-wise, all-gracious Jesus, be jealous for thine honour! Let me not, O let me not cloud its brightness, or obstruct its progress, by any unjudicious touches of my pen.—I now feel the loss of our valuable friend Dr. Doddridge, to whose judgment I ever paid the highest deference; but since he is gone, and we can have no more of his personal counsels, let us redouble our attention to his writings.

---

[1]  Letter CXX, *Works*.

[2]  Letter CXXIII, *Works*.

**Theron and Aspasio is published in 1755. A good year for the gospel**

The first edition of Hervey's *Theron and Aspasio* was published in January, 1755 and was immediately a success being read not only by Christians but men and women who would otherwise never touch a religious book. Indeed, it became fashionable reading amongst the so-called 'polite' people of 'quality' and assisted the work of those such as Whitefield and Lady Huntingdon who wished to evangelise the nobility. Criticism was rare and Hervey found his post bag full of letters of praise from all walks of life. Needless to say, Hervey answered all the theological and literary accolades with a plea that the writers should allow him to take up their suggestions and criticisms in a second edition which followed speedily on the first.

1755 was, indeed, a good year for the gospel and most of the evangelical leaders of this time leave records of great blessing. Whitefield wrote to William Cudworth on June 7 to say:

> It will rejoice you to hear that the glorious gospel of Jesus Christ gets round apace. Several of the clergy, both in town and country, have been lately stirred up to preach Christ crucified, in the demonstration of Spirit, and with power. This excites the enmity of the old Serpent. The greatest venom is spit against Mr. Romaine, who, having been reputed a great scholar, is now looked upon and treated as a great fool, because he himself is made wise unto salvation, and is earnestly desirous that others should be. Methinks I hear you say, 'O happy folly!' May this blessed leaven diffuse itself through the whole nation! The prospect is promising. Many students at Oxford are earnestly learning Christ. Dear Mr. Hervey has learnt and preached Him some years; his loving and truly catholic heart cheerfully complied with the notion about your future correspondence. As for myself, I can only say, 'Less than the least of all,' must be my motto still. I labour but feebly, and yet, O amazing condescension! Jesus owns and succeeds such feeble labours. People still flock to the gospel, like doves to the windows. Next week I begin to take my country range. Be so good, my dear Sir, to add to my obligations, by continuing to remember a poor but willing pilgrim, and to salute all my dear friends as they come in your way.[1]

**William Cudworth becomes Hervey's friend**

One of the first to react in writing to reading *Theron and Aspasio* was Whitefield's friend, (though with ups and downs), William Cudworth, now independent minister of Margaret Street, Oxford Road, London. Cudworth

---

[1]   *Whitefield's Works*, vol. iii, p. 122.

had been nurtured in the faith through reading John Owen, Ralf and Ebenezer Erskine, Fisher and Boston and, as he had been reared mostly on Scottish Presbyterian and Independent theology, he longed to see an Anglican theologian and writer of the same calibre. On reading Hervey's new book, he realised that he had, at last, found what he wanted. Many have criticised Cudworth negatively, influenced by John Wesley's extraordinary aversion to him. Tyerman, for instance, in his Whitefield biography[1], says that Cudworth angered Wesley by becoming Whitefield's successor at the Norwich society and, in the same breath, says that he became a dangerous friend to Hervey. Tyerman's anti-Cudworth bias is obviously merely because Wesley did not like him. This bias has caused many readers of Tyerman to be critical of Cudworth, though they have not familiarised themselves with Cudworth's works. Cudworth had also come under great criticism by Methodists and over-moderate 'Calvinists' for holding to views of imputation, reconciliation, faith and justification which they felt made too much of God's sovereignty and too little of man's agency. Strangely enough, those who admired Hervey for these very doctrines had criticised Cudworth for holding the very same views. This is perhaps because Cudworth tended to use the battering-ram where Hervey used gentle persuasion. Now this man, similar to sturdy William Huntington in many ways, wrote to tender Hervey who was more of a gentle William Cowper, with the result that the man who did not fear facing anyone and the man who confessed that even a grasshopper on his shoulder was a burden to him, found that they were deeply one in the faith and formed a sincere friendship of physical opposites.

When Hervey received Cudworth's letter, he was as delighted as its sender and replied in a letter from Weston-Favell, dated April 15, 1755:

> Dear Sir,—Last night I received your kind letter; and this morning I have but a moment's space in which to acknowledge it. However, I cannot neglect the first opportunity. Are you the author that has given us an abridgment of Mr. Marshall? Truly, I think you have well bestowed your labour, and well executed your work. I wish you had not given yourself the trouble of sending me the book, because I have it, and highly prize it—the abridgment, I mean.
>
> I should be very glad if you would read that Dialogue you mention with a critical attention—if you would point out the places where you think I am confused in my apprehensions, injudicious in method, or weak in argument. As you have so thoroughly studied the point, and so often taught the doctrine, you must easily see where the essay lies most open to objection, and where the point

---

[1]    Vol. ii, p. 347.

might receive additional strength. You would much oblige me if
you would do this with the utmost impartiality and freedom; and I
hope you would do service to the truth as it is in Jesus. Several
persons, I find are dissatisfied with my opinion on this head. Do,
Sir, review Dialogue 16 and favour me with your free remarks and
friendly improvements. Whatever of this kind is done, I beg may
be done speedily; because a new edition is in the press, and the
printers will soon come to that part. When I hear from you again, I
will speak my sentiments with relation to your well calculated design of an evangelical library[1]. At present, I have leisure only to
assure you, that I am, dear Sir, your affectionate friend in Jesus
Christ, JAMES HERVEY.

Cudworth replied within a few days and pleased Hervey so much that
he wrote to Cudworth twice again in April, enclosing letters which he had
received from objectors, asking Cudworth how he would deal with them.
Hervey's editor gives a footnote here saying that the objections in the
letters did not deal with revealed truths but were 'an attempt to overthrow
the solid foundation laid for the hope, confidence, and salvation of guilty
sinners; that which makes the gospel glad tidings indeed to such.' Hervey
was thrilled with Cudworth's planned evangelical library but warned him
not to gallop before he walked on the project as John Wesley had rushed
into attempting a similar thing but had merely jumbled together whatever
was within his reach at the time, leaving out the very works which ought to
have been included. He confessed to Cudworth that he could not understand why godly people rejected their doctrine as it was the very doctrine
which was 'so eminently conducive to the comfort, recovery, and happiness of a sinner, that I cannot be persuaded to relinquish it.' It is not quite
clear from the general context, if Hervey is referring to the doctrine of
faith or of imputed righteousness. Most likely he is referring to the former
as he came under some criticism at the time for his view of faith as being
a gift of God enabling the approbation of justification rather than it being
the *sine qua non* leading to a later justification. Hervey saw faith as 'a
persuasion of our reconciliation to God, previous to our performance of
holy duties' (Romans 5:10) and 'a persuasion of our future enjoyment of
the heavenly happiness, previous to our performance of holy duties.' The
foundation of this persuasion being in 'our free justification through Jesus
Christ, which we receive under the character of ungodly persons; consequently before the performance of good works'(Romans 4:5, 1 John 5:11).
Thus faith, reconciliation and justification which lead to eternal life are

---

[1]    A collection of evangelical works in 'marrow' form from the Reformation to Cudworth's
day was planned. Little of this work was accomplished but Marshall and Hervey became
part of it.

not founded on our own duties and obedience but 'on the duties and obedience of our great Mediator. "This life is in his Son."'[1]

Hervey's new friend felt that he ought to tell him how unpopular he, Cudworth, had become with his fellow ministers because of his views, but Hervey, writing in May, was not at all put off by this. He told Cudworth that he knew quite well of his reputation among 'moderates' but believed firmly in the very same doctrines himself. Although he knew that people would not look into further editions of *Theron and Aspasio* if they felt he had any connection whatsoever with Cudworth, Hervey refused to drop a good friend on such grounds. He did, however, advise Cudworth to act prudently and be as wise as a serpent, not announcing the fact of their friendship from the housetops in his usual open zeal but giving readers the chance to buy further editions of *Theron and Aspasio* and let the doctrines speak for themselves.

### Evangelical criticism confusing law and gospel

March to June 1755 saw the second edition of *Theron and Aspasio* in print, the volumes being released individually. There was an immediate demand for a third as only three thousand copies of the second edition had been published. Again, Hervey wrote to his dozen or so friends, informing them that the altered and extended version was the genuine sentiments of his heart but if they felt that they receded a hair's breadth from the unerring standard of Scripture then his friends should inform him and pray that he would have grace to retract whatsoever was not of the finest gospel standard. Hervey often wrote at this time concerning John Brine who had given him good advice on *Theron and Aspasio*. He was dismayed to find how strong was the reviewers' criticism of Brine's works, which made him rather worried about what they would make of his own books. He thus tells Ryland, 'I find, from an advertisement in the Northampton newspaper, that the writers of the review have treated Mr. Brine with virulence and scurrility. What may I expect at their hands? Pray for me, that I may receive their censures and invectives with calmness, and neither be exasperated in my temper, nor intimidated in my spirit. May this be the language of my heart, *Though they curse, yet bless thou.*'[2] In the same letter, Hervey says he has heard that the Prince of Wales and other royals have received his *Theron and Aspasio* well so that he could say, 'May the divine Redeemer open their hearts; give them admission into their souls; and make them not merely a matter of amusement, but a savour of life unto life!'

Hervey did not experience much criticism from the literary reviewers but several leading evangelicals felt they had a bone to pick with him.

---

[1]  Letter CIII, *Works.*

[2]  Letter XV, Ryland's collection in his memoir of Hervey.

These serious-minded believers, of various denominations, held a common view that faith in Jesus Christ was the outcome of fulfilling the duties of the law. They could not envisage that one must partake of the comforts and strength of the gospel before duty to the law can be truly and freely practised and interpreted the law as a schoolmaster who brought them to Christ in the sense that allegiance to the law automatically revealed Christ to the law-doer. Hervey taught that the law drove men to see what failures they were. Such men, chosen of God, were then drawn to Christ by the Spirit to experience that Christ's faith and righteousness could provide what they never could have gained from the law which had damned them but could not acquit them. The law could never be a fulfilled standard in fallen man but could only be a standard fulfilled in saved sinners by the imputed righteousness of Christ. He equips those who are judged perfect in Him to walk according to the rule of faith and the rule of Christ which are not abrogations of the law but the means of vitalising and fulfilling the law. Hervey was dismayed at the weak doctrine of holiness shown by a number of his fellow evangelicals as they stressed what they did for the Lord as signs of holiness rather than what they received from the Lord, keeping humbly quiet about their own actions. These thoughts moved Hervey to plan a supplement to his three volumes dealing with the doctrines of obedience, assurance and vital 'evangelical holiness'.

## The difficulty of acknowledging that there is no good thing in the flesh

What was at fault in the evangelism of his day, Hervey believed, was an unwillingness to accept that there was no good thing in the flesh. Current views of holiness seemed to have been centred on making the man of sin, i.e. the flesh, 'good' instead of centring holiness in the new man created in Christ's righteousness. They thus interpreted the word 'mortify' as used by Paul in Romans 8:13 and Colossians 3:5, meaning to subdue and put to death, as 'make righteous' which not only turns Scripture upside-down but the dictionary, too. One writer early in 1755, whose name Hervey at first keeps secret, objected to Hervey's view of Romans chapters 7 and 8. He complained of Theron saying that he defiled himself afresh, though cleansed and 'was struck with horror' at Aspasio's arguing 'my best hours are not free from sinful infirmities, nor my best duties from sinful imperfections.' The pious but rather popish gentleman maintained that when Paul speaks of his sin, he is referring to himself in the natural state before conversion. He argued that if Paul were speaking as a Christian, then we must believe that 'good Christians' are more holy than Paul as they are becoming perfect by degrees, yet Paul remains a sinner.[1] It was obvious

---

[1]    See Collection of Letters appended to Ryland's biography of Hervey, Letter XVI, dated March 15, 1755.

that Hervey regarded the Arminian author of the letter highly and was at pains not to break peace with him but even to learn from him, if possible. He thus decided not to change his doctrines but to make them less open to the charge of Antinomianism. He then told Ryland that he would alter the phrase 'I defile myself afresh' as it could be interpreted as meaning that Theron wilfully and voluntary defiled himself, believing that he could do so with impunity as a Christian. Nothing, of course, could have been further from Hervey's mind but this is the very accusation which John Wesley brought against Hervey in a later, extant letter dated October 15, 1756. Indeed, it is quite certain that the criticism Hervey takes up here was from Wesley's pen. The latter wrote at least four letters of criticism to Hervey based on *Theron and Aspasio*, a very short one first and, some time later, three more lengthy ones as Hervey had asked him to be more specific. Wesley's letters of 1756 and 1758 have been preserved but the first letter or letters of 1755 are only mentioned indirectly by Hervey. The sentiments Hervey refers to in this March 5, 1755 letter to Ryland were identical with Wesley's overall criticism of Hervey's work[1] and were repeated almost verbatim in Wesley's subsequent printed attacks on Hervey. Further evidence for this unnamed person being Wesley is that five months later, Ryland requested the name of a critic Hervey had mentioned in a previous letter and begged to be allowed to examine the whole document. Hervey replied that the critic to whom he had previously referred was Wesley who was preparing to go to the press against Hervey at the time. Hervey also told Ryland that two former preachers of Wesley's had heard that he was in Ireland and was preparing a lengthier answer to *Theron and Aspasio*. This is obviously a reference to Wesley's third letter, based on a pirated Irish copy of Hervey's works, which caused Hervey to write *Aspasio Vindicated*.[2]

## Opposition from a most unexpected quarter

Hervey decided to expound Romans 7 for his new edition in order to show how the new man in Christ is perfectly cleansed but the flesh is sinful.[3] Whilst he was working on it, he received fierce opposition from an entirely different and very local, source. It was the time of republican and revolutionary thinking and one of Hervey's tenants was caught up into

---

[1]   See Hervey's *Aspasio Vindicated* for Wesley's second (or possibly third) letter and also Hervey's letters numbers CXCVI, CXCVII, CXCIX and CCV.

[2]   See Ryland's collection, Letter XXI. Also Letter CLXXXIII in Hervey's *Works*. Judging by the sentiments expressed in Wesley's *Preventative against Unsettled Notions in Religion*, this letter also refers to Wesley's criticisms.

[3]   In all fairness it must be stated that Hervey's view of Romans 7 fluctuated, at times he felt that the chapter portrayed Paul before conversion, at other times the strife between the new man and the old.

believing that as all men are equal, no man ought to have responsibilities and commitments to another. He thus formally dismissed Hervey as his landlord and refused to pay his rent. If Hervey so much as stepped on 'his land' the tenant would rush out with an ancient rifle and threaten to blow Hervey's brains out. The man had forgotten that Hervey was not one of the 'idle rich' but the rent from his tenants was part of his £180 salary per annum which had to be split between him and several other family members and was meant for the upkeep of the estate and the salary of a curate. The tenant's poor mother strove to intervene but she had no power over her son. Any other landlord would have had the man whipped, deprived of his tenancy and put into the debtor's prison. Hervey was different. He told Ryland of the difficult situation he was in:

> My thoughts have been so engaged, and my weak spirits so hurried, about a troublesome vexatious affair of a secular nature, that I have had but little power, and as little leisure, to consider more important points. The tenant, whose mother you saw at my house, continues obstinate and revengeful to the very last, and will leave me no possibility of getting my money for the time past, or my land for the time to come, but only by arresting him, and throwing him into gaol; and this I cannot be prevailed on to do: it would grieve me extremely to reflect, that a man, who has a wife and two small children, lies in prison, confined by my order.[1]

**The assurance of faith**

The next batch of criticism Hervey had to cope with was concerning the assurance of faith. Some writers felt that a saved sinner must be fully assured, whereas others, Hervey felt Brine was to be included here, taught that the saved sinner can never go beyond a conviction that if Christ wills, then He can make the sinner clean. Brine was warning against a sinner feeling that his rational interest expressed in 'a conclusion, springing up in my mind of my own interest in him, and his saving benefits' was a sign of faith. Hervey accepted much of the teaching shown by both sides but felt they were as theoretical as they were highly systematic. He wished to aim rather at an explanation of faith that was both Biblical and useful, that is, practical and experiential. Writing to Ryland for advice, Hervey says: 'Now I would so conduct my treatise, that it should establish my own opinion, without opposing the judgment of these and other eminent divines: I would recommend and promote the assurance of faith, yet allow that a soul, destitute of this gift, may be really safe, though not truly happy. If you could suggest some method of maintaining the Christian's privilege, without

---

[1]    Letter XVII, Ryland's *Character of Hervey*.

offending the brother of high or low endowments, I should be glad. What you do of this kind, pray let it be speedy, otherwise it cannot take place.' He had just heard that the publishers were speeding up the publication of the next edition and making it 4,000 copies instead of the planned 3,000.[1]

Hervey's correspondence with Ryland on the subject of faith produced an essay on that doctrine from Ryland's pen called *The Full Assurance of Faith* with Hervey's stylistic and theological additions and corrections.[2] Of the finished product, Hervey confessed that it contained the most grand and important truths that could ever enter into the heart of man and he assured Ryland that he subscribed to them all without the least hesitation or reserve. He ordered a dozen copies for distribution but warned Ryland that the work might appear 'rant and enthusiasm' to carnal minds and would be completely new to many an established Christian. Such established Christians, particularly those who thought that faith was either a mere rational acceptance of Christ's saving work or that faith was a trust in earned deserts did indeed challenge Hervey. Foremost of these were Robert Sandeman (1718-1771) and John Wesley. John Brown looked upon Hervey's doctrine of faith as a pure expression of Biblical truth and says of it:

> Mr. Hervey viewing faith as being founded in the *self-evidenc-ing light of the word*, as being the effect of the demonstration of the Spirit, and in its very nature implying an assurance of the divine all-sufficiency and grace, he apprehended it gave the soul a *con-scious enjoyment* of the Saviour, and that it was the best means of knowing our actual interest in him, and that we are under no delusion. He thought, with other evangelical divines, that *so far* as a believer is in the exercise of this direct and assured faith, under the influence of the Holy Spirit, he needeth not the support of other marks and evidences of grace within himself, because his mind rests entirely and quietly in the divine all-sufficiency, grace, and faithfulness; and this he reckoned the most desirable way to keep all other marks and evidences of a gracious state clear and distinct. To use his own words; 'As faith is such a persuasion of the heart, and such a reception of Christ (as above described), it assures the soul of salvation by its own act, antecedent to all reflection on its fruits and effects, or works and evidences. It assures the soul of acquittance from guilt, and of reconciliation to Christ; of a title to the everlasting inheritance, and of grace sufficient for every case

---

[1]    Ibid, Letter XVII.

[2]    This work is often appended to Hervey's works as, though it might be an exaggeration to call it a joint production, it reveals Hervey's views on faith as if he had written the work himself.

of need.' He was happy that his sentiments of the appropriation of faith were not only scriptural, but confirmed by a multitude of eminent witnesses. 'If the reader,' says he, 'inquire after their names, he will find some of them enumerated in the following catalogue:- Luther, Calvin, Melancthon, Beza, Bullinger, Bucer, Knox, Craig, Melvil, Bruce, Davidson, Forbes, &c, Ursinus, Zanchius, Junius, Piscator, Rollock, Wendelinus, Chamierus, Bodius, Pareus, Altingius, Triglandii, Arnoldus, Maresius, Wollebius, Heideggerus, Essenius, Turretinus, Witsius, &c. Many British divines; among others, Perkins, Pemble, Willet, Gouge, Rogers, Owen, and Marshall.' He farther adds, 'If we were apparently and demonstratively in an error, yet, to err with such company, and in the footsteps of such guides, must very much tend to mitigate the severity of censure. But I believe few serious persons will venture to charge error and delusion upon such a venerable body of Protestant divines, so eminent for their learning, and so exemplary for their holiness; whose labours were so remarkably owned by God, and whose sentiments have been adopted by so many reformed churches. The declarations of the English and Palatine churches are produced in the Dialogue (*Theron and Aspasio*). I have in my hand an extract from the confessions and standard doctrines of the Church of Scotland—of Ireland—of France—of Helvetia; with all which Aspasio has the happiness to agree. Only some of them are much stronger in displaying and maintaining the special *fiducia*, or the appropriating persuasion of faith.[1]

### Hervey, Cudworth, Ryland and Lady Francis on Tobias Crisp

Meanwhile, Hervey was keeping up his correspondence with Ryland and exchanging manuscripts with him for correction as also books as loans or gifts. Hervey had become an avid reader of Tobias Crisp whose doctrine of no wrath displayed to saved sinners by God, though rejected at first, was now a great comfort to him. Cudworth, however, had queried this teaching and now Hervey approached Ryland on the subject, quoting Crisp who said, 'There is no wrath to believers; Christ has bore it all; exhausted it wholly, and carried it—clean away.' This Hervey compared with Micah who said, 'I will bear the indignation of the Lord, because I have sinned against him.' Hervey explains that the words are obviously spoken by a believer who speaks in faith to the God of his salvation, claiming, 'The Lord will bring me forth to light: I shall behold his righteousness.'[2] He asks Ryland, if the one contradicts the other. Ryland does not

---

[1]    Brown's *Memoir of Mr. Hervey*, pp. 63, 64.

[2]    Micah 7:9.

record his answer in his *Memoirs* of Hervey but whatever he said, it obviously reassured and even strengthened Hervey's love and respect for Crisp as witnessed by several letters to Lady Francis written some time after his appeal to Ryland.[1] Apparent contradictions with the Word of God found in Crisp, Hervey argues, generally reveal the pre-conceived and legal views of the critic rather than errors in Crisp's doctrine.[2] Hervey confesses to Lady Francis that he previously thought otherwise of Crisp but had matured into believing he was one of the very greatest evangelical writers and carer of souls. The fact that Hervey went his own way in his high view of Crisp and did not follow Cudworth is very important in assessing later Methodist criticism that Hervey became theologically a pawn in the hand of Cudworth, a man whom John Wesley personally abhorred. The odd thing about Wesley's criticism, however, is that, in the case of Cudworth, it loses all its strength as it can be clearly shown that where Cudworth disagreed with Hervey, he agreed with Wesley, as, for instance, in their attitude to certain doctrines of Crisp.

### Continuing prison work

Though Hervey was very busy at this time and again bound to his room and often to his bed for weeks on end, he still thought of his Christian duties to the lost and corresponded at length with prisoners in Northampton jail as he could not visit them. One such letter has been preserved, written about the middle of July, 1755. Immediately on commencing the letter, Hervey places himself where the condemned criminals stand, bemoaning his own depravity and addressing the condemned criminals as 'fellow-sinners'. He tells them that they have been condemned to death by both an earthly and a heavenly tribunal but, horrible as the earthly condemnation is, the wrath of God which brings eternal destruction is more terrible still. After describing the killing nature of sin and the law, Hervey tells the criminals how Christ has taken pity on such deplorable sinners as themselves. He did not leave things at that, however, but worked out a way in which pity could be joined by relief for the accused. Hervey tells them, 'Because we had broke the commandments of the law, he fulfilled them in their perfection. Because we deserved the punishment of the law, he sustained it in its utmost extremity.' Hervey now outlines the saving sufferings of Christ, leaving out no Scripture detail, pointing out that here is a door of hope for the condemned for there is no condemnation for those who are in Christ Jesus. He shows how a righteousness is wrought for believers in Christ which is perfect and everlasting 'such as brings

---

[1]  Letters LXXXIV, XCIII and XCVI.

[2]  See the next chapter for Hervey's overall opinion of Crisp.

incomparably greater honour to God's law, than all our transgressions bring
dishonour. By all this, he has merited and obtained a full deliverance, and
a complete redemption.' After explaining their eternal state and the eternal promises of the gospel, Hervey goes through the Bible doctrines ap-
pertaining to salvation one by one asking the condemned men to check
them with their own state and their own longings and hopes. He tells them
that they are unpardonable before men but Christ is able to save to the
uttermost those who come to Him. He is also able to save the chief of
sinners as indeed, everyone coming to Christ should feel they are. Of those
coming to Christ, He will refuse none as He says, 'Him that cometh to me,
I will in no wise cast out.' Then Hervey adds a postscript: 'What I have
written, I shall beg of God to bless; and will attend you with my prayers,
though I cannot visit you in person.'[1]

## Writing for 'ordinary people'

Hervey's reputation as a literary figure and a writer to the upper classes
always troubled him somewhat as his main pastoral care lay with the poor.
He thus decided to collect a few of his sermons together and print them
with a view to distribution to the poor. As Hervey rarely made extensive
notes for his sermons, he found little material to prepare for the press.
Early in 1757, ashamed that so many sermons published by members of
his own church lacked the one thing needed, he told Ryland that he was
about to sacrifice any reputation he may have had with the 'elegant and
polite' and publish sermons for ordinary folk. He confessed that he could
let his reputation freely disappear 'if any honour may redound to the Lord
our righteousness.' His friendship with Ryland had now grown so strong
that he naturally turned to him for guidance on this matter. It was a great
comfort to Hervey to know that a mind so astute as young Ryland's, accompanied by a strong trust in Christ, saw Christian doctrine in the same
light. At this time, Hervey was greatly pleased to find that Ryland, too,
saw Romans 7 as the testimony of a Christian man as his Arminian friends
had urged him to accept that Paul was speaking of himself in his former
unconverted state and this had influenced some of Hervey's corrections
for a further edition of *Theron and Aspasio*. It was a comfort to both Hervey
and Ryland to know that Paul, too, suffered as they did in the battle to
mortify the flesh. This instance shows that Hervey was still growing in
grace and in a knowledge of the truth and we find him, with Ryland's
backing, re-correcting new additions he had made to *Theron and Aspasio*
to make the message of Romans 7 stand out more clearly.[2]

[1]   Letter CXLI, *Works*.
[2]   Letter XXVIII, Ryland's collection.

**Placing his will in the will of the Lord**

In the same letter, Hervey confesses that his health is deteriorating. Though he often experienced attacks of extreme weakness, Hervey usually suffered more from aches than smarting pain, but now he experienced times of agonising pain which made him irritable, soon angry and call upon the Lord to keep his mind and speech calm. It also strengthened his prayer for a safe entry into a better world as he was weary of the old one. Nevertheless he always added, 'In thy good time, O Lord,' and 'Only be it thy will,' and asked to be given strength to testify to Christ's righteousness. Because of his physical state, Hervey tells Ryland in a following letter that his entire strength is concentrating now on improving his *Theron and Aspasio* with the assistance of some eight men who were helping him prepare the manuscript for a new edition. Though he is now one of the most read British authors, he confesses to Ryland that his work is 'a thing of nought'. He begs Ryland, however, to pray that, in God's good providence, it will not appear to the readers as dust upon the hedges but as dew upon the grass. For the next few weeks, there was some improvement in Hervey's health so he was able, for a while, to repay Ryland's attention to *Theron and Aspasio* by intensively correcting works of Ryland and rewriting a line here and there.

It is now time to look at Hervey's later works in detail and see what earned for them the praise of the reformed established church and the evangelical Calvinists of the Dissenting churches.

# Chapter Eight:
# Later Works of Maturity and Depth[1]

## Witnessing to a noble infidel

Whilst preaching to a congregation of dukes, duchesses and prominent politicians at Lady Huntingdon's in 1748, George Whitefield noticed
a new face amongst his hearers. The man seemed greatly moved by what
he was hearing and approached Whitefield after the sermon to invite him
to his home on the following morning. Whitefield was only too pleased to
accept the invitation and on visiting the man, found that he behaved 'with
great candour and frankness.' The man was Lord Bolingbroke whom J. H.
Overton says was known as 'a violent partisan of the established faith and
as a persecutor of Dissenters.' To add to the picture, Overton also mentions that Dr. Johnson called Bolingbroke 'a scoundrel and a coward.'
Lady Huntingdon, despite the fact that he occasionally attended her circle
freely called Bolingbroke 'an infidel'. Perhaps the best that can be said of
Bolingbroke from a theological point of view is that he was the last of the
more well-known Deists.

There is no doubt, however, that Bolingbroke regarded Whitefield
highly. A letter has been preserved in which he tells Lady Huntingdon:

> Mr. Whitefield is the most extraordinary man in our times. He
> has the most commanding eloquence I ever heard in any person;
> his abilities are very considerable; his zeal unquenchable; and his
> piety and excellence genuine—unquestionable. The bishops and
> inferior orders of the clergy are very angry with him, and endeav-
> our to represent him as a hypocrite, an enthusiast; but this is not
> astonishing—there is so little goodness or honesty amongst them.
> Your ladyship will be somewhat amused at hearing that the King

---

[1]  Not all Hervey's later published works will be dealt with here as some are mentioned at
length in other chapters and, in particular, discussed in the chapter on Hervey's library.

has represented to his Grace of Canterbury, that Mr. Whitefield should be advanced to the Bench, as the only means of putting an end to his preaching. What a keen, what a biting remark! but how just, and how well earned by those mitred lords![1]

When he penned these words, Bolingbroke was perhaps thinking of the great good Whitefield had done for his own half-brother Lord St. John who had come to know the Lord of Lords through Whitefield's preaching, became a changed man and a shining example to his brother. Lord Bolingbroke was present at his brother's death in 1749 and heard him say before he breathed his last, 'To God I commit myself. I feel how unworthy I am; but Jesus Christ died to save sinners; and the prayer of my heart now is, God be merciful to me a sinner!'[2]

There is also no doubt that Bolingbroke considered Calvinism to be the best interpretation of Christianity, a point he used to make when discussing religion with the Arminian clergy. On July 30, 1775, the Countess of Huntingdon told Augustus Toplady the following story:

> The late Lord Bolingbroke was one day reading in Calvin's Institutes. A clergyman of his Lordship's acquaintance coming on a visit, Lord Bolingbroke said to him, 'You have caught me reading John Calvin. He was indeed a man of great parts, profound sense, and vast learning. He handles the doctrines of grace in a very masterly manner.' 'Doctrines of grace!' replied the clergyman, 'the doctrines of grace have set all mankind together by the ears.' 'I am surprised to hear you say so,' answered Lord B.; 'you who profess to believe and to preach Christianity. Those doctrines are certainly the doctrines of the Bible: and, if I believe the Bible, I must believe them. And, let me seriously tell you, that the greatest miracle in the world is, the subsistence of Christianity, and its continued preservation, as a religion, when the preaching of it is committed to the care of such unchristian wretches as you.'[3]

### Lord Bolingbroke attacks the Bible and Hervey defends it

Lady Francis Shirley read Bolingbroke's *Letters on the Study and Use of History* and found it not so much a study of history as an out and out attack against the integrity and witness of the Bible. Her Ladyship, shocked by the person who appeared in Lady Huntingdon's home church as a wolf in sheep's clothing, asked Hervey for advice on the matter. Hervey bought the book and began a series of letters to Lady Francis on the subject. The

---

[1]   Taken from Tyerman's *Life of Whitefield*, p. 194.

[2]   Ibid., pp. 214, 215.

[3]   *The Complete Works of Augustus Toplady*, p. 51.

recipient realised that Hervey had the correct qualifications to openly refute Bolingbroke and, over a period of many months, slowly persuaded
Hervey to appear in print against his Lordship.

In his Preface to *Remarks on Lord Bolingbroke's Letters on the Study
and Use of History*, Hervey briefly mentions how the work came to be
written but stresses that he is fulfilling the wishes of a friend so that he
may 'support the dignity of the divine word; may raise its esteem, and
promote its study among men: because then he may reasonably hope to
promote the best interests of his fellow-creatures, and subserve that grand
designation of the Almighty Majesty expressed by the Psalmist, 'Thou
hast magnified thy word above all thy name.' Psalm 138:2.

## The Old Testament allegedly less reliable historically than other 'con-temporary' works

Bolingbroke's first aim was to persuade his readers that, in comparison to other ancient records, the Old Testament was unreliable in its chro-
nology and in no way illustrated the history of time from creation onwards. Hervey asks him what alternative account is available to the
chronologer which depicts such memorable date-fixing events in such a
closely ordered sequence as the Pentateuch and the later Biblical writings.
Going into great detail, Hervey shows how the genealogies of the ten eminent patriarchs are carefully outlined up to the flood. From the flood to the
time of Abraham, in whose 'seed shall all the nations of the earth be
blessed,' careful records are displayed. The Egyptian captivity and deliverance of the Children of Israel is outlined in the closest of accounts and
the history is continued until the building and destruction of the Temple.
Then, progressing through time to the Babylonian captivity and later restitution, the world is made aware of not only the history of salvation but
how this was historically prepared. Bolingbroke was convinced of the superior accuracy of ancient historical and extra-Biblical works over and
against the Scriptures. He referred to *The Remains of Tacitus*, for instance,
as 'precious' full of 'integrity and lustre' but to the Biblical account as
'dark and imperfect', and even 'a heap of fables . . . useless to mankind.'
This led Hervey to take the learned Lord through all the historical and
literary annals of other ancient peoples, and ask him wherein this superiority lies. Quoting from the works of historians, Hervey shows that they
have a completely different, and far more negative, view of Tacitus than
Lord Bolingbroke presents in his undocumented praise of the writer.

## Scripture records have always portrayed history accurately, even before its time

As a further indication of the Scriptures' unparalleled historical value,
Hervey shows how one can not only trace the history of the Jews and,
indeed, the world, back to their origins but one can trace the history of

God's people in a forward direction before the events take place as one prophecy after another comes to pass. This prophetic portraying of history before its time even extends into times to come. As these prophesies have proved true in past times, there is every reason to believe their records of future events. This is especially the case when dealing with the failures of the Jews and the establishing of the Messianic hope. Hervey cannot help point out that the very fact that the history is so unfavourable to the Jews, hardly suggests that it is the product of legends designed by them for self-aggrandisement. Hervey also points out that not only did ancient peoples come and go over the centuries, always merging or separating and creating new nations and peoples, this was the same after Biblical times as witnessed by the history of Europe and the merging of Danes, Saxons and Normans with the British. The Jews, however, remained a people throughout the ages, with a continuing record of their history, and are a people still.

## Bolingbroke separates doctrinal truths from their historical origins

Bolingbroke's next surmise is that the historicity of the Scriptures has nothing to do with the doctrines therein expressed which are obviously the work of the Holy Spirit. This statement Hervey finds a mere contrivance to keep up an orthodox appearance. The one, he argues, stands or falls with the veracity of the other. Again, Hervey demands Bolingbroke's criteria for believing that God has preserved Holy Spirit inspired doctrine in the works of blundering forgers and fable-writers who were not only unaware of the purport of the doctrines they recorded but completely ignorant of the world around them. If the origin and compilation of the Scriptures were as Bolingbroke so dogmatically asserts, Hervey argues, 'who would depend on their testimony in any point whatsoever?'

Hervey now shows how such a naive belief is quite contrary to what the Scriptures portray of the inter-link between history and revelation. Such texts as 2 Timothy 3:16, John 5:39 and Romans 15:4 are proof enough for Hervey of how close the historical records are intermingled with the inspired Word. Using the testimony of Christ Himself in Luke 24:44, Hervey points out how all the single parts of the historical and doctrinal writings, comprising the whole of the Old Testament, are given decisive authority and declared unquestionably true.

## Demythologising Bolingbroke's view of Scripture

Next Hervey takes up Bolingbroke's more hidden means of disparaging Scripture. He refers to the nobleman's repeated allusion to the Scriptures as fables, traditions or legends. He wonders how Bolingbroke would react if his *Sketch of the History and State of Europe* would be referred to as '*Lord Bolingbroke's Written Legends.*' Hervey then alludes to Bolingbroke's method of interspersing his criticism with 'idle tales and scandalous stories' which he uses to cheat the reader into depreciating the pure testimony of the divine Word. Bolingbroke's third method was to presume that the Scriptures were 'full of additions, interpolations, and transpositions'. Such criticism, Hervey explains is more easily asserted than evinced. Of all the 'add-ons' that Bolingbroke alleges are in the Scriptures, he actually gives only one concrete example and that is the story of Moses death at the end of the Pentateuch. Either we are to suppose that Moses wrote of his own demise, which would be preposterous, says Bolingbroke, or someone has tampered with his five books. Hervey cannot follow this logic, explaining that Joshua could have added the account to Moses work or even a writer unknown to us. To argue that the fact that we do not know who penned these words proves that they are the work of an impostor, is strange argumentation indeed. Hervey mentions two of Bolingbroke's works which had been printed anonymously and denies that they must be regarded as impostures for that reason alone.

### Noah's curse seen as 'un-Christian'

Bolingbroke's major trump card in affirming the absurdity of the Scriptural records was Noah's curse pronounced on Canaan found in Genesis 9:25[1]. Although his Lordship was not too particular about the scandalous tales he told to discredit Scripture, he suddenly becomes highly sensitive and moral concerning Noah's action and says, 'One is tempted to think that the patriarch was still drunk, and that no man in his senses could hold such language or pass such a sentence.' This reminds Hervey of Acts 2:13 where the miraculous preaching of the Apostles was put down to the excessive drinking of wine. Again, knowing that holy men have been used in the past as the oracles of God, speaking out what God has ordained and planned, Hervey can accept Noah's utterance as indicating rather what God ordains than what Noah wishes i.e. 'cursed be' in the sense of 'cursed is'. Hervey asks, considering the word 'curse', 'What name then can be bad enough for a profane and unnatural wretch, who makes sport with a parent's folly, a parent's sinfulness, a parent's misery? Surely this was a most flagrant violation of filial reverence, filial love, and filial duty? Proverbs 30:17.' Again, Hervey brings in the works of various scholars in refuting Bolingbroke's wider exposition of this passage. Bolingbroke had also left himself open to Hervey's criticism by pronouncing authoritatively on the Hebrew text without having any knowledge of that language. Hervey, an expert in the Hebrew language, soon cleared up Bolingbroke's faulty claims concerning Hebrew syntax and semantics. Bolingbroke, however, argues dubiously in ridiculing the idea that a man can be cursed or punished through what happens to his offspring. Hervey quickly uses the story

---

[1]    'Cursed be Canaan; a servant of servants shall he be unto his brethren.'

of David and Absolom in 2 Samuel 18:33 along with several others which were perfectly designed to explode Bolingbroke's theory.

### His Lordship is shocked by Jewish cruelty

Bolingbroke finds himself shocked by the campaigns of Joshua and the cruelty he discovers in the Jews' treatment of their enemies. Oddly enough, contrary to the main thrust of his book, Bolingbroke is here arguing as if he accepted the accounts of the battles as history! Hervey points out how loathsome Israel's enemies were so that 'the land itself vomiteth out her inhabitants.' Quoting Genesis 15:16, Deuteronomy 9:5 and Leviticus 18:25, Hervey shows how, 'For the wickedness of these nations, the Lord thy God doth drive them out from before thee.' Nevertheless, in most of these cases, Hervey argues, there was an ignored chance of a reprieve or a settlement. Furthermore, the condemnation of nations in the Old Testament is a warning finger in the history of salvation, 'a presage of the misery and ruin which will sooner or later fall upon individuals and nations that reject the glorious gospel, and vilify its sacred repository, *The Bible*.' This should have been warning enough for Lord Bolingbroke!

### Hervey shows how the Bible reveals the very kind of history that Bolingbroke desires

His Lordship presents Davilla, who wrote the history of the French civil wars, as the doyen of historians because he traces all he relates to its sources and its 'inner springs of action.' As Bolingbroke is so impressed by the Italian writer's skill in discovering the inner secrets and motivating powers of the people he describes, Hervey recommends to him the Holy Scriptures which reveal both the unsearchable counsels of heaven and the innermost thoughts of the human heart. Quoting Scripture after Scripture, Hervey shows how man's actions in history are evaluated and discerned, praised and judged and analysed in regard to their sources and development in the greatest of detail. This is exactly, Hervey complains, what Bolingbroke requires in a historical work but his own work is made conspicuous by the absence of this essential feature. For instance, he has attempted to describe the entire history of the Jews without due regard for their messianic teaching which is present throughout the entire Old Testament from the account of the fall to the later prophets' references to the coming of the Redeemer. Bolingbroke, Hervey argues, writes history in the same way as a charlatan would give a lecture on anatomy without dealing with the nerves, the muscles and the heart. He also compares him to a map-maker who leaves out all the rivers, towns and cities.

### Scripture endures the gaze of critics

Hervey's conclusion is that the pages of Scripture not only endure the test of critics such as Bolingbroke but would appear to improve under the trial as any open consideration of their testimony can only end in an impression of their high value both as a historical document and a manual of right conduct. Hervey proclaims himself thankful for the energies the nobleman has spent on denouncing the Scriptures as, in examining Bolingbroke's complaints, Hervey has found new treasures in the Word of God. In closing, Hervey does not fight shy of applying the truths of the Scriptures to the spiritual needs of his hearers as he concludes his historical discussion which, in reality, all along, was a message designed to awake a lively hope and trust in the Lord Jesus Christ.

## Keeping the Christian Sabbath holy

After tackling Bolingbroke, Hervey went on to promote Sabbath keeping amongst his readers by writing *Considerations on the Prevailing Custom of Visiting on Sundays*. Hervey was accused by his Wesleyan friends of being an Antinomian because he stressed that the Christian was not under the law but under grace and that Christ's obedience to the law was imputed to the believer. They concluded, quite contrary to the Scriptures, reason and Hervey's own testimony, that those who held such views had no interest in performing good works and upholding the sanctity of the law. Hervey believed that he was not saved by good works but saved to do good works. He also believed strongly in the Christian's duty of strict Sunday observance. He believed that Sunday had become the seventh day to Christians through Christ being raised on that day and the early church's setting that day apart for their Sabbath remembrance. To Hervey the fact that the Sabbath was a memorial day, part of the eternal covenant, not just the covenant of works, and a pointer to the Christian's eternal rest to come, made it an ordinance of the Church to be observed with particular devotion. For him, the Sabbath embraced both law and gospel, pointing to its original institution in time before the fall and to the full restitution of the people of God in their resurrection life. Indeed, it was customary in the preaching of eighteenth century Evangelicals to emphasise that the Sabbath was an ordinance practised from before the fall to the giving of the law under Moses. They pointed out, for instance, that Moses forbade the gathering of manna on the Sabbath before the ceremonial law was given. It was also usual for them to argue from their understanding of Scripture, that the original Sabbath day was the same day as the Christian Sabbath. The original creation Sabbath was altered after the Jews left Egypt and made the Saturday in the ceremonial law.[1] They could thus argue that Christ lay in the grave on the Jewish Sabbath but was raised on the original creation Sabbath.

---

[1]    See, for instance, William Romaine's sermon on Exodus 31:12-14, Sermon IV in his *Works*.

### Talking vanity with one's neighbour rather than sharing fellowship with God

If one had visited Hervey's home whilst he was rector of Collingtree on a Sunday, he would have probably found the house empty as every person able to walk out of the house, be it a family member or a servant, would be at church. Thus no cooking was done and no household chores performed apart from those pertaining to the bare necessities of hygiene and health. Once a neighbour, a would-be Sabbath visitor, sent along a side of venison with the promise that he was following it in time for the Sunday dinner. He was no doubt surprised to read Hervey's quick reply informing him that no meat could be dressed on the Sabbath and it would be thus better if his friend delayed the visit until the afternoon, obviously giving the gentleman the opportunity to have a cooked meal at home before visiting Hervey.

Hervey viewed the 'polite' and 'people of quality' of his day as the chief profaners of the Sabbath. Sunday had become their day of social visiting, parties, picnics and entertainment. Hervey was no legalist in these matters. If all these occasions had been used to honour Christ and spread the knowledge of Him abroad, Hervey argued, he would have had no complaint. He, however, knew human nature all too well and, backed by Psalm 12:2, he complained that 'They talk of vanity every one with his neighbour.' This, to Hervey, was dishonouring the day God had specially given His creation for the purpose of fellowship with Him.

In his *Considerations on the Prevailing Custom of Visiting on Sundays*, Hervey shows how remembering the Sabbath includes keeping it holy which does not mean seeking one's own pleasure outside of Christ. He quotes Isaiah 58:13,14 to back up his argument, 'If thou turn away thy foot from the sabbath, from doing thy pleasure on my holy day; and call the sabbath a delight, the holy of the Lord, honourable; and shalt honour him, not doing thine own ways, nor finding thine own pleasure, nor speaking thine own words: Then shalt thou delight thyself in the Lord; and I will cause thee to ride upon the high places of the earth, and feed thee with the heritage of Jacob thy father: for the mouth of the Lord hath spoken it.' To those who ask what harm is done through engaging in trivial pursuits and entertaining relaxation, Hervey asks them if they are really saying that at times one must take a holiday from active Christian service. 'True refreshment for the soul,' he tells his readers, 'consists in having our faith increased, our hope elevated, and our views of heaven enlarged; in contemplating the infinite perfection and glory of our Redeemer, the infinite grandeur and fulness of his propitiation, and our complete, I might have said our infinite security from wrath and vengeance, by being interested in his merits.'

**Excuses for misusing the Sabbath met**

To those who argue that Sunday is the 'best part of their time' for
visiting, Hervey argues that they ought to dedicate the best part of their
time to the best of Beings. He tells those who say that Sunday visiting is a
sociably accepted convention, indeed, 'the done thing', that they ought to
try being a little unconventional for Christ's sake who died in a most unconventional way for their sakes. Nor is Hervey much impressed by the
complaint that life would be irksome and dull without Sunday pastimes
and entertainment and Christian life would become a burden. Quoting
Malachi 1:13, Amos 8:5 and Psalm 54:10, Hervey shows how such thinking is from a mind alienated from God. Rather should he say of keeping
the Sabbath, 'One day thus employed is better than a thousand.' Those
people who find the Sabbath irksome would find Heaven eternally irksome as, 'In the regions of immortality they (true Christians) find a heaven,
because there they have an uninterrupted and everlasting Sabbath.'

Hervey rarely entertained any political thoughts and there is little in
his letters which might reflect the political nature of Britain at the time.
One exception Hervey made was concerning the laws governing penalties
for the profanation of the Sabbath. In Hervey's day, anyone found doing
business on the Sabbath, no matter how seemingly helpful this was, as for
instance the work of a barber, were liable to a fine of five shillings or two
hours in the stocks. Public houses breaking the law would lose their licences. Anyone found selling goods on the streets or loitering outside
when services were in progress would have their goods confiscated or
fined five shillings as the case may have been. Public houses and inns
which allowed gambling on the Sabbath were fined ten shillings. Hervey
found it wrong that these laws were relaxed and even ignored by the mag-
istrates of his day and said, 'It is a pity that these (laws) should be unknown to the common people; and still a greater pity, that our justices of
peace should not exert themselves vigorously in an affair of such consequence to the present and eternal welfare of their fellow-creatures. I wish
a spirited pamphlet was judiciously drawn up and published on this occasion; setting the sins of omission in a true light. It grieves me to think how
much good might be done, especially by gentlemen who have leisure and
abilities to plan schemes for the public benefit; but so far are they from
applying themselves in good earnest to promote religion, that they too
generally ridicule or discourage any attempts of this kind. Ah! how little
do they reflect, that the night is coming on apace, when no man can work,
John ix. 4.; and that for all these things God will bring them into judgment.'[1]

---

[1]    *Works*, Letter CXCIII.

## Home schooling for ladies of society

The lack of obvious holiness in the lives of many Christians troubled Hervey greatly so he began work on a supplementary volume to his *Theron and Aspasio* on personal holiness and sanctification. Part of this book was to be dedicated to the fair sex who were permanently shut out from the academic and therefore theological world of his day. Many girls were not even allowed to partake in the basic education enjoyed by their brothers. Hervey, like Cowper after him, was convinced that it was inhuman to neglect the education of girls and women, which, to him, meant education in the nurture and admonition of the Lord. By dedicating several works to lady-friends and writing hundreds of doctrinal letters to ladies of all walks of life, Hervey strove to fulfil a pastor's and Christian's responsibility to make sure that those neglected in spiritual matters might learn the ways of holiness without which no person shall see the Lord, whether male or female. The only part of the planned supplement to be published was Hervey's *Treatise on the Religious Education of Daughters* which he based on Proverbs 22:6, rendered by him as, 'Train up a child in the way *she* should go, and when *she* is old, *she* will not depart from it.'[1]

## Education opens the door to religion

Rather than believe the old adage that education shows religion the door, Hervey depicts the epoch-making discoveries and feats of intelligence and learning that Biblical characters and Christians through the ages have been empowered to perform. Indeed, Hervey says he is staying at the house of one of these intellectual giants of the faith whilst writing these very lines. Hervey goes on to describe how this secularly employed man leads family evening worship at which no family member or servant is absent. Males and females, whatever their state, are taught to read the Scriptures and take part in the devotions and then Hervey's friend, whom he calls Camillus for anonymity's sake, 'explains, applies, and affectionately urges upon their consciences' the Word of God which has been read. The servants and children especially are now coached in making preparations for the morning prayers of the following day when they will be required to show what they have learnt. In this way the whole household learns to read, be articulate, train the memory and be educated in the most important things of life. In particular Camillus has the education of his two daughters at heart over which he presides with the eye and ear of a true pedagogue. Hervey, as always, is writing with the gentry in view and

---

[1]    This is not a bending of the original to serve a didactic purpose as, according to Gesenius and Wigram, the word for child in the context is used in the O.T. for a female child or girl though the 'masculine' form is used.

is gently hinting that those fathers that pamper their sons in matters of learning but neglect their daughters are neither acting intelligently nor in a Christian way.

## A surprising piece of broad-mindedness

Surprisingly enough, Hervey approves of his friend taking his daughters to the theatre on odd occasions and having them taught to dance. This is because he knows that what one has not experienced in social life always seems better from the distance of no experience and, after visiting the plays, Camillus discusses intensively their pros and cons with his daughters, comparing what they have seen with the Christian life they themselves lead. The dancing steps they learn is to teach them correct carriage and pose but not to shine at a ball and learn to tempt the coxcombs. This may all seem naive to some readers and even worldly to others but if one compares this to a modern school curriculum in which the most disgusting works are put on the syllabus and perhaps never discussed by Christian parents with their children, Camillus' methods may not seem too impractical. Whoever has seen their budding-adult daughters forced to wrestle, lightly clad, in various ways with the boys as part of so-called Physical Training, may wonder whether Camillus did not provide a more practical physical training for his girls and the modern co-ed fanatics are the naive ones.

## Teaching girls what the boys were never taught

Camillus' daughters are also taught the classics, poetry, world history, geography, zoology and biology alongside their Bibles, subjects still unknown in most boys'-schools of the day. This is to show them how Providence works in creation and how Christian responsibility should be used to meet the problems and cares of the world to which they are called as stewards. The present school curriculum throughout Europe, including Britain, has almost forgotten that poetry and classical literature exist. History, and, indeed, literature in general, are almost solely related to the home country. Geography has become limited to commerce and trade and political ethics is taught as a feeble imitation of basic Christian responsibility to God, mankind, nature and true religion. Zoology and biology, if taught, are more designed to convince the students that life is a means of mechanics caused by chemistry rather than a living creation of God. There was no such narrow-mindedness in the eighteenth century educational reforms implemented by a growing number of evangelicals. A marked feature of the new interest in home schooling today is that the curriculum has broadened out no end and methods are being used that remind one of the enlightened educational views of a Hervey, Ryland, Doddridge, Cowper or Adam Smith rather than the politico-educational theories which led to the dubious teaching reforms of the early 1960s to late 1980s.

**Learning by experience**

Learning by doing and learning by playing are two major factors in Camillus' curriculum for his daughters in which he does not neglect their creativity in practical craftsmanship, language training and elocution. The girls are taught mathematics by managing the everyday financial affairs of a large household and trained in responsibility by their father's committing to them sums of money for the regulating of these affairs. Though still of what is commonly called 'school age' the girls are now able to take on responsibility for managing the tenant's accounts on their father's estate, trained not to neglect generosity to the poorer tenants in exercising that function.

Camillus' daughters are encouraged and coaxed to learn rather than drilled and they are taught to organise their own time for study, recreation and relaxation. Much of their leisure time, however, is taken up by visiting and caring for the needy or reading entertaining and instructive books such as those of Samuel Richardson whose works, especially *Clarissa* are happily still on school and university curricula today. When the girls were obviously in danger of putting good looks and fine dress before good sense and a fine character, Camillus did not give his girls a severe generation-gap dressing down but helped them to their senses in a way that made them fully conscious of both the fault and how to amend it. He presented each of his daughters with a decorative knife with handles of ivory and blades of glass, covered in dazzling coloured decorations. The girls were delighted with the pretty gifts. Camillus then gave the girls an orange apiece and said they could try out their new knives. To the dismay of the girls, the knives could not cut through the skin of the fruit. Their father then gave them two ordinary knives with sharp metal blades which did what they were designed to do at great speed. The point was soon applied and the girls realised that God would have them to be useful in this world rather than merely be decorative and that if they wished to be respected by others and their names blessed, it would be by helping in a practical way rather than dazzling their neighbours.

Blood sports were almost the chief occupation of the gentry in Hervey's days, rivalled only by card-playing and other time-killers. Camillus was no hunter for sport's sake and encouraged his daughters to see all animals and even insects as living, feeling beings, capable of experiencing both pain and joy. Thus the girls should follow their own Creator's example whose 'tender mercies are over all his works'. To this end, Camillus equipped his children with microscopes to help them become aware of the beauties and intricacies of nature. In this way they discover that life-forms which they had thought common and contemptible will display great complexity of design and beauty. They will also see that if they study the varnish and carvings of human works of art under the microscope, they will see nothing but scratches and rough hewn designs.

190 _James Hervey_

**'More desirable partners the heart of man cannot wish'**
In all these educational reforms, Hervey was years before his time. Indeed, it is most uncertain whether times have caught up with Hervey yet. This is all frankly and humbly recognised in Hervey's treatise. The two young ladies enjoyed an education which few boys of their age had even dreamed could be possible and it troubled Camillus greatly when suitors started appearing who praised the beauty and vivaciousness of the girls, being in no way competent themselves to comment on their learning, education and knowledge of the Lord. This worry was deepened when ladies of fashion told Camillus that he had spoilt his girls and robbed them of their pride and fondness of pleasure which was essential to a lady of fashion. Hervey closes his treatise by saying 'more desirable partners the heart of man cannot wish.' We trust that those most desirable young ladies eventually found partners worthy of them.

**Visiting widows in affliction**
The next short work in the standard editions of Hervey's collected writings is his _Preface to Burnham's Pious Memorials_, already mentioned. The author begins with a fine definition of all that makes life purposeful and the means of attaining to it:

> Religion, or an affectionate and firm connexion of the soul with God, is the highest improvement of the human mind, and the brightest ornament of the rational nature. It is the most indissoluble bond of civil society, and the only foundation of happiness to every individual person.
>
> The gospel, by which we have access to the King immortal, invisible, through the merits of Jesus Christ; by which we are conformed to his amiable and holy image, through the operations of the blessed Spirit—the gospel is, of all other religions, most exquisitely adapted to compass those desirable ends.

Hervey explains how these truths are clearly outlined in the work he is prefacing through the consecrated lives and death-bed testimonies of men of God from Ignatius to Dr. Watts depicted in it. Here are histories proving fact mightier than fiction as they are not only true accounts but the finest examples of fortitude, rational tranquillity and well-grounded hope in the face of death afforded by the Holy Spirit through divine propitiation and the power of Christ's righteousness. Here is portrayed concrete testimony of the power of God in Christian lives which is able to keep them from falling in spite of their own weak and feeble natures. They show how God can remove the sting of death from the most fearful saint and equip him with unfeigned faith and vital holiness.

Before anyone begins to think that such pious lives have nothing to do with him, Hervey reminds his readers that they have something very much in common with the future of these saints as they, too, must die. How to die well, is thus the theme of the book; a theme anyone would neglect at his peril.

### Recommending Marshall on Sanctification

Hervey was never tired of recommending Marshall's *Gospel Mystery of Sanctification*. When he realised that death was near and he would never be able to write the fourth volume on holiness which he had planned for his *Theron and Aspasio*, Hervey advised his publisher to append Marshall to his work with the argument that; 'Mr Marshall expresses my thoughts; he prosecutes my scheme; and not only pursues the same end, but proceeds in the same way.' Both Marshall and Hervey have been criticised for seeing holiness as God's sovereign work in man rather than man's exercise of his Christian duties, as if these aspects had nothing to do with each other. The two Bible scholars knew of no such teaching but saw the Christian's awareness of his responsibility to live righteously as growing from God's sovereign work in him. To them, the Christian who did not believe that his calling was to 'labour to enter into this rest, and allow all diligence to the full assurance of hope,' was a sham. In order to limit any misunderstanding which may arise from presenting Hervey's views of Marshall on this very sensitive subject in words which are not his own, and recognising that few could put doctrine so succinctly as Hervey, it is necessary to quote him at length verbatim from his *Marshall Recommended*:

> Mr. Marshall represents true holiness as consisting in the love of God, and the love of man; that unforced, unfeigned, and most rational love of God, which arises from a discovery of his unspeakable mercy and infinite kindness to us; that cordial, disinterested, and universal love of man which flows from the possession of a satisfactory and delightful portion in the Lord Jehovah. These duties of love to our Creator and our fellow-creatures are regarded as the sum and substance of the moral law; as the root from which all other branches of pure and undefiled religion spring. Holiness thus stated, is considered not as the means, but as a part, a distinguished part, of our salvation; or rather as the very central point in which all the means of grace, and all the ordinances of religion, terminate.
>
> Man, in a natural state, is absolutely incapable of practising this holiness, or enjoying this happiness. If you ask, What is meant by a *natural state*? It is that state in which we are under the guilt of sin and the curse of the law, are subject to the power of Satan, and

influenced by evil propensities. From this state none are released,
but by being united to Christ ; or, as the apostle speaks, by 'Christ
dwelling in the heart through faith.' Eph. iii. 17.

Faith, according to Mr. Marshall, is a real persuasion that God
is pleased to give Christ and his salvation; to give him freely, without any recommending qualifications, or preparatory conditions;
to give him, not to some sinners only, but to *me* a sinner in particular. It is likewise an actual receiving of Christ, with all the benefits,
privileges, and promises of the gospel; in pursuance of the divine
gift, and on no other warrant than the divine grant. This last office
is particularly insisted on, as an essential part, or as the principal
act of faith; to perform which there is no rational, no possible way,
unless, as our author declares, we do in some measure persuade
and assure ourselves that Christ and his salvation are ours.

As faith is such a persuasion of the heart, and such a reception
of Christ, it assures the soul of salvation by its own act, antecedent
to all reflection on its fruits or effects, on marks or evidences. It
assures the soul of acquittance from guilt and reconciliation to God;
of a title to the everlasting inheritance; and of grace sufficient for
every case of need. By the exercise of this faith, and the enjoyment
of these blessings, we are sanctified; conscience is pacified, and
the heart purified; we are delivered from the dominion of sin, disposed to holy tempers, and furnished for an holy practice.

Here, I apprehend, our author will appear singular; this is the
place in which he seems to go quite out of the common road. The
generality of serious people look upon these unspeakable blessings as the reward of holiness, to be received after we have sincerely practised universal holiness; not as necessary, previously
necessary, to perform any act of true holiness. This is the stum-
bling-block which our legal minds, dim with prejudice, and swol-
len with pride, will hardly get over. However, these endowments of
our new state are, in our author's opinion the effectual, and the
only effectual expedient, to produce sanctification. They are the
very method which the eternal Spirit has ordained, for our bringing
forth those 'fruits of righteousness which are by Jesus Christ unto
the glory and praise of God,' Phil. i. 11. Whereas, if there be any
appearances of virtue, or any efforts of obedience, which spring
not from these motives and means of practice, Mr. Marshall treats
them as 'reprobate silver'; he cannot allow them the character of
gospel holiness.

This is the plan, and these are the leading sentiments of the
ensuing treatise. To establish or defend them, is not my aim. This is
attempted, and I think executed, in the work itself. My aim is, only

to exhibit the most distinguishing principles in one sketch and clear point of view, that the reader may the more easily remember them, and by this key enter the more perfectly into the writer's meaning. Let him that is *spiritual* (I Cor. ii. 15,) judge, and reject or admit, as each tenet shall appear to correspond or disagree with the infallible word. Only let candour, not rigour, fill the chair; and interpret an unguarded expression, or a seemingly inconsistent sentence, by the general tenor of the discourse.

We are not to expect much pathos of address, or any delicacy of composition. Here the gospel diamond is set, not in gold, but in steel—not where it may display the most sprightly beam, or pour a flood of brilliancy, but where it may do the most signal service, and afford a fund of usefulness. Neither is this book so particularly calculated for careless insensible sinners, as for those who are awakened into a solicitous attention to their everlasting interests, who are earnestly inquiring, with the Philippian jailer, 'What shall I do to be saved?' Rom. viii. 24 or passionately crying, in the language of the apostle, 'O wretched man that I am who shall deliver me from the body of this death?' Rom. vii. 24. If there be any such, as no doubt there are many in the Christian world, I would say, with regard to them, as the Israelitish captive said concerning her illustrious but afflicted master, 'Would God my master were with the prophet in Samaria for he would recover him of his leprosy,' II Kings v. 3. O that such persons were acquainted with the doctrines, and influenced by the directions, contained in this treatise! They would, under the divine blessing, recover them from their distress, and restore them to tranquillity; they would 'comfort their hearts, and thereby establish them in every good word and work.' II Thess. ii. 17.

### Theron and Aspasio

All Hervey's life up to his conversion can be summed up under the title 'self-righteousness'. All Hervey's life after conversion both in his teaching and actions was a life of humble and holy thankfulness to Christ for placing His righteousness at man's service and thus providing a means of communion for man with his holy God who will not look on unrighteousness. For Hervey, as he says in his Dedication to Lady Francis Shirley in his greatest work *Theron and Aspasio*, 'To be reconciled to the omnipotent God; to be interested in the unsearchable riches of Christ; to be renewed in our hearts, and influenced in our lives, by the sanctifying operations of the Spirit—this is evangelical righteousness; this is genuine religion.' Thus the main theme of *Theron and Aspasio* is the main theme of Hervey's redeemed life—the imputed righteousness of Christ.

**Modern readers' difficulties with *Theron and Aspasio***

This three-volumed work may not be to every reader's taste, although it remained one of the best selling set of books in the kingdom for well over a hundred years; a success equalled by very few. There are a number of features, however, which might render the book less palatable for modern readers. First, there is its length. Anything that runs into volumes sells badly nowadays and multi-volumed books of an instructive nature have become an absolute rarity. A bedside 'who-done-it?' of a mere two hundred pages seems to sum up the maximum workload of a modern average reader.

Then there is the scholarly depth of the work. It was written at a time when knowledge of classical literature and languages was more widespread than today. In Hervey's day, even Dissenting colleges expected their pupils and students to debate publicly on Hebrew and Greek literature in Latin and even compose original works in these languages. Happily for us, most of Hervey's comments on Hebrew, Greek and Latin texts are placed in lengthy footnotes and though today's generation might know little of the writings of 300 B.C. to 300 A.D., our public libraries and many homes include informative and compact encyclopaedias on their shelves which quickly convey the necessary information to understand Hervey fully.

The story of Theron and Aspasio might put others off by the way it is told. At first sight, it seems to be lacking in any form of a plot or rational scheme or plan. The work is really a collection of seventeen dialogues and twelve letters which seem as if they have been penned as the ideas arose. In one way, this is perfectly true as the dialogues are the conversational records of two good friends as they visit each other at their country seats. Though the framework is imaginary, much of the contents are faithful records of actual conversations and experiences Hervey has had over the years as witnessed by his letters and earlier works. Aspasio is obviously Hervey himself.

**Parallels with *Theron and Aspasio* in contemporary literature**

The account begins with Theron's arrival at Aspasio's mansion and a long after-dinner conversation which is continued during a walk in the park after breakfast on the following day. The outings, country walks and fire-side chats form the basis of the ensuing dialogues. The letters represent the correspondence of the two companions when separated by business or whilst visiting other friends. Here we see parallels in other great eighteenth century literary works such as in Young's *Night Thoughts*, Thomson's *The Seasons* and Cowper's *Task*. It is interesting to note that Hervey, called the Poet of Prose, had such close affinities with these major poets. In prose realms, we find similarities in the works of Jonathan Swift (1667-1745), Laurence Sterne (1713-68) and the so-called stream of consciousness writers. Readers familiar with the works of Izaak Walton (1593-1683), especially his *Contemplative Man's Recreation,* better known as *The Complete Angler*[1] will see a kindred method in Hervey's writings. A near resemblance to the style and composition of *Theron and Aspasio* can be found in the works of clergyman Gilbert White of Selborne (1720-93), who gives his books the framework of a naturalist's diary and letters.[2] Hervey, too, takes on the role of a chronicler, diary-keeper and letter-writer, describing thoughts as they enter the mind or recording events as they present themselves to the senses. In *Theron and Aspasio,* the reader is treated with a wide variety of literary genres, including narrative description, scientific records, inner monologue, anecdotes, autobiography, eye-witness reports, pen-portraits, short stories, sermons, linguistic studies, nature portrayals, journals, poetry and hymns. There is also much in the work that is reminiscent of a modern film-script. This makes the work many-sided and never monotonous but as the genre changes from page to page, it is certainly not the kind of work that can be read easily at one sitting. A welcome side-line to lovers of the Scriptures in the volumes are excellent expositions of some three hundred and fifty Bible texts, most editions listing all the references with their pagination.

### Nature as the handmaid of God pointing to a need for the Word of God

The main framework of *Theron and Aspasio* is perhaps the most foreign to the modern reader. Though some Christian writers such as Walton and White seldom dwell on the theological in their pastoral tales, this was far from typical for the period. Hervey gently sets his theological discussion against the background of the splendours, beauties and orderly patterns of nature. He sees nature as the hand-maid of God to aid the observer in his spiritual contemplation and instil in him a longing to find more about nature's Creator in the Word of God. One might say that this was the general pattern of evangelical writers of the eighteenth century, a good number of whom reached national and international fame in literary circles. One only has to think of Thomas Parnell's *Night-Piece,* Robert Blair's *Grave,* Edward Young's *Night Thoughts,* James Thomson's *Seasons,* William Cowper's *Task* and the works of John Byrom, Moses Brown and John Newton.[3] Critics usually include Thomas Gray (1716-1771) in this

---

[1]   First published 1653. One of the very best of nature and especially piscatorial books, perhaps the most often reprinted of its kind.

[2]   The letters were real, being sent to naturalists Thomas Pennant and Daines Barrington who returned them so that White could use them in his works.

[3]   Their dates are: Parnell (1679-1718), Blair (1699-1746), Young (1683-1765), Thomson (1700-1748), Cowper (1731-1800), Byrom (1692-1763), Brown (1704-1787), Newton (1725-1807).

circle because of his *Elegy Written in a Country Churchyard*, though his works do not reflect the spiritual depth of, say, Young and Hervey. Nevertheless, those who only see graveyard melancholy, rather than the spiritual thoughts it ought to engender in the soul, identify these two evangelicals with Gray and say with that critic of all things Christian, William Kenrick (c1725-1779):

> 'Twas thus enthusiastic Young;
> 'Twas thus affected Hervey sung;
> Whose motley muse, in florid strain,
> With owls did to the moon complain.[1]

William Cowper gives a more balanced picture as he preaches from earthly to heavenly themes in his poem *Hope*:

> The just Creator condescends to write
> In beams of inextinguishable light,
> His names of wisdom, goodness, pow'r and love,
> On all that blooms below or shines above,
> To catch the wand'ring notice of mankind,
> And teach the world, if not perversely blind,
> His gracious attributes, and prove the share
> His offspring hold in his paternal care.
> If led from earthly things to things divine,
> His creature thwart not his august design,
> Then praise is heard instead of reas'ning pride,
> And captious cavil and complaint subside.
> Nature employ'd in her allotted place,
> Is hand-maid to the purposes of grace,
> By good vouchsaf'd makes known superior good,
> And bliss not seen by blessings understood.[2]

### Man is God's under-gardener and steward of the earth

Christian poets in the eighteenth century looked upon man as being the essential element in nature, in deep empathy with it. Their more secular fellow-poets looked on nature as if it were a thing apart. The poet was not one with nature, but an observer standing aside. The great poet Alexander Pope (1688-1744), for instance, could write his *Pastorals* without projecting himself into what he was describing. Much modern so-called 'green' thinking is of this kind. Man is portrayed as being at enmity with nature

---

[1]    Fairchild's *Religious Trends, Wits and Scoffers*, p. 43.

[2]    Lines 133-148.

and a foreign body amongst the flora and fauna. If nature is to survive, they argue, it must be left alone by man who has no business with it. The eighteenth century Christian writers saw man not only as the crown of nature but nature's chief steward whose God-given task it was to restore in nature, as in man, what sin had marred. This oneness of man with nature and God's overall purpose for His people is quite lost to Hervey's third and latest major biographer Luke Tyerman. This writer sees Hervey falling at times between two stools. He believes he has written a nature story *and* a theological treatise and, although both are written well, they obstruct and collide with each other. If the reader, however, sees the book of nature as a pictorial, but nevertheless factual, illustration of God at work in his entire creation, he will be able to understand Hervey all the better when he turns to his teaching concerning God's two covenants with man as revealed in the Bible. Any reader who fails to bear this in mind will most likely be put off by what must appear to be abrupt breaks between theological thinking and monologues in praise of nature. Hervey would have argued that such abrupt breaks were in the mind of the reader and a true hindrance to learning from both the Word of God and the Book of Nature.

Such thoughts were fully acceptable to the general reader in Hervey's day. Indeed, writing a hundred years later, Luke Tyerman could still say of Hervey, 'few books have passed through more editions than his have done; and after the lapse of a hundred years since their author's death few are greater favourites at the present day.'[1] The great change in literary appreciation, or rather the great decline, came in the twentieth century so that a hundred years on after Tyerman's confession that Hervey had enjoyed a century of being a best-seller, Laurence Porter writes, obviously with regret, in his bi-centenary article, 'Hervey of course falls strangely on our ears, but we of the age of atom bombs and man-made moons cannot capture the impressions made on contemporary ears by the *Meditations* and *Theron and Aspasio*.'[2]

### The main characters of the books presented as the story opens

Theron is a naturalist, scientist and God-fearer but he uses the arguments of the Socinians and Deists. He is too cock-sure by far in his trust in his own 'ethics of a true gentleman' and there is obviously one thing lacking in his life. This is an awareness of how Christ has wrought out salvation and how this applies to him personally. His much older friend Aspasio is also well-qualified in the sciences and natural history but he has learnt

---

[1]   Rev. James Hervey, M. A. Parish-Priest, *The Oxford Methodists*, New York, 1873, p. 201.

[2]   James Hervey (1714-1758): A Bicentenary Appreciation, *Evangelical Quarterly*, 31, 1959, p. 13.

to love the Word of God, the study of which, in his retirement, has now become his major occupation. After the first evening meal of Theron's visit to Aspasio's, he comments admiringly on the guests who have just left. Aspasio agrees with his friend but surprises him by saying that he missed conversation on higher things. Aspasio skilfully steers the conversation into literature and the various genres in the Word of God with its heroic poetry and dramatic performances and the conversation begins to centre around the 'magazine of nature' and the 'book of Scripture' and their complimentary messages. By the second day Theron is admitting with Aspasio how nature is ever labouring to serve man and provide him with all that he needs for his bodily care. This gives Aspasio the lead he has been waiting for and he tells Theron of the economy of redemption:

> Even the Son of the most high God, through all his incarnate state acted the very same part. He took flesh, and bore the infirmities of human nature, not for himself, but for us men, and our salvation. He suffered want and endured misery in all its forms, that we might possess the fulness of joy, and abound in pleasures for ever more. When he poured out his soul in agonies, under the curse of an avenging law, was it not with a compassionate view to make us partakers of eternal blessedness? When he fulfilled, perfectly fulfilled the whole commanding law, was it not for this gracious purpose that his merits might be imputed to us, that we by his obedience might be made righteous? Yes;
> ... For us he liv'd,
> Toil'd for our ease, and for our safety bled.

### Theron thinks the doctrine of imputation is ridiculous

Theron interrupts Aspasio here to tell him that the doctrine of imputed righteousness is ridiculous. The older man then tells Theron that he, too, held the doctrine in contempt until God opened his eyes to his own sinful nature and ruined state and now he blesses God for this 'sovereign restorative' because nothing counts so little before God as our unrighteous deeds but nothing counts so much with him as the righteousness of Christ which he freely imputes to us. This doctrine is thus, he says, 'the source of my strongest consolations, and the very foundation of my eternal hope.' Theron cannot accept the fact that a person can do a thing on behalf of another, thus freeing the one assisted from his unfulfilled obligations and unpaid debts. Aspasio surprises him by arguing that this is what the gospel is all about. The sinner stands condemned because he has broken the law and is without righteousness. He has no justification before God because he has no holiness, but:

> Justification is an act of God Almighty's grace; whereby he acquits his people from guilt, and accounts them righteous, for the

sake of Christ's righteousness, which was wrought out for them, and he imputed to them.

Using the illustration of Paul and the rebel slave Onesimus in the epistle to Philemon, Aspasio shows how the one was ready to take over the entire debts of the other, saying, 'If he hath wronged thee, or oweth thee ought, put that on mine account.' Hervey can thus go on to argue:

> That which the zealous preacher of Christianity offered, the adored Author of Christianity executed.—We had revolted from the Lord of all lords, and broke his holy commandments. The Son of God, infinitely compassionate, vouchsafes to become our Mediator. That nothing might be wanting to render his mediation successful, he places himself in our stead. The punishment which we deserved, he endures: The obedience which we owed, he fulfils.— Both which, being imputed to us, and accepted for us, are the foundation of our pardon, are the procuring cause of our justification.

**Theron questions the Biblical doctrines of satisfaction and redemption**

The next conversation finds the two friends returning from a distant visit. As the weather is so fine, they decide to send their horses on with the servants and walk the last few miles home. Theron is so taken up with the scenery that he begins to quote from the Song of Solomon 'The winter is past; the rain is over and gone; The flowers appear on the earth; the time of the singing of birds is come; and the voice of the turtle is heard in our land; The fig-tree putteth forth her green figs, and the vine with the tender grapes, give a good smell.'[1] Aspasio is quick to point out that all the beauties of nature, as testified by the rural scenery depicted in such works is a pointer to its Creator Jesus Christ who is the fairest of ten thousand. Theron is prepared to accept that nature testifies to a Creator and the Scriptures lead to moral improvement but he is sceptical of the satisfaction and redemption which Christ is supposed to work out in our stead as he finds them against the dictates of reason and perfections of God. Their conversation continues:

> **Aspasio:** Let gentlemen be candid in their inquiries, and truly liberal in their way of thinking; then, I flatter myself, these scruples may be removed without much difficulty.
>
> God, the almighty Creator and supreme Governor of the world, having made man, gave him a law, with a penalty annexed in case of disobedience. This sacred Law our forefather Adam presumptuously broke; and we, his posterity, were involved in his guilt. Or,

---

[1]   Song of Solomon, 2:11-13.

should that point be controverted, we have undeniably made, by
many personal transgressions, his apostasy our own; insomuch that
all have sinned, have forfeited their happiness, and rendered themselves obnoxious to punishment.

Man being thus ruined, none could recover him, except his injured Maker. But shall he be recovered, shall he be restored, without suffering the punishment due to his crime, and threatened by
his Creator? What then will become of the justice of the divine
Lawgiver? and how shall the honour of his holy law be maintained?
At this rate, who would reverence its authority, or fear to violate its
precepts? Sinners might be emboldened to multiply their transgressions, and tempted to think, that the God of immaculate holiness,
the God of unchangeable veracity, is 'altogether such an one as
themselves.' Does it not appear needful, that some expedient be
devised, in order to prevent these dishonourable and horrid consequences?

**Theron:** Proceed to inform us what the expedient is.

**Aspasio:** To ascertain the dignity of the supreme administration,
yet rescue mankind from utter destruction, this admirable purpose
was formed, and in the fulness of time executed. The second person of the ever-blessed Trinity unites the human nature to the divine, submits himself to the obligations of his people, and becomes
responsible for all their guilt. In this capacity he performs a perfect
obedience, and undergoes the sentence of death; makes a full expiation of their sins, and establishes their title to life. By which
means the law is satisfied, justice is magnified, and the richest grace
exercised. Man enjoys a great salvation, not to the discredit of any,
but to the unspeakable glory of all, the divine attributes.

This is what we mean by Christ's satisfaction. And this, I should
imagine, wants no recommendation to our unprejudiced reason; as
I am sure it is most delightfully accommodated to our distressed
condition. It is also confirmed by many express passages of Scripture, and illustrated by a variety of very significant images.

**Union with Christ the key to the doctrine of imputation**

Theron demands Scriptural proof for this exegesis and Aspasio leads
him on to consider passages such as 'The Son of Man came not to be
ministered unto but to minister; and to give his life a ransom for many.'
Mark 10:45, backing this up with 1 Peter 1:18,19, 1 Corinthians 6:20 and
Galatians 3:13. Knowing that the Grotian and Latitudinarian view had
infiltrated evangelicalism, Hervey stresses in a footnote that this ransom
is in no way metaphorical or 'as if' because the Scriptures stress that this
is a fulfilment of prophecy and the price that Christ actually paid is actually stated. Against this, Theron objects, arguing that the price could have

only been paid to the devil, which is a preposterous idea. Aspasio corrects his friend, quoting Revelation 5:9, 'Thou hast redeemed us to God,' showing how satisfaction was made to the divine law which had been offended and to the divine justice which had been violated, both these factors having concurred to pronounce the transgressor's doom should not God intervene.

Theron still cannot understand how God can treat a man as righteous when he is nothing of the kind. He argues that sins can neither be transferred to Christ, nor righteousness to man. Aspasio explains how Theron does not considers man's oneness with Adam nor redeemed man's oneness with Christ. He thus outlines the Scriptural doctrine of union with Christ which answers the problem of how God can view the redeemed sinner as if he had never sinned:

> For Christ and his people are actually considered as one and the same person. They are one mystical body; he the head, they the members; so intimately united to him, that they are 'bone of his bone, and flesh of his flesh,' (Eph. 5:30; Col. 1:20.) by virtue of which union, their sins were punished in him, 'and by his stripes they are healed,' (Isa. 53:5.) they obtain impunity and life.

Thus, in the work of redemption, God was in Christ reconciling the world to Himself 2 Corinthians 5:19 i.e. not to some third party, and certainly not to the devil!

### What has happened to the believer's sin?

Theron is far from being satisfied and still wants to know what has happened to the sin which must naturally separate man from God. Aspasio explains that the Biblical doctrine of sacrifice and atonement teach that the just penalty has been enacted in Christ's sufferings and death and the just obedience has been enacted in Christ's life lived on behalf of His people, enabling Him to present His people spotless before God. This is because, in God's atonement plan, it is possible for sin, when the correct satisfaction is given, to be completely covered (according to the root meaning of 'atonement'), and thus removed from its role under the covenant of works, making way for the covenant of grace. This new covenant sees no condemning sin in believers but recognises Christ's representation before the Mercy Seat (literally the covering seat) for us and deals with believers as fully acquitted and thus fully innocent. God refuses to hold anything against His elect.

### Theron sees Christ's sacrifice as a great example to be followed

In Dialogue IV, there is another delightful portrayal of appreciation of nature before Theron again takes on a doubting position. He still cannot

accept Aspasio's view of ransom and righteousness and confesses that to
him Christ's death was 'to confirm the truth of his doctrines, and leave us
a pattern of the most perfect resignation.' Aspasio protests that this pulls
Christ down to the level of the martyrs whose death was supposed to bring
them personal saving merit, but what about all the non-martyrs. Christ was
slain before the foundation of the world, thus gaining salvation for all His
people from the beginning of time until time ceases. Christ's blood was
not shed merely to give credibility to his gospel or provide an example of
complete resignation but it was shed for the remission of sins. Matthew
26:28. Again, this does not seem to move Theron who insists that 'It is
inconsistent with the acknowledged principles of justice, that the innocent
should be punished instead of the offender.' Aspasio guides Theron back
to the Word of God and says:

> The Bible, that authentic transcript of the counsels of heaven,
> avows, and by avowing, vindicates the practice, 'The Lord hath
> laid on him the iniquity of us all.' When all we like sheep had gone
> astray, and were exposed to the stroke of vengeance, as those wan-
> dering creatures to the ravenous beasts; the good shepherd inter-
> posed, and the just God made that vengeance to fall upon him,
> which must otherwise have been executed upon us. 'He suffered,'
> says one inspired writer, 'the just for the unjust,' that, by expiating
> our guilt, 'he might bring us to God;' now to his gracious favour,
> hereafter to his blissful presence.

### Theron cannot conceive of a Christ who lowers Himself for any purpose

Theron, always ready to extol the excellencies of Christ, cannot imagine that the Son of God could make himself so base as to suffer vicariously
for His people. The very idea of vicarious punishment in relation to Christ,
Theron argues, means that we have a mean and lowly view of Him. Needless to say, Aspasio shows how this very factor of Christ's humbling Himself to save us, proves the immeasurable depths of His perfect love towards us. This enhances Christ's greatness rather than subtracts from it.
Theron, however, does not accept the point but goes on to argue that guilt
cannot be vicariously transferred. He is again forgetting the doctrine of
union with Christ which is a great stumbling block for Socinians and Deists.
Aspasio also argues that Theron is begging the question. He is assuming a
proposition which involves the conclusion. One ought to ask what God
does, rather than say dogmatically, without evidence, what God cannot
do. Obviously, argues Aspasio, Christ carries no guilt in the sense of consciousness of having committed sin but He does voluntarily accept the
charge of criminal action on behalf of others and the obligation to suffer
their penalty. This is an acceptance of guilt. Thus, 'the Lord laid on him
the iniquities of us all.'

## Does God exercise vengeance on His own Son?

Now Theron begins to argue that in order to accept Aspasio's theology, we must presume that God is prepared to take vengeance and that on His own Son whereas God is all love. Aspasio rejects Theron's view of a God who is always amiable and tells him that this would not be in keeping with God's justice and, besides, Scripture tells us that, 'The wrath of God is revealed from heaven, upon all ungodliness and unrighteousness of men.' Romans 1:18, and 'Who can stand before his indignation? and who can abide in the fierceness of his anger?' Nahum 1:6.

It seems that Theron is influenced by the Baxterian view that God would suspend the legal requirements of the law and its condemnatory function in order to display his amiable nature and where else was this more appropriate than in the case of His Son? Theron thus finds it shocking that Aspasio should teach that Christ felt the full force of the broken law and God's wrath upon sinners. Aspasio reminds Theron of Gethsemene and asks him why Christ declared that his soul was 'sorrowful, exceedingly sorrowful—even unto death,' why Christ was in great anguish if there was no wrath to fear and no punishment to undergo. Subsequent events, of course, only underline the immensity of God's wrath so that even His Son thought Himself absolutely forsaken, sweating drops of blood in his sufferings.

## Theron's objections become less harsh

Gradually, we see a change in Theron's attitude. He still confesses that he cannot accept the doctrine of Christ's satisfaction but he does see its reasonableness, its cheering nature to the distressed sinner and how it can influence moral conduct. Aspasio is pleased at the confession but reminds his friend that, 'To deny the expiation made by our Redeemer's sacrifice, is to obscure the brightest manifestation of divine benignity, and to undermine the principal pillar of practical religion; it is to make a desperate shipwreck of our everlasting interests, and to dash (such, I fear, it will be found in the final issue of things) ourselves to death on the very rock of salvation.'

## He begins to concede to truths of the gospel

In Dialogue V, we find Theron morose and argumentative. Those who counsel sinners welcome such attacks as they often show that the Word is taking effect on the soul and natural man is making his last stand before being defeated by the grace of God. Aspasio, skilled in these matters, is not ruffled by Theron's outbursts but grows more optimistic that his friend will also begin to yearn for the righteousness of Christ. Indeed, we soon hear Theron telling his friend that he accepts that Christ was punished in our stead and that His death worked the expiation of our sin through penal suffering but he cannot believe that our sins were imputed to Christ and His righteousness to us. Aspasio is now able to explain to Theron that the one doctrine depends on the other. No expiation without imputation, otherwise how could Christ have expiated our sins if our iniquities were not laid on Him and how could we be declared righteous if Christ's righteousness was not imputed to us and thus cause us to stand spotless before God? Aspasio then goes on, amid protests from Theron, to explain the Biblical doctrine of being, by imputation, in Adam as the federal head of mankind and being, by imputation, in Christ as the federal head of all the elect.

**The difference between imputation and inherence**
    Theron obviously understands imputation in terms of inherence alone. Aspasio explains the difference. Christ's inherent righteousness is the essence of our sanctification but this imputed to the sinner, is the ground of his justification. We are not justified through the deeds of the law which only Christ in His inherent righteousness could accomplish, but we are justified freely by His grace given to us on the basis of His fulfilling the law and bearing the penalties of a broken law on our behalf. This leaves Theron thinking that if all our debt has been paid, the believer is under no compulsion to live a life of righteousness and, if he does so, it is only out of his own generosity. Aspasio explains how faith is expressed in the words, 'What shall I render unto the Lord for all the benefits that he hath done unto me?' It incorporates good works as to this end the believer has been born again.[1] Those who do not live the practical life of faith do not belong to the Lord and will experience God's damning words, 'Depart from me, for I never knew you.' Matthew 7:23.

**Have all believers the same righteousness?**
    This gives Aspasio's friend food for thought and he now changes his tactic by arguing that if all believers in Christ are accounted righteous, then all have the same righteousness, yet the Scriptures teach various degrees of rewards in heaven which must be based on various standards of righteousness. Aspasio shows how all who are found in Christ are equally justified and it is the same righteousness that justifies them all. Thus, in respect to the privileges, there is no difference between babes, young men or fathers in Christ. As to a possible variety of rewards, Aspasio, never claiming to know everything, reflects Hervey here, who never came to a settled opinion as to possible degrees of future glory. He feels, however, that he can confidently leave such matters to the One who, 'meteth out the heavens with a span, and setteth a compass upon the face of the deep.' Meanwhile, he advises Theron that we ought to be practising the faith

---

[1]    See Titus 3:8, Psalm 116:12 and Ephesians 2:10.

which 'purifies the heart, overcomes the world and sets its affections on things above' and presses Theron to anchor his soul on the Rock of Ages.

## Motives for learning and the pursuit of virtue

Dialogue VI opens with Aspasio's return-visit to Theron's country seat where their discussion continue in the well-stocked library which also displays Theron's architectural blue-prints and models. Aspasio praises the combination of usefulness and beauty in Theron's works. Theron confesses that all his work is dedicated to virtue and the improvement of morals and introduces his eldest son, Eugenio, to Aspasio who is also something of an artist and a student of history. Theron is called away and soon Eugenio and Aspasio are deep in conversation concerning the history of Palestine, Greece and Rome. Inevitably the conversation turns on the motives of the great ones of old in putting their ideals into practice and Eugenio asks Aspasio what motives for learning and the pursuit of virtue he could recommend. The elderly man does not hesitate to come to the point of all points quickly and tells the boy, 'that you may please God, your Almighty Creator; that you may glorify Christ, your infinitely condescending Redeemer; that you may yourself attain what is the true dignity and only felicity of your nature; and may be serviceable to the best interests of your fellow creatures—even their present holiness and their eternal happiness.'

## Faith expressed in works

Theron rejoins the conversation and leads it on to consider his scientific instruments which deepen his knowledge of the visible world. This gives Aspasio the opportunity to explain how the revelation of God's Word opens doors to truths of which we would be otherwise ignorant. Theron now confesses that he has been reading the Bible diligently of late and has seen that if the wicked man turns from his wickedness, he will 'save his soul alive' Ezekiel 18:27 and that God rewards us according to our works, Psalm 62:12. Aspasio explains how God's reward is one of mercy as no man can reach this Biblical norm. The wages of sin brings death but God has provided a life giving way by a merciful gift of faith in Christ which works righteousness in us. Arguing that he has still not found the doctrine of Christ's imputed righteousness in the Scriptures, Theron quotes James, Chapter 2, claiming that this proves that we are justified by our own works. He still has not seen the point James is making concerning the relevance of faith which is expressed in works.

Aspasio tells Theron that they are talking about two different gospels. Theron will have favour bestowed on the innocent, the pure and the holy, but where are these among men? 'The gospel of Christ runs in a very different strain. This brings pardon for the condemned, and blessings for the accursed: This is health to the sick, and recovery to the ruined.' Aspasio confesses that he belongs to the condemned and naturally accursed set himself, so may be forgiven for taking their part.

## The best things in life are free

In Dialogue VII, we find the two friends discussing how the beauties of God's creation are free and Aspasio is explaining how the gifts of God in Christ shown in pardon from sin are equally free. Theron is still not convinced and claims that Aspasio makes salvation too cheap. If a man wishes to have a cleansed soul, he must be prepared to do something to attain it. Aspasio asks his friend what he did to attain his first birth and what he has done to be kept in God's good providence ever since. Theron seems truly to believe that 'social accomplishments and moral virtues, completed by the performance of religious duties' have kept him in good standing with God. Aspasio patiently asks his friend if he has really performed all these duties perfectly. Theron, however, believes God will respect the sincerity of his endeavours. This is not gospel or saving sincerity, argues Aspasio. Paul argues that we must be sincere in Philippians 1:10,11, 'That ye may be sincere, being filled with the fruits of righteousness, which are by Jesus Christ, unto the praise and glory of God.' True, sincerity, Aspasio explains, does not terminate in self-justification but in the glory of God. This sincerity does not spring up within sincere man whose sincerity, he believes, will save him, but it flows from the grace of the Son and glorifies the Father. This shocks Theron who now accuses Aspasio of rejecting moral endowments and evangelical obedience. Indeed, Aspasio denies that these elements have anything to do with the justification of the ungodly. Salvation is 'Not of works . . .' Expounding Ephesians 2:8, Aspasio affirms, 'Grace, like a magnificent sovereign, from the riches of his own bounty, and without any respect to human worthiness, confers the glorious gift. Faith, like an indigent petitioner, with an empty hand, and without any pretence to personal desert, receives the heavenly blessing.' This is all in keeping with Hervey's three great experimental rules which he maintained throughout his Christian life as 'a touchstone to distinguish evangelical truth.' These are to honour the doctrines that humble the sinner, exalt the Saviour and promote holiness.' Whatever claims to be Christian and yet fails to keep these standards, is not the genuine thing.

## Confusing cause and effect

It is obvious that Theron is now changing his ground, though he still has not set his feet on the solid rock of hope in Christ's grace and faith in His righteousness. Quoting Ouranius, he suggests that the believer is justified, not by the merits of Christ imputed to him but more directly by Christ being formed in the hearts of believers. Quoting Romans 4:5, Aspasio shows how sinners are justified by God's free grace before there is a spark of anything Christ-like in their natures. We are not acceptable to Christ because He finds or forms something of Himself in us but we are justified through Christ's action in shedding His blood for our sakes on the Cross.

Aspasio now patiently tells Theron that he keeps turning the gospel back to front and confuses the results with the causes. There is no super-structure of faith which is not built on Christ, the corner-stone. In his epis-tle to the Romans, Paul shows the depravity of human nature and the mis-ery of the human condition. He then points out the way of recovery in Christ and the blessings freely vouchsafed by the gospel. He shows how any fruit which faith's blossoms produce is through the free unbounded loving-kindness of the Saviour. Peter drives home this truth in 1 Peter 1:2 when he tells us that we are 'Elect, according to the foreknowledge of God the Father, through sanctification of the Spirit, unto obedience, and sprin-kling of the blood of Christ.' By this time, Theron is confessing that he is not so enamoured of his own ideas but he is prepared to stick to them, come what may. He confesses that he had never studied Romans too closely and was unaware of the stages in salvation as presented by Paul. Aspasio ends Dialogue VII by telling Theron that he has, up to now, merely taken up his objections and promptings but now he is going to give Theron's citadel of protest the full charge of the gospel that he might become 'cap-tive unto Christ,' arguing that it will be to Theron's eternal triumph to lose the victory and subject himself to the Saviour's righteousness.

**The law condemns us but cannot save us**
In Dialogue VIII we find Theron submitting himself to the tribunal of the holy law and realising that this is not able to justify any man because all have fallen short of the standards of God's righteousness. Aspasio sug-gests that though this law is needful to mirror our corrupt nature to us, it is no help whatsoever in saving us. This is not its God-given purpose. Let us then see if there is a more workable way. Let us win Christ and find in Him, not our own righteousness which is of the law 'but the righteousness which is of God by faith in Jesus Christ,' Philippians 3:8,9 as the founda-tion of our hope. By Dialogue IX, Theron is now doubting his view of 'sincere obedience' which is the Neonomian view of a milder law given to Christians to promote a righteous life of which they are capable. He is beginning to see that the law is not an instrument of salvation but of con-demnation. It is never a justifier but an accuser. The function of the law as the schoolmaster to bring us to Christ is to make us aware of our lost state and our sin and, having condemned us, deliver us over to a Redeemer's merits that we might be saved. The law does not reveal saving grace but reveals the necessity of salvation in the sinner's life which cannot be ob-tained in the law. In this sense, Christ is the end of the law. Hervey con-cludes Dialogue IX by quoting Milton 'whose divinity is as faultless as his poetry is matchless:'

So law appears imperfect; and but giv'n
With purpose to resign them, in full time,
Up to a better cov'nant; disciplin'd
From shadowy types to truth; from flesh to spirit;
From imposition of strict laws, to free
Acceptance of large grace; from servile fear
To filial; works of law to works of faith.[1]

**Theron now accepts the passive role of Christ in the gospel but not the active**

Though Theron now accepts that forgiveness of sins is alone a work of active grace, he still has difficulty with Hervey's conceptions of the active and passive obedience of Christ, passive in reception of suffering but active in obedience to the law. He sees Aspasio as indicating that forgiveness of sins, wrought through Christ's passive suffering, is then only half of what justifies the sinner before God, whereas Theron holds that if he is pardoned, all should be well. Hervey explains that before a sinner can be justified in God's sight, there must be a remission of sins to take care of his obligation to punishment and there must be an imputation of righteousness to give him a title to happiness. There is no real righteousness and therefore no true justification where the sinner is merely pardoned. He must not only be pardoned but proclaimed guiltless and sinless. He can only be done so by having Christ's righteousness replace His own. These aspects are all part of the same work of justification. Hervey, amongst other Scripture references, gives Acts 26:18 here, where Paul distinguishes between the remission of sins and the inheritance of the saints, i.e. between the pardon that delivers from hell and the justification that entitles to heaven.

Theron's problem is that he feels that Christ's sufferings were all that were required by the law as the wages of sin is death and Christ bore that death vicariously. Hervey shows how this is wrong because Christ wished not only to save us from death but fit us out for heaven, too. He not only took on Himself our penalty but also made Himself under the law and obeyed it vicariously for us. Thus through Christ's incarnation the filth is removed and a new, spotless robe is given. Theron feels that he has the edge on Aspasio who insists that no one is justified by the works of the law by showing that, according to his friend, Christ justifies us through His obedience to the law. Exactly, says, Aspasio. No man can be justified by the law which only condemns him. Christ is not condemned by the law and has performed all its requirements for our sakes. We are saved, in-

---

[1]   *Paradise Lost*, Book xii, line 300-306.

deed, by works, but not ours. The works which Christ has performed on our behalf and which are put to our reckoning, save us.

### A righteousness which is not make-believe

This causes Theron to ask what good could such an imputation be to us. What is the use of a make-believe righteousness, bringing with it make-believe pardon and justification? Aspasio explains that this is not a make-believe transaction which remains in the 'as if' stage, because through Christ's righteousness being imputed to us, His benefits are literally and actually imparted at the same time. The pardon from sin is real and the justification is actual. Our nature is also truly sanctified because it is set apart for God's use and to His glory. Thus these benefits are not merely pro-forma reckoned to us but they are enjoyed by us, they are not merely the Divine estimation of us but our proper and personal possessions.

Theron now confesses that when he listens to Aspasio, he is 'half a convert' and would go a long way with him. Where Theron accepts his friend's argument, it is in acknowledging that human righteousness must always be insufficient for our justification, thus any hopes of everlasting happiness must lay, not upon works of our own but 'upon the free-goodness and unbounded beneficence of the Supreme Being, pursuant to that maxim of Scripture, "The gift of God is eternal life."' Aspasio rejoices that his friend has come thus far but tells him, he has still to add the vital factor to his statement of belief, 'through Christ Jesus our Lord.' This seems to cause Theron some embarrassment and he changes the subject abruptly, suggesting he needs time to think.

### The doctrine of the fall comes as a shock to the 'righteous overmuch'

Dialogue XI is a discussion on history, art and nature as if the two friends cannot return to their central theme. Even though the conversation comes round to the Fall of Babylon, which, of course, Aspasio sees as a picture of the fall of man, there seems to be little prospect now in the conversation that the two friends will be able to speak of the rise of man in Christ as there is in referring to a Babylon raised again. Indeed, now Theron is talking once more about the excellencies of the work of man's hands as if he had taken no part in the former conversations. Though he obviously is trying to avoid the topic, after much discussion about other things, he suddenly asks Aspasio to explain the doctrine of the Fall to him and is quite shaken when he hears how deep that fall was. Theron protests that all this is Pauline theology and we must take particular notice of James to obtain a more balanced position. James spoke of man 'made after the similitude of God' (3:9), which can only mean that man has moral endowments which distinguish him from the brute and the devil and thus confute the doctrine of total depravity and original sin. If Theron had read on in

James, he would have found his own picture of man, which he thrust onto James, greatly warped. It is human nature to pick and choose arguments to make man appear better than he is. Aspasio soon shows Theron how James would have been the last to 'set aside the sanctification of the divine Spirit, and the propitiation of the Redeemer's death.' James, Aspasio points out, was speaking of man in the collective as they were included in their first parent, Adam. Just as all were created after the similitude of God in Adam, so all have marred that similitude with and in Adam in the fall. Theron interrupts Aspasio, however, telling him that he ought not to bore into that which was only worth forgetting. Aspasio retorts that it is strange logic indeed to believe that forgetting a disease is the best remedy for it which prompts Theron to ask, 'Where is this remedy to be had?' Aspasio replies:

> Not on earth, but from heaven. The school of science cannot discover it. The courts of kings are unable to procure it. The college of physicians know not how to prescribe it. But the gospel of our salvation prescribes, prepares and dispenses it. The language of Christ in the holy word is 'I will bring her health and cure,' Jeremiah 33:6. And the beginning of our cure is, to be sensible of our disorder.

### Letting sin be seen as sin

This leads Aspasio to advise Theron to look upon his own sin as it really is and not blind himself to the fact that man is not morally as he supposes. This would only bring on a feeling of wretchedness, Theron argues. This is needed, Aspasio urges, as a preparative for redemption in Christ and reception of His gospel as a sovereign remedy. This causes a cry of protest from Theron who professes to accept the gospel as a display of moral excellency. 'You should add,' Aspasio gently tells his friend, 'as revealing that great Mediator, who has fulfilled all righteousness, to effect our justification; who has also the fulness of the Spirit, to accomplish our regeneration. Otherwise, what you mention is infinitely short of the gospel. It brings no glad tidings to fallen creatures. It administers no succour to ruined sinners. It is like writing a copy for the blind, or setting a task to the disabled; which would rather be an insult on their impotence, than a relief of their distress.' Aspasio now presses Theron to a confession of his own need of Christ but Theron, pleading that evening has come, asks for time to think before continuing on the following day.

### From darkness to the day-spring on high

Dialogue XII opens on the following day with one of Hervey's typical poetic descriptions of nature which has earned him respect from generations of literary critics, lovers of descriptive writing and nature enthusiasts besides readers who have progressed from the Book of Nature to the Book of God's Word. Hervey describes the scene:

The sun was fiercely bright, and the sky without a cloud. Not a breath fanned the woods, nor a gale curled the stream. The fields, exposed to all the fiery beams, were like a glowing hearth. The little birds, overcome by the potent influence, lost, for a while, their tuneful notes. Nothing was heard in the garden but the drowsy hum of bees, and the moan like buzz of winged insects. All nature seemed to languish: The flourishing meads looked sickly: the gayest blossoms began to fade, the sprightliest animals, if not reposed under some cooling shelter, panteth for breath and hung their drooping heads amidst the all-surrounding blaze and the unsufferable heat. Aspasio disappeared ever since dinner, and none could tell whither he was gone. Theron, as soon as the tea equipage was removed, took his way to the wood. Desirous of the thickest shade, he hastened to the centre. A serpentine walk composed the avenue; which, after several windings, delivered him into a large circular area, not covered with a Grecian or Roman temple, unmeaning imitation of pagan idolatry, but surrounded with aged and princely oaks; the coalition of whose branches threw over the grassy plat a majestic, rural dome, and their unpierced foliage 'unbrowned'[1] the noontide hours.

Needless to say, Theron finds Aspasio in this idyll of the privileged few with his head deep in a Latin tome. The conversation centres at first around the classical writers but soon we find Aspasio speaking of the providence of God and the fact that their religion is not based on a set of sacrificial rules to pacify 'lascivious, debauched and scandalous deities;' but on 'the tender mercies of our God; whereby the day-spring from on high hath visited us;' Luke 1:78 and 'brought us out of darkness into the marvellous light of the gospel.' Aspasio was reading Cicero on the Nature of the Divine Being. He seems to have had an evangelistic purpose in this regarding Theron as the two friends now delve deeply into a technical conversation on the anatomical structure of man, with Theron taking the lead as a very observant and diligent scientist. Soon Theron is speaking of the 'Master Builder' in his wonder at the amazing creation of man. Aspasio has let Theron take on the lion's share of the conversation, but now, as his friend comes to the end of his eulogy on creation, he tells him that there is a still greater honour given the human body of which he has not mentioned a word. On Theron's objecting, Aspasio tells him of the Lord's taking on Himself a human body as a display of His love towards man and how man's body can become a temple of the Holy Spirit. These two facts, for Aspasio, are the crowning features of God's creation of man and cause him to express in the words of Addison:

---

[1]    Take away any 'brown study' i.e. any thoughts of melancholy.

When all thy mercies, O my God,
My rising soul surveys,
Transported with the view, I'm lost
In wonder, love, and praise.

**The doctrine of original sin allegedly contrary to nature**
Dialogue XIII starts with another of Hervey's descriptive pen-portraits
of feelings produced by nature:

> The morning had been wet. At noon, the rain ceased; but the
> heavens still continued gloomy. Towards evening a gentle eastern
> gale sprung up, which dissipated the dead calm, and cleared the
> face of the sky. The sun, which had been muffled in clouds, dropped
> the veil. Disengaged from the dusky shroud, he shone forth with
> peculiar splendour. His beams, endeared by their late suspension,
> were doubly welcome, and produced unusual gaiety.

With this transformation of nature before their eyes, Theron and Aspasio
resume their discussion with Theron professing that all this beauty shows
'that God is good, and men are made to be happy,' whereas Aspasio would
turn all humans into spiritual lepers and the world into a hospital for the
sick. The doctrine of original sin, he affirms, is contrary to nature. Though
Aspasio now gives Theron one passage of Scripture after another to show
that all have sinned and fallen short of God's glory, his friend parries every
Scriptural blow with arguments that the passage either did not refer to a
man of virtue or was such that God would draw a veil of love over the sin
and not take it seriously. Theron sees sin as inattentiveness rather than
blindness or defect in man's nature. Though he believes the 'vulgar rab-
ble' would be careless in these matters, he feels 'persons of rank and education think in a more exalted manner.'
    Theron is here displaying the one great flaw in his own armour—he is
a snob. Aspasio tells him plainly that if he thinks that 'Unless a man be
born again, he cannot enter into the kingdom of heaven' John 3:3, refers to
all others but not himself, there is, if not a cloud, total darkness on his
mind. Theron asks Aspasio how many other human faculties he is going to
put through the mangle as Aspasio's admonitions seem to have no effect
whatsoever. We notice, however, that, rather than dismiss all that Aspasio
says about the depravity of man, Theron is willing to accept it in all cases
except his own. Whenever the conversation settles on his own case, Theron
either changes the subject or confesses that he is sick of it. In all this, it is
astonishing that he does not lose his temper. He certainly does not lose his
sense of humour as he tells his friend that whatever could be said of him,
no one could say he was a flatterer! Theron does become rather passionate

when Aspasio asks him if his personal pride is in the way of his right understanding of Christ's work. He is soon accusing Aspasio of lack of Christian charity and 'insufferable censoriousness'. The dialogue ends at Theron's request with Aspasio summing up the Biblical doctrine of the Fall.

## Almost persuaded

Before Dialogue XIV takes place, we read that Aspasio is spending the largest part of the day packing for an intended journey, which gives Theron a good deal of time to go over all that he has discussed with his friend. True to his love of nature, he finds nowhere better to meditate than under the open skies. He finds that, though not convinced, he is silenced by Aspasio's arguments. He sees that even if Aspasio's forecast of doom for mankind is accepted, there is still his way of hope for mankind to be considered which displays Christ as freely providing a title to pardon and to a life of true spiritual blessing. Theron finds himself saying, 'My prejudices are wearing away. I am almost a convert!' As Theron breaks out with these words, Aspasio joins him and with Isaiah 54:17 begs him to become a full convert and experience that 'Their righteousness is of me, saith the Lord.' Theron turns to his friend, as if he had fully expected him to come at the right moment and says, 'If, by this doctrine, the claims of the law are answered—if the perfections of God are glorified—if the interests of morality are secured—I must acknowledge, it will be more worthy of acceptance than I could once have imagined.'

Hervey, remembering his own conversation with the old ploughman who warned him against the snares of righteous self, begs Theron in the person of Aspasio to leave his own ideas of his moral and righteous self behind and measure himself against the holy law of God, realising that even he, with all his high ideals, falls short of God's high standards. As a parting wish, he advises Theron to keep a diary of his spiritual life, registering all that happens in his walk with God. Then he will soon see how impotent he is to do that for himself that only Christ can do effectively for him. He will learn to know himself.

## Theron begins to understand his own heart

The second part of Theron and Aspasio is taken up with twelve letters, nine from Aspasio and three from Theron. The correspondence opens with Aspasio's letter from the house of Camillus, reminding his young friend of what they have discussed and, probably because of Theron's belief that James represents the true gospel rather than Paul, quotes James to show that he is quite in line with the Scriptures in general. Theron replies in words that show he is a changed man. There is not a trace of his former 'stiff upper-lip' morality and trust in his personal virtue. He can now only say:

If I look back, and review the years of youth and manhood, what has been the tenor, what is the aspect of my life? More like a desolate and horrid wilderness, than a cultivated garden, or a fruitful vineyard. In youth, what sordid gratifications of appetite! In manhood, what base compliances with a wicked world! In both, what shoals of evil inclinations have polluted my heart! what swarms of vain imaginations have debased my thoughts! what frothy and unprofitable words have dropt from my lips! By all which, how have I disobeyed, and how dishonoured God! how have I denied, and how crucified the Lord Jesus Christ! and yet supposed myself, all the while, to be good enough.

Two elements in Theron's life which were formerly quite lacking, now become very evident in his writing. His old religion was neither centred in Christ nor in an objective view of himself. Instead of following a religion based on his own sincerity; Theron is stepping out into a faith which sees his own failures and the merits of the Saviour. He ends his letter by admitting:

I now see the necessity of an imputed righteousness. Without some such object for my trust, I am undone. I long, therefore, to hear your arguments in its behalf. And I must declare to you, if it can be satisfactorily proved from the scriptures, it is the most comforting doctrine in the world, and worthy of all acceptation.

### The teaching of orthodox Christianity on Christ's righteousness imputed to the believer

Theron had formally declared that the doctrine he was now so interested in was against the teachings of his church and contrary to the entire Scriptures. Aspasio's next three letters to his friend contain the teaching of the Church of England on the subject, the testimony of the Old Testament and that of the New. Going through the Book of Common Prayer, the Collects, the Homilies and the Articles, Hervey shows how his church teaches clearly that 'Christ is the righteousness of all them that do truly believe. He, for them, fulfilled the law in his life. So that now, in him, and by him, every true Christian may be called a fulfiller of the law; forasmuch as that which their infirmity lacked, Christ's righteousness supplied.'[1] Then, quoting Bishops Beveridge, Hopkins, Reynolds, Davenant, Sanderson besides Prebendary Hooker, Clemens, Justin and Chrysostom, Hervey shows how the doctrine of imputed righteousness is central to the

---

[1]    *Homily on the Salvation of Mankind.*

teaching of the Church of England. Aspasio introduces the topic in his second answer to Theron's plea with a quote from Romans 3:21,22, 'Now the righteousness of God without the law is manifested, being witnessed by the law and the prophets; even the righteousness of God which is by faith of Jesus Christ unto all and upon all them that believe.' Starting at Genesis 3:14, he combs through the entire Old Testament with particular reference to Abraham, Job, David, Isaiah and Jeremiah, tracing the history of revelation concerning 'The Lord our Righteousness,' Jeremiah 23:6; 33:16, and showing that the Old Testament church gloried in being able to say, 'Blessed are the people that know the joyful sound: they shall walk, O Lord in the light of thy countenance. In thy name shall they rejoice all the day; and in thy righteousness shall they be exalted.' Psalm 89:15,16.

For Aspasio, turning to the New Testament, the Christian faith is through the righteousness of the Father and the Son, 2 Peter 1:1; Romans 1:17. The only plea a saved sinner can have before God is Christ's righteousness, i.e. a perfect righteousness, which is imputed to him for faith. Just as the Father will not impute the sin to us which we have received through our federal unity with Adam and our disobedience to the law, so he wills to impute to us that perfect righteousness, displayed in Christ's vicarious suffering and obedience, which we have through union with Christ, the federal Head of all believers. Expounding Romans 5:12 to the end of the chapter, Hervey (in the role of Aspasio) sums up by saying:

That Christ, in pursuance of the covenant of grace, fulfilled all righteousness in the stead of his people: That this righteousness being performed for them, is imputed to them: That by virtue of this gracious imputation they are absolved from guilt and entitled to bliss; as thoroughly absolved, and as fully entitled, as if in their own persons they had undergone the expiatory sufferings and yielded the meritorious obedience. Lest it should seem strange in the opinion of a Jew or Gentile, to hear of being justified by the righteousness of another, the wary apostle urges a parallel case, recorded in the Jewish revelation, but ratified by universal experience; namely, our being condemned for the unrighteousness of another. In this respect, he observes, Adam was a type of our Lord, or 'a figure of him that was to come.' Romans 5:14. The relation is the same, but the effect is happily reversed. Adam the head of his posterity; Christ the head of his people. Adam's sin was imputed to all his natural descendents; Christ's righteousness is imputed to all his spiritual offspring. Adam's transgressions brought death into the world, and all our woe; Christ's obedience brings life, and all our happiness. The whole closes with the very obvious and no less weighty inference: 'Therefore, as by the offence of one, judgment

came upon all men to condemnation; even so, by the righteousness
of one, the free gift came upon all men unto justification of life.'
Romans 5:18.[1]

## Theron begins to see with new eyes

Theron's response to what is happening to him may come as a surprise
to those unused to the ways of God with man. Alone with his thoughts of
his own lack of righteousness and the need for the righteousness of another, he finds that he is viewing the scenery in which he lives with renewed eyes. He finds the charms of nature heightened by the knowledge
that Christ is behind and in it all as Creator and Preserver. Everything he
sees now reminds him of Christ's love and he can even say of the rushing
hillside stream as it forces its way down the hill-side into the river near his
mansion and which he has observed a thousand and more times without
really understanding its purpose, 'Reminded by this watery monitor, of
that constancy, and vigour with which the affections should move towards
the great centre of happiness, Christ Jesus; of that determined ardour with
which we should break through the entanglements of temptation, and ob-
stacles of the world, in order to reach our everlasting rest.' But Theron,
though Christ has become precious to him, is still thinking in terms of his
own fight with sin rather than Christ's conquering righteousness. Be this
as it may, Theron can draw true spiritual parallels from nature and say, 'If,
amidst these ordinary productions of the earth, God appears so 'great in
counsel, and mighty in work,' Jeremiah 32:19, what may we expect to see
in the palaces of heaven, in the hierarchies of angels, and in that wonderful
Redeemer who is, beyond all other objects, the 'power of God, and the
wisdom of God?' 1 Corinthians 1:24.

## Checking whether one is in the faith

Aspasio now renews his efforts to help searching and seeking Theron
to his goal and gives him Scripture after Scripture to help him on his way.
Summing up the state of a sinner 'unawakened from carnal security', and
to prompt Theron to see on which side of salvation he stands, Aspasio
says:

> Loads, more than mountainous loads of guilt, are upon his soul,
> and he perceives not the burden. For this reason, he is in no appre-
> hension of the vengeance and fiery indignation which he deserves:
> he has no superlative esteem for the atonement and merits of the
> Redeemer, which alone can deliver him from the wrath to come.

---

[1]    Hervey also deals with much of Romans 4 and 5; Romans 8:5; 9:2, 30-32; 10:2-4;
1 Corinthians 1:30; 6:11; Philippians 3:8, 9 and a number of other texts to illustrate these
truths.

But if once his conscience feels, what his lips, perhaps have often repeated, 'We do earnestly repent us of these our misdoings, the remembrance of them is grievous unto us, the burden of them is intolerable;' then will he prize such a text, 'The Lord laid on Christ the iniquity of us all!' How will he long for an interest in the Lamb of God 'which taketh away the sin of the world!' Then that Jesus who has 'finished the transgression, and brought in everlasting right-eousness,' will be all his salvation and all his desire.[1]

Should Theron be now standing in the ranks of sinners made saints and fitted out for glory, Aspasio adds:

'Ye are complete in Him,' Colossians 2:9,10. Never was any conclusion more weighty in itself, or founded on more solid princi-ples. Ye are not only pardoned, but reconciled; and not only recon-ciled, but justified; nay, ye are—and what can be said or desired more?—'ye are complete': And not barely before men or angels, but before infinite purity, and omniscience itself, 'Ye are made,' (amazing and charming truth!) 'the righteousness of God,' 2 Corinthians 5:21. in this wonderful Saviour. What a fountain is this, or rather what a sea of fathomless depth, to obliterate all sins, and supply all wants? What a mirror of God's stupendous grace, and ever to be adored loving-kindness.[2]

Theron's reply does not show on which side of salvation he stands but he is obviously in the right place for a work of God to be done. He con-fesses, 'So superficial are my views of Christ; so scanty is my acquaint-ance with the gospel.' It is obvious that Theron is still struggling with the Bible's teaching on faith and thus in the next three letters Aspasio goes step by step through the Bible, dealing with faith, especially in its refer-ence to Christ's righteousness, union with Him and personal assurance. Aspasio winds up his affairs with Camillus, whose daughters had been benefiting from his knowledge of the Bible and skills in science, and now revisits Theron and finds him in a highly nervous and perplexed state, full of anxiety. He was longing, using the words of Isaiah 60:17, to trade in his brass and iron for Aspasio's gold and silver 'hoping that some proper conversation on the grace and privileges of the everlasting gospel might compose and comfort his mind, might, while his heart was softened by humbling convictions, fix the stamp of Christianity, and deliver his whole soul into the mould of evangelical religion.'[3]

---

[1]  Letter vii.

[2]  Letter viii.

[3]  Dialogue XV. 'Deliver into the mould' is the literal translation of Romans 6:17

**Theron's former bridge to a false hope in salvation has broken down**

Theron admits that the method of salvation in which he formerly trusted is a broken bridge and he confesses that he was blinded with prejudice, intoxicated with pride and full of conceit concerning his own moral powers. Aspasio comforts him with the words of Scripture concerning Christ's call to those who hunger and thirst after righteousness. Using the parable of the Prodigal Son, Aspasio shows his friend how a new robe of Sonship is prepared for those whose sins are blotted out, which must be accepted as a gift and not grasped at as a thing to be bought or earned. Theron can only cry out that this is the gift of all gifts he needs, 'To be interested in all the merits of Christ! to have his immaculate righteousness imputed to my soul! so that from henceforth there shall be no fear of condemnation, but a comfortable enjoyment of freest love, and a delightful expectation of completest glory!' Dialogue XV thus ends with Theron confessing, 'Lord, I believe; help thou mine unbelief!'

**A pupil in the school of Christ**

Aspasio's friend has now entered into the school of Christ and has become a most willing pupil. His teacher now begins to build him up in the faith with the assistance of the Scriptures and sound advice from such writers as Owen and Alting,[1] supported by the confession of his own and the Palatinate Church. John Owen had defined faith as 'a gracious resting upon the free promises of God in Jesus Christ for mercy, with a firm persuasion of heart that God is a reconciled Father to us in the Son of his love,' and the Palatine Catechism answers the question, 'What is true faith?' with the words 'It is not only an assent to all the truths which God hath revealed in his word; but it is an assured trust, wrought by the Holy Spirit in my heart, that remission of sins, complete righteousness, and eternal life are given, freely given, not to others only, but to myself; and all this from the mere mercy of God, through the alone merits of Christ.' Theron hears this impatiently because he wants to know what the Scriptures say directly rather than via a creed which could include human interpretation. Aspasio, beginning at Hebrews and going on through 1 Corinthians 15 shows Theron what the Bible has to say about the life of faith, the perseverance of faith and the end or reward of faith. The joy with which Theron absorbs all these truths shows that he is living out the joys of faith himself. Then Hervey's most famous book ends with Theron proclaiming what the Son of Righteousness means to him and Aspasio tuning in with the words:

---

[1]   Dr. John Owen (1616-83), Dean of Christchurch, Oxford, Independent theologian of great renown. Prof. Johann Heinrich Alting (1583-1644) of Heidelberg and Groeningen Universities, usually known in England as 'Altingius', author of *Expicatio Catecheseos Palatinæ*.

What a gift then is the righteousness of Christ! Blessed be God for all the indulgent dispensations of providence! Blessed be God for all the beneficial productions of nature! But, above all, blessed be God for the transcendent and unspeakable gift of Christ—for the unsearchable and infinite treasures of 'his righteousness'.

## Hervey's plans for a fourth volume to *Theron and Aspasio*

Hervey wrote often to his friends of the fourth and last volume which was to bring the story of Theron and Aspasio to a close with the triumphant death of Aspasio and a Theron, rooted and grounded in the faith, taking over his work. Hervey's last year, however, was so taken up by his continual work on revising the first three volumes and his preparation of an answer to John Wesley's attacks on orthodoxy, hindered by the heightened onslaughts of a terminal consumption that the fourth volume was never completed. Hervey, however, sent a rough sketch of his plans for the final volume to several of his friends so we gain some insight into Hervey's thoughts on the matter. These are published appended to Letter CXLII in *Hervey's Works,* dated Sept. 10, 1755.

Pleasure and happiness of Christ's religion; (for I am of the same mind with Mr. Marshall in his *Treatise on Sanctification,* namely, that we must partake of the comforts of the gospel, before we can practise the duties of the law.) Theron oppressed with fears, on account of his numerous sins. Discouraged with doubts, on account of his imperfect obedience. The cordials of the gospel re-administered, with some additional spirit and strength. Objections to assurance of faith stated, discussed, answered. Vital holiness; its nature, necessity, excellency. Its grand efficient, the blessed Spirit. Its principal instrument, true faith; mixed with which, the Scriptures, the Lord's supper, prayer, the divine promises, are powerful and effectual means; disunited from which, they are a dead letter and insignificant ordinances. The evangelical principles of holiness, such as, 'I beseech you by the mercies of God—Ye are bought with a price—Ye are the temples of the living God,' &c; all these privileges, though not hereditary, yet indefeasible; or the final perseverance of the believer. Our friends part; renew their correspondence; Theron desires to glorify the God of his salvation, asks advice concerning the best method of family worship, educating children, instructing servants, edifying acquaintance. On each of these particulars Aspasio satisfies his inquiry, enlarges on the subject of education, especially of daughters; as that seems to be most neglected, or the proper way of conducting it least understood. Letter on the covenant of grace, comprising the substance, and being a kind of recapitulation of the three foregoing volumes. Aspasio seized with a sudden and fatal illness; his sentiments and behaviour in his last moments.

With his usual humility and willingness to be corrected, Hervey adds the request: 'If, dear sir, you see anything in this plan that is improper, correct it; anything that is defective, supply it; and if any thoughts occur on any of the topics, be so kind as to suggest them.'

## A good friend of Hervey's testifies to the truths maintained in *Theron and Aspasio*

Commenting on Hervey's doctrine of Christ's righteousness with which he thoroughly agreed, William Romaine said in his public tribute to Hervey's life and work:

In this all-glorious righteousness of the God-man Christ Jesus consists the sinner's salvation; for he is accepted and justified by it: the fruits of this righteousness are his sanctification, and the robe of this righteousness is his glorification. So that salvation in time and in eternity depend on the righteousness of the incarnate God. This is the fundamental doctrine of the Christian religion, for which our dear brother was a noble champion. He saw, he experienced the importance of it, and therefore in his conversation and in his preaching it was his favourite topic. How sweetly, how profitably have I heard him dwell upon it, and how excellently has he defended it in his writings? Read his *Theron and Aspasio*, and when you are thoroughly convinced that Christ is the end of the law for righteousness to every one who believeth, and can say with faith, 'in the Lord have I righteousness and salvation,' then your mind will be settled in peace and comfort, and you will be delivered from those dangerous errors which are now propagated concerning the righteousness of the Lord Jesus. Thank God for the masterly defence of it in these dialogues. In them Mr. Hervey, being dead, yet speaketh the praises of his adorable Redeemer, and clearly proves that we have our salvation through his righteousness. Immanuel the Saviour is the justifier, as he says himself, (Isaiah 45:21,22) 'There is no God else beside me; a God that gives righteousness and a Saviour there is none beside me. Look unto me, and be ye saved, all the ends of the earth: for I am God, and there is none else.' How could they be saved by looking unto Christ? Certainly not by a look of their bodily eyes. Simeon's joy did not arise from having Christ in his arms, and looking upon him; but from being able to look upon him by an act of faith. He knew him to be his Saviour. Thence arose his joy, and from thence must yours arise. It is the look of faith which saves; the eye of faith kept in exercise upon its proper object, even upon Jesus, the author and finisher of the faith. It is this act of faith which our Lord requires—'Look unto me,' with this promise annexed, 'and be ye saved.' There is salvation in the look of faith: for it sees and receives Jesus, as he is offered in scripture, for a free, full, and complete Saviour. And whoever keeps the eye of faith in constant exercise is prepared with good old Simeon to depart in peace; because, by having an interest and property in the salvation of our God, he is thereby delivered from every thing that can make death dreadful, and is in possession of everything that can make death desirable.[1]

---

[1]  Romaine's *Works, The Knowledge of Salvation Precious in the Hour of Death: A Sermon on the Death of the Rev. James Hervey,* p. 806.

# Chapter Nine:
# The Parson in his Parish

## Hervey's daily routine

When well, Hervey got up before six in the morning and busied himself with written work and sermon preparation. At eight o'clock he called the members of his family, any visitors to his home and his servants to morning devotions. The servants were asked to repeat the texts which he had expounded the day before and he then added further thoughts on them so that they might be impressed on their memories all the more. Often he would catechise those present to make sure that his point had been understood. After this he spent a time of prayer with his wider family before breakfasting with them at nine.

During the rest of the morning and early afternoon Hervey would either work in his study or visit his flock amongst whom he witnessed by catechising them on doctrine and teaching them the scriptures. During these visits, Hervey distributed Bibles, books, household goods and clothing to his poorer parishioners, believing that this was, on the whole, better than distributing money.

Dispensing with lunch, Hervey took tea early in the afternoon and once again gathered his family and servants around him, inviting his neighbours to join in and being careful to invite five or six converted people to assist him with the witness. This time he took his Hebrew Old Testament or Greek New Testament and expounded several verses of Scripture. Hervey recorded for Lady Francis a verbatim report of how he conducted his tea-time witness and catechised those sharing the meal with him. Modern families could do well to go back to the kind of Table-Talk practised by true Christian divines in the years of reformation and awakening. Perhaps quoting Hervey in full here might help to foster such a fountain of spiritual nourishment.

The weather being wet and tempestuous, brought on our re-membrance that cheering and comfortable passage, where it is said of CHRIST JESUS; *He shall be for a place of refuge, and for a covert from storm and from rain.*

How, or in what respects, shall CHRIST answer these desirable purposes?—Because, He is our Surety. He has put himself in our stead. He has undertaken to answer all accusations, that may be brought against us; and to satisfy all demands, that may be made upon us.

Has the Law of GOD any charge against us?—It has. The Law saith, *Cursed is He that continueth not in all things that are writ-ten in the Book of the Law to do them.* And instead of continuing in ALL, we have continued in none. We have not *perfectly* kept any, but repeatedly broke all the commandments. Broke them, if not in the outward act, yet in our hearts—If not in the sight of our fellow-creatures, yet before the all-seeing GOD—If not in the literal, yet in the spiritual sense of the Precepts. Therefore, the Law pronounces Us accursed: and the Law cannot be broken. Heaven and earth may pass away, sooner than one iota or tittle of its commands shall be unfulfilled, or of its threatenings unexecuted. To rescue us from this dreadful condition, the blessed JESUS said; 'Upon me be their curse. I am content to be treated as an accursed creature. Let all that ignominy and wrath, which are due to the vilest transgressors—let it all fall upon me.'

Had the *Justice* of GOD any controversy with us?—It had. Jus-tice solemnly declared, *The soul that sinneth, shall die.* All we have sinned, and dealt wickedly. Death therefore is our due: Death temporal, spiritual, and eternal.—But our adorned Redeemer put Himself at our Head; became responsible for all our provocations; and said, as it is most sweetly recorded in the Book of Job, Deliver them from going down into the pit; I have found a ransom. 'Here am I; prepared and determined to expiate their iniquities: though it cost me tears and groans, agonies and blood.'—Accordingly, the sword of inflexible justice awoke; sheathed itself in his sacred heart; and took full vengeance on the royal and immaculate LORD, that it might spare his mean and sinful servants.

The *authority* of GOD had a demand upon us; That we should keep the divine law, or else never expect a title to eternal life. *This do, and thou shalt live*; is a decree, that will never be repealed.—It was impossible for our *fallen* nature, to perform the heavenly com-mandment, in all the extent of its requirements. Therefore, our ever-gracious Master became our Surety. HE, who gave the Law, was

made under the Law. HE, who is ruler over all, subjected Himself
to our obligations: in our place, and in our stead, He fulfilled all
that the Law commanded. On purpose, that He might answer that
amiable character, THE LORD OUR RIGHTEOUSNESS. On purpose, saith the inspired writer, That by *His* obedience *we* might be
made righteous. Rom. v. 19.

In these respects, the LORD JESUS is a refuge and shelter. A
*refuge*, ever open and free of access to all sinners: a shelter, inviolably secure and never to be penetrated by any danger. Lot was
safe, when he fled to Zoar. Noah was safe, when he was shut up in
the Ark. The prophet was safe, when chariots of fire and horses of
fire were all around him. And are not they equally safe, who fly to
this divinely excellent MEDIATOR? Who are interested in his atoning death, his justifying righteousness, his prevailing intercession?
They may boldly say; they may rejoice and sing; *We have a strong
city*, in our Redeemer's grace and love. *Salvation*, salvation itself,
hath GOD appointed for *our walls and bulwarks.*[1]

After telling her Ladyship of what went on at the tea-time service,
Hervey gets down to the application:

While Others, therefore, are hastening to gay Amusements:
Others are pushing their Way to Preferments, or aspiring after
worldly Honours: may You, Madam, be pursuing the heavenly Plan,
and *flying for Refuge to the Hope set before You.*

The remaining hours until the main evening meal and evening devotions were usually taken up by study and preparation as Hervey was not
strong enough to be out and about much. At eight he would dine and at
nine expound the Scriptures again for about 15 minutes to those present in
his household. He did not take the texts which were appointed for reading
by the Church of England but chose texts which he believed were applicable to the particular situation of the hour. If visitors were present or special
guests, these evening expositions and times of prayer would often take
half an hour or so as Hervey dealt with their particular needs. During these
evening family services, Hervey asked his servants to read passages from
the Bible by turns, thus bringing them into the worship and assisting them
in their education.

Wednesday evenings were a special time for the inhabitants of Weston
as Hervey gave an open lecture in which he departed from the strict for-
malities of the Prayer Book services and merely spoke his heart out on a

---

[1]   *Letters to Lady Francis*, Letter LXI.

Biblical theme. His major aim was to help those who had come to know the Lord through his Sunday preaching and build them up in the faith. Thus he tells a friend;

> My text on Wednesday evening will be a complete description of a Christian; viz. 'We are the circumcision which worship God in the spirit, and rejoice in Christ Jesus, and have no confidence in the flesh,' Phil. iii. 3. A fine subject for your meditation: Why should I not add for your conversation also?[1]

The time of this lecture varied with the time of the year according to what agricultural work was being carried out. The general rule was to wait until darkness gathered which meant the service was held in the late afternoon in autumn and winter and in the evening in the summer. Then Hervey would speak to a full church, the building being lit by candles which he paid for out of his own pocket. It was always a wonder to Hervey that no matter how weak he was, his church was always full. After preaching to such a congregation at the end of October, 1753, Hervey tells a friend:

> I have this afternoon been preaching to a crowded audience. The Lord Jesus Christ grant that it may be an edified one! You would be surprised, and I believe everybody wonders, that I am able to officiate myself. I am so weak, that I can hardly walk to the end of my parish, though a small one; and so tender, that I dare not visit my poor neighbours, for fear of catching cold in their bleak houses; yet I am enabled on the Lord's day to catechize and expound to my children in the morning and to preach in the afternoon. And every Wednesday evening, hay time and harvest only excepted, I read prayers, and give them a lecture-sermon in Weston church. This is the Lord's doing, or, as your favourite book expresses it, this is owing to 'the good hand of my God upon me.' Join with me, my dear friend, in adoring his grace, and pray, that if my life is spared, my capacity for his services may be prolonged; that if it be his blessed will, the day which he puts an end to the one may put a period to the other.

### Hervey, the poor man's friend
Hervey had a good business head and bought linen, worsted, shoes and stockings at wholesale prices or at trade or bulk discount for his parish poor which they would never have been able to obtain themselves. If he found out, however, that a family was in great financial straits and had

---

[1]    Letter CXXXIV, *Works*.

medicine bills etc. to pay, Hervey would dig deep into his own pocket and settle the family's bills. Because of this service to his Lord, Hervey, who was by no means a poor man, gave away the bulk of his earnings and lived very Spartan himself. Hervey, for instance, earned £700 on his *Meditations* alone but gave every penny of it to charity. When he died, Hervey left very little money but stipulated that the little he left should be used to provide food and clothing for the poor.

Of his work amongst the poor, Ryland says:

> His love and compassion for the poor, rose to such an astonishing degree, as I never discerned in any other human being: he appeared to be nothing but bowels of mercy: he had a powerful disposition to feed them, to clothe them, and instruct them in the true method of salvation, by our Lord, Jesus Christ: he did but just allow himself the necessities of life, in order that he might have the more to bestow on the people of God, and ministers of Christ. He kept no money by him, any longer than he could dispose of it to some good use; yet he made no account of the money that he gave away; he tried to forget every thing he did, and could not bear to have any body mention any charitable action he had done.[1]

## Finding employment for his people

Hervey took special care that his people were well-employed and in a position to be able to care for themselves and their families adequately and solicited employment for his parishioners wherever he could. Lady Francis preserved one such letter in which Hervey says:

> Does your Ladyship want a maid-servant? Or know of any mild-tempered, condescending, serious Lady that wants a maid to wait on her? There is in my parish a young woman, who, I think, would make in all respects, a valuable servant. Very neat and has a genteel air. Good-natured and perfectly honest. Quite sensible, and has a fine hand with her needle, or at ironing. Some years ago, being out of place, she lived in our family, rather than have no employ. Continued with us more than a year, but deserved a much better place. A better place she got, and for several years held. But is now out of service again. I verily think, she would give great satisfaction, where-ever she was employed; otherwise, I would not presume to mention her, in this manner to your Ladyship.[2]

---

[1]  *The Character of Mr. Hervey,* p. 27.

[2]  *Letters to Lady Francis,* Letter XCV.

We may presume that the industrious lady in question soon obtained a post with such a glowing reference!

## Looking after the bodily health of his parishioners
Hervey, being a semi-invalid himself for the major part of his adult life, was particularly concerned for the health of his flock and would consult the best doctors in the country to obtain help for them. Whenever he heard that a prominent doctor was passing by Weston-Favell, he would send messengers to him, begging him to visit those of his flock who were ill, promising to meet all expenses himself. He refused to follow the example of many of his fellow Evangelical ministers and distribute medicine himself as he argued that this was the task for the expert. He did, however, make sure that the doctors examining his parishioners were provided with cut-price medicine which he bargained for with the local chemists, who often refused to make a profit on their mixtures as they were used for charitable purposes.

## Catechising the children
Though Hervey catechised the children in their homes when he was well enough, he always reserved a part of the service for catechetical work, never being satisfied with a mere 'correct answer' but always pressed the child to explain what he meant. Much of what he said to the children did not escape the adult's notice in the congregation and this was also Hervey's intention. Letter LXIII in Hervey's *Works* was written during his earlier days as a curate and perhaps does not reflect his full theological maturity but it serves to show how thorough the young clergyman was in this important work for the gospel:

> My Dear Friend,—I received your letter; am sorry to hear you have been ill, heartily wish you a re-establishment of your health, and shall be glad, when it suits your inclination and conveniency, to see you at Weston.
> I am glad you are beginning to catechize your children. I hope you will be enabled to feed Christ's lambs, and dispense to them the milk of the word as they may be able to bear it. Indeed you apply to a wrong person for advice. I make some efforts it is true, to discharge this duty, but not to my own satisfaction; and great will be the glory of divine grace, if it is to the edification of my people My time for catechizing is during the summer; when the days are long, and the weather is warm. But I think you do right to conform to the usual custom of catechizing in Lent.
> My method is to ask easy questions, and teach the children very short and easy answers. The Lord's prayer was the last subject of our explanation. In some such manner I proceeded:—Why is this

prayer called the Lord's prayer? Because our Lord Jesus Christ taught it us. Why is Christ called our Lord? Because he bought us with his blood. Why does he teach us to call God Father? That we may go to him as children to a father. How do children go to a father? With faith, not doubting but he will give them what they want. Why is our Father in heaven? That we may pray to him with reverence. What is meant by God's name? God himself and all his perfections. What by hallowed? That he may be honoured and glorified. How is God to be honoured? In our hearts, with our tongues, and by our lives, &c. &c.

On each question I endeavour to comprehend, not all that may be said, but that only which may be most level to their capacities, and is most necessary for them to know. The answer to each question I explain in the most familiar manner possible; such a manner, as a polite hearer might perhaps treat with the most sovereign contempt. Little similes I use, that are quite low, fetched *non ex academia, sed e trivio*. In every explanation I would be short, but repeat it again and again. Tautology, in this case, is the true propriety of speaking; and to our little auditors, the *crambe repetita* will be better than all the graces of eloquence.

I propose to explain to them principally the creed, the Lord's prayer, and the commandments. What relates to the two sacraments at present, I do not attempt to set before them; let them first have some tolerable notion of the former. I fancy you had better proceed in the same method. If I know your sentiments about baptism aright, with which our catechism begins, I should apprehend it would be most prudent to go immediately to the great fundamentals. However, pray to the Lord, whose work you work; and he who is all-wise will direct you, he who is all-powerful will prosper you. Pray give my very affectionate compliments to —, Through the everlasting righteousness of our Redeemer, I hope to meet them in the world of glory; and there he that is feeble will be as David.
Yours sincerely, &c.

## Hervey's views of religious societies

Even in his student days, Hervey had been keenly interested in societies for the improvement of manners and the Christian walk. In 1747, he helped found a meeting with the aim of 'promoting religion in ourselves and others' for those living in the Northampton area and drew up guidelines concerning how to witness, deal with swearers, the unchaste etc., pray, conduct Christian conversation, study the Bible, spend the Sabbath, witness in writing and how to keep a diary as a means of personal discipline. These friends strove to attend public services every day where possible and take their stand for the Lord in all walks of life. The fellowship was mainly Anglican but close connections were maintained with Reformed Independents and Baptists. Hervey attended these meetings regularly as long as he had the strength to travel on horseback, but in times of illness, his home was always open for their fellowship of which many members availed themselves. Realising the brevity of life, Hervey always pressed on his friends the necessity not to delay in working for Christ but to utilise every opportunity for witness given as soon as it presented itself. Typical of such encouragement were the words, 'Let us all remember, my dear friends, that time is upon the wing; eternity is at our door; therefore what we do for our blessed Master we must do quickly.'

**Hervey was blessed with two fine curates[1] who became men of the eighteenth century revival themselves**
When he was too ill to go visiting himself, he would make sure that his two curates, Brown and Maddock showed the same pastoral spirit. At times his curates were far too parsimonious for his taste and needed to be taught the basics of pastoral work. Even during his terminal illness, he had his curates report to him concerning whom they had visited and what they had said. A visitor from Scotland was taking down a preface dictated by Hervey for a new edition of Erskine because Hervey was too weak to write when one of his curates came in. Hervey asked if he had visited a certain sick woman and the curate replied that he had. 'Did you pray with her?' was Hervey's next question. This, too, was answered in the affirmative but the curate added that he had read prayers to her. Hervey asked if anyone else were present and heard that the Dissenting minister was there, too. 'How did he pray?' was Hervey's next question. The curate admitted that he liked the Dissenter's prayers very much but found that he took great liberty with God and did not bother to read his prayers but prayed spontaneously. Hervey could only say, 'I fear, I fear, he is better acquainted with the object of prayer than you are.'

**Bringing comfort to the sick and afflicted**
Hervey was most practical and sober in his counselling. He never approached a person on the sick bed or one suffering from loss of a dear one or great personal problems without talking about human sin and divine grace. He never gave a seeker or suffering person reason to feel sorry for himself or feel that circumstances were being extra hard on a person. Nor did he ever sit down by an individual who was complaining about his lot and complain with him. At times, his counsel will certainly seem harsh to a modern spoilt mind who believes that sympathy with the nature of the sufferer is the best sign of a good Christian counsellor. Whilst showing

---

[1] Abraham Maddock (sometimes Maddox) and Moses Brown. Maddock subsequently pastored a very large congregation which, after his death, joined the Northamptonshire Baptists.

strong Christian love for a soul and understanding of his predicament, Hervey never hesitated to look to God as the instigator of afflictions for a purpose often hidden in the divine love. Writing to one suffering friend at the end of 1747, he says:

> You well know that all afflictions, of what kind soever, proceed from God: I form the light, and create darkness; I make peace, and create evil; I the Lord do all these things, Isaiah xlv.7. They spring not from the dust; are not the effects of a random chance, but the appointment of an all-wise, all foreseeing God, who intends them all for the good of his creatures. This I think, is the Fundamental argument for resignation and the grand source of comfort. This should be our first reflection and our sovereign support. He that gave me my being, and gave his own Son for my redemption, he has assigned me this suffering. What he ordains, who is boundless love, must be good; what he ordains, who is unerring wisdom must be proper.
>
> This reconciled Eli to the severest doom that ever was denounced: It is the Lord and though grievous to human nature much more grievous to parental affection, yet it is unquestionably the best; therefore, I humbly acquiesce I kiss the awful decree, and say from my very soul, let him do what seemeth him good, 1 Sam. iii. 18.
>
> This calmed the sorrows of Job under all his unparalleled distresses: The Lord gave me affluence and prosperity; the Lord has taken all away: rapacious hands and warring elements were only his instruments; therefore I submit, I adore, I bless his holy name.
>
> This consolation fortified the man Christ Jesus at the approach of his inconceivably bitter agonies: The cup which, not my implacable enemies, but my Father, by their administration, has given me, shall I not drink it? It is your Father, dear sir, your heavenly Father, who loves you with an everlasting love, that has mingled some gall with your portion in life. Sensible of the beneficent hand from which the visitation comes, may you always bow your head in patient submission; and acknowledge, with the excellent but afflicted monarch Hezekiah, *Good is the word of the Lord concerning me,* 2 Kings xx. 19.
>
> All afflictions are designed for blessings; to do us good at the latter end, however they may crop our desires, or disquiet our minds at present. Happy (says the Spirit of inspiration, and not wretched) is the man whom God correcteth, Job v. 17; and for this reason, because his merciful chastenings, though not joyous but grievous, yieldeth the peaceable fruit of righteousness unto them that are exercised thereby, Heb. xii. 11. God's ways are not as our ways.

The children whom we love we are apt to treat with all the soft blandishments and fond caresses of profuse indulgence; and too, too often cocker them to their hurt, if not to their ruin. But the Father of spirits is wise in his love, and out of kindness severe. Therefore it is said, *Whom he loveth he chasteneth, and scourgeth every son whom he receiveth,* Heb. xii; 6. Would you not, dear sir, be a child of that everlasting Father, whose favour is better than life? Affliction is one sign of your adoption to this inestimable relation. Would you not be an 'heir of the inheritance incorruptible, undefiled, and that fadeth not away '?

Affliction is your path to this blissful patrimony. Through much tribulation we must enter into the kingdom of heaven, Acts xiv. 22. Would you not be made like your ever-blessed and amiable Redeemer? He was a man of sorrows, and acquainted with grief; and every disciple must expect to be as his master.

Perhaps you may think your affliction peculiarly calamitous; and that, if it had been of some other kind, you could more cheerfully submit, more easily bear it. But you are in the hands of an all-wise Physician, who joins to the bowels of infinite love the discernment of infinite wisdom. He cannot mistake your case. He sees into the remotest events; and, though he varies his remedies, always prescribes with the exactest propriety to every one's particular state. Assure yourself, therefore the visitation which he appoints is the very properest recipe in the dispensatory of heaven. Any other would have been less fit to convey saving health to your enjoyment of the temporal blessings which may, perhaps, be yet in store for you.

Should you inquire what benefits accrue from afflictions. Many and precious. They tend to wean us from the world. When our paths are strewed with roses, when nothing but music and odours float around; how apt are we to be enamoured with our present condition, and forget the crown of glory, forget Jesus and everlasting ages : But affliction, with a faithful though harsh voice, rouses us from the sweet delusion. Affliction warns our hearts to rise and depart from these inferior delights, because here is not our rest. True and lasting joys are not here to be found. The sweeping tempest, and the beating surge, teach the mariner to prize the haven, where undisturbed repose waits his arrival. In like manner, disappointments, vexations, anxieties, crosses teach us to long for those happy mansions, where all tears will be wiped away from the eyes, Rev. xxi.4; all anguish banished from the mind; nothing, nothing subsist, but the fulness of joy, and pleasures for evermore.

Afflictions tend to bring us to Christ. Christ has unspeakable and everlasting blessings to bestow: such as the world can neither

give nor take away; such as are sufficient to pour that oil of glad-
ness into our souls, which will swim above the waves of any earthly
tribulation. But are we not, dear sir, are we not most unhappily
indolent and inattentive to these blessings, in the gay hours of uninterrupted prosperity? It is very observable that scarce any made
application to our divine Redeemer, in the days of his abode with
us, but the children of affliction. The same spirit of supineness still
possesses mankind. We undervalue, we disregard the Lord Jesus,
and the unspeakable privileges of his gospel, while all proceeds
smoothly, and nothing occurs to discompose the tenor of our tranquillity. But when misfortunes harass our circumstances, or sorrows oppress our minds;—then we are willing, we are glad, we are
earnest, to find rest in Christ.

In Christ Jesus there is pardon of sins. Sin is a burden, incomparably sorer than any other distress. Sin would sink us into the
depths of eternal ruin, and transfix us with the agonies of endless
despair. But Christ has, at, the price of his very life, purchased
pardon for all that fly to him. He has borne the guilt of their sins in
his own body on the tree, 1 Pet. ii. 24. Have they deserved condemnation? He has sustained it in their stead. Are they obnoxious
to the wrath of God? He has endured it as their substitute; he has
made satisfaction, complete satisfaction for all their iniquities,
Rom. iii. 25, 26. So that justice itself, the most rigorous justice, can
demand no more. O that distresses may prompt us to prize this
mercy! may incite us to desire ardently this blessedness! then it
will be good for us to have been afflicted, Psalm cxix. 71.

Christ has obtained for us the gift of the Holy Spirit, Gal. iii. 2,
to sanctify our hearts, and renew our natures. An unrenewed carnal
mind, is ten thousand times more to be lamented, more to be
dreaded, than any external calamities. And nothing can cure us of
this most deadly disease but the sanctification of the Spirit. The
divine Spirit alone is able to put the fear of God in our souls, and
awaken the love of God in our hearts, Jer. xxxii. 40. His influences
suggest such awful and amiable thoughts to our minds, as will be
productive of these Christian graces. This sacred principle subdues our corruptions, and conforms us to our blessed Redeemer's
image. How is this best gift of Heaven disesteemed by the darlings
of the world, who have nothing to vex them? But how precious is
it, how desirable, to the heirs of sorrow? They breathe after it, as
the thirsty hart panteth for the water brooks. They cannot be satisfied without its enlightening, purifying, cheering communications.
This is all their request, and all their relief, 'that the spirit of Christ
may dwell in their hearts,' Rom. viii. 9; may enable them to possess their souls in patience, Luke xxi. 19, and derive never-ending
good from momentary evils. Before I close these lines, permit me

to recommend one expedient, which yet is not mine, but the advice of an inspired apostle. If any be afflicted, let him pray. Dear sir, fly to God in all your adversity, pour out your complaints before him in humble supplication, and show him your trouble. Psalm cxlii. 2. When I am in heaviness, says a holy sufferer, I will think upon God, Psalm lxi. 2,—his omnipotent power, his unbounded goodness, whose ear is ever open to receive the cry of the afflicted. When the psalmist was distressed on every side, without were fightings, within were fears, the throne of grace was the place of his refuge; I give myself to prayer, Psalm cix. 4, was his declaration. This method, we read, Hannah took, and you cannot but remember the happy issue, 1 Sam. i.10. Let me entreat you to imitate these excellent examples; frequently bend your knees, and more frequently lift up your heart to the Father of mercies, and God of all consolation; not doubting, but that through the merits of his dear Son, through the intercession of your compassionate High-priest; he will hear your petitions, will comfort you under all your tribulations, and make them all work together for your infinite and eternal good.

In the mean time, I shall not cease to pray, that the God of all power and grace may vouchsafe to bless THESE CONSIDERA-TIONS, and render them as balm to your aching heart, and as food to the divine life in your mind. I am, dear sir, with much esteem, compassion, and respect, your very sincere well-wisher, &c.[1]

### Hervey the preacher

Hervey took over his late father's work amongst a very faithful flock. The poor walked as much as twelve miles to the Lord's Day services, and the rich drew up in their coaches from far wider afield. Though marked by illness and often only able to recline on a couch whilst preaching, the more Hervey's health weakened, the more church attendance grew. It was as if everyone wished to capture as much as possible of the blessing which emanated from weak Hervey's display of strong faith. His portrayals of Jesus and His salvation were so moving that his hearers longed also to depart from this life and be with Christ for ever. Writing in 1747, when he realised for the first time that he would never recover from his permanent illness, Hervey confessed that he wanted now only to live to commune with Christ and preach the gospel. Of his work as a preacher he said:

> With regard to my public ministry, my chief aim should be, to beget in my people's minds a deep sense of their depraved, guilty, undone condition; and a clear believing conviction of the all-suffi-

---

[1] *Works*, Letter XLVII.

ciency of Christ, by his blood, his righteousness, his intercession, and his Spirit, to save them to the uttermost. I would also observe to labour for them in my closet, as well as in the pulpit; and wrestle in secret supplication, as well as to exert myself in public preaching, for their spiritual and eternal welfare. For unless God take this work into his own hand, what mortal is sufficient for these things?[1]

When preaching, Hervey never used notes except on rare occasions such as when a bishop made a visit of inspection and would demand to see Hervey's preparation work. This method of preaching occasionally had its drawbacks, and reports of one of these had reached Lady Francis' ear which she aired with Hervey. The country parson replied:

How does your Ladyship know, that I 'speak to my people an hour together'?—I must confess, I do sometimes. But I always blame myself for it. It detains the congregation too long. It renders the discourse tiresome to be heard, and almost impossible to be remembered. This is one of the inconveniences attending the extempore method of preaching. We forget how the time passes away; We advert not to the length of our harangue; and, being desirous of impressing our hearers, are insensibly betrayed into an undue prolixity.[2]

Hervey never minded being criticised in this way, indeed, he encouraged it, arguing that it was better to have one's mistakes corrected than have one's praise trumpeted about.[3]

Knowing that he had many farm-labourers in his congregation, Hervey never made his sermons too technical and had rarely more than two points to expound. He always encouraged his hearers to bring their Bibles to church and would mention a text which he asked all to look up and, at times, he told them to fold over the page so that they could easily find the passage again for their home study. He insisted that the sermon was merely preparatory to this and that when his congregation returned home, they should turn to the text and explain it to their children and to family members who were not at church.

The young Ryland and his wife had ample opportunities to hear Hervey preach as on their two visits a year to stay with Hervey, they did not attend the Baptist church which was only a few miles away but sat under the word as preached by their host. Of those times Ryland writes:

---

[1]    Letter XL, *Works*.

[2]    *Letters to Lady Francis Shirley,* Letter XCI, p. 216.

[3]    Ibid, Letter XCV, p. 227.

In the course of six years that I visited him twice a year; what astonishing charms of eloquence have I heard from him at family worship, as well as in the pulpit. Never did I hear from any other man such new turns and elevated range of thought and passion as I have heard from him times more than I can recollect, in the parlour, at family devotions. In a word, they were some of the best divinity lectures that ever were given to young students. . . He knew as well as any man the best figures which contained a beauty, or expressed a painful or pleasing commotion of the soul, and he seized with ardour the most glowing images of all things. He relished the most daring and striking ideas, and painted them in so lively a manner, as though you saw them before your eyes. . . his manner of addressing the understanding and conscience, the imagination, memory, and passions of his different kinds of hearers, were unboundedly new; and he could afford to blot out, and throw away riches, superior to other authors.[1]

Writing on Hervey's eloquence as a preacher, Ryland says:

We have very able divines, who have stated the great doctrines of the Gospel, and improved them in a masterly manner. Witness Dr. Waterland, Dr. Abraham Taylor, Dr. Calamy, and Mr. Sloss, on the Trinity. Dr. Owen and Mr. Hurrion on particular redemption. Mr. Richard Rawlin on Justification, by Christ's righteousness. Dr. Doddridge's sermon on Regeneration. Edward Polhill, Esq. on Christ, as the mirror of the divine perfections, and vital union with Christ. The Rev. Thomas Hall, on Final Perseverance. Dr. Gill on the Resurrection of the Dead: With many other great and good authors; but in point of eloquence and beauty, Hervey exceeds then all.[2]

It was not that Ryland felt that Hervey was all soothing beauty in his preaching. 'He could sting like a bee', said Ryland but 'he always affords a drop of honey to assuage the smart.'[3]

Hervey had few of his sermons published but he felt compelled to print his fast sermons according to the usual Church of England custom but with his own evangelical touch. He explains his reasons in his Preface:

'What then is his motive?'—This is the very truth. In several of the sermons published on this occasion, the *one thing needed* seems

---

[1]   *The Character of Mr. Hervey*, pp. 5-7.

[2]   Ibid, p. 14.

[3]   Ibid, p. 16.

to be overlooked. Christ and his free grace, Christ and his great salvation, are either totally omitted, or but slightly touched.—Where these are but slightly touched, the door of hope and the city of refuge are shewn, as it were, through a mist, dimly and indistinctly. We have no more than a transient glimpse of the desirable objects; and only so much light as is sufficient to bewilder, rather than direct.—Where they are totally omitted, the door of hope is barred, and the city of refuge withdrawn from our view. In this case, being without Christ, we are without consolation; and may justly complain, with the mourning prophet, *the Comforter, that should relieve our souls, is far off.*

Through the following discourses, a constant regard is paid to the redemption which is in Christ Jesus; to his all-atoning blood, and his everlasting righteousness; which are the grand means, both of comforting our hearts, and sanctifying our nature.—Indeed, the principle aim of the whole is, to display the unsearchable riches of Christ, the matchless efficacy of his death, and that perfect freeness with which all his invaluable benefits are bestowed.—*To those who believe he is precious*; and to those who are convinced of sin, these salutary truths will be their own best recommendation. Such readers will excuse a multitude of blemishes, provided they find Jesus who was crucified; Jesus, who is the desire of all nations; Jesus, than whom no other foundation can be laid, either for present holiness, or future happiness.

The titles alone of these sermons show how Hervey preached the whole counsel of God, covering the entire aspects of law and gospel, leaving out nothing. He begins with *The Time of Danger* opening his hearers eyes to the approaching doom for those not found in Christ. He goes on to outline *The Means of Safety*, showing how Christ's precious blood was shed to reconcile His people to God. Here Hervey emphasises that it was not merely the death of Christ which saves, thus producing mere pardon, but the obedience of Christ which made such an atoning death possible and a means of justifying sinners whom He covers in His righteousness and vouchsafes through His suretyship. Hervey does not recommend his hearers to saunter into these doctrines, gradually appropriating them and making them part of their mental apparatus. Using Proverbs 18:10, he urges those affected by his message *to run* to the strong tower of the Lord of righteousness and thus find a secure hiding place from the wages of their own sin.

Under *The Way of Holiness*, Hervey puts to flight all the Arminian errors heaped against him, condemning him for introducing Antinomianism because he taught that man can have no holiness of his own but only that which is imputed to him by Christ. Preaching on Ezekiel 18:27, Hervey teaches plainly that 'When the wicked man turneth away from his wickedness that he hath committed, and doth that which is lawful and right, he shall save his soul alive.'

Hervey argues that when he emphasises the righteousness of Christ imputed to us as the only saving claim we have before the judgment seat of God, he is not neglecting but promoting vital holiness. Leaning on 2 Peter 1:3, he tells his hearers and readers that 'It is through the knowledge of our adorable Saviour, as calling us to glory and virtue, that we have all things pertaining unto life and godliness.'

Hervey speaks firmly to those sinners who believe they can mortify their sin by keeping it in check and not letting it grow. What a foolish man a gardener would be if he pruned the tares in his garden so that they would equal the very choicest plants. No pruning of a briar can turn it into a lily-of-the-valley! Tares, like all wickedness, must be torn up by the roots. The wicked man with a heart of weeds must have that heart crucified and become a new creature in Christ so that he might receive a new nature, even more beautiful than the lilies.

Gentle Hervey is terrible to behold as he denounces in God's name the self-righteous pleas of any man. Commenting on the natural catastrophes that have been warning sinful man of his impending doom, Hervey pronounces God's verdict:

> Behold then, sinners, inconsiderate and insensible sinners, you are this day impleaded at God's bar: you are found guilty before the Judge of the world: you are upon the very brink of everlasting destruction.—Not the earth, but *hell*, is opening her mouth to devour you; not the stones and timber of your houses, but the *vengeance* of the Most High, is rushing down upon you. The sword, not of an enraged adversary, but of God's most *tremendous* displeasure is drawn, perhaps stretched out to destroy you: the pestilence, or what is infinitely more to be dreaded than the pestilence that walketh in darkness, the *curse* of God is ready to break forth upon you.—And will not these terrors awaken you, alarm you, persuade you? Thou God of the world, and God of our souls, let not thy judgments and thy threatenings go forth in vain!

Hervey renounced the Arminian teaching that the act of believing is that which enables God to count us righteous and emphasises the spiritual impotence of man, even when he is aware of his plight. Commenting on the wicked man's need to turn from his evil ways and do that which is lawful and right, Hervey says:

> But you are guilty, ruined, impotent creatures.—*Guilty*, and can you, under a load of trespasses, arise and do your Lord's will?—*Ruined*, and can you, amidst such discouraging circumstances, have

any heart to set about the work of reformation?—*Impotent*, and can you, under the most deplorable weakness, perform the most difficult of all services?—No; you must first be relieved and enabled, before you can be sufficient for these things. Like the woman bowed down with a spirit of infirmity, or like the impotent man at the pool of Bethesda, you must receive restoration and strength from God your Saviour. Turn then to Christ, who says by his prophet, *O Israel, thou hast destroyed thyself, but in me is thy help.*

Hervey then expounds fully how Christ removes guilt by blotting out the sinner's transgressions and how he restores his ruined nature in Christ:

Because you are ruined, and have nothing that may recommend you to the most high God, Christ has brought in a righteousness—a complete righteousness—a divine righteousness. Consider the unspotted purity of his nature, and the unsinning obedience of his life; consider his fervent charity to man, and his patient resignation to God; consider all his exalted virtues, and all his exemplary actions; these, all these, in their utmost perfection, are not only for the imitation, but for the justification also, of such sinners as you and I. His name is Jehovah, which speaks incomprehensible grandeur in him; Jehovah our righteousness, which speaks unutterable comfort to us. In this righteousness we may be fully accepted, and entitled to life eternal. Of this we make our boast, and say, *In the Lord have I righteousness*; I, a transgressor, have a real righteousness; I, a defective creature, have a consummate righteousness; I, a frail relapsing Christian, have an invariable and everlasting righteousness. O! what a treasure is this! what an unspeakable gift is this! Is there a cordial that can revive our spirits, is there a motive that can animate us to duty, like justification through Immanuel's righteousness?—Blessed Lord! this makes thy yoke easy and thy burden light.

The prose poet then goes on to relate how there is grace sufficient in Christ. Whatever hinders us from living a holy life, He removes; whatever we desire in his name, He bestows. In a life led by the Spirit, He delivers us from all that embarrasses us and discourages us so that we might serve Him without slavish or disquieting fear, in holiness and righteousness, all the days of our lives.

Should the seeking sinner cry out that he cannot burst the chains of his corruption and he be brought to that point where he cries out, 'Oh, that Christ would break them!' The preacher tells him, 'Fear not: he will, he will. He that sends his ministers to give you this exhortation; he that sends his Spirit to work this desire in your soul; he that spilt his blood to obtain all blessings for you; he will put forth his strength and turn you to himself.

He stretched his beneficent hand and saved Peter from sinking in the tempestuous sea. What he did for him, is a pattern and a pledge of what he is ready to do for you. . . he will bring you spiritual health and cure; he will carry on what he has begun, and enable you to grow in grace. He will comfort your hearts, and stablish you in every good work.'

Though Hervey always preached under great difficulty and had often breathing difficulties because of his consumption, he kept a careful but energetic eye on his congregation and noted who was present and who was absent. During his sermon on holiness, he spotted some people who were not too diligent in their attendance and was moved to show how serious this could be for their own spiritual safety. We thus find Hervey saying:

> I observe several persons here, on this day of humiliation, who very rarely attend the public worship.—Why, my friends, why do you withdraw yourselves from the preaching of the gospel? Know ye not, that Jesus passeth by, in the way of his ordinances? Here you may, like Bartimeus of old, approach the Son of David; here you may obtain faith and holiness. Faith cometh by hearing, and holiness by the word of God. And are not these blessings worth your attendance? can you live happily without them? can you die comfortably without them? or can you, without them, be prepared to meet your God, when he cometh to judge the world?—Why should you forsake the assembling yourselves together? Do you hear terrifying or distressing doctrines in this place? is this not the house of praise, as well as of prayer? does not the *joyful sound* echo under these roofs? Is not Christ set forth crucified before your eyes? crucified for such offenders as you! crucified, that such offenders as you may be pardoned, may be accepted, may be glorified? and will you despise such a divinely-compassionate Saviour? will you refuse such astonishingly-rich mercies? O! that hereafter you may *be glad when they say unto you, Let us go into the courts of the Lord.*
>
> Should my wishes prove vain, I have at least delivered my message. If you perish through obstinacy and unbelief, I am clear from your blood. I call heaven and earth to witness, you have been *warned*, you have been *instructed*, you have been *exhorted*. You cannot say, you perish for lack of knowledge; for life and salvation have been set before you, have been brought to your very door, and you are importuned to lay hold of them. You will therefore be without excuse, and have no cloak for your guilt.

The fourth and last sermon in this series, a so-called visitation sermon, was preached before Archdeacon John Brown at All Saints Church in Northampton on May 10, 1753. It was the natural outcome of the three previous messages entitled *The Cross of Christ: The Christian's Glory.* After the sinner has been ransomed, healed, restored and forgiven, what then? Hervey used Galatians 6:14 to answer that question in the presence of one who had come to supervise and check his proficiency as a shepherd of souls: 'God forbid that I should glory, save in the cross of our Lord Jesus Christ.' Hervey skilfully divided the text under three headings: 1. In what the apostle would not glory; 2. In what he did glory; and 3. What reason he had to glory in the cross of Christ.

Under the first heading, Hervey showed how Paul did not glory in his scholarly achievements, nor his natural upbringing as a Jewish Pharisee. Nor did he stress his great gifts and his wide usefulness in the Lord's service. He gloried in the scandalous cross on which rebellious slaves and crooks of the lowest order were hung to die. It must have reached his hearers ears as if Paul was saying that he glorified in a noose, or the gallows, or the gibbet. Indeed, when Hervey first used this comparison, some hearers, thinking of the cross as a beautiful ornamented church artifice, objected to Hervey's comparing it to the gallows. They told him they were disgusted at his contemptible language and begged him to leave out such comparisons in future from his sermons! But this is the very point that Hervey wished to make. We glory as Christians in those very things that make self-righteous sinners feel we are disgusting and contemptible. Hervey was glorying in the cross before the bishop's official representative and thus his superior. In spite of the risky business this was, he refused to make the cross a glittering, bejewelled crucifix to be worshipped and kissed by doting hypocrites and held aloft in procession by false shepherds. The cross, to Hervey, was where Christ was brutally wounded and killed in that very place that is our only rightful end. He died the death we had earned. Thus Christ's cross has become no ordinary cross to the saved sinner. It has become not an ignominious but hallowed and honoured place. It is the cross of Christ! It is the place where the elect's sin was conquered and lost its total power. Only those elect sinners can glory in the cross. Not even the angels can do so as it is possible to say, 'Angels, he rules over you; but he died on a cross for me.' How can we thus not 'exult in such transporting beneficence'?

Thus in dealing with his third point, Hervey shows how the rebel's wooden scaffold has become the tree of life, bearing divine and everlasting fruit and justifying men from all things. It has become the place of reconciliation where those that were afar off have been drawn nigh to their God, having their enmity blotted out. With justification and reconciliation comes holiness. This Hervey calls 'true morality', distinguishing between this and slavish obedience to the Mosaic law. 'True morality', he tells us, 'is most charmingly delineated throughout the whole Bible; it is the beginning of heaven in the human soul; and its proper origin is from the cross of our divine Master.—For, through the merits of his death, sinners are made partakers of the Holy Spirit: who writes upon their hearts, and makes legible in their conversation, what was anciently written upon the mitre of the high priest, Holiness to the Lord.' This is the teaching that men of God such as Gill, Romaine and Huntington taught but which was ridiculed as Antinomian by their law-bound critics. But Hervey knew that the old law was but a schoolmaster to bring the soul to Christ. Once in Christ's hands, the soul is in the hands of the Lawgiver Himself who does not need to teach by proxy. True followers of the law are followers of Christ. Sinai has been caught up in Calvary where Christ completed His fulfilment of it. Instead of stone tablets we have the voice of God Himself through His Holy Spirit indwelling our lives. Instead of remaining slaves and hirelings, we have become sons of the living God. Instead of merely seeing God as our Judge, He has become our Father. This is real (as Hervey calls it) justification, reconciliation and holiness. This is actually how God sees us and actually what Christ makes of us.

### Hervey and the communion of the saints

One of the most salient features of the pioneers of the eighteenth century revival was that they put inter-church fellowship before their denominational differences. To them sharing union in Christ as head of the Church universal and taking the Gospel to all was more important than personal preferences regarding modes of church government and order. Thus we find Baptist Gill working hand in hand with Independents in his Lime Street and East Cripplegate lectures, Anglican Augustus Toplady supporting his Baptist friends, Dissenting William Jay working closely with Hannah More of the Established Church, Whitefield the Church of England clergyman preaching at Doddridge's Dissenting Academy, John Newton, Vicar of Mary Woolnoth writing the curricula for Independent William Bull's college, Dissenter Risdon Darracott working with the Parish Council and the prison reformer John Howard opening his doors, his heart and his pocket to all Christians who put the Lord's work first. James Hervey stood in this worthy tradition and some of his closest friends were Independents, Baptists and members of Scottish denominations. Amongst Hervey's closest friends on the Anglican side were William Romaine, George Whitefield, Walker of Truro, Moses Brown who became Newton's Vicar at Olney and Thomas Jones[1]. Perhaps Hervey's most faithful companion was John Ryland Sen., a Baptist minister, and apart from Gill and Darracott who stood very close to Hervey, he enjoyed good fellowship with Doddridge, Watts, Pearsall, Brine, Evans, Medley and Cudworth amongst non-Anglicans. Witherspoon of Beith and Thomas Gillespie of Carnock were two of Hervey's many Scottish correspondents who also included members of

---

[1] Thomas Jones of Southwark not of Clifton.

the Traill and Hog families. The Anglican was especially open to evangelical Baptists and could not tolerate bigotry on baptismal matters on either side. Usually he had a Baptist to dinner one day and an Anglican the next. Sometimes when he invited both parties at once, difficulties, not of his making, would arise. Once when he had invited ministers of various denominations to share dinner with him together, he was shocked to hear a ministerial friend, a Mr. H. launch into a sharp attack against a Baptist Mr. S. present.[1] The offender, probably Hartley, who was staying with Hervey at the time, had not reckoned with his host. Hervey told John Ryland how he reacted, 'I thought it a breach of delicacy and propriety of conduct, especially to do this to my guest, and at my table; therefore I took up the cudgels, and personated a baptist.' Hervey was very critical of the Prayer Book concerning baptism and the visitation of the sick and campaigned for a reform in the language and theology. Of this effort he wrote, 'In an affair of the highest consequence, how negligent is the community, I mean in the long expected reformation of the liturgy, in which, excellent as it is upon the whole, there are some passages so justly exceptionable, that every bishop in the kingdom will tell you he wishes to have them expunged; and yet, I know not for what political or timid reasons, it continues just as it did. Had our first reformers been thus indolent, we still had been Papists.'[2] Hervey's defence of the Baptist position did not go unheeded by his congregation. After Hervey's death, a minister took over who had married Hervey's younger sister without apparently taking over her gospel faith. When John Newton visited Weston-Favell a few years later to preach, he found no evangelicals in Hervey's church—they had all left and become Baptists!

Writing in 1748 to a friend who had written comforting him in his physical frailty, Hervey tells him:

> You are not ignorant of my sentiments with regard to our dissenting brethren. Are we not all devoted to the same supreme Lord? Do we not all rely on the merits of the same glorious Redeemer? By professing the same faith, the same doctrine which is according to godliness, we are incorporated into the same mystical body. And how strange, how unnatural would it be, if the head should be averse to the breast, or the hands inveterately prejudiced against the feet, only because the one is habited somewhat differently from the other? Though I am steady in my attachment to the established church, I would have a right hand of fellowship, and a heart of love, ever ready, ever open, for all the upright evangelical dissenters.

---

[1]   Letter XXII, Ryland collection.

[2]   Letter CLVI. Hervey wrote this in a general criticism of laws and rules both secular and ecclesiastical.

Whilst Hervey was convalescing in London, he had numerous visits from Dissenters, other than his friend John Gill, pastor of Goat Yard Baptist Church, and tells of such a visit in a letter dated November 15, 1750:

> Yesterday a serious dissenter from the country came to see me. God had freed him from a spirit of bigotry, and made my book acceptable to him. O that we may all love one another, and bear with one another! so fulfil the law, and follow the example of Christ. In the new Jerusalem, that city of the living God, all our little differences of opinion as well as all the remainders of corruption, will fall off. In the light of God's countenance we shall see the truth clearly, and enjoy the life, the life of heaven and eternity perfectly. O that we may love that amiable and adorable Being every day, every hour, more and more! who, though the king immortal and invisible, gave his own Son to bleed and die for worms, for rebels; for you, my dear friend, and for your unworthy, but truly affectionate, &c.

Casting a glance at those who made an issue concerning non-essential differences between Dissenters and Anglicans Hervey spoke of a Dissenting friend, saying:

> I dearly love him, and rejoice in the expectation of meeting him in the everlasting kingdom of our glorious Redeemer. How inconsiderable, what a perfect nothing, is the difference of preaching in a cloak or in a gown, since we both hold the Head, both united to the same Saviour, and have access by the same Spirit to the Father. I assure him his name has been constantly mentioned in my poor intercessions, ever since he favoured me with his friendly and edifying epistle. Tell him I am making some faint attempts to recommend to the world a doctrine which is music to his ears, and better than a cordial to his heart--the righteousness of Immanuel, freely imputed to wretched sinners for their complete justification and everlasting acceptance.[1]

Writing to Ryland on October 23, 1756, Hervey told him:

> Yesterday my old friend, Mr Hartley (an Anglican), dined with me, and brought a pious clergyman with him; the day before, your brother, (and why should I not add my brother) Mr. Evans (a Baptist), was content with a morsel at my table. O! for that hour, when

---

[1]   Letter LXI

we shall all sit down at the marriage feast of the LAMB! May we taste it by faith, till our souls are 'satiated with its fulness in glory.'[1]

Often Hervey's insistence on the need for imputed righteousness and the doctrines of grace caused him to be better understood amongst his Dissenting friends than amongst those of his own denomination. A Dr. Free, lecturing to his fellow clergymen, took great exception to Hervey's belief that the Christian has no righteousness of his own and is thus solely dependent on Christ's and announced on hearing of Hervey's death, 'James Hervey, rector of Weston-Favell, was permitted to go on in his own way, till death put an end to his blasphemies.' One would have thought that his own view that raised the works of Christians to the status of righteousness in their own right would have been thought blasphemous by any orthodox Christian as it took the sinner's gaze from Christ and turned it to his own strivings to please God. This point was taken up by fellow-Anglican Erasmus Middleton in his four-volumed *Biographia Evangelica* when outlining Hervey's life and work. Concerning criticism of Hervey's theology from within his own denomination Middleton says, 'Some have, with absurdity enough, objected to Mr. Hervey's what they are pleased to call Calvinism, forgetting or not observing, that all the doctrines of free grace, fervently preached by Calvin, and therefore meant to be abused by his name, are the doctrines of the church of England, which every minister of that church is bound to observe and teach upon OATH. Hence, if he omit to preach them, and much more if he dare to preach contrary to them, he is not only a doctrinal Dissenter from that church, but an impiously perjured person in the sight of God and man.' He goes on to say, 'Our Dissenters in general have had but too much reason to say, "that they have kept our own articles for us"; and to the honour of many among them it must be added, that they have adorned the doctrines too by their lives and writings.'[2]

Hervey put all the strength and influence that he could into the work of evangelical prayer that was going on amongst the various denominations in the eighteenth century. In 1744 a number of Scottish ministers, following the pattern of Continental missionary-minded Christians, called for a special regular time of prayer concerning the spread of the Lord's Kingdom. This was followed in 1748 by Jonathan Edward's *Call to United Extraordinary Prayer* in America. In 1757 a number of London Evangelicals, under the leadership of Romaine gathered together to discuss how they, too, could best promote true evangelical fellowship and the spread of the gospel. Hervey was one of the first they asked for support. These friends subsequently published *An Earnest Invitation to the Friends*

---

[1]   Letter XXII, Ryland collection.

[2]   Vol. VI, pp. 331, 332.

*of the Established Church, to join with several of their brethren, clergy
and laity, in setting apart one hour in the Sunday of every week for prayer
and supplication, especially during the present troublesome times.* This
was later extended to 'all the well-disposed Christians (laity as well as
clergy) throughout this nation,' and was seen as prayer for repentance
because of private and national sins before going on to pray for the growth
of God's kingdom amongst the nations. Such earnest prayer was instrumental in furthering much Independent, Presbyterian and Anglican world-
wide evangelistic work and was followed in 1784 by the *Prayer Call* of
the English Particular Baptists which resulted in their overseas missionary
endeavours and which sparked off a number of denominational and inter-
denominational inner missions and foreign mission societies.

## John Ryland sums up Hervey's ministry

After minutely analysing all the aspects of Hervey's ministry in words
which could not possibly be more full of praise—even wonder and mar-
vel—and giving thanks to God for Hervey's personal testimony to him,
Ryland concludes:

> He was governed in his whole temper and conduct by the su-
> preme ends of his ministry, which were the utmost glory of CHRIST,
> and the union of immortal souls to him. All his thoughts and stud-
> ies were tinctured with this design. All his writings and his ser-
> mons were animated by this principle. CHRIST was, in the highest
> sense, his whole life; and he lived *from* CHRIST as the fountain of
> his life; he lived *like* CHRIST, as the pattern of his life; and he
> lived *to* his glory, as the end of his life. His great aim and passion-
> ate desire, was to bring souls to *know* CHRIST, to make them *wise*
> men; to bring souls to *love* CHRIST, to make them *good* men; and
> to bring their souls to *possess* CHRIST, to make them *happy* men.[1]

---

[1]   Ryland's *The Character of the Rev. James Hervey*, p. 18.

# Chapter Ten:
# A Peaceful Departure

### Final preparations

By the end of 1757, it was obvious that Hervey's earthly vessel was breaking up and his letters are full of reports of his frailties and wishes that he would soon be absent from the body but present with the Lord. The very thought of over-demanding guests coming to visit him made him tremble as he knew that he had little energy to cope with them. One letter of several with death and departure as its theme must be quoted to show how Hervey was labouring towards triumph in preparation for his last call:

> My Dear Friends,—Sincerest thanks for your benevolent offices; may they, through our great High Priest, and in the incense of his atonement, go up as a memorial before God; not as a demand, (we may observe), not as a bill drawn upon heaven, but only as a memorial.
>
> I had a very restless night, tore almost to pieces by my cough. Strange! that these flimsy vessels can bear such violent straining! that none of them will burst, and let the battered soul slip away to her eternal rest in Christ!
>
> Here are two sets of the Meditations, with which you may gratify some of your acquaintance. The Lord Jesus Christ grant that they may promote his glory. Do not you often wish, often pray, that the same blessed effect may be produced by your book? We authors should not be like the ostriches in the wilderness, cruel and forgetful of their young, Lam. iv. 3.
>
> If you have Dr. Grey's translation of Hawkins Browne's Latin poem on the Immortality of the Soul, favour me with the sight of it: it is a grand subject; it is a glorious subject; and, when considered

in connexion with Jesus Christ, it is a delightful subject. Oh! that it may incite us to aim, not at the things which are seen, for they are temporal; but at the things which are not seen, for they are eternal.

I have found the little treatise, entitled, *Recovery from Sickness*. It is one of the most pertinent and rational, the most animating and encouraging, that I have seen on the occasion. Few properer pieces, I think, can be put into a sick person's hand. May the Lord God, omnipotent and gracious, accompany it with his blessing!

I am always complaining; complaining of my poor body; but, I trust, more and more resigned to the unerring and gracious will of my Lord.

I beg, I entreat you, if you value the honour of the gospel, that you will dissuade those polite persons you mention, from coming to hear me to-morrow. My spirits sink more and more. I am visited with some returns of my hacking cough, perhaps I shall not be able to speak at all. Such disagreeable circumstances will only expose me, and create in them very unpleasing ideas of what I shall deliver. My imagination is gone. I am sensible my sermons are flat and my voice spiritless. Why therefore should you bring persons of taste to see the nakedness of the land? The poor country people love me tenderly, and therefore bear with my infirmities; else I should no longer attempt to preach even before them. I am now unfit to appear in the pulpit.

I hope Dr. Swan's journey will be blessed to the restoration and establishment of his health. I wish I may never forget the text on which he heard the minister of Weston preach; I wish we may all enjoy the blessing comprised and promised in it: 'I will pray the Father, and he shall give you another Comforter, that he may abide with you for ever.' Do not you, my dear friend, think of such things? talk of such things to your lady, and instruct your children in such things? O! let us remember the Judge is at the door, and eternity is near.

I heartily wish Mrs.—a speedy recovery, and a sanctified improvement of her affliction. See, my dear friend, how all flesh is grass ; but Jesus and his great salvation endureth for ever; here is indeed an everlasting possession. The text particularly fit for me and for you to meditate on; (viz. Heb. i. 2, 8.) I will preach on next Sunday. Can any be more grand in itself; or more consolatory to us sinners?

How go you on? do you see any opening in the affair we last talked about? are you come to any determination? Remember him who sees, this very moment, all the consequences of every step we take; and who hath said, in tender compassion to our ignorance, 'The Lord shall guide thee continually.' Pray, beware of precipitate resolutions; *festina lente*. Whatever we do, whithersoever we go, may we say with the Psalmist, 'This God is our God for ever and ever; he shall be our guide even unto death.' My weak state of body dispirits my mind, and enervates my hand. Oh that I may be strong in faith, joyful through hope, and rooted in charity! and not I only, but my dear friend, whose I am cordially and inviolably, while, &c.[1]

## Wesley burdens dying Hervey

It was obvious that Wesley's private attacks against Hervey's gospel doctrines, which he was now making public both from the pulpit and in print, lay heavy on Hervey's mind. Those who blame Hervey for even thinking of taking up Wesley's challenge when he should have been preparing for the grave are all on Wesley's side and under his lasting influence. To Hervey, however, the doctrine of Christ's vicarious righteousness resting on an atonement that really redeemed those for whom it was intended was the only truth that could reclaim man from the wages of sin. Men who sought to gain holiness by personal effort and thus please God could never cleanse themselves from their pollution and find salvation in God. Every good work of man put forward as a sign of holiness, to Hervey, was a denial of the righteousness that Christ had worked out for us. Man's shame ought to be centred around his own filthy-ragged righteousness and his boast should be in the perfect righteousness of Christ. Hervey, too, thought that Wesley's holiness doctrine, with its stages in attaining justification and perfection, denied the grace and love of God as 'The vilest of men have just the same right to Christ and his merits, as the best of men, a right founded not on their awakened desires, not on anything in themselves but purely, solely, entirely on the free grant of a Saviour.' Hervey saw no difference between Socinians and Wesleyans in their insistence that salvation was according to conditions to be fulfilled by man. To him they were both ardent enemies of the truth as it is in Jesus. This error, he believed, smacked of the Classical writers but had nothing to do with the Bible.[2]

## The only preparation for heaven is to secure the favour of Christ in pardon and justification

Friends who visited Hervey in 1758 testified that they had never caught such a profound glimpse of heaven as when talking to terminally ill Hervey. Though wishing to depart and be forever with the Lord, he felt that he should not go before he was called and thus followed the advice of his doctor carefully. In 1755, he had read the testimony of a believer who so

---

[1]   *Works*, Letter CLXXXI.

[2]   These sentiments are expressed in *Works*, Letter CLXXXIII.

longed to die and be with Christ that he refused to take medicinal aid when ill and forbade his friends to pray for his recovery. Of his stubbornness, Hervey wrote, 'Life and health are mercies in the esteem of Heaven; and the dying Christian ought to esteem everything as God esteems it. Suppose such a one desires to die, yet still he ought to use every lawful means to live, to make the will of God his own, and to be willing to continue even out of heaven, as long as his heavenly Father pleases.'[1] In the same letter Hervey gave sound advice concerning seeking consolation in illness, thanking the Lord for improvement and preparing for the home-call. Concerning the latter, Hervey says, 'The only preparation is to secure the favour of Christ, and an interest in his merits, by which we are pardoned and justified. A participation of the Spirit of Christ, by which we are made fit for heaven.' There was no doubt in the minds of those who knew Hervey in his final illness that their friend possessed Christ's favour and a participation of His Spirit to a high degree.

### 'Calvinistical' preaching by terminally ill Hervey

William Bull, friend of Cowper and Newton, was taken to hear Hervey preach in 1758 when a young boy. Years later, Bull told his grandson Josiah how 'Mr Hervey was then in the last stage of consumption, was pale and thin, and when he stretched out his hand, as the sun shone upon it, it was rendered almost transparent,' and relates how, though it was no special occasion, the church was 'crowded to excess' and the windows had to be removed so that the crowds outside could hear. Bull, a man whose memory was so great that he could learn the sermons of others off by heart as they were being given, told Josiah how Hervey warned his congregation about the deep sin that was present in the flesh of God's saints on earth, saying to them:

> You have observed the walls on either side of the path leading to this church. They are covered, as you know, with ivy. Now, you may pluck off the leaves, and break off the branches, so that none of them shall be seen on the outside; but the roots of the plant have so worked themselves into the wall, that, it would be impossible entirely to eradicate them without taking down the wall, and not leaving one stone upon another. And so must this frail body be taken down; and then, and not till then, shall we get rid of the remains of a degenerate nature.[2]

---

[1] Hervey could not accept the fact that Burnham refused all assistance when dying, even prayer for his recovery. It was seen as entirely wrong by Hervey who nevertheless helped print the Memoirs and added a Preface. This was to assist Burnham's destitute widow who was able to earn a little cash on the sales. This caused Hervey some difficulty as the rumour was spread that he was the author.

[2] *Memorials of the Rev. William Bull*, p. 8.

This is the story that Tyerman, true to his own Wesleyan perfectionist convictions, removed from its touching context to show how 'Calvinistical' Hervey's preaching was and how, 'Hervey's metaphor was striking; but metaphors are not arguments!' Tyerman could not accept Hervey's view of the perpetual sinfulness of human nature. Yet here, knowing his own end was near and knowing his own heart, Hervey could not afford to give his hearers false hope in themselves as he knew that they would follow him soon to the grave and it was his duty to give them a concern about their own filthy-ragged righteousness that they might long for the righteousness of Christ. This is not 'Calvinistical' preaching to be mocked as Tyerman sees it, but preaching the truth as revealed in Christ which is preached to be believed.[1]

**What thou dost, do quickly**

As the summer of 1758 turned into autumn, we find Hervey warning his friends that he would not 'live to see the approaching Christmas.' After taking prayers in the evening of Sunday, October 3 he became very ill and had to be helped upstairs by his mother and sister, never to leave his bedroom again. His body from now on was perpetually wracked in pain due to attacks of cramp, coughing and general weakness. Often his pulse was so faint that the doctor could only perceive it with great difficulty. It was amazing that he still could write. To a friend he says, 'I now spend almost my whole time in reading and praying over the Bible. Indeed, indeed you cannot conceive how the springs of life in me are relaxed and relaxing. "What thou dost, do quickly," is for me a proper admonition, as I am so apprehensive of my approaching dissolution.' A fortnight later, Hervey replies to a friend, 'Glad I am to be informed, that you are so very zealous for the honour and interest of our Lord Jesus Christ. What can make mankind happy, but his gospel? What is worthy of our sedulous application, but his interest? What will be a substantial reward, but his acceptance, favour, and love? I am now reduced to a state of infant weakness, and given over by my physician. My grand consolation is to meditate on Christ; and I am hourly repeating those heart-reviving lines of Dr. Young, in his fourth night:

This, only this, subdues the fear of death;
And what is this? Survey the wondrous cure;
And at each step let higher wonder rise!
Pardon for infinite offence! and pardon
Through means that speak its value infinite!
A pardon bought with blood with blood divine!

---

[1]    *The Oxford Methodists*, pp. 278,279.

With blood divine of him I made my foe!
Persisted to provoke! though woo'd and aw'd
Bless'd and chastis'd, a flagrant rebel still!
A rebel 'midst the thunders of his throne!
Nor I alone, a rebel universe!
My species up in arms! not one exempt!
Yet for the foulest of the foul he died;
Most joy'd for the redeem'd from deepest guilt,

These amazingly comfortable lines, I dare say, you will treasure up in your heart; and when you think of them, will think of me; and I hope, dear sir, pray for me, that I may not disgrace my ministry, or dishonour the gospel of my Master in my last moments, by unbelief! base provoking unbelief! This probably is the last time you will ever hear from me: for indeed it is with some difficulty I have wrote now; but I shall not fail to remember you in my intercessions for my friends at the throne of Christ; and I humbly beg of God Almighty, that the love of his Son may sweetly constrain you, and that his promises may be ever operative on your mind.'[1]

## Arminian accusations of Antinomian do not trouble Hervey's refuge in the law's Fulfiller

Just a matter of days before his death, Hervey came under harsh criticism by free-willers for his doctrine of imputed righteousness which was claimed to promote lasciviousness and make a Christian so sure of the mercies of Christ that he would be encouraged to live an Antinomian life, knowing that nothing could separate him from Christ's love. The idea that Hervey could be taken for an Antinomian is preposterous but this is what was being rumoured by those who knew Hervey was dying. Hervey was always shocked at this accusation not being able to imagine how one caught up in Christ should misuse that intimate fellowship with his Master in such a way. To one who warned him of what was being rumoured, Hervey said:

In spite of the sarcastical reflections you say are thrown upon me, I must recommend to every one Marshall on *Sanctification*, and Jenk's *Submission to the Righteousness of God*. These are with me the two fundamental books; these teach vital religion. Do they who would decry faith, and extol their good works, distinguish themselves by the practice of them? If not, I must beg leave to say, they are self-condemned. Only observe for the next month (by their fruits you will know them) the conduct of those who are such loud advocates for the merit, the dignity of man, and the freedom of his ac-

---

[1]   *Works*, Letter CCVII.

tion; and of those who rely on the active and passive obedience of Christ; and then tell me ingeniously, which are the people that pay the greatest reverence to the word of God; and in particular, to the fourth commandment? Inquire which of them use family prayer? whose conversation is most edifying? which of them visit and travel on Sundays? and which of them pass that holy day as becomes those who have named the name of Christ? I will be bold to say, that, on an impartial examination, the majority will be found on the side of those who embrace the doctrine of the imputation of Christ's righteousness, and who expect salvation by him alone, and not by deeds which they have done.[1]

In the same letter, thought to be the last he ever wrote, Hervey tells how his cough is very troublesome and medicines give him no relief, yet his never-failing cordial is the love of Christ.

### Hervey's enemies spread more evil rumours concerning the dying saint

At the same time, Hervey's curate, Abraham Maddock, came to him with the news that the rumour was being spread that Hervey had renounced his belief in justification through faith in Christ's imputed righteousness and had confessed that Sandeman's view of faith as mere acceptance of Scriptural axioms was correct. Hervey assured his curate that he had not become a Sandeman by any means and Maddock tried to persuade him to have an article placed in a London paper affirming his orthodox stance. Hervey replied that he had taken up the matter in his *Answer to Mr Wesley*[2], which he hoped to publish soon and the matter should be left at that.

### Hervey's one sadness was that he had not served Christ well enough

Hervey's last experiences were not all mountain-top. At times he was filled with remorse as when he told Maddock in tears, 'O! what has Christ, how much has Christ done for me, and how little I have done for so loving a Saviour! If I preached even once a week, it was at last a burden to me. I have not visited the people of my parish as I ought to have done, and thus have preached from house to house. I have not taken every opportunity of speaking for Christ.' Lest his friends took this to be a sign that Hervey feared death, he was quick to add, 'Do not think I am afraid to die; I assure you I am not; I know what my Saviour hath done for me; and I wish to be gone, but I wonder and lament to think of the love of Christ in doing so much for me, and how little I have done for him.'

---

[1]    Ibid, Letter CCIX.

[2]    Published as *Aspasio Vindicated*.

## The only invaluable riches are in heaven

On December 20, 1758 Dr. Stonehouse visited Hervey and, after his examination, told him that he had only three or four days to live. The dear doctor began to relate to his patient what the joys of heaven were. 'True, Doctor, true,' replied Hervey, 'the only invaluable riches are in heaven. What would it avail me now to be Archbishop of Canterbury?[1] disease would show no respect to my mitre. That prelate not only is very great, but, I am told, has religion really at heart; yet it is godliness, not grandeur, that will avail him hereafter. The gospel is offered to me, a poor country parson, the same as to his Grace: Christ makes no difference between us! Why, then, do ministers thus neglect the charge of so kind a Saviour, fawn upon the great, and hunt after worldly preferments with so much eagerness, to the disgrace of our order? These are the things, Doctor, and not our poverty or obscurity, which render the clergy so justly contemptible in the eyes of worldlings. No wonder the service of our church (grieved am I to say it!) is become such a lifeless thing, since it is, alas! too generally executed by persons dead to godliness in all their conversation, whose indifference to religion, and worldly-minded behaviour, proclaim the little regard they pay to the doctrines of the Lord who bought them.'

Even when on the verge of death, Hervey felt for the souls of others and, as Dr. Stonehouse was about to leave, Hervey reminded his doctor that he had recently suffered a serious fall from his horse and was badly bruised and still looking shaken and pale. He pointed out that Stonehouse should take this as a warning from the Lord to be very careful how he used his life in the Lord's service as one never knew when one could be called home. The words were highly relevant to Stonehouse who was about the same age as his patient now being called to Glory.

### George Whitefield says farewell

When Whitefield heard that Hervey was dying, he wrote his last farewells to him from London on December 19. There was nothing in Whitefield's words which reflects usual human nature to put off thoughts or words about death and strive to fill the person dying with false hopes of recovery. Whitefield knew where Hervey was going and came to the vital point straight away,

And is my dear friend indeed about to take his last flight? I dare not wish your return into this vale of tears; but our prayers are

---

[1]   Dr. Thomas Secker (1693-1768) gained his doctorate in medicine at Leyden before going on to study for the ministry at Oxford. He took a stand very near to that of the Evangelicals and Bishop Porteus prefaced a biography to the 12 volumes of Secker's *Works*.

continually ascending to the Father of our spirits, that you may die in the embraces of a never-failing Jesus, and in all the triumphs of an exalted faith. O when will my time come! I groan in this tabernacle, being burdened, and long to be clothed with my house from heaven. Farewell, my very dear friend, f-a-r-e-well! Yet a little while and we shall meet,

> Where sin, and strife, and sorrow cease,
> And all is love, and joy, and peace.

There Jesus will reward you for all the tokens of love which you have showed, for His great name's sake, to yours most affectionately in our common Lord,
George Whitefield

P. S. God comfort your mother, and relations, and thousands and thousands more, who must bewail your departure.[1]

On Christmas Eve, Hervey tried to get up and walk but had only taken a few steps when he began to fall due to general weakness. His sister caught him but he fainted and was thought to be dead. When he came round, his brother said, 'We were afraid you was gone.' Hervey replied 'I wish I had.'

### Hervey's last Christmas message
On Christmas Day Hervey's brother came into the dying man's room to hear him complain of his own ingratitude to God for what he had done for him. When his curate arrived, Hervey could only whisper, 'Sir, I cannot talk with you.' and said that he was in inner conflict. He was heard to say several times, 'When this great conflict is over, then.' When Dr. Stonehouse entered the suffering saint was almost suffocated from phlegm and vomit and his pulse was growing weaker, yet now Hervey would not stop talking about the blessings he was receiving. He encouraged Stonehouse to seek for the essential things in life and be prepared for his own home-call, not letting the affairs of this world pull him down. Stonehouse begged him to conserve his energies but Hervey replied, 'No, Doctor, no. You tell me I have but few minutes to live; oh let me spend them in adoring our great Redeemer. Though my flesh and my heart fail me, yet God is the strength of my heart, and my portion for ever.' He then went on to quote 1 Corinthians 3:22, 23 which he gave as 'All things are yours, life and death: for ye are Christ's.' and said, referring to Philip

---

[1]   Tyerman's *Life of Whitefield*, p. 413.

Doddridge's exposition of the text, 'Here is the treasure of a Christian. Death is reckoned amongst this inventory;—and a noble treasure it is. How thankful am I for death, as it is the passage through which I pass to the Lord and Giver of eternal life, and as it frees me from all this misery you now see me endure, and which I am willing to endure, as long as God thinks fit! for I know he will, by and by, in his own good time, dismiss me from the body. These light afflictions are but for a moment, and then comes an eternal weight of glory. Oh welcome, welcome death!—Thou mayest well be reckoned amongst the treasures of the Christian.—To live is Christ, but to die is *gain.*'

As the doctor was going, Hervey thanked him for his tender care. He then lay so still that even the doctor thought he was dead and took a mirror out of his pocket and applied it to Hervey's lips. The doctor saw that he was still breathing, though faintly, and Hervey recovered for a few moments more. The pangs of death then took hold of Hervey and he knew he was going home. With a look of expectant joy on his face he spoke in chorus with Simeon of old, saying, 'Lord, now lettest thou thy servant depart in peace, according to thy most holy and comfortable word: for mine eyes have seen thy precious salvation.' and added, 'Here, Doctor, is my cordial. What are all cordials to the dying, compared to the salvation of Christ? This, this supports me.' After a short while, Hervey was heard to say 'The conflict is over; now all is done.' He then said two or three times, 'Oh precious salvation' and then leaned his head to one side on the arm-chair in which he was sitting and fell asleep in Jesus aged forty-four.

Hervey's first biographer ended his account of Hervey's death by writing, 'God grant that we might all live the life, and die the death of the righteous, and that our last end may be like his!' Combining these thoughts with those of Hervey's on his death-bed and those he expressed in *Theron and Aspasio*, William Cowper identifying Hervey with his own hero, Aspasio, wrote:

Oh most delightful hour by man
Experienc'd here below;
The hour that terminates his span,
His folly and his woe.

Worlds should not bribe me back to tread
Again life's dreary waste;
To see my days again o'erspread
With all the gloomy past.
My home, henceforth, is in the skies,
Earth, seas, and sun adieu;
All heav'n unfolded to my eyes,
I have no sight for you

Thus spake Aspasio, firm possest
Of faith's supporting rod
Then breathe'd his soul into its rest,
The bosom of his God.

He was a man among the few
Sincere on Virtue's side,
And all his strength from Scripture drew,
To hourly use applied.

That rule he priz'd, by that he fear'd,
He hated, hop'd, and lov'd,
Nor ever frown'd, or sad appear'd,
But when his heart had rov'd.

For he was frail as thou or I,
And evil felt within,
But when he felt it, heav'd a sigh,
And loath'd the thought of sin.

Such liv'd Aspasio, and at last,
Call'd up from earth to heaven,
The gulph of death triumphant pass'd,
By gales of blessing driven.

*His* joys be *mine*, each reader cries,
When my last hour arrives:
They shall be yours, my verse replies.
Such ONLY be your lives.

The *Northampton Mercury* produced one of the finest pieces of Christian obituary to come from a secular newspaper by reporting:

> On Christmas-day, in the afternoon, died, in the 45th year of his age, the Rev. Mr. James Hervey, rector of Weston-Favell, near Northampton, and author of *Meditations among the Tombs, Flower Gardens*, &c. He was one of the most eminent instances of the power of Christianity upon the human mind. In his ministerial province he was pious, fervent, and indefatigable. In his ordinary connexions with the community he was ever cheerful, conscientiously punctual in all his dealings, and amiably candid to persons of every denomination. To his charities he set no bounds, scarcely leaving himself the mere requisites of his station. Under the severest trials of infirmity, for several years he displayed the highest

example of fortitude, serenity, patience, and an entire resignation to the divine will. His writings most abundantly evidence his learning and ingenuity: But, reader, it is not the acquisitions of his understanding, but the improvements of his heart, and his confidence in the great Redeemer, which will now avail this most excellent man.

# Chapter Eleven:
# Aspasio Vindicated

**An interesting theory**

In 1940 T. B. Shepherd published a Ph.D. thesis entitled *Methodism and the Literature of the Eighteenth Century*, featuring a chapter on James Hervey whom he introduces as the next famous Methodist writer to the Wesleys. This oft-quoted but badly researched work provides some very imaginative background information which must cause many smiles if not much head-shaking from those familiar with Wesley's and Hervey's works. One of Dr. Shepherd's theories, in particular, provides for much pleasant speculation. Shepherd argues that Hervey used his correspondence with Wesley on the subject of Calvinism as a basis for his *Theron and Aspasio*. No details are given but the reader is left to imagine that the dialogues and letters in the work depict conversations between Hervey the Calvinist, in the person of Aspasio and Wesley the Arminian in the person of Theron. As Shepherd is a professing Methodist, his is a very noble gesture as everyone knows that Theron was soundly converted through Aspasio's testimony and saw through his own self-righteousness, rejecting it for the righteousness of Christ. The fact that Shepherd does not seem to have read *Theron and Aspasio* all the way up to its happy ending rather spoils our brown study, but the thesis provides us with an insight as to what might have happened if Wesley had suddenly found himself free of his self-centred views of righteousness, law-obedience, justification, perfect love, sinless perfection, imputation and the covenant of grace. We are allowed to speculate on what would have become of Wesley and his movement if he had followed Theron at last and had testified to having his sins imputed to Christ and Christ's righteousness to him. How this experience would have strengthened the faithful and the newly converted throughout the Evangelical Revival and up to the present day! If only Wesley had clearly testified that free justification from all sin is because of God's perfect love demonstrated by the sinless perfections of Christ in fulfilling the Law for the sake of His Bride; a Bride bound to Him through the covenant of grace. Sadly, Dr. Shepherd's pipe-dream was just that and no more. The naked truth is that when John Wesley read *Theron and Aspasio*, he became so over-wrought and upset and took the fact that Hervey disagreed with him so to heart personally that he quite over-reacted and in publishing against dying Hervey, rejected not only Hervey's doctrines, but in his anger, rejected many a doctrine which he had formally held with him, such as the imputed righteousness of Christ.

### Hervey's last major task

Thus the last year and a half of Hervey's short life, were outwardly troubled times for him. During this time, Wesley was denouncing his doctrines in letters, from the pulpit and in print, proclaiming that Hervey was an Antinomian and made Christ 'a minister of sin'. This action alone was a great breach of fellowship and friendship and showed that Wesley had utterly turned against his saintly brother in Christ who had never wronged him. Hervey sadly felt that he must prepare a defence of evangelical truths and publish against Wesley. It was the last task he was given of God to do.

Though Hervey feared that he would not live long enough to complete this new work, he nevertheless persevered as he felt that Wesley, with his enormous influence, was well able, if unrestricted, to redirect the entire history of evangelical faith and turn thousands of pilgrims to the Heavenly City back on their tracks to worldly Rome. He was fully convinced, on strong Scriptural grounds, that what Wesley deemed 'Antinomian' in his work *Theron and Aspasio* was the faith of Christ in all its splendour and Wesley's emphasis on the sincere Christian's merits and deserts was the way of all flesh as traditionally sponsored by the strictest Papists. What was at stake was not only the reputation of true Bible Christianity but the Reformation itself which had brought this true religion back into the minds of the populace.

### Wesley's dogmatic denunciations

Hervey was anxious to avoid the use of the same methods of argumentation that Wesley had adopted in his various letters against *Theron and Aspasio*[1]. These gave Hervey no concrete material to work on as they were mere jumbled collections of dogmatic assertions without the slightest trace

---

[1] It is commonly thought that Wesley only wrote twice to Hervey on the subject of *Theron and Aspasio* but he obviously wrote four times in all. He first wrote at Hervey's request after receiving an early unfinished manuscript of *Theron and Aspasio* but merely replied with a short word of criticism. Hervey wrote again, asking Wesley to be more specific and Wesley replied with two letters after publication, the first being more critical than the last, which was critical enough. Hervey did not reply to these letters. Finally, Wesley wrote in November, 1758 some three weeks before Hervey's death, warning his friend, whom he knew was dying, against reacting in print against his own public criticisms of Hervey's work.

of evidence being provided. As he told Wesley later, no 'satisfactory explanation' was given and the criticisms had 'rather the air of a caveat, than
a confrontation; and we are often at a loss to discern, how far your remonstrance is either forcible or apposite. Brief negatives, laconic assertions
and quick interrogatories, supported by no scriptural authority, are more
likely to stagger, stun, and puzzle, than to settle our notions in religion.
You seem, Sir, to have forgotten, that propositions are not to be established with the same ease as doubts are started; and therefore have con-
tented yourself with a brevity which produces but little conviction, and
more than a little obscurity.'[1] This attitude had initially moved Hervey not
to reply to Wesley's private comments—as there was nothing to reply to.
Having prepared an answer, based on Wesley's criticism of *Theron and
Aspasio* which Wesley had now published, Hervey wrote to Ryland in
January, 1758, complaining:

> You enquire after my intended answer to Mr. Wesley: I am tran-
> scribing it for the press, but find it difficult to preserve the decency
> of the gentleman, and the meekness of the Christian: there is so
> much unfair dealing running through my opponent's objections,
> and the most magisterial air all along supplying the place of argu-
> ment. Pray for me, dear friend, that I may not betray the blessed
> cause, by the weakness of my reasoning; nor dishonour it by the
> badness of my temper.[2]

Referring to Wesley's published letter again in the following March,
Hervey confesses to Ryland that Wesley 'urges no argument, either to establish his own opinion, or to overthrow mine; only denies the validity of
my reasons.' As an example, Hervey gave Wesley's rejection of the doctrine that the salvation of the believers was determined before the foundation of the world, and his argument that there was no pre-creation covenant between Christ and the Father concerning the reconciling work of
the Saviour. Wesley, in his zeal for his own opinion had neither examined
Hervey's proof texts concerning 'Christ slain before the foundation of the
world'[3] nor had he given evidence to back up his own dogmatism.

### Wesley contra Aspasio

*Aspasio Vindicated,* containing Hervey's eleven letters against Wesley's
criticisms was not published before his death, yet no sooner was he buried

---

[1]   *Aspasio Vindicated,* Letter V.

[2]   Letter XXXIV, Ryland collection.

[3]   See Matthew 13:35; 25:34; Luke 11:50; John 17:24; Ephesians 1:4; Hebrews 4:3; I
Peter 1:20 and Revelation 13:8.

than John Wesley began a vigorous campaign to denounce Hervey's theology. This was at the risk of his own reputation as he knew full well that Hervey was just about the most popular Christian writer of the time. But worse was to come. After Hervey's death, Wesley contacted Hervey's brother William and wrung from him a promise not to publish his brother's defence. William, however, had not been involved in the preparation of *Aspasio Vindicated*. Indeed, he was probably quite unaware that at least a dozen of Hervey's closest friends had copies which Hervey had prepared for publication. Meanwhile, Wesley not only published edition after edition of his attack on Hervey but he had raised this jumbled mixture of dogmatic utterances, void of all Scriptural evidence, to the status of a systematic outline of Arminian Methodist doctrine, making it compulsory study for all his preachers and commanded it to be read out in all his societies. Though *Theron and Aspasio* had run into a good many English editions, readily available to Wesley, he used the dubious strategy of quoting from the pages of an Irish pirate edition which did not coincide with the pagination of the English editions and contained a number of careless mistakes and editorial alterations. This meant that only the most industrious of Wesley's hearers could check Wesley's arguments with the English original. Soon gentle James Hervey, whose one ambition was to live at peace with all men and be a stone of stumbling to none, was being portrayed as an Antinomian without a mask and as one who had had the audacity to challenge the definitive teaching of John Wesley himself! Indeed, as one who had died cursing Wesley! When Wesley actually read Hervey's defence, which was couched in the most guarded language, he proclaimed abroad that Hervey had libelled him.[1] When Toplady, Romaine, Cudworth, Ryland, the two Hills (Sir Richard and Rowland) and Dr. Erskine came to Hervey's defence, Wesley charged these champions with 'acrimony, bitterness, forgery, violence, palpable dishonesty and mischief.'

**The 'original' and the 'official' version of *Aspasio Vindicated***

Given this background, it is to be expected that Hervey's friends were very keen to publish his *Aspasio Vindicated* as soon as possible. The enemy, however, were already spreading rumours which made this a diffi-

---

[1] See especially *Wesley's Remarks on Dr. Erskine's Defence of the Preface to the Edinburgh Edition of Aspasio Vindicated*, his *A Letter to Dr. Erskine* (vol. XIII), his *Some Remarks on Mr. Hill's Review of all the Doctrines taught by Mr. John Wesley*, his *Some Remarks on Mr. Hill's Farrago Double-distilled*, his *A Letter to the Rev. Mr. Hervey* and *Second Letter to Ditto* (vol. XV) in Wesley's *Works*. Wesley also published the views held in these works in his *A Preventative against Unsettled Notions in Religion*. This work was published whilst Hervey was terminally ill and Wesley knew it. Nevertheless Wesley told Hervey that it would be wrong of him to reply in print. What is sauce for the goose is obviously not sauce for the gander!

cult proposition. The most harmful tale spread was that Hervey's friends
would be only too eager to publish as anything from the pen of Hervey
would make the publishers rich. This is why three of Hervey's friends
decided to publish *Aspasio Vindicated* without revealing their names but
they assured the public that they would not accept a penny of the profits.
This became a tradition amongst Hervey's editors; some years later, we
find, for instance, Toplady making public other as yet unpublished works
of Hervey and stressing that, despite rumours to the contrary, he had neither asked for nor received any fees for his work.[1]

This action on the part of Hervey's closest friends did not please his
brother William who had never shared James' confidence as they had done.
It appears that William did not even share James' faith as his brother was
always particular to state that William was his 'brother in the flesh' rather
than his 'brother of my heart'.[2] Nevertheless, for various perfectly understandable and acceptable reasons, William felt that if anyone should publish his brother's posthumous works, he should be the one to do so. Furthermore, though James had died and was buried as a pauper, causing no
financial burden on his family, his death annulled any income his wid-
owed mother and unmarried sister had and there was no money to keep
their house and home together. Thus William concluded that the copyright
for his brother's works should remain within the family and any income
raised should go towards their financial needs. William had approached
the subject only a matter of hours before James died and had understood
that the *Aspasio Vindicated* manuscript could not be published as there
were some parts left in short-hand which had not been transcribed. He
had, rather unwisely in the circumstances, passed on this information to
John Wesley. The latter, however, apparently broke a tacit cease-fire with
William who had understood that he was under a mutual agreement with
Wesley not to continue the controversy. He would not publish *Aspasio
Vindicated* if Wesley refrained from publishing against Hervey's *Theron
and Aspasio*. Believing that the matter was settled in an amicable way,
William decided to suppress his brother's last great work. On finding that
Wesley was breaking what he had understood as a gentleman's agreement,
William decided to print an 'official version'. Being an honest man, William
refused to attempt at a transcription of some of the short-hand, which was
beyond his powers and those of a friend he called in for expert help, and
left them out. He rather exaggerates however, when he complains that the

[1]  See Toplady's *To the Reader*, dated July 1769, *The Works of the late Rev. James Hervey*, vol. v., pp. 126,127.

[2]  See Letter LXVI in which Hervey states that he is staying with Whitefield and not William.

work originally published, differed in many ways from his own.[1] Here Wesley's statement that the original version and William's version showed hardly any difference must be accepted. Wesley's view was also shared by the original publishers who, out of respect for the wishes of the Hervey family, produced no new 'rival' edition.

## John Ryland's view of the matter

Ryland Sen., did not in the least share either Wesley's or William Hervey's view of the history of *Aspasio Vindicated* as he had followed its progress from the very beginning and had been one of Hervey's chief advisors concerning it. In Ryland's biography of Hervey, he praises his friend's defence of Christ's satisfaction and righteousness as the grounds of our acceptance with God. In view of the prevailing swing in alleged Reformed thinking which stressed human agency in salvation, Ryland added, 'Not so our author and dear Friend: no man in the whole world had a more piercing sense of the impurity of his nature and his guilt before God. This he has demonstrated in his eleven letters, beyond any other man that has ever written on the glorious subject (i.e. Christ's satisfaction and righteousness).' Ryland gave his views on the propriety of the first publication, in which William Hervey took no part, in a footnote to this comment in which he said:

> These eleven letters were just upon the point of being suppressed, and lost to the Christian world for ever. If that had been the case, I should have reason to regret the loss to the day of my death. Soon after Mr. Hervey's death, these excellent letters were put into my hands for twelve or fourteen weeks. From a principle of foolish and false delicacy, I did not take a copy of them, which I ought to have done. Happy for the church, the manuscript fell into the hands of three of my friends, who had more sincerity, zeal, and courage, than I had; and thus the manuscript was rescued from destruction: and the original copy at last brought to light. This is such an event as I shall bless God for to all eternity.[2]

This testimony ought to be proof enough that it was Hervey's original work that was eventually printed and that Wesley's repeated, but never substantiated, claim in his works that it was a forgery was pure panicky self-defence on Wesley's part. William Romaine, along with several other witnesses who wrote to the *Gentleman's Magazine* on the matter shortly

---

[1]    See William's preface to *Aspasio Vindicated*.

[2]    Ryland's *The Character of the Rev. James Hervey, A. M.*, pp. 101,102.

after Hervey's home call, testified that Hervey's *Aspasio Vindicated* had been completed by Hervey for the press. Romaine announced the forthcoming publication of *Aspasio Vindicated* in his printed funeral sermon on Hervey's death.

## Wesley promises Hervey's defenders a thrashing

When Wesley received a copy of *Aspasio Vindicated*, his shock and anger knew no bounds. 'Mr. Hervey has painted me as a monster!'[1] he cried. When he heard that Whitefield, Romaine and Madan 'from their hearts subscribe to Mr. Hervey's eleven letters,' Wesley replied, 'I hope not: from any that do, I expect no more mercy than from a mad dog.'[2] Wesley treated all those who felt Hervey had been Biblical and objective in his work as if they were all in debt to him but were now acting like rabid dogs, biting the hand which had fed them. Hervey, he claimed, owed his soul to him and when Dr. Erskine backed Hervey, Wesley referred to the Scotsman with the words, 'O Absalom, my son, my son!'[3] and marvelled at Hill's cheek in attempting to 'measure swords', with him in his defence of Hervey in *Some Remarks on Mr. Hill's Review of All Mr. Wesley's Doctrines*. Wesley answered Hill's criticism with *Tandem extorquebis ut vapules.*[4] This is some indication of the enormous importance Wesley gave himself, yet in the very anti-Herveyan works in which Wesley lifts himself above all his opponents, he boasts how humble the Lord has kept him throughout his Christian life.

It is admitted that Wesley had been Hervey's tutor, but what he had taught his pupil had ruined his health and made him 'righteous overmuch'. Nevertheless Hervey always confessed his indebtedness to Wesley's kindness at this time. Wesley, however, was quite ignorant of the way of salvation himself during his Oxford days and never came to understand the gospel at the same experimental depth that Hervey did. So for Wesley to suggest that he had fathered Hervey's Christian soul was a real flight of imagination. For Wesley to view Dr. Erskine, who was not indebted to Wesley in any way, as an Absalom who had parted from his father David, alias John Wesley, was presumption indeed. When Wesley eventually wrote against Hill's defence of Hervey and strove to refute Hill's list of one hundred contradictions found in Wesley's doctrines, only Wesley's fondest admirers claimed it was the 'thrashing' promised. Wesley merely quoted

---

[1]    *Works*, vol. xiii, *A Letter to Dr. Erskine* (printed with *Remarks on Dr. Erskine's Defence,*), p. 125.

[2]    *Works*, vol. xv, *Some Remarks on Mr. Hill's Review of all the Doctrines Taught by John Wesley*, p. 43.

[3]    *Works*, vol. xiii, *Remarks on Dr. Erskine's Defence of Aspasio Vindicated.*, p. 121.

[4]    You will at last compel me to give you a thrashing.

the one hundred alleged contradictions one by one and denied them one by one, now and then adding a sentence which only confused the issue further. In other words, he handled Hill exactly like Hervey. He gave his own dogmatic and officious opinion, backed by nothing but his own authority to confute what Hervey and Hill had maintained on strong Scriptural evidence.

### Wesley likens *Aspasio Vindicated* to the Koran

Yet Wesley's remarks on Hervey and his friends grew more and more extreme as he penned more and more pamphlets to ward off criticism which had risen through *Theron and Aspasio, Aspasio Vindicated* and his reactions to them. Criticising, for instance, Hill's exuberant support for Hervey, Wesley says, 'As to that most excellent and "evangelical work", as you term it, the eleven letters ascribed to Mr. Hervey, Mr. Sellon has abundantly shewn, that they are most excellently virulent, scurrilous, and abusive; and full as far from the evangelic spirit as the Koran of Mohamet.'[1] And so the abuse went on and on. When Wesley heard that Augustus Toplady admired *Aspasio Vindicated*, Wesley retorted that the letters were, '*bitterness* double distilled! Which overflow with little else but *calumnious expressions*, from the beginning to the end!'[2]

In his *Letter to Dr. Erskine* concerning his publishing Hervey's work in Scotland with a personal evaluation of the author's doctrines, Wesley told his correspondent that *Aspasio Vindicated* was, 'one of the most bitter libels that was ever written against me: written by a dying man.' He went on to say,

> Mr Hervey, who had been a man of peace all his life, began a war not six months before he died. He drew his sword, when he was just putting off his body. He then fell on one to whom he had the deepest obligations, (as his own letters which I have now in my hands, testify) on one who had never intentionally wronged him, who had never spoken an unkind word of him, or to him, and who loved him as his own child. O tell it not in Gath! The good Mr. Hervey (if these letters were his) died cursing his spiritual Father.

Here again, we are provided with a deep insight into Wesley's psyche. Hervey's personal indebtedness to himself, he believed, put himself above any criticism from that quarter. Again, Wesley emphasises that he was Hervey's spiritual father whereas this honour obviously goes to Darracott, Orchard, Thomson and, especially, Whitefield, not forgetting the humble

---

[1]  *Works*, vol. xv, *Some Remarks on Mr. Hill's Farrago Double-Distilled*, p. 106.

[2]  *Some Remarks on Mr. Hill's Review*, p. 64. Emphasis Wesley's.

ploughman, all, with perhaps the exception of Orchard, who were converted and preaching righteousness before him. Wesley had obviously made
a large bubble of his own self-esteem which needed to be burst for the
good of his soul in the way Hervey pricked it.

## The emptiness of Wesley's case against Hervey

When all the froth and verbal abuse is removed from Wesley's defence
of his attitude to Hervey, it becomes very plain how remote his accusations are from the solid evidence at hand. This fact is underlined by John
Brown who finds ample proof that Hervey in no way dishonoured the
cause of Christ either in weak reasoning or strong temper on any page of
*Aspasio Vindicated*. The Scotsman thus says of Hervey's work:

> In his *Aspasio Vindicated* against Mr. Wesley, we have one of
> the best patterns of polemic divinity. 'This is, indeed,' says the
> venerable Dr. Erskine, 'an excellent piece. The subject is infinitely
> interesting; the manner in which it is managed, scriptural, judi-
> cious, and animated.' His works at large have a rich evangelical
> strain. He well knew the gospel, both in the restricted and enlarged
> sense of the terms, and this appears in its matter and glory in all his
> writings. Here all qualifications to prepare us for the Saviour are
> entirely discarded; justification through his righteousness alone,
> received by faith, is exactly stated, duty always founded upon privi-
> lege, and sinners as such called to receive Jesus and his blessings.
> Not only are his sentiments entirely evangelical, but his language
> is unexceptional, and extremely guarded and precise. There is, per-
> haps, no modern divine before him, if equal to him, in his excel-
> lency.[1]

## Wesley's self-felt innocence in attacking Hervey

Another point that Wesley clothes in innocence is the fact of his most
unkind statements in at least three letters to Hervey. In his letter to Erskine,
Wesley professes never to have used an unkind word against his former
pupil. Hill took Wesley up on this matter, reminding him of the number of
times he had spread abroad that Hervey was an Antinomian. In his defence, Wesley agrees that he had asked Hervey why he had gone 'to such
pains to increase the number of Antinomians' and also admits that Hervey's
teaching concerning Christ's satisfying all the demands of the law was, for
him, 'the very quintessence of Antinomianism.' Furthermore, he affirmed
that Hervey's doctrine regarding the claims of the law all being answered
in Christ was 'Antinomianism without a mask.' Wesley also conceded

---

[1]    *Memoirs of Mr. Hervey*, pp. 425,426.

saying that Hervey used many expressions in *Theron and Aspasio* which 'directly lead to Antinomianism.' Nevertheless, Wesley can still conclude, after the pattern of his very own logic, which Hill called '*logica wesleiensis*', that he 'does not condemn him (Hervey) as an Antinomian.'

**Further examples of Wesley's abilities at dodging the issue**
To accuse Hervey, who emphasised holiness, sanctification and righteousness in all he wrote, of deliberately being at pains to promote Antinomianism seems like unkindness itself to one who cannot follow Wesley's self-exonerating logic. Hill also uncovered some strange contradictions in Wesley's condemnation of imputed righteousness in which, as Hervey had also pointed out, Wesley formerly believed. Wesley had told Hervey not to dispute for the term as it caused 'immense hurt' and argued at length against its meaning. In his defence, Wesley said that he did not *deny the term* but he dare not dispute for it, so could see no contradiction. The reader is left with the idea that Wesley has wriggled out of the situation with an ambiguous statement. He does not deny *that there is such a term*, but does not believe it. In *Some Remarks on Mr. Hill's Farrago Double-Distilled*, Wesley takes up quotes from his own works, provided by Hill, given as evidence to show that he not only believed in imputed righteousness but also in the imputed righteousness of Christ. The way Wesley strives to escape from this dilemma is also very enlightening regarding Wesley's skill as a debater. He maintains that when he denied imputed righteousness in his writings against Hervey, *it was in the Antinomian sense*. Of course, Wesley never told Hervey that he was denying the term in such a sense, nor did he tell Hervey what he meant by that sense. Nor does he now inform Hill as to what he means by 'imputed righteousness in the Antinomian sense.' Concerning the doctrine of 'the imputed righteousness of Christ', which he had apparently previously believed, Wesley, in his work against Hill, denies in the strongest language that he had ever believed such a doctrine but adds that they are talking about *phrases*, not *doctrines*, and that he does believe in the *phrase* 'imputed righteousness of Christ' but means by that 'every believer is justified for the sake of what Christ has done and suffered.'[1] Of course, this is a far cry from the interpretation given the term by our Reformers, the bulk of the Puritans, including Bunyan and Hervey himself. The doctrine of the imputed righteousness of Christ, *as the phrase itself* informs us, declares what it is that causes sinners to be made righteous before God and therefore justified. Wesley's definition, however, leaves everything open. He does not say whose righteousness saves us. Indeed, it is obvious when reading Wesley's letter against Hervey which sparked off *Aspasio Vindi-*

---

[1]    See *Some Remarks on Mr. Hill's Farrago Double-Distilled*, pp. 89, 90.

*cated* that Wesley considers justification all along without taking imputed righteousness into any account at all.

## Wesley's charge of forgery

Another interesting point is Wesley's dating of Hervey's commencement of his *Aspasio Vindicated* in the above-mentioned letter to Dr. Erskine and the hint that the work was not Hervey's. These two suppositions are strategically linked. Hervey received Wesley's letter on which he based his *Aspasio Vindicated* in either October or November, 1756. He was greatly handicapped at the time by the tremendous pressure of work in completing edition after edition of *Theron and Aspasio* and the fact that for months on end, he was too ill to work at all. Nor was there any great reason to reply at first as Hervey had already replied personally to Wesley regarding a similar, though briefer criticism. Furthermore, he had probably received a dozen such detailed comments on his work from friends whom he had asked for assistance, not as a basis for further correspondence but in order to help him produce as good a work as possible. When in the following year, however, Wesley began to preach and print against Hervey, the matter of a formal reply became urgent. It is obvious from Hervey's letters that he had prepared the bulk of a reply by the end of 1757, over a year before his death. Wesley either did not know this or ignored it when altering his later defence against *Aspasio Vindicated*. It is obvious from Wesley's correspondence that at first he accepted that Hervey wrote against him. He then spread the rumour that the bulk of the work was Hervey's but a few remarks were added by others. When *Aspasio Vindicated* became something of a best-seller, Wesley changed his tactics completely to save his reputation and proclaimed, without the slightest evidence being given, that *Aspasio Vindicated* was the 'lively words of Mr. Cudworth, graced with the name of Mr. Hervey.'[1]

## Cudworth could not have written *Aspasio Vindicated*

Now this was a sheer impossibility and Wesley knew it. He had known before Hervey's death that he was going to publish and had written to Hervey, warning him against this move. Hervey's letters also show that: a. he was preparing his *Aspasio Vindicated* for publication by the end of 1757; b. the initiative was solely his and c. the matter was not discussed with Cudworth at the time. This is very important to note in the face of Wesley's ridiculous charges of forgery and his accusation that Cudworth poisoned Hervey's mind against him. Hervey was in correspondence with Cudworth throughout 1756 and criticised Wesley's *Christian Library* in a letter to Cudworth dated April 21, 1756, saying it was performed in a

---

[1]   *Some Remarks on Mr. Hill's Review*, p. 36.

'confused, inaccurate, slovenly manner' and thought it must be a discredit to Wesley. Tyerman, in his Hervey biography, says that this criticism is unjust and a sign that Hervey was already alienated from Wesley, an alienation which was either created or widened by Hervey's contact with Cudworth. Hervey's criticism of Wesley's *Christian Library* was, however, a general criticism which was shared by Wesley himself. In his pamphlets against the Hills, Wesley admits time and time again that the Library has been very badly edited and corrected and contained (Calvinist) views radically opposed to his own. Hervey had spoken of Wesley's *Christian Library* in this manner as Cudworth was planning a similar project and Hervey was warning him how difficult such a task would be but how necessary it was that Cudworth should succeed where others had failed. Hervey had always combined a balanced criticism of Wesley with great respect for him and his remark can hardly be taken as unbalanced or even as a sign of enmity. Tyerman has also left out of consideration the fact that Wesley had written a highly critical letter to Hervey in 1755 so that Hervey had just cause to be upset at Wesley's treatment. In spite of this, there is no evidence in the Cudworth collection of Hervey's letters, or in the other numerous collections, that Hervey complained at this early date to Cudworth about Wesley's criticism at all. Even after Wesley sent Hervey his second letter of criticism on October 15, 1756, Hervey still did not broach the subject to Cudworth although he did air his criticisms of Sandeman's views of *Theron and Aspasio* in no less than three letters. Indeed, we first find Hervey telling Cudworth of his reply to Wesley on July 15 and July 27, 1758, almost two years after hearing from Wesley. By this time *Aspasio Vindicated* was already complete in manuscript form. Cudworth obviously became very interested in the work in the latter half of 1758 and sent Hervey his thoughts on the subject. Wesley dates the composition of *Aspasio Vindicated* wrongly from the time of Cudworth's proposed emendations.

Wesley first heard of Cudworth's interest in Hervey's *Aspasio Vindicated* in November, 1758, less than a month before Hervey's death, when it was general knowledge that Hervey had written against Wesley but not yet published his work. Wesley then wrote to Hervey on November 29, 1758, saying:

Dear Sir,
A WEEK or two ago, in my return from Norwich, I met with Mr. Pierce, of Bury, who informed me of a conversation which he had had a few days before. Mr. Cudworth, he said, then told him, 'that he had prevailed on Mr. Hervey to write against me, who likewise in what he had written referred to the book which he (Mr. Cudworth) had lately published.'
Every one is welcome to write what he pleases concerning me.

But would it not be well for you to remember, that before I published any thing concerning you, I sent it to you in a private letter. That I waited for an answer for several months; but was not favoured with one line: that when at length I published part of what I had sent you, I did it in the most inoffensive manner possible; in the latter end of a larger work, purely designed to *preserve* those in connexion with me from being tossed to and fro by various doctrines. What therefore I may fairly expect from my friend, is, to mete me with the same measure. To send to me first in a private manner, any complaint he has against me; to wait as many months as I did; and if I give you none, or no satisfactory answer, then to lay the matter before the world, if you judge it will be to the glory of God.

But whatever you do in this respect, one thing I request of you. Give no countenance to that insolent, scurrilous, virulent libel, which bears the name of William Cudworth. Indeed, how you can converse with a man of his spirit, I cannot comprehend. O leave not your old, well-tried friends! The new is not comparable to them. I speak not this because I am *afraid* of what any one can say or do to *me*. But I am really concerned for *you*: an evil man has gained the ascendant over you, and has persuaded a dying man, who had shunned it all his life, to enter into controversy as he is stepping into eternity! Put off your armour, my brother! You and I have no moments to spare, let us employ them all in promoting peace and good-will among men. And may the peace of God keep your heart and mind in Christ Jesus! So prays,

Your affectionate Brother and Servant,
J. WESLEY.[1]

One can sympathise with Wesley in his argument that Hervey ought to have responded to his last letter although it must not be forgotten that Wesley, after receiving a second letter from Hervey on the subject, had sent two letters to Hervey on *Theron and Aspasio*, the first one being, in Hervey's words, more stinging and sarcastic than the second but neither providing the constructive criticism with Biblical support which Hervey had solicited. Wesley merely refers to the second, less distasteful, of the two lengthier letters, which was harsh enough. Wesley never published the first letter and always displayed the one which he felt put him in the best light as if this had been his only correspondence with Hervey. Needless to say, this was the only letter Wesley published, at first in part, then

---

[1]    *Works*, vol. xv, *Letter to the Rev. Mr. Hervey*, pp. 412,413.

the whole. Hervey, too, rejected the first letter fully and though he said in a letter written May 4, 1758 'I have taken no notice of either, being very unwilling to embark in controversy,' he concentrated his reply on the less offensive letter i.e. the one that showed more 'candour and temper' than 'sting and sarcasm'.[1]

**Not doing as one would like to be done by**
Nevertheless, Wesley's other words in his letter reveal a total lack of tact that one would hardly expect from a minister of the gospel who knew he was speaking to a dying man. If Wesley had really thought that the matter was Hervey's own business and that he did not fear what Hervey might say in any way, it is difficult to see why Wesley went to such extraordinary lengths to put Hervey off publishing against him. It is difficult to rule out that Wesley's gross attempt to interfere in Hervey's plans was caused by his acute fear that his reputation might be damaged. Wesley protested loudly in the works mentioned above that Hervey, the Hills, Toplady and Erskine were striving to blacken his character, showing a depth of bad conduct to which Wesley confesses he himself could never sink. Yet Wesley is here insulting Hervey's ability to chose his friends for the best of purposes and his blackening of Cudworth's character could hardly be more extreme. This letter also shows that Wesley knew very well that Hervey was writing against him and he did not regard Cudworth, whatever his influence on Hervey was, as the author.

Wesley seems to have either been misinformed by Pierce or he has misunderstood the information given. He was obviously frightened of Hervey publishing against him because he feared that he would recommend, or quote from, a book written by Cudworth which he considered was an 'insolent, scurrilous, virulent, libel' against himself. Actually, Hervey mentioned no such work and disclosed no such information, whether Cudworth had written such material or not. Wesley had completely underestimated the integrity of his former student. Nevertheless, when Wesley read Hervey's *Aspasio Vindicated*, which received wide praise for its balanced and well-founded criticism, Wesley greeted it with exactly the same unbalanced vocabulary that he used against Cudworth. This would make any unbiased reader feel that Wesley's highly-peppered language against Cudworth was equally without foundation. Wesley's suspicion that Hervey would allow himself to be influenced by Cudworth rather than, say, Whitefield, Ryland, Thomson, Gill or Brine was equally ill-founded as Hervey stood far closer to many of his other friends in theology than Cudworth, who, however, proved a most sturdy friend to Hervey in the promotion of his works and written defence of them. Cudworth, however,

---

[1]  Letter CXCIX.

was Wesley's 'favourite enemy' alongside younger Augustus Toplady and Rowland Hill.[1]

## Clearing Cudworth's name as a possible forger

It was quite unnecessary for Wesley to presume that Cudworth was behind Hervey's *Aspasio Vindicated* as Cudworth published his own vindication of Aspasio under his own name, calling it *A Defence of Theron and Aspasio*. There are very many factors revealed in this work which speak out loudly against Wesley's contention that Cudworth influenced Hervey's theology and writing negatively, a contention which has become a dogma of later Wesleyan apologetics. The amendments which Cudworth discussed with Hervey concerning doctrine and its wording in *Theron and Aspasio* were never utilised by Hervey and were first printed by Cudworth as part of his *Defence* and as an appendix to it.[2] Whereas Hervey's language in *Aspasio Vindicated* is identical with that of his other works, given the different emphasis and subject matter, the language Cudworth uses in his own version is vastly different. It is less polished, more firm and tense and more economical in its wording. It is completely void of what one might call 'the classical touch' and there is a total absence of Hebrew, Greek and Latin, though the topics are exactly the same. Cudworth also goes further than Hervey would go in emphasising a number of points, especially in his dealings with the Marrow Men, where Hervey always showed more caution. In other words, Cudworth is more blunt and steps into theological areas where Hervey would fear to tread.[3] Though more plain than Hervey and more economical in his descriptions, he is far more detailed in the build-up of his argument in matters of doctrine. Thus it is quite obvious that Cudworth's *Defence* and Hervey's *Aspasio Vindicated* are the works of two quite different authors who, nevertheless, complement and supplement each other to a very marked degree.

The last possible suspicion that Wesley might have had concerning a Cudworth authorship of *Aspasio Vindicated* ought to have been removed through reading his *Defence* as Cudworth explains enthusiastically that James Hervey's work has been published by William, his brother. Unless Cudworth were the greatest of deceivers, which his works[4] and his friend-

---

[1]    See, for instance, Wesley's tracts against Hervey's works mentioned in this chapter, his *The Consequence Proved* and *Journal* entry for June 29 1784.

[2]    See Cudworth's *Defence of Theron and Aspasio*, especially *Amendments proposed* included in the 1837 edition of Hervey's *Works*. The amendments are, however, so excellent that one ought to have no difficulty in believing Cudworth's statement that Hervey would have added them had he survived.

[3]    This does not, of necessity mean that Hervey would have disagreed with Cudworth.

[4]    See the many gems culled from Cudworth's works reproduced by John Brown in his *Memoirs of Hervey*.

ship with Hervey do not suggest he is, this confession rules out that he was the author. According to another of Wesley's hunches, Cudworth was one of the original three publishers who issued a 'pirate version' of Hervey's eleven letters. Cudworth's reference to William Hervey also refutes this theory. In this connection one might also think of Toplady's and Rowland Hill's association with Cudworth but that was a friendship to come. In 1758 Hill was only fourteen years of age and Toplady eighteen and they had no personal connections with Hervey.

It is interesting to note that Wesley makes no reference to the Rev. R. Yates, who was a good friend of Hervey's and published his own defence of Aspasio as early as September 1755 in the *London Magazine*. It is obvious that Wesley had no personal axe to grind against Yates, who in his works seeks to present Hervey as open to Arminianism as possible, so he left him alone.[1] Other defenders of Aspasio such as Cudworth, the Hills and Toplady, were already marked out as Wesley's chief enemies and therefore he used their love for Hervey to fit him out with ammunition to settle old scores.

**Toplady's summary of the Wesley-Hervey controversy**
When all is said and done, the relationship between Wesley and Hervey has been, most likely, best summed up by Augustus Toplady who wrote a decade or so after Hervey's death. The author of the well-known hymn *Rock of Ages* and Editor of the *Gospel Magazine* wrote:

The world have long seen, that unmixed politeness, condescending generosity, and the most conciliating benevolence, can no more soften Mr. Wesley's rugged rudeness, than the melody of David's harp could lay the North wind, or still the raging of the sea. Mr. Hervey, in his famous Eleven Letters, has handled Mr. Wesley with all the delicacy and tenderness that a virtuoso would shew in catching a butterfly, whose plumage he wishes to preserve uninjured; or a lady, in wiping a piece of china, which she dreads to break. Did Mr. Wesley profit by the engaging meekness of his amiable and elegant refuter? nay, but he waxed worse and worse: like Saul, he strove to stab the name of that inestimable friend, whose gospel music was calculated to dispossess him of his evil spirit. Like the animal, stigmatized in the 58th Psalm, he stopped his ears, and refused to hear the voice of the charmer, though the strains were no less sweet than wise. Every artifice that could be invented has been thrown out, to blacken the memory of the most

---

[1] See Yates' defence of Hervey in the 1771, 6 vol. edition of Hervey's *Works*. John Brown was highly critical of Hervey's editors as a number of them, throughout the many editions of his works, sought to bend Hervey to suit their own theological interpretation.

exemplary man this age has produced. Mr. Wesley insulted him, when living, and continues to trample on him, though dead. He digs him, as it were, out of his grave, passes sentence on him as an heretic, ties him to the stake, burns him to ashes, and scatters those ashes to the four winds. Rather than fail, the wretched Mr. Walter Sellon is stilted to oppose the excellent Mr. Hervey; and most egregiously hath the living sinner acquitted himself against the long-departed saint! In much the same spirit, and with just the same success, as the enemy of mankind contended with Michael the archangel, about the body of Moses.

Every reader may not perhaps, know the true cause (at least, one of the principal causes) of Mr. Wesley's unrelenting enmity to Mr. Hervey; an enmity, which even the death of the latter has not yet extinguished. When that valuable man was writing his *Theron and Aspasio*, his humility and self-diffidence were so great, that he condescended to solicit many of his friends to revise and correct that admirable work, antecedently to its publication. He occasionally requested this favour even of some who were enemies to several of the doctrines asserted in the dialogues; among whom was Mr. John Wesley. The author imagined, that the unsparing criticism of an adversary might observe defects, and suggest some useful hints, which the tenderness and partiality of friendship might overlook, or scruple to communicate. Several sheets having been transmitted to Mr. John Wesley(an honour of which he soon shewed himself quite unworthy,) he altered, added, and retrenched, with such insolence and wantonness of dictatorial authority, as disgusted even the modest and candid Mr. Hervey. The consequence was, Mr. Wesley lost his supervisorship, and in return, set himself to depreciate the performance he was not allowed to spoil.[1]

## All for the furtherance of the gospel

Hervey's biographer John Brown of Whitburn, sees all this controversy as being for the common good and the positive spread of the gospel and concludes his chapter on Hervey's writings by saying, 'By these means *Aspasio Vindicated* was more prized and read than likely it would have been, had it been published in Mr Hervey's lifetime, and met with no opposition.'[2]

## Hervey's defence against Wesley's criticisms: the doctrine of imputation

What then were Wesley's complaints against Hervey and how did the latter meet them? Hervey begins his defence by stating that though he had

---

[1]    *Complete works of Augustus Toplady, Introduction*, p. 49.

[2]    P. 449.

originally decided to remain silent on the issues taken up by Wesley for the sake of peace,[1] he was now being summoned to the bar of the public by Wesley's bringing the controversy to their notice. He was thus replying, believing that, in the case of Wesley, it would be a question of 'Give admonition to a wise man, and he will be yet wiser.' In the case of others, believers would rejoice in the truths contained in the vindication and it was his desire that the sinner might learn to long for them.

Wesley's major arguments are centred around Hervey's view of righteousness, imputation, justification and the place of good works in salvation. In Dialogue II, Aspasio argues that Christ has met the requirements of the Law and yet taken upon Himself our penalties so that our sins were imputed to Him and His righteousness was imputed to us. He argues furthermore that 'Justification is an act of God's Almighty's grace; whereby he acquits his people from guilt, and accounts them righteous for the sake of Christ's righteousness, which was wrought out for them, and is imputed to them.' Theron asks what Aspasio means by 'Christ's righteousness' and the term 'imputed'. Aspasio replies, 'By Christ's righteousness, I understand the whole of his active and passive obedience; springing from the perfect holiness of his heart, continued through the whole progress of his life, and extending to the very last pang of his death.—By the word imputed, I would signify, that the righteousness, though performed by our Lord, is placed to our account; is reckoned or adjudged by God as our own. Insomuch, that we may plead it, and rely on it, for the pardon of our sins, for adoption into his family, and for the enjoyment of life eternal.'

## Taking the Lord's Name in vain

Wesley reacts strongly to these words saying, 'For *Christ's* sake, and for the sake of the immortal souls which He has purchased with his blood, do not dispute for that *particular phrase*, The imputed righteousness of Christ, it is not scriptural; it is not necessary; men who scruple to use, men who never heard the expression, may yet "be humbled, as repenting criminals, at his feet, and rely as devoted pensioners on his merits". But it has done immense hurt. I have abundant proof, that the frequent use of this unnecessary phrase, instead of "furthering men's progress in vital holiness,"[2] has made them satisfied without any holiness at all; yea, and encouraged them to work all uncleanness with greediness.'[3] When commenting on Dialogues II and IV, Wesley goes so far as to say, 'The nice, metaphysical doctrine of imputed righteousness, leads not to repentance, but to licentiousness.'[4] When the Hills challenged Wesley on this point, the

---

[1]    As Wesley had insisted.

[2]    The quotation marks within the quote show where Wesley is quoting Hervey verbatim.

[3]    See Wesley's *'A Preventative*, his *Letters to Hervey* in vol. XV of his *Works* and, *Mr. Wesley's Letter* in Hervey's *Works*.

[4]    *Works*, vol. XV, p. 393.

Arminian leader refused to comment, merely retorting that the thought was unscriptural[1] but his arguments against Hervey show that he cannot accept the doctrine because it contradicts the Arminian doctrine of faith which works righteousness. Hervey asks Wesley why he is so reluctant to use the word 'imputed' and says, 'How can we be justified by the merits of Christ, unless they are imputed to us? Would the payment made by a surety procure a discharge for the debtor, unless it was placed to his account?' Concerning Wesley's argument that the doctrine of imputed righteousness was not Scriptural, not necessary and leads to licentiousness, Hervey quotes Romans 4:6 and 4:11 and asks him what is the difference between 'righteousness imputed' and 'imputed righteousness'? If this phrase 'does immense hurt' as Wesley argues, Hervey says he is quite willing to use other ways of saying the same thing such as 'reckoned as our own' or 'placed to our account'. However, Hervey continues, he would prefer to keep the term 'imputed' as it describes the doctrine precisely and is a long tested and proved word. Thus to Wesley's suggestion that he should drop the term 'imputed righteousness' because it is not worth bothering about, only causes strife with Arminians and leads to Antinomianism, Hervey says that he will continue to use the phrase and promote the doctrine because he has come to see that those who would do away with the word, hate the doctrine. This doctrine is not only Scriptural but it is the very spirit and essence of the gospel and the brightest jewel in Christ's mediatorial crown.

### Pardon, removal of guilt and justification secured and sealed in the work of Christ

Wesley has been arguing all the time that Christ's full work was done at His death and by His sufferings alone the law was satisfied.[2] Hervey agrees that the death of Christ is the crux of our faith but it was not *a* death alone which ransomed us but the death of one who both bore our punishment and through his imputed righteousness removed our guilt. Christ not only voluntarily took upon Himself the punishment that we had earned, gaining our pardon but worked out a way by which we could receive justification in our union with Christ. Thus when God views the elect sinner, He views him as being in Christ and thus pardoned and freed from guilt and therefore justified. This is the essence of Christian faith which 'is ever desirous to see more of Christ's worthiness, that the soul may rejoice in his excellency, and be filled with all his fullness.' Somehow, Wesley cannot imagine a soul hungering and thirsting after righteousness thinking in

---

[1]    *Works*, Vol. XV, *Some Remarks on Mr. Hill's Review of All the Doctrines Taught by Mr. John Wesley* and *Some Remarks on Mr. Hill's Farrago Double-distilled*.

[2]    See also *Some Remarks on Mr Hill's Review, Works*, vol. xv, p. 43.

this way. He argues instead that such teaching is unscriptural and would only turn hungering souls into Antinomians. Hervey argued in return that people who have found fullness in Christ and His righteousness, will not make the aim of their lives to live as if they had never experienced Christ but, on the contrary, they will serve the Lord out of a happy and willing heart.

## Christ's vicarious obedience establishes the law

Referring to Dialogues III and IV, Wesley cannot understand the Reformed doctrine of Christ's obedience to the law. Here, Hervey is dealing with the doctrine of redemption arguing that Christ has redeemed us to God (Revelation 5:9) and that satisfaction was made to the divine law and to the divine justice. Wesley cannot accept this as being Biblical theology and says, "'Satisfaction was made to the Divine law." I do not remember any such expressions in Scripture. This way of speaking of the law as a person injured and to be satisfied, seems hardly defensible.' Thus Wesley takes offence at the law being regarded as a personal active agent. Hervey feels he ought to remind Wesley that he has hitherto spoken of the law as a person himself in his *Explanatory Notes on the New Testament* and re-emphasises that this is quite in keeping with Scriptural usage. Indeed, Wesley had only to think of what Paul says concerning the righteousness of God which is witnessed by the law, that we are judged by the law, that the law works wrath in the sinner, has dominion over him, wars against him and takes him captive and slays him besides being a schoolmaster to bring him to Christ. This is all a personalising of the law's functions without anyone possibly making the mistake that the law is truly a person. The point Hervey is making is clear, the law demands full obedience, man has failed to perform this, but Christ has answered the demands of the law in every jot and tittle. This is, Hervey explains, what is meant in Galatians 4:4 with 'Christ was made under the law,' i.e. He placed Himself subject to the law, to obey it, that is to fulfil its precepts, and undergo its penalty. In this way, Hervey argues, Christ established the law and provided for its honour by His perfect obedience to it.

The doctrine of Christ's full obedience to the law has always been a stone of stumbling for Arminians. Thus Wesley protests concerning Hervey's interpretation of Paul's words 'we establish the law', 'Can you possibly think St. Paul meant this? That such a thought ever entered into his mind?' and argues that the phrase merely means 'we establish both the true sense and the effectual practice of it; we provide for its being both understood and practised in its full extent.' It would have helped matters if Wesley had explained what he meant by 'the true sense' and 'effectual practice' if he meant anything other than Christ has fulfilled the law on our behalf. But as Hervey complained, Wesley constantly used dogmatism in place of argument. Romans chapter 3 shows that no flesh can be justified via the law in the sight of God. However, it also says that the law witnesses to Christ's righteousness through His redemptive act with reference to the remission of sins committed against the law. In other words it was Christ who 'declared' what true righteousness was in relation to what the law demanded but to which no man can attain. Wesley thinks all this merely means that the way is now open to prove that all flesh can live by the law. Again, Wesley is taking what is attributed to Christ's work and basing it on man's efforts. Against this, Hervey argues that because Christ submitted Himself to the obligations of the law, 'The law says, I am fulfilled: Justice says I am satisfied. While both concur to expedite and ascertain the salvation of a believer.'[1]

## Wesley's defective view of the law

Though Wesley accuses Hervey of Antinomianism repeatedly in his letter, it is obvious that his own view of the law must be at fault, otherwise he could not imagine that it were humanly possible not only to live a life of sincere obedience to the law but also to do so in order to be 'perfected' and finally accepted by God. The fact that Wesley is always ready to belittle sin in those whom he claims are made perfect in love, by referring to 'things not quite right' or 'petty offences', confirms Hervey's opinion so that he feels bound to tell Wesley:

> It is, I apprehend, one of your leading errors, that you form low, scanty, inadequate apprehensions of God's law; that law which is a bright representation of his most pure nature, a beautiful draught of his most holy will, and never since the fall has been perfectly exemplified in any living character, but only in the man Christ Jesus. From this error many others must unavoidably follow:—a disesteem of imputed righteousness, and a conceit of personal perfection; a spirit of legal bondage, and, I fear, a tincture of pharisaical pride.[2]

Wesley quotes Hervey's words, 'We establish the law, as we expect no salvation without a perfect conformity to it—namely by Christ,' and says of this gospel truth:

> Is not this a mere quibble? and a quibble which, after all the laboured evasions of Witsius, and a thousand more, does totally make void the law? But not so does Paul teach. According to him, without holiness, personal holiness, no man shall see the Lord. No

---

[1]    Letter II.

[2]    Letter IV.

one who is not himself conformed to the law of God here, shall see the Lord in glory.

This is the grand, palpable objection to the whole scheme. It directly makes void the law. It makes thousands content to live and die transgressors of the law, because Christ fulfilled it for them. Therefore, though I believe he hath lived and died for me, yet, I would speak very tenderly and sparingly of the former, (and never separately from the latter) even as sparingly as do the Scriptures, for fear of this dreadful consequence.

The objection to Wesley's scheme is obviously that his 'perfect' Christians show a standard of establishing the law which is far from the Scriptural norm as made evident in Wesley's report on such perfectionists in his Journal dated Monday, April 3, 1786. Here he refers to up to a dozen who simultaneously pray aloud, scream at the tops of their voices, use indecent language, drop down as if dead and jump up crying 'Glory' twenty times in succession. Wesley assures his readers, however, that these mockers of true Christian conduct have been 'awakened, justified and soon after perfected in love.' His excuse for their deplorable behaviour is that, 'Satan strives to push many of them to extravagance.' One would think this fact should have made Wesley more intent on pleading the merits of Christ's perfect righteousness. Wesley's perfection is typical of a religion that seeks such perfection outside of union with Christ.

### Imputed righteousness does not negate the law

Wesley would apparently speak very sparingly of Christ's obedience to the law and establishment of the law because he feared, paradoxically enough, that this would put the believer off living a moral life. Hervey could not speak enough of Christ's righteousness, first enacted in His vicarious keeping the law and then imputed to us, because he felt this was the only way to make a man truly holy and be able to live a law-honouring life in Christ. Rather than speak sparingly of Christ's life and triumph over the claims of the law, the Scriptures make a great point in emphasising it. The Christian does not serve the law as it is in the hand of Moses. This would mean defeat. He serves the law as it is in the hand of Christ, which means that in Christ he fulfils and establishes the law, 'bringing into captivity every thought to the obedience of Christ.'[1] The new covenant is that the laws on the external tablets of stone are now in the minds and hearts of believers. The author to the Hebrews calls this 'a more excellent ministry' and says it was 'established upon better promises.'[2] This doctrine of a

---

[1]     2 Corinthians 10:5.

[2]     See Hebrews 8:6-10.

vicarious fulfilling of the law on the sinner's behalf was a beam in the eye to Wesley. He felt it meant that as Christ has fulfilled the law for us, the believer could live as he liked. Wesley gives what he feels is an irrefutable example of the folly of Hervey's doctrine and which proves that it is 'the very quintessence of Antinomianism.' If Christ has met all the demands of the law, says Wesley, then when the law says 'Thou shalt love thy neighbour as thyself', the Christian has no obligation to love his neighbour as Christ has loved his neighbour for him. As Wesley has a very weak idea of the Biblical doctrine of union with Christ, apparently, he can neither envisage Christ acting through the believer nor imagine the believer acting in Christ.

## Union with Christ makes the believer a fulfiller of the law

All this is the result of Wesley's rejection of the doctrine of Christ's imputed righteousness and the gospel teaching of Christ's federal oneness with His Church. Obviously, if Christ's righteousness is imputed to the believer, making him a new creature and filling him with the Holy Spirit, that believer has every encouragement to live a holy life. He can now say with Paul 'I am crucified with Christ: nevertheless I live; yet not I, but Christ liveth in me: and the life which I now live in the flesh I live by the faith of the Son of God, who loved me, and gave himself for me.'[1] God's law becomes part and parcel of his mental, moral and spiritual makeup. Hervey stresses these biblical doctrines in his Dialogue III where he says, 'Christ and his people are actually considered as one and the same person. They are one mystical body; he the head, they the members; so intimately united to him, that they are "bone of his bone, and flesh of his flesh," (Eph. 5:30; Col. 1:20) by virtue of which union, their sins were punished in him, "and by his stripes they are healed," (Isa. 53:5,) they obtain impunity and life.' Wesley rejects Hervey's teaching of union with Christ arguing that we are not justified *in* Christ but *by* or *through* him. Indeed many of the passages which Hervey quotes to prove the justification of the ungodly, Wesley argues are proof of the sanctification of the godly. Whenever Hervey sees God's work in salvation, Wesley turns it on its head and speaks of man's agency in his efforts to become 'perfected in love'.

Wesley was the one who had formerly taught Hervey Hebrew but now Hervey is compelled to give his old tutor a lesson in that language. The passage in question, Isaiah 45:24-25, reads as follows in English:

> Surely, shall one say, in the Lord have I righteousness and strength: even to him shall men come; and all that are incensed against him shall be ashamed. In the Lord shall all the seed of Israel be justified, and shall glory.

---

[1]    Galatians 2:20.

Wesley, with his novel translation of the holy Word was radically altering the basic meaning and the traditional interpretation of '*In the Lord* have I righteousness' and '*In the Lord* shall all the seed of Israel be justified, and shall glory.' Hervey tells him that after a month's Hebrew, most students know that the Hebrew prefix b (ב) basically means 'in' and not 'by'. This is seen in the opening words of the Bible which read 'In the beginning, God', the first word being 'ב' or 'in'. 'By the beginning, God,' would make a very strange translation. When David speaks of fruit in season, he did not really mean, 'fruit through season'. Similarly when it is said that certain people 'shall not stand in judgement', it cannot be translated 'shall not stand by/through judgement.' The text shows not only that our righteousness and justification are found in Christ but that it is *in* Him (not merely *by* Him) that we should glory. It is to Christ that all men shall come and find righteousness in Him and they cannot possibly find righteousness anywhere else 'by' or 'through' Him. This is also made abundantly plain by verse 22 which reads, 'Look unto me, and be ye saved, all the ends of the earth.' Salvation is found '*in* Christ'.

Just as Wesley would not accept the phrase 'in the Lord', he also objected to Hervey saying 'Ye are complete in Him',[1] especially as Hervey uses this phrase to show that we receive our justification because of our oneness in Christ. The phrase must be translated, 'Ye are filled with him,' Wesley argues, and this meaning points to the believer's sanctification. Now he strives again to better the English translation and transform the meaning of the Greek. Wesley argues that 'en' (εν) in the Greek, as in '*In* the beginning was the Word,' really means 'with'. Hervey admits that 'en' sometimes has this transferred meaning but its literal, basic, meaning is obviously 'in', especially in the phrase in question, which is 'in him' (εν αυτω). This is supported by the entire context. Having said that, Hervey points out that even if the translation 'Ye are filled with him' were correct, this would not speak against the Christian being 'complete *in* him', nor would it speak against the text having bearing on our justification. But Hervey wants to know why Paul's words to the Colossian church have nothing to do with justification. The only reason Wesley had provided is 'any unprejudiced reader may observe it', which is sheer presumption and not evidence at all. Hervey then expounds the wider text in Colossians 2 to show how it deals with both sanctification and justification so that one can sum the teaching up in the words, '*In* him ye are completely justified, *in* him also ye are truly sanctified.'

**Wesley re-channels salvation along lines of grace super-added to works**
It is, of course, of great interest to a Christian reader to know why Wesley constantly fought shy of interpreting a text in the traditional sense

---

[1] Colossians 2:10.

of the words, and also constantly quarrelled with the Authorized Version, where that text presents Christ, to use Hervey's words, 'as the fullness of our sufficiency. In him and in him alone, there is enough to answer all the purposes of wisdom, righteousness, sanctification and redemption.' The answer can only be that Wesley re-channelled the means of salvation along lines of sanctification caused by grace being super-added to the believer[1] in his life of faith. The grace to live this life of faith was given by Christ, Wesley believed, but this was not a once and for all time sanctifying grace and thus not a once and for all time justifying grace. The grace was merely made available as long as the sincere believer kept using this grace to work out his salvation and therefore merit it. This was the way to perfection for Wesley, which must be attained fully in this life, otherwise there will be no perfection in the life to come. Again, Hervey can show that this is a new development in Wesley's theology as he once must have believed differently, otherwise he would not have written:

> Let us for this faith contend,
> Sure salvation is its end:
> Heaven already is begun,
> Everlasting life is won.

Any other view of salvation than that displayed in Wesley's former words reflects a very imperfect and highly theoretical knowledge of sanctification and justification. It also means that those of Wesley's followers who were pronounced 'perfect in love' and 'freed from sinful thoughts' and, indeed, felt themselves to be such, must therefore be seen as mere babes in Christ as they had no idea of the sinfulness of sin. These, however, Wesley called 'fathers' and it was people such as Hervey who knew where true righteousness was to be found, that Wesley called 'babes'.

Hervey explained to Wesley that he had lost his experimental knowledge of his faith because he had lost the knowledge of the supremacy of Christ and the experience of being partakers of him. Hervey is confident that Wesley once knew this better way as he had found it recorded in an early hymn of Wesley's:

> Join earth and heaven to bless
> The Lord our righteousness.
> The mystery of redemption this.
> This the Saviour's strange design;
> Man's offence was counted his,
> Our's his righteousness divine.

---

[1]    Wesley's phrase.

In him complete we shine,
His death, his life is mine.
Fully am I justified;
Free from sin, and more than free;
Guiltless, since for me he died,
Righteous, since he lived for me.[1]

Here is embedded the whole rainbow of gospel colours that Wesley later discarded for his drab, heavily-yoked gospel of sincere obedience. Here we have the Christian Wesley at his brightest and best, but it is unhappily a side of him that was kept in the dark in his arguments with Hervey and his friends. Indeed, Wesley sadly came to deny all the glorious, joyful teaching found in these two triumphant verses which he himself had penned.

**Arguing for the sake of the argument**
There is also much proof in Wesley's letter to Hervey that he is arguing for the sake of the argument. To win the argument over his pupil rather than gain the truth is his obvious goal. Time and time again, Wesley boasts in his works that he is an able debater but he quite forgets that he is not in a university debating society, debating for the sheer exercise but contending against gospel truths. This is shown in the meticulously pedantic way in which he demands that Hervey keep to the very language of the Authorized Version, though he reserves the right to retranslate the Bible at liberty himself. It is seen in the way he often misquotes Aspasio merely to create a basis for a further argument which really does not ensue from *Theron and Aspasio*. Also in the way he argues that Aspasio deals with doctrines that belong together as if they were exclusive though Aspasio emphasises particularly that such doctrines (e.g. Christ's active and passive work), reflect one work of salvation. We see it in the way Wesley picks on Hervey's language as misleading where it is perfectly understandable as when Aspasio states that we have a righteousness that is imputed and Wesley says the indefinite article should not be used. This is what Hervey meant by Wesley's 'unfair dealings' and 'magisterial air'. Another typical example is Wesley's insistence that he ought to speak, to be exact, of 'righteousness imputed' rather than 'imputed righteousness'. In his letter, Wesley now claims that Hervey's reference to 'the world of believers' is not Scriptural because it is not found in the Scriptures and, indeed, has 'no countenance from the Scriptures'. Referring to a hymn of Wesley's in which he says,

---

[1]  Though some 'experts' have doubted John Wesley's authorship of this hymn, Hervey who knew Wesley intimately, believed Wesley was the author. Wesley never denied this and he was usually very quick to deny anything wrongly attributed to him. The hymn appeared in the Wesleys, hymn book though it is often left out of modern Methodist collections.

For every man, 'tis finished, 'tis past,
The *world's* forgiven for Jesus' sake.

Hervey tells Wesley that it is obvious from this hymn that Wesley did
not mean that unbelievers were included in the 'world' so why should he
object to Aspasio believing that the world Jesus saves is the believing
world. Actually, Hervey might also have cited Wesley's *Christian Library*
of which he said, 'I believe, (it) is all true, all agreeable to the oracles of
God.' In this work, those whom Christ has saved are referred to as 'the
elect world of his church.' When Hill pointed out to Wesley that he had
criticised Hervey's 'world of believers' though he believed in using the
phrase 'the elect world' himself, Wesley merely commented that this was
no contradiction as when he said he believed everything in the *Christian
Library*, he was referring to the tracts in it but not to every word in those
tracts.[1]

**Wesley argues that the atonement merely makes salvation possible**
Having discussed righteousness, sanctification and justification, Hervey
now turns to Wesley's teaching on the atonement as a work of Christ that
did not secure salvation for any man. To find the Arminian leader teaching
that if a sinner does not believe in Christ, then Christ died in vain for him
was evidence to Hervey that Wesley had quite departed from the Word of
God and the gospel once committed to the saints. Wesley had written to
him, 'The plain truth is, Christ lived and tasted death for every man,' and
followed this up with the surprising statement, 'To be sure, then, since
every man is not saved by him, he lived and died only to make their salvation possible.' Wesley seems to be actually saying, 'Christ has done His
bit, now it is up to you to give it all purpose and fulfilment.' To this,
Hervey says:

> From this, and other hints, I guess your opinion to be, that Christ,
> by his life and death, obtained only a possibility of salvation; which
> salvation is to become our own, upon performing terms and condi-
> tions, bringing with us prerequisites and qualifications. If I mistake
> you, Sir, in this case, you have nothing more to do, than simply to
> deny my supposition. This exculpates you at once. I shall rejoice to
> hear you say, as Christ made us, and not we ourselves; in like man-
> ner he saves us and not we ourselves. No human endowments, no
> human performances, but Christ alone, is the author of eternal sal-
> vation.
>     Should you reply, True, Christ is the author of eternal salva-
> tion, but *to those* only who *obey Him*: I must then ask, what obedi-

---

[1]    *Works*, vol. xv, *Some Remarks on Mr. Hill's Review*, pp. 37-39.

ence Christ requires? the law says, Do and live. Christ, the end of the law, says, Believe in me, and live. Be verily persuaded, that I am sufficient for thy salvation, without any working of thine at all. Is not the Son, the Son of the most high God, given unto thee in the divine record? Be satisfied with *his* doing and suffering, without wishing for or thinking of any thing more to procure thy final acceptance.—Let no one account lightly of this obedience. It is the obedience of faith; the obedience suited to the name of Jesus; obedience to the first and great command of the gospel. Beyond all other expedients, it excludes boasting; and at the same time produces that genuine love, that filial fear, which the law of works requires in vain.

Only to make a thing possible, and effect it, are widely different. When our king fits out a fleet, and gives his admiral commission to harass the French coasts, and destroy the French shipping, he makes the thing possible; but to carry the design into execution, to accomplish the enterprise now become practicable, is a far more arduous task and a far more honourable achievement. How strangely do those writers derogate from the dignity and glory of the Redeemer who would ascribe to him what corresponds with the former, and attribute to man what bears a resemblance to the latter!

If Christ only made our salvation possible, then we are to execute the plan; we are to face the enemy, to sustain the charge, and silence the battery; we are to climb the steep, to enter the breech, and bring off the standards; and so, in all reason, the honour and praise must be our own. Whereas, the gospel gives all the honour to the Captain of our Salvation: He bore the heat and burden of the dreadful day: He made reconciliation for iniquity, and brought in everlasting righteousness: So that all our officious attempts, like a pinnace arriving after the victory, should be told, 'it is finished'; the great salvation is already wrought. And instead of being dissatisfied or disappointed, methinks we should rejoice, unfeignedly rejoice, in the accomplishment of the glorious work.[1]

### The perseverance of the saints

Wesley now takes up what Hervey has to say concerning the perseverance of the saints. Not only is the act of believing solely the responsibility of the Christian, according to Wesley, but also the process of remaining in Christ. Aspasio had remarked on some professors of religion who had fallen away, believing them never to have been converted. Wesley objects to this and says, 'Not so; They who turn back as a dog to the vomit, had

---

[1]   Letter III.

once escaped the pollutions of the world by the knowledge of Christ.'
When Aspasio argues that it is impossible for God's elect to fall again into
total apostasy, Wesley replies 'How pleasing this is to flesh and blood,'
and denies the doctrine outright. One would have hardly thought that flesh
and blood had any interest in being one with Christ for ever, according to
the Scriptures, but here, again, we have an example of what Richard Hill
called *logica Wesleiensis*. Hervey asks Wesley if he really believes that
those whose names God has put in the Lamb's Book of Life can have them
rubbed out. Can those sheep who hear God's voice and to whom he gives
eternal life, suddenly lose their eternal salvation because Satan has plucked
them from the hand of Christ? John, Hervey tells Wesley, shows the futil-
ity of his argument by stressing that those who apparently deserted the
gospel way had never walked along it 'They went out from us, but they
were not of us.'[1] Wesley, presumably, Hervey adds, would say to John,
'Not so; they were of you, but they fell away from you.' But the apostle
proceeds to prove what he has said by adding that if those who left had
been really one with the believers, i.e. one in Christ, they would have
continued with them. Concerning the quote from 2 Peter 2:22 where the
topic is the rejection of the way of righteousness, illustrated by the dog
returning to its vomit and the pig to its wallowing in the mire, Hervey asks
Wesley since when knowledge alone saved. The apostle tells us that if we
have all knowledge but no faith, we are nothing. Simon the Sorcerer had
'knowledge of the things which concern the kingdom of God, and the
name of Jesus Christ' but he had neither lot nor portion in salvation. Hervey
points out that Peter is not referring to those who have become partakers
of the Divine nature with their souls purified by the Spirit but of those who
have made morals their religion and thus subdued their lusts for a time.
These people are referred to by Peter, not as one time Christians but as a
dog and a sow that were such then and are such still. He is referring to
those who deserted their own for a time, only to return to them, but they
were of their kind all along. Hervey then explains to Wesley the difference
between notional knowledge and experimental Christianity.

As so often in his letter against Hervey's doctrines, Wesley refutes the
faith, seemingly for the sake of the argument, which he had continually
maintained previously and, indeed, once again professed after denying
these very doctrines to Hervey. One Sunday, July 1778, Wesley entered
into his Journal, a note saying how God poured on the assembly a spirit of
grace and supplication when singing the concluding hymn:

To us the covenant blood apply,
Which takes our sins away;

---

[1]    1 John 2:19.

And register our names on high,
And keep us to that day.

Indeed, a far better case could be made out for arguing that Wesley's letter, had it not been so clearly testified to by Wesley himself, was a forgery as many of the doctrines denied in it were otherwise approved of by the Methodist. This is why Hill constantly asked Wesley to make a definite statement, without dodging the issue, as to what he really believed.

### A nice metaphysical doctrine

Wesley's next point shows him once more arguing in a way that bars all objectivity as he picks on a subject with which he really agrees and uses it as an excuse for returning to the topic of imputed righteousness, a theme he never seems to be able to drop and professes he does not believe in the least. With a logic that is hard to follow, Wesley quotes Aspasio's words, 'The goodness of God leadeth to repentance,' and comments, 'This is unquestionably true but the nice metaphysical doctrine of imputed righteousness, leads not to repentance, but to licentiousness.' Perhaps these are the words that gave Shepherd the idea that Theron had taken on the role of Wesley as it was Theron who claimed that imputed righteousness was metaphysical. He dropped this claim, however, on becoming a Christian. Hervey asks Wesley to explain how the words, 'I am acquitted and counted righteous before God, only through the imputation of my Saviour's obedience and death.' could be described as metaphysical. Were they not rather truly evangelical? This question illustrates Hervey's difficulty with Wesley. How can one defend Christian doctrines against a man who brings no arguments whatsoever to bear on the subject under consideration apart from a dogmatic denial? Hervey explains how contemplating on the righteousness of Christ and the divine goodness which causes God to accept this in lieu of our imperfections, rather than drive him to licentiousness, leaves him lost in wonder at the condescension of Christ. Rather than drive him into loose living, the revelation of it shows up his own sin and forces him to cry out for mercy. This doctrine, and this alone, he believes, leads a sinner to repentance.

### Laying a good foundation for eternal life

Now Wesley turns to the subject of Christian obedience. Hervey had maintained that 'we no longer obey, in order to lay the foundation for our final acceptance,' meaning that the foundation of our acceptance lies in God's grace and not in our works. Wesley appears to accept this, saying, 'that foundation is already laid in the merits of Christ.' These words caused Hervey real pleasure but this pleasure turned to dismay when he read how Wesley interpreted this to mean the exact opposite of his own understanding of saving grace. Wesley continued by saying, 'Yet we obey, in order to

James Hervey

secure our final acceptance through his merits. And in this sense, by obeying we lay a good foundation, that we may attain eternal life.' Hervey tells Wesley, 'if you obey in order to attain your final acceptance, surely you must expect final acceptance and eternal life on account of your own obedience.' This causes Hervey to quote from the canons of the Council of Trent, 'If any one shall say that the righteous ought not for their own good works to expect the eternal reward through the merits of Jesus Christ, let him be accursed.' If we take away the words 'let him be accursed,' which Wesley always abhors in his writings on Romanism, the dogma of Trent is identical with his own. Hervey goes on to say:

> By this time, I believe, the thoughtful reader will guess the reasons why you oppose and decry imputed righteousness. You are solicitous, it seems, not barely for works of obedience, but for their value and credit in the affair of salvation; for their significancy and influence in winning the good will of Jehovah. Since this is your notion, you may well be offended at Christ's imputed righteousness. This will admit of no partner or coadjutor. This, Sir, in the case of justification, pours contempt upon all your most laborious exercises, and admired attainments. Yea, this being divine and inconceivably excellent, pours all around a blaze of glory, in which all our puny doings are lost, as the stars in the meridian sunshine.[1]

**Justification by augmentation refuted**

Now Wesley returns to the topic of justification, arguing that Aspasio is wrong to say 'Justification is complete, the first moment we believe; and is incapable of augmentation.' Wesley suggests that justification comes in stages. As a Christian grows into the image of God, his degree of justification grows. This is in keeping with Wesley's Christian evolution programme whereby a newly converted person is a babe in Christ and is at the start of being saved and needs to grow into a father in the faith, perfected in love and able, with a good conscience, to be declared fully justified. Again Hervey quotes the Council of Trent which so clearly backs up Wesley's doctrine.

Justification, Hervey argues, is a single act of God's grace, therefore it must be done or not done. If it is done, it is completely done. There is no such thing as incomplete justification, says Hervey, quoting Paul in Romans 3:24-26 and other passages of Scripture to prove it. Wesley seems to be arguing here against the doctrine of conversion, viewing the would-be believer as acquiring degrees of justification (as he terms the process) as he practises sincere obedience and grows nearer his spiritual goal. Hervey

---

[1]    Letter III.

stresses that justification and sanctification are gifts that Christ has 'wrought out' (a term which Wesley finds unscriptural) on Calvary. Thus we can say with the author of Hebrews, 'For by one offering he hath perfected for ever them that are sanctified.' The author emphasises that no further sacrifice is necessary because a once and for all time justification has been worked out. If Wesley wishes to follow Arminius and maintain that justification has both divine and human elements, then his logic holds but this is not the voice of the inspired Word.

Now Wesley objects to Aspasio referring to good works (beneficences) as 'transient bubbles'. Hervey explains that Aspasio is not speaking absolutely but relatively. They have their purpose but in God's service alone. As far as earning justification, which is the point Aspasio is making, they are but 'bubbles'. If you do not like the word, Hervey suggests, then we shall take Paul's word. He called them 'dung'.[1] Wesley obviously does not like calling good works bad names because he believes that they are an expression of doing the commandments of God and thus 'the way to, though not the cause of, eternal life.' Hervey tells him that Christ kept all God's commandments, thus providing a way to the Father for us. This way is now found in Him who says, 'I am the Way, the Truth and the Life, no man cometh to the Father but by me.' In Christ we have a 'new and living way' and we are told to 'walk in Him'.

### Wesley alleges that Abraham's righteousness is different to the Christian's

Wesley and Hervey could not have disagreed more concerning their interpretation of John 8 and Romans 4. To Hervey, Abraham rejoiced to see the day of the Lord and, in faith, foresaw it. His faith i.e. faith in Christ was imputed to him for righteousness. Time and time again in his works, Wesley denies that Abraham's faith, that was imputed to him for righteousness, had anything whatsoever to do with Christ. Knowing how Jesus risked being stoned to death for saying that Abraham trusted in Him, it is amazing that Wesley shows so much antagonism on this point. Nor did Wesley ever change his mind on the issue. Writing nineteen years to the month after his letter to Hervey, i.e. on Thursday October 9, 1777, Wesley entered into his Journal the words, 'I was desired by some of our friends to clear up the point of Imputed Righteousness: I did so, by preaching on, "Abraham believed God, and it was imputed unto him for righteousness." In opening these words, I showed what that faith was, which was imputed to him for righteousness, viz., faith in God's promise to give him the land of Canaan; faith in the promise that Sarah should conceive a son; and the faith whereby he offered up Isaac on the altar. But Christ is not in any of

---

[1]    Philippians 3:8.

these instances the direct or immediate object of that faith.' It is strange here that Wesley does not link Abraham with covenantal and messianic promises concerning his 'seed'. Here the servant Wesley, begs to differ from his Master Christ!

Yet Wesley did not always have this faulty belief concerning Abraham. In his sermon *The Righteousness of Faith*, although he denies much that is orthodox, which will be discussed below, he clearly states, 'Even so Abraham "believed in the Lord, and he counted it to him for righteousness."'[1]

Referring to Aspasio's belief that Abraham's faith overcame the world and answered its proper end, so that one can say of him, 'by works his faith was made perfect,' Wesley drops a theological bombshell. 'You are wrong,' he tells Hervey, 'The natural sense of the words is, by the grace superadded, while he wrought those works, his faith was literally made perfect.' Of course, Hervey wanted to know where 'grace super-added' was to be found in the texts Aspasio quotes. James talks about works but Wesley about 'super-added' grace. Here Wesley is quite obviously disagreeing now with James. James clearly says that Abraham applied his faith to doing works, i.e. his faith was demonstrated in the works he did. Thus Hervey explains, quoting several other commentators, that James 2:23-26, refers to 'faith illustriously displayed by works.'[2]

### Considering Christ's death exclusive of His fulfilling the law

In Letter VI, Hervey deals with another of Wesley's apparent quibbling over words which obviously is a cover-up for his own unorthodox doctrine. Wesley objects to Aspasio referring to Christ's *accomplishing* justification on the sinner's behalf. The word 'purchase' should be used, he argues. The context again refers to the obedience of Christ which accomplished justification for us, a doctrine with which Wesley never came to terms. To Wesley's question, 'Is the death of Christ insufficient to purchase justification,' as if Hervey were arguing on these lines, Hervey answers, 'If you consider the death of Christ as exclusive of his obedience, it is insufficient. If you do not, there is no great reason your starting a doubt where we are both agreed.' Hervey explains that he had used the word 'accomplished' to distance himself from the Popish teaching whereby 'the righteousness of Christ purchases, but does not accomplish; it merits our justification, but does not constitute our justifying righteousness.' Obviously Hervey is saying that if the Popish cap fits Wesley, he is entitled to wear it but then must stand outside of Reformed Christian theology.

---

[1]   *Works*, vol. vii, pp. 80, 81.

[2]   See Letter V.

### Providing for rather than securing salvation

Wesley now builds another of his disagreements with Hervey on an apparent agreement, though a connection is not explained. Aspasio states that which no Christian could deny, 'The saints in glory ascribe the whole of their salvation to the blood of the Lamb.' Wesley answers, 'So do I, and yet I believe he obtained for all a possibility of salvation.' Here, of course, what Wesley affirms has no logical connection with what Aspasio has stated. Furthermore, Aspasio's statement is hardly capable of misunderstanding, whereas Wesley's statement, in view of what he has already said about the atonement merely *providing for* but not *securing* salvation, is extremely ambiguous. Aspasio is saying that the salvation of all the saints in glory is secured at Calvary. Although Wesley, here, affirms that he accepts Aspasio's statement, it seems he has misunderstood it as he has already stated that he does not believe that Christ secured the salvation of those for whom He died. Hervey asks Wesley to be less ambiguous in his statements as it is clear that he means, 'Yet I believe that Christ obtained no more than a possibility of salvation for any.' This, Hervey argues, would be neither sound sense nor sound doctrine. It would not make sense as it would mean that salvation was according to conditions placed on man thus the saints in glory could not then say that salvation was all of Christ. Wesley's view is not sound doctrine because, according to the Scriptures, when Christ cried out, 'It is finished,' full and complete salvation was worked out. This salvation is never acquired but is always given absolutely. 1 John 5:11, 'God hath given us eternal life.'

### Wesley accuses Hervey of making Christ the servant of sin

When commenting on the Ninth Dialogue Wesley forgets good manners and becomes insulting in his arguments. Hervey insists that the true believer longs for purity of heart. Hervey's believers do no such thing, claims Wesley, as his doctrine 'makes the Holy One of God a minister of sin'. One wonders how Wesley can possibly accuse saintly Hervey of such blasphemy? The cause is obviously to be found in Wesley's faulty view of the doctrine of the union of the believer with Christ, his unorthodox views of imputation, his unscriptural views of the Second Adam and his imperfect teaching concerning the new man in Christ. For him the very fact that Hervey can say 'Christ has done everything necessary for my salvation.' indicates that he must automatically live a lawless life. Thus when the Hills accused Wesley of maintaining that those who taught that the claims of the Law were answered in Christ were Antinomians, Wesley confirmed this and said they were 'Antinomians without a mask'.[1] Wesley even goes

[1]   *Works*, Vol. XV, p. 42.

so far as to argue that Christ's fulfilling of the Law as 'requisite *in order* to his *purchasing* redemption for us' could not be proven.

## The conditions of salvation

Now Wesley takes a look at the conditions of our salvation. Hervey, through Aspasio, had stated, 'The terms of acceptance for fallen men were a full satisfaction to the divine justice, and a complete conformity to the divine law.' In other words, Christ has died for us and Christ has fulfilled the law for us. This is salvation accomplished and applied. Wesley retorts by saying that this is taking for granted what cannot be as the terms of acceptance before God in Scripture are clearly repentance and faith. Hervey asks Wesley how then fallen man is to meet these conditions as he is dead to God and has no more the powers to perform the actions of a living Christian as a dead body has the powers to perform the functions of a living man. He reminds Wesley that he is quoting Wesley's own words from a sermon he once preached. Obviously, according to Scripture, God grants to those whose salvation is accomplished the grace to repent and the gift of faith. This seems to have been Wesley's own faith when he preached the sermon referred to. Hervey argues that he does not like to use the word 'conditions' applied to fallen man and referring to what is Christ's work because it darkens the sinners soul and fills him with anxiety as to how well he has performed the conditions and it takes away the bright lustre of grace as it takes the eyes from Christ and centres them on one's own deeds. It also affords too much occasion for boasting.

## Satisfaction of Divine justice *and* conformity to the law needed

Quoting from another sermon of Wesley's on the *Righteousness of Faith*, Hervey says, 'According to your gospel, faith will say to the righteousness of the Redeemer, "Depart hence, I have no need of thee. I myself act as the justifying righteousness. I stand in the stead of perfect obedience, in order to acceptance with God."[1] To this may we not reply, Was

---

[1] Hervey seems to be summing up Wesley's sermon here but a footnote, either by Hervey or a later editor, claims that 'these are Wesley's very own words, in his explanation of this very doctrine.' The sermon entitled *Righteousness of Faith* in Wesley's various collections which was preached along with a series of sermons exhibiting the same views of righteousness, does not give verbatim the words Hervey quotes. Wesley informed his readers in 1771, however, that these sermons were preached 'during the last eight or nine years.' Hervey wrote in 1757 at the latest, so he must be referring to an earlier sermon, or at least an earlier version. In his sermon on *The Lord our Righteousness*, which is also open to Hervey's criticism but which was written later, Wesley mentions that he had preached on the subject in 1738, which could be the sermon Hervey is referring to. There is no earlier sermon of this title, however, included in Wesley's complete works. The footnote gives vol. i., p.111 as the source of Hervey's quote but no date or edition is given. In the 1808, xvi volume edition of Wesley's works, the sermon *Righteousness of Faith* is found in vol. vii, Sermon vi, p. 76 ff..

faith then crucified for you? Has faith magnified the divine law? Or is it by means of faith, that not one jot or tittle of its precepts pass unfulfilled? If faith, in this sense, is imputed for righteousness how can you subscribe that emphatical article which declares, "We are accounted righteous before God, only for the merit of our Lord and Saviour Jesus Christ."'

Hervey argues that man is fallen because he has failed to keep the Law that God made for him. If he had kept it, he would have gained eternal life but in breaking it, he lost this privilege. But God still demands of man full satisfaction to the Divine Justice, and a complete conformity to the Divine law. This man is unable to give but Christ fulfils these requirements on behalf of His Church. Wesley cannot agree and claims that 'What Christ has done is the *foundation* of our justification, not the *term* or *condition* of it.' He hotly denies that Christ has fulfilled all conditions in order to save His elect, claiming that man must have an 'interest in Christ' and that 'every man shall receive his own reward, according to his own labour.'

Again Wesley is forgetting the union of the believer in Christ. It is in Christ that the believer is given repentance for breaking God's standards and it is in Christ that he is enabled to believe. This is what Hervey means by saying that the believer's full justification was wrought out at Calvary. Wesley, however, argues that justification is not complete until the believer exercises faith which then, and only then, is imputed to him for righteousness. Thus the atonement, for Wesley is not a once and for all time absolute event on Calvary but applications of separate events each time a believer exercises faith. This is not even a once and for all time event in the life of a believer as such believers are liable to become unbelievers again as their will moves them and thus need, for every fall from faith, a newly applied atonement. Justification for Wesley appears to be a growth whereby the believer in part becomes the believer in full. Thus the believer exercises faith and by the grace that is 'superadded' whilst works are wrought, faith is 'literally made perfect'. Hervey reminds Wesley that this perfect faith is Christ's gift as the author and finisher of our faith, not merely the foundation of it. Our salvation is *all* of Christ. Once more, Hervey is forced to see a comparison with what Wesley teaches and what the Council of Trent maintained. In the Roman Catholic findings at the council, it was held that though Christ has laid the foundation, faith is procured by the believer fulfilling certain conditions. This, believes Hervey, 'bears the greatest opposition to the truth of his gospel, and the freeness of his redemption.'

## Wesley's 'perfect' Christians

Wesley's view of perfection is displayed in his argument concerning Hervey's quote of Ecclesiastes 7:20, 'For there is not a just man upon the earth that doeth good, and sinneth not.' Wesley says that this might be said of Solomon's days but cannot be said of New Testament times. Quoting

John and James 'Whosoever is born of God sinneth not.'[1] and 'in many things we offend all,' Wesley seems to be arguing for a sinless perfection whereby the believer is perfect yet guilty of 'offending'. It is equally clear that he feels Solomon's words do not apply to James and, what he calls, 'real Christians', 'adult Christians' or 'fathers'.[2] Hervey points out that James is indicating that those who are born of God do not make a point of practising sin, sin does not *reign* in the mortal body (Romans 6:12). Though sin may assault a believer, it does not have dominion over him (Romans 6:14). Besides, Hervey argues, John does not speak of the highest rank of Christians but says 'whosoever' is born again does not sin. In this sense 'babes' are included as well as 'adults'. Solomon, Hervey explains, had his eye on the 'inconceivable purity and spirituality' of the law which is God's standard in all ages, not only in the old dispensation but in the new heavens and new earth to come. On the other hand, when James says we offend all, he is referring both to himself and all Christians, a fact which Wesley denies though James proves by referring expressly to his brethren and himself as the subjects of those who 'offend all'. Contrary to this view, Wesley argues, 'No Scripture teaches that the holiness of Christians is to be measured by that of any Jew.' He says this, of course, in union with his belief that the faith expressed by the Old Testament heroes, including Abraham, David and Solomon, was a different faith to that of a Christian. Hervey, referring to the nature and fruits of faith expressed in Hebrews 11, shows how the lives of the patriarchs illustrate how 'faith is the substance of things hoped for, the evidence of things not seen,' and that this faith was pleasing to God. Contradicting Wesley's argument that the faith of the Old Testament heroes was not in Christ, the author of Hebrews argues that 'By faith Moses . . . choosing rather to suffer affliction with the people of God, than to enjoy the pleasures of sin for a season; Esteeming the reproach of Christ greater riches than the treasures in Egypt: for he had respect unto the recompense of the reward.'

Wesley, however, clung to his doctrine of Christian perfection, arguing that Hervey was wrong in his belief that the best of Christians must say with Paul, 'When I would do good, evil is present with me,'[3] arguing that 'If sin remains in us till the day of judgement, it will remain in us for ever.' Wesley, however, had a Neonomian view of perfection, far lower than the standards Christ set in fulfilling and establishing the law. He says, referring to the words of John, 'If we were perfect in piety, we should still be encompassed with infirmities, and liable to mistakes, from which words or actions might follow, even though the heart was all love, which were

---

[1]   See 1 John 3:9, 'Whosoever is born of God doth not commit sin,' and James 3:2.

[2]   See also *Some Remarks on Mr. Hill's Review, Works*, vol. xv, pp.52, 53

[3]   Wesley obviously believed that here Paul is speaking as a non-Christian.

not exactly right.' This utterance is typical of Wesley's low view of sin in the Christian, arguing it away as 'infirmities', 'mistakes' and 'things which are not exactly right'.

## Wesley sees righteousness as a method and not God's standard

Hervey's view of righteousness is incomprehensible to Wesley, shown by the fact that whenever he returns to the subject, he misquotes Hervey in his effort to understand him. He cannot see righteousness as the standard which Christ has set us in His own life and imputed to us. Righteousness, he argues, is a method, namely a method whereby God justifies sinners. He feels this is the teaching of Paul in Romans. Wesley often uses the word 'method' to describe righteousness but he never really defines what this righteousness entails or to whom this righteousness belongs. Obviously he is not speaking of Christ's righteousness when viewing his 'method of justification' but the life-long obedience of man. Actually, for Wesley, only dead Christians are really justified because only then have they fulfilled the conditions to the end. Hervey asks Wesley to be more specific in his arguments, asking him if one can speak of God's attributes such as holiness and wisdom as being 'methods'. One must rather speak of God's righteousness revealed in Christ as God's *gift* or as the *object* of justifying faith. Wesley, however, seems to be saying that God's righteousness is one thing, Christ's righteousness is another and the believer's righteousness is a third. Here Hervey quotes 2 Peter 1:1 'to them that have obtained like precious faith with us through the righteousness of God and our Saviour Jesus Christ,' showing that there is only one righteousness which is the object of and establishes our faith. Hervey backs this up with 2 Corinthians 5:21, 'For he hath made him to be sin for us, who knew no sin; that we might be made the righteousness of God in him.' Could you possibly understand this as meaning, 'That we may be made God's method of justifying sinners?' Hervey asks Wesley. What upsets Wesley is the fact that Hervey says it is this righteousness and this alone which, when imputed to us and made ours by faith, makes us acceptable before God. Of this doctrine, Wesley says, 'I cannot allow it at all.' Again, Wesley is using his 'magisterial air' to confute all opposition without further argument, whereas Aspasio gives one Scriptural passage after another which ought to be consulted. Such refusal to accept the Biblical teaching on the atonement moved Sir Richard Hill to argue that Wesley had seemingly no doctrine of atonement at all.[1]

## Mistaking the effect for the cause

Wesley constantly interprets imputed righteousness as 'interest in Christ', whereas Hervey explains that Wesley is mistaking the effect for

---

[1]  See his *Imposture Detected.*

the cause. He argues that the interest in Christ can only be found in those
who have tasted imputed righteousness. As so often, Hervey must remind
Wesley that he, too, once taught the same doctrine. This time, he quotes
Wesley's hymn,

> Let faith and love combine
> To guard your valiant breast,
> The plate be righteousness divine,
> *Imputed* and imprest.

**Christ gained for His people not only pardon but also acceptance**
In arguing for the righteousness of Christ being displayed in His obedience to what was 'requisite', Hervey says through Aspasio, 'If it was
requisite for Christ to be baptized, much more to fulfill the moral law.'
Surprisingly, Wesley says, 'I cannot prove that either the one or the other
was requisite in order to his purchasing redemption.' Wesley here, for
once, explains what he means. He maintains that the law was satisfied by
Christ's death alone. The law did not require Christ to suffer and obey but
merely to suffer. Thus Wesley interprets 'He was obedient to the death,' as
meaning 'He died in obedience to the Father.' Here Wesley has missed the
purport of the text, namely that Christ was obedient 'unto' death and not
'in' death or 'in' dying. Here also Wesley has missed the dual purpose of
redemption. a. Christ came to suffer our penalties vicariously, and b. He
came to present us perfect before God clothed with a righteousness which
has established the law through obeying every jot and tittle. Christ's death
took away the penalty but Christ's righteousness makes us meet to have
our guilt removed so that we are sinless in God's eyes of mercy and justice. This is why Wesley speaks so much of falling from grace. His believer is only pardoned so is free at any time to go back to his former life.
In Hervey's theology, the elect sinner is both pardoned and made a new
creature in Christ. Pardon and acceptance go together in redemption. This
makes it impossible for the believer to return as the sow to the mire or the
dog to its vomit.

**The surety of salvation covenanted before the foundation of the world
challenged**
The next complaint on Wesley's agenda is against Hervey's statement,
'Christ undertook to do everything necessary for our redemption, namely,
in a covenant made with his father.' He asks Hervey for proof that Christ
undertook all these necessary things before the foundation of the world
and this by means of a covenant with His Father. Oddly enough, Wesley
denies that there was ever a covenant made between Father and Son in
their plan of redemption. He overlooks completely the covenant duties

which Christ took upon himself as outlined by the author of Hebrews[1], as Hervey points out, comparing this with Isaiah 42 where Christ is given 'for a covenant to the people.' It is easy to see in what direction Wesley is arguing. If there is a covenant between God and Christ, then it is up to the Father and the Son to keep the conditions. Hervey would say that this is correct. Wesley, however, will not accept that the conditions for salvation are divinely met. Thus he argues that all God's covenants are with man and the conditions of fulfilling them are repentance and faith which Christ has not fulfilled for us.

Arguing against Hervey's phrase that 'the obedience of our Security is accepted instead of our own,' Wesley says he prefers the Scriptural expression, 'we are accepted through the Beloved.' Again, the suretyship of Christ can hardly appeal to one whose surety lies in the life-long obedience of the believer. Hervey tells Wesley that we are acceptable because of Christ's suretyship. Though Wesley is claiming to be more Scriptural than Hervey, he again re-translates Scripture to suit his own theology, as Hervey is quick to point out. The Scriptures say that we are accepted *in* the Beloved, that is *in* Christ. Wesley sees Christ merely as a means which man may use and therefore prefers the preposition 'through'. Hervey explains that we are accepted because of our union in Christ and not because Christ becomes a means for us to perform some end. He drives this home by quoting John 17:22, 23, 'And the glory which thou gavest me I have given them; that they may be one, even as we are one: I in them, and thou in me, that they may be made perfect in one; and that the world may know that thou hast sent me, and hast loved them, as thou has loved me.'

In Letter IX, Hervey takes up Wesley's repeated insistence that Christ has not fulfilled all the conditions of salvation on our behalf and is thus not our Surety before God. 'If we allow this,' Wesley says, 'Antinomianism comes in with a full tide.' The conditions of salvation, Wesley emphasises anew, are repentance and faith. These gifts, Hervey stresses, are not conditions required but blessings bestowed. They are 'not conditions on which depends the accomplishment of the covenant, but are happy fruits, or precious effects of the covenant, made, and making good to sinners, who are wholly without strength.' Going through over thirty passages in Scripture, Hervey outlines how the believer has nothing but what has been freely given him by the grace of God so that he might convince Wesley that all human conditions and pre-requisites have been put aside so that we might be saved by a divine act. Needless to say, Hervey is able to quote from Wesley himself to show that this was the true faith which Wesley formerly held dear. In summing up, Hervey points out in the words of Zechariah 9:11, 'By the blood of thy covenant I have sent forth the prison-

---

[1]    See especially Hebrews 1 and 10:7-9.

ers out of the pit wherein is no water.' From a position of helplessness, where there was nothing to be done by us because we could do nothing, so hopeless was the situation; God rescued us by the atoning ransom of Christ's blood shed for us for the remission of our sins.

## Pardon complete and irrevocable

Now Wesley comes up with an amazingly logical statement which he yet fails to grasp and uses as evidence against Hervey. He argues, 'If Christ's perfect obedience be ours, we have no more need of pardon than Christ himself.' No, not any more, is Hervey's comment. 'By one offering, he hath perfected for ever them that are sanctified.' (Hebrews 10:14). Believers, Hervey explains, are not reconciled for one day or one year, according to how they fall in and out of grace; they are reconciled for ever. 'The pardon is irrevocable; the blessing inalienable.'

Being at a loss to find Scripture to support him, Wesley hides behind what he feels is the teaching of his church, maintaining it is Christ's death alone which gains full satisfaction. Anyone familiar with the Articles and the Homilies of the Church of England will notice how Wesley, without a blush, cuts all the appropriate passages out and then triumphantly declares that the Church is on his side. Hervey takes up the challenge and has Wesley read more carefully the very homily which he quotes from, which says:

> The apostle toucheth three things, which must go together in justification. On God's part, his great mercy and grace: On Christ's part, the satisfaction of God's justice, or the price of our redemption, by the offering of his body and shedding of his precious blood, with fulfilling of the law perfectly: On our part, true and lively faith in the merits of Jesus Christ, which yet is not ours, but by God's working in us.

In a like manner, Hervey deals with the Articles. Thus sound Anglican theology joins hands with Scripture to confute Wesley, yet Hervey, as an Anglican to an Anglican, cannot help but tease Wesley and tell him that Aspasio had not appealed to the Church but to the Scriptures alone.

## Putting into Hervey's mouth words he never used

Now Wesley attacks Hervey on 'absolute predestination' which was the topic of his first 'stinging and sarcastic' letter against *Theron and Aspasio* and a topic Hervey hardly touches on. Needless to say, when Wesley accuses Hervey of believing in absolute predestination and that nine-tenths of mankind are reprobate, this is all in Wesley's imagination as Hervey neither mentions the one not the other in his *Theron and Aspasio*. Thus Hervey must ask Wesley for the umpteenth time, 'Is it fair, is it honest, to put into your friend's mouth words which he never used, and then exclaim against them?' Hervey, no doubt, had also in mind the first letter he received from Wesley concerning his *Theron and Aspasio* some time just before or after the beginning of 1755. Writing to Lady Francis about this quite unfair attack on his work, Hervey says:

> He takes me very roundly to task, on the score of predestination. At which I am much surprised. Because a reader, ten times less penetrating than he is, may easily see, that this doctrine (be it true or false) makes no part of my scheme; never comes under consideration; is purposely and carefully avoided.[1]

Here the reader can draw parallels with Wesley's treatment of Augustus Toplady[2] and John Gill. So great was Wesley's anti-predestination phobia that when the author of *Rock of Ages* maintained that the number of the elect were 'fixed and determined', Wesley accused Toplady of saying that 'nineteen in twenty' will be damned. Needless to say, Toplady was as innocent as Hervey of such a ridiculous claim to know the will of God. When John Gill wrote his *The Doctrine of the Saints' Final Perseverance* in 1752, Wesley immediately attacked the work as if it had been a treatise on predestination and published his *Predestination Calmly Considered* showing his total inability to understand and represent Gill's theology correctly. When Gill replied with his *The Doctrine of Predestination, Stated and Set in the Scripture Light*, Wesley retired from the combat and turned to Toplady and Hervey.

### The Biblical word 'righteousness' challenged

In Letter X, Hervey takes up Wesley's claims that where he refers to righteousness, indicating the righteousness of Christ, he is misinterpreting the original Hebrew or Greek texts which either refer to mercy or justification. When the Bible refers to '*everlasting* righteousness', Wesley claims, this should be translated '*spotless* holiness', a meaning the Hebrew word cannot possibly bear. Especially the latter, Wesley maintains is a condition set upon Christians in order that they might be saved rather than on Christ in order that He might save them. After Hervey has referred Wesley

---

[1]   Letter to Lady Francis, LXXIV, Jan. 9, 1755.

[2]   See Wesley's *Works*, vol. xiv, *The Consequence Proved*. Toplady's protest at this dishonest attack which shows Wesley in the worst possible light is found in his *More Work for Mr. John Wesley; or A Vindication of the Decrees and Providence of God, from the Defamation of a Late Printed Paper, entitled 'The Consequence Proved.'* Generations of Methodists have protested at Toplady's use of such words as 'defamation' when speaking of their beloved founder but the *The Consequence Proved* is such a vulgar piece of diatribe, comparing Toplady with an executioner who first deflowers an innocent virgin and then strangles her, that one feels that Toplady answered in a way that does honour to his self-control.

to all the dictionaries, showing how the basic word for righteousness saddîq (צדק)[1] is quite different to those for mercy, holiness etc., he points out that the best interpreter of this is the Bible itself. Quoting from Hebrews 5 and 7, Hervey shows how Melchi*sedec* is translated King of Righteousness, after whose order Christ took up his work of righteousness. Even if the word were to be translated mercy, justification or holiness, Hervey argues, mercy is shown to a sinner only on account of the righteousness of our Security; we are justified equally only on account of that righteousness and if there is any spotless holiness in this world, it is only that which Christ has proved to be His. Referring to Daniel 9:24 'to finish the transgression, and to make an end of sins, and to make reconciliation for iniquity, and to bring in everlasting righteousness,' which Wesley insists on completely re-translating, Hervey relates this eternal righteousness (lit. Righteousness of the ages), along with the other Messianic characteristics, to that of Christ in eternity as it denotes:

> the perpetuity of this righteousness, and of its beneficial effects. It was from the beginning, it is at this day, and it will be even at the end, mighty to save. It is the one refuge and hope of sinners, in every age of the world, and under every dispensation of religion. Through all the changes of time it has been, and through the unchangeable eternity it will be, their chief joy, and their crown of rejoicing.

Again, Wesley, though giving no Scriptural authority for his reasoning, clearly indicates why he re-translates all texts to do with Christ's eternal righteousness given us as our shield. Righteousness is two-fold, he explains; part imputed and part inherent. Hervey gently calls Wesley's attention to the words of the Prayer Book and their original source in the testimony of Paul in Philippians 3:9 when he says, 'That I may be found in Christ, not having mine own righteousness, which is of the law but that which is through the faith of Christ, the righteousness which is of God by faith.' Hervey, recognising that Wesley's zeal as a debater has again won the mastery over him, points out that this is the very Biblical doctrine that Wesley put so well in verse:

> My righteous servant and my Son
> Shall each believing sinner clear,
> And all who stoop to abjure their own,
> Shall in his righteousness appear.

---

[1] The word is translated some 400 times in the O. T. as 'righteousness'.

### Making and accounting the ungodly righteous

Hervey's last two letters are taken up with linguistic explanations, a defence of Calvinism against the charge of Antinomianism and a criticism of Wesley's practice of misquoting Aspasio and then basing his argument on his own misquotes, using extraordinary strong language. Hervey also re-examines his belief that we are made righteous imputatively, then accounted for what we have been made. Wesley reverses this order, arguing that God merely accounts us as righteous and then through sincere obedience the believer is made righteous. Hervey asks:

> How! does God account us righteous, before he makes us so? Then his judgement is not according to truth; then he reckons us to be righteous, when we are really otherwise. Is this not the language of your doctrine? this the unavoidable consequence of your notion? But how harsh, if not horrid, does it sound in every ear! Is not this absolutely irreconcilable with our ideas of the Supreme Being, and equally incompatible with the dictates of Scripture? There we are taught that God 'justifieth the ungodly'. Mark the words: 'The ungodly are the objects of the divine justification.' But can he account the ungodly righteous? Impossible! How then does he act? He first makes them righteous. After what manner? By imputing to them the righteousness of his dear Son. Then he pronounces them righteous, and most truly; he treats them as righteous, and most justly. In short, then he absolves them from the guilt, adopts them for his children, and makes them heirs of his eternal kingdom. In the grand transaction, thus regulated, mercy and truth meet together; all proceeds in the most harmonious and beautiful consistency with the several attributes of God, with his whole revealed will, and with all his righteous law.

Hervey finishes his eleven letters by quoting a former statement of Wesley's, written at a time when he was more clear on Bible doctrine:

> for neither our own inward nor outward righteousness is the ground of our justification. Holiness of heart, as well as holiness of life, is not the cause but the effect of it. The sole cause of our acceptance with God is the righteousness and death of Christ, who fulfilled God's law, and died in our stead.

> To this Hervey remarks, appealing to Wesley: 'Excellent sentiments! In these may we ever abide. To these may you also return.'

In summing up the teaching of Hervey's *Aspasio Vindicated* and the life of Hervey himself, no better words can be found than those of John Ryland who said:

Hervey was no Antinomian. He loved and practised every branch of moral virtue in the best manner, and on the purest and most noble principles. No man upon earth exceeded him in love to holiness, in heart, lip, and life.

He was no Arminian. He did not depend for one moment on himself for wisdom, righteousness, sanctification, and redemption. No man loved virtue *more*; no man depended on it *less*, than himself.[1]

---

[1]   *The Character of the Rev. James Hervey*, p. 103.

# Character of Mr. James Hervey's Writings[1]

The Reverend Mr. James Hervey being now dead, yet speaketh to us in his valuable writings; writings which, for importance of subject, weight of argument, sublimity of thought, justness of sentiment, and elegance of diction, are equalled by few, and excelled by none.

His strain is truly evangelical; his method inviting, entertaining, and edifying; calculated both to profit and to please : and a spirit of meekness, candour and modesty, breathes through and beautifies the whole.

His favourite topic is the *righteousness* and *atonement* of the Redeemer. On this he expatiates with inexpressible satisfaction, and dwells with rapturous delight. By this he 'touches the finest movements of the soul, and strikes all the inmost springs of action, with the most persuasive, the most commanding energy,' and sweetly constrains to the obedience of love.

He ransacks the mansions of the dead, turns the grave into a pulpit and makes putrefaction and mortality preach lessons to the living. He surveys, with Newtonian exactness, the *starry expanse*, and the countless radiant worlds that roll in the nocturnal sky: from these he investigates the glory and perfections of the creating and sustaining God; and from these he enhances the wonders of *redeeming love*. He mounts the believer on the summit of creation, as upon a stupendous eminence, to enlarge his prospect, and exalt his conceptions of the majesty and glory of that God, who *redeemed his church with his own blood*. When imagination itself, with all the assistance of science, is lost in the immensity and awful grandeur of the works of nature; immediately he contracts the universe into a span, and the enormous orbs into fleeting atoms, or the small dust that remains in the balance, when the works redemption are brought in view.

---

[1]  Anonymous addition to the 1837 Edinburgh edition of Hervey's *Works*.

Thus, he unites the most improved philosopher with the sound believer; and makes reason and nature *subservient* to faith and revelation. Whilst he allows reason its freest inquiry and fullest scope, he gives up with none of the peculiarities of the gospel; but holds forth, with the clearest light, and in various points of view, those truths wherein the *offence of the cross* consists.

May these heavenly doctrines, and precious truths, which flowed in such copious, gladdening streams, from his lips be transmitted pure and unadulterated to the latest posterity; and may that divine Spirit, which gave them their proper energy and influence upon his heart and life, ever accompany them to remotest ages!

# Further Gems from Hervey's Literary Treasury

### The ideal pastor

Hervey believed strongly that he was called of God to preach the gospel and often could not wait to climb into his pulpit and spread the good news of Christ's redeeming love. Yet he could never accept that he came anywhere near to being the ideal pastor and initially turned down an offer to become his father's successor because he believed that he was such a long way from fulfilling the necessary qualifications. Though but a babe in Christ on June 29, 1737 when he wrote to decline the offer from Collingtree, he penned the mature words of the following letter to guide the church in its choice of a pastor:

My Dear Friends, the inhabitants of Collingtree, near Northampton, —

I received the letter wrote in your name, and signed with your hands, and was very well pleased with its contents. I am glad that you are all in good health, and am obliged to you for retaining so honourable a remembrance of an unworthy youth. Your desire to have a careful clergyman settled among you, is perfectly right and laudable. But I fear you make an over-favourable and mistaken judgment, when you imagine me to be such a one, and pitch upon me for that purpose. However, letting this pass, it is, I say, well and wisely done of you, to be solicitous in this matter. For a minister is a person of the greatest importance imaginable; his office is of the most universal concernment; and his demeanour therein of the most beneficial or prejudicial tendency. Beneficial, if he be able, faithful, and watches for his people's souls, as one that must give account. Prejudicial, if he be unskilful, inactive, and unconcerned about the spiritual welfare of his people. The things that pertain to salvation, and the means of obtaining everlasting life, are lodged in his hands. He is the steward of the mysteries of Christ, and so the guardian (under divine grace) of your best and most abiding interests. If through ignorance he mismanage, or through idleness neglect this weighty trust, it may be the ruin of immortal souls; whereas, if he be both discreet and diligent in his holy vocation, he may be the instrument of the richest benefits to those committed to his charge. His praying to God, and his preaching to them, may be attended with such a blessing from on high, as will fill them with heavenly wisdom, form them to true holiness, and fit them for the future glory. Benefits these, not inconsiderable or momentary, but such as are great beyond all expression, and lasting to eternity. For these reasons, it will be your wisdom and your happiness to procure a pastor whose life is exemplary; whose doctrine is sound, whose heart is warm with zeal for God; and whose bowels yearn with compassion for men. If your bones were broken, or if you were brought to death's door by the force of some violent disease, you would not be content with the prescription of a quack, but seek out for the best advice. If your wives were in hard labour; if the children were come to the birth, and there was not strength to bring forth, you would not spare to ride for the most experienced midwife. Oh! be as prudent and careful of the salvation of your souls, which endure for ever, as you are for the life of your bodies, which is but as a vapour. Remember that you are sick of sin, sadly disordered by sundry corruptions and must necessarily be cured before you go hence and are no more seen. Remember that you must be regenerated and born again, or you cannot enter into the kingdom of heaven. And be not willing to trust such matters, which are of infinite and everlasting moment, to the management of any that comes next.

Now, that you may be the better able to make a right choice in this important particular, I will lay before you two or three of the distinguishing characters of a true minister. First, He has a tolerable stock of knowledge: Though not enough to explain all mysteries, or to answer every perplexing question, yet enough to make himself and his hearers wise unto salvation. He may be ignorant of many things, without much disparagement to himself, or prejudice to his people; but he must be acquainted with, and able to teach others, all that is necessary for them to know. He has not only some understanding, but some experience also, in the way of godliness. He has learned to subdue, in some measure, the pride of his nature, and to be humble in his own eyes, and not fond of applause from others. He has broke the impetuosity of his passion, and generally possesses his soul in patience; or if, upon some very ungrateful and provoking usage, he cannot calm his temper, yet he can curb his tongue, and though his spirit be ruffled, yet his words will be gentle. He is most commonly meek, after the manner of his blessed Master, and will always return blessing for cursing, according to his holy command. He has often looked into the shortness of time, and the length of eternity; he has weighed the greatness and richness of heaven, with the insignificant and despicable meanness of earth; and discovers such a mighty difference, as helps him to live above the world, even while he is in it. So that he is no lover of filthy lucre, no hunter of carnal pleasures, but his hopes, his desires, and all his views of happiness, are hid with Christ in God. He is courteous and condescending, and will stoop with the utmost cheerfulness to the lowest person in his parish. He will be affable and kind, and seek to please, not himself, but his neighbours, for their good to edification. But you must not expect to find him trifling or ludicrous; he will not preach to you on the Sunday, and play with you on the week-days, but carry the spirit of his sermons into his ordinary conversation. He will maintain a uniform gravity of behaviour, without suffering it to be frozen into moroseness, or thawed into levity. He will love his parishioners, not for their agreeable persons or amiable qualities, but because they are redeemed by the blood of Christ. It will be his business and constant endeavour, I had almost said his meat and drink, to set forward their salvation; that, by their being made meet for the inheritance of saints in light, his crucified Lord may see of the travail of his soul, and be satisfied. He will never forget the importunate request of his Saviour, but those winning and commanding words, 'Feed my sheep, feed my lambs,' will be engraven upon the tables of his heart.

To fulfil this earnest request, and execute this last charge of his dearest Redeemer, will be the fixed and invariable scope of all his designs. If at any time he hits this desirable mark, by bringing home to the fold any that have gone astray, he will be as glad as one that findeth great spoils. To see the people of his care persisting in profaneness, sensuality, and an unconverted state, will be the greatest grief that he feels: but to see his children walking in the truth, mortifying their evil affections, and growing up in goodness as the calves of the stall, this will be his joy and crown of rejoicing; better to him than thousands of silver and gold. It is his work to win souls, and by the former of these qualifications he is fitted for it, by the latter he is wholly devoted to it. And, in order to prosecute it with the greater success, he will first take heed to himself, that his life be a fair and beautiful transcript of his doctrine such as may remind men of, and be daily reinforcing his instructions. He will not bind the yoke upon your shoulders, till he has wore it himself; and should the paths of religion prove ever so thorny, he will go first, and beat the way. As far as human infirmities permit, he will strive to be unblamable and irreproveable, that he may renew the apostle's challenge, 'Be ye followers of me, even as I am of Christ.'

Secondly, his preaching will he plain; full of such useful sense as may be edifying to the better learned, and yet delivered in so easy a manner as may be intelligible to the ignorant. It will not only be plain, but powerful also; if preceding prayers and tears; if words coming warm from the heart, and accompanied with an ardent desire of being attended to; if to feel himself what he speaks, and to long that it may be felt by others, can make it such, he will declare the whole will of God, without withholding or mincing any. Be the truth ever so disagreeable, contrary to your profits, or contrary to your pleasures, you will be sure to hear it. He will indeed show it in as lovely a light, and make it as palatable as he can, but nothing will prevail upon him to conceal or disguise it.

Thirdly, he will not confine his teaching to God's day or house, but will exercise his care of you every day, and will bring it home to your own houses, whether you invite him or no he will frequently visit you, and for the same end as he meets you at church. Now, shall you like this part of his duty, or bid him welcome when he comes on such an errand? Nay, he will think himself bound to proceed farther, and to inquire into the state of your souls, and your proceedings in your families; whether you are competently furnished with saving knowledge, and are careful to increase it daily, by allowing a daily portion of your time for reading the Scriptures? what virtues you are deficient in, what vices you are subject to? what evil tempers, what vile affections, what unruly passions are predominant in you, and want to be suppressed? whether your children are catechized and your servants instructed? whether you are constant in family-worship, and at your closet devotions? how you spend the Sabbath—whether you squander it away in impertinent visits, idle chat, or foolish jesting; or whether you consecrate it to the better exercises of prayer, praise, holy discourse, reading and meditation? These, and other points of the like nature, he will examine into, and exhort you to amend what is amiss, no less than encourage you to persevere in that which is good. Nor will he exhort you once or twice only, but again and again, and hardly leave off till he has won your consent.

In things that relate to himself he will be easily said nay; but when the great God insists upon obedience, and a blessed immortality will be lost by disobedience, he will be constant in season, and out of season he will solicit with unwearied applications the important cause, and press you to perform your duty, as the poor widow importuned the unjust judge to avenge her of her adversary; he will add to his exhortations reproofs. His eye will be open, and his ears attentive to what passes in his parish and when any one walks disorderly, he will meet him as Elijah did Ahab, 1 Kings 21:20, with a rebuke in his mouth. This I can promise, that he will not rail at, nor accost you with reproachful words, but he will certainly set before you the things that you have done. He will not defame you behind your backs, but whether you be rich or poor, whether you be pleased with it or not, he will bear in mind the commandment of the Lord, and show his people their transgressions, and the house of Jacob their sins, Isaiah 58:1. He will tell you with tenderness, but yet with plainness, that such courses are a sad and too sure a proof that grace has not had its proper work on your souls; that ye are carnal, and have not the Spirit of Christ. So that a true minister of the gospel will be a constant inspector of your actions, a faithful monitor of your duty, and an impartial reprover of your offences. He will guide you by his counsel, and animate you by his example, and bless you by his prayers. If you be willing and obedient, he will conduct you safely through a troublesome and naughty world, and bring you to the land of everlasting felicity; but If you be perverse and obstinate, he will be a standing terror to your consciences here, and a swift witness against you hereafter; he will be the unhappy means of increasing your guilt, and aggravating your future account, and of making it more tolerable for Tyre and Sidon, in the day of judgment, than for you.

And now, my kind and dear friends, are you, upon second thoughts, desirous of having such a pastor placed amongst you? Shall you be glad to have the aforementioned vigilance and diligence exerted in the holy function? Can you willingly submit to an oversight so narrow, to admonitions so incessant, to corrections so close and particular? If, after due consideration, you are willing; give me leave to inform you how you may procure such a man of God to come unto you, and take up his abode with you. He is an exceeding great and precious blessing to any people, too precious to be purchased with money, and is the free gift of God; so that the way to obtain him is to address yourselves to Heaven, and make supplication to the Almighty. What cannot prayer, fervent and believing prayer, do? I scarcely know any thing that is above its power, or beyond its reach. Prayer has locked up the clouds, and opened them again, made the earth as iron, and the heavens as brass; prayer has arrested the sun in his race, and made the moon stand still in her march, and reversed the perpetual decree; prayer has fetched down angels from above, and raised up the dead from beneath, and done many wonderful works. In like manner, prayer will get for you an useful and worthy teacher; if he be ever so far off, this will

bring him near; if he be ever so averse, this will overrule his inclination. Do you doubt of this? I own you would have good reason if
you had nothing but my word to support it; but what if God, who
cannot lie, has testified, and given you assurance of the same? Why,
then, I hope ye will be no longer faithless but believing. Hear, therefore, what he himself hath said by his own beloved Son, 'Ask, and
ye shall receive; seek, and ye shall find,' Matthew 7:7. Again he
saith, 'If ye shall ask any thing in my name, I will do it,' John
14:14. Here you see the Almighty has passed his word, and he, to
whom all things are possible, has pawned his veracity, that he will
not deny you the request of your lips. And dare you not trust in the
All-powerful? Can you have a better security than his, whose title
is faithful and true? The divine promises are all immutable, stronger
than the strong mountains; and heaven and earth shall pass away,
sooner than one jot or tittle of them shall pass unfulfilled. When
you desire a pious and able minister, ye desire a good thing, such
as will be for the honour and glory of God to grant. Therefore,
encouraged by this, and confiding in his most sure promise, beg of
the Most High to give you a true pastor and shepherd for your
souls; one that may love you like St. Paul, rule you like David,
teach you like Samuel, and lead you like Joshua to the heavenly
Canaan, that blessed and blissful country, where we all would be!

O God, great and glorious, infinite in thy wisdom, and incon-
trollable in thy power! thy providence is over all thy works; thine
eyes run to and fro through the earth, to behold the condition, and
supply the wants of thy servants: 'Thou sentest Moses to deliver
thy children out of Egypt, Philip to instruct the ignorant eunuch,
and Peter to preach to the devout centurion. O blessed Lord, who
art the same yesterday, and today, and for ever, vouchsafe the same
mercy to us of this parish, that we also may have a teacher come
from God: Grant us, O thou Giver of every good gift, a faithful
shepherd for our souls, who may feed us in a green pasture, and
lead us forth beside the waters of comfort; one that may be wholly
devoted to thy service, and intent upon nothing but the due discharge of his important office; who may be a light to our paths by
his godly directions, and as salt to our corrupting souls by his
unblamable conversation. Let such a minister, we beseech thee, be
placed over us as will watch for our spiritual welfare, that will love
us with an affectionate and parental tenderness, that will cherish us
as a hen cherisheth her chickens under her wings; one that may be
able as well as willing, to instruct us in our duty; to whom thou hast
revealed the wondrous things of thy law, and the glorious mysteries of thy gospel; whose lips may preserve knowledge, whose tongue
may be continually dealing it out, and whose mouth may be unto us

a well of fire; whose discourses may be milk to the babes, meat to the strong, and medicine to the sick; who may have a skilful as well as a compassionate zeal, and know how to divide rightly the word of truth; who may be an example as well as an exhorter, a pattern as well as a preacher, of every charitable action, and every devout temper; under whose guidance we may walk in the ways of peace and piety, of meekness and humility, of righteousness and salvation, till we all come to the city of the living God, to an innumerable company of angels, and to the spirits of just men made perfect. O grant us such a priest, and clothe him with such qualifications, and make thy chosen people joyful. Hear us, most merciful Father, for his sake whose sheep we are, who bought us with his blood, who died for us on earth, and maketh intercession for us in heaven, even Jesus Christ; to whom, with thee and the Holy Ghost, be all honour and glory, world without end. Amen.

**Recommending the Word of Life**

*The London Magazine and Gentleman's Monthly Intelligence* was a newspaper supported by those who wished to preserve the airs of a gentleman and the learning of a classicist. In February, 1755, only a month after *Theron and Aspasio* had been published, the magazine featured a long extract from Hervey's work to 'give a specimen of his elegant performance' and present an exercise in 'style and manner'. The anonymous editor of the excerpt did a marvellous job of finding quotes from Hervey which completely circumnavigated all signs of Hervey's gospel message. The magazine had promised mere elegance, style and manner and that is all its readers were given. In the following April, a reader felt called to correct this inattention to Hervey's real purpose and requested that the newspaper should not just look at Hervey's elegance and style in a vacuum but also consider Hervey's Christian message. Instead of snarling at Hervey's religion, the subscriber, who signed himself Verus, argued, the newspaper should dare to publish Hervey on the subject of the superiority of the Scriptures over classical literature. The newspaper kindly obliged and published the following quote from *Theron and Aspasio*, Dialogue I:

**Asp.** When Secker preaches, or Murray pleads, the church is crowded and the bar thronged. When Spence produces the refinements of criticism, or Young displays the graces of poetry, the press toils, yet is scarce able to supply the demands of the public. Are we eager to hear, and impatient to purchase, what proceeds from such eloquent tongues and masterly pens? And can we be coldly indifferent, when, not the most accomplished of mankind, not the most exalted of creatures, but the adorable Author of all wisdom, speaks in his revealed word? Strange! that our attention does not hang[1] upon the venerable accents, and our talk dwell upon the incomparable truths!

**Ther.** I admire, I must confess, the very language of the Bible. In this, methinks, I discern a conformity between the book of nature and the book of Scripture.

In the book of nature the divine Teacher speaks, not barely to our ears, but to all our senses. And it is very remarkable how he varies his address! Observe his grand and august works. In these he uses the style of majesty We may call it the true sublime, It strikes with awe, and transports the mind. View his ordinary operations. Here he descends to a plainer dialect. This may be termed the familiar style. We comprehend it with ease, and attend to it with pleasure. In the more ornamented parts of the creation, he clothes his meaning with elegance. All is rich and brilliant. We are delighted; we are charmed. And what is this but the florid style?

A variety, somewhat similar, runs through the Scriptures. Would you see history in all her simplicity, and all her force, most beautifully easy, yet irresistibly striking? See her, or rather feel her energy, touching the nicest movements of the soul, and triumphing over our passions, in the inimitable narrative of Joseph's life. The representation of Esau's bitter distress, (Genesis 27:30 &c.); the conversation pieces of Jonathan and his gallant friend, (1 Samuel 18-20); the memorable journal of the disciples going to Emmaus, (Luke 24:13 &c); are finished models of the impassioned and affecting. Here is nothing studied; no flights of fancy; no embellishments of oratory. Yet how inferior is the episode of Nisus and Euryalus, though worked up by the most masterly hand in the world, to the undissembled artless fervency of these scriptural sketches!

Are we pleased with the elevation and dignity of an heroic poem, or the tenderness and perplexity of a dramatic performance? In the book of Job they are both united, and both unequalled. Conformable to the exactest rules of art, as the action advances the incidents are more alarming, and the images more magnificent. The language glows, and the pathos swells; till at last the Deity himself makes his entrance. He speaks from the whirlwind and summons the creation—summons heaven and all its shining host, the elements and their most wonderful productions—to vouch for the wisdom of his providential dispensations. His word strikes terror, and flashes conviction; decides the momentous controversy, and closes the august drama with all possible solemnity and grandeur.

---

[1] St. Luke, in his evangelical history, uses this beautiful image, 'The people hung upon the lips of their all-wise Teacher.' Luke 19:48. Which implies two very strong ideas, an attention that nothing could interrupt, and an eagerness scarce ever satisfied.

If we sometimes choose a plaintive strain, such as softens the mind and soothes an agreeable melancholy are any of the ancient tragedies superior, in the eloquence of mourning, to David's pathetic elegy on his beloved Jonathan, (2 Samuel 1:19, &c.) to the most passionate and inconsolable moan over the lovely but unhappy Absalom; or to that melodious woe, which warbles and bleeds in every line of Jeremiah's Lamentations.

Would we be entertained with the daring sublimity of Homer, or the correct majesty of Virgil? with the expressive delicacy of Horace, or the rapid excursions of Pindar? Behold them joined, behold them excelled, in the odes of Moses, and the eucharistic hymn of Deborah; in the exalted devotion of the Psalms, and the glorious enthusiasm of the Prophets.

**Asp.** Only with this difference, that the former are tuneful triflers, and amuse the fancy with empty fiction; the latter are teachers sent from God, and make the soul wise unto salvation. The Bible is not only the brightest ornament, but the most invaluable depositum. On a right, a practical knowledge of these lively oracles, depends the present comfort and the endless felicity of mankind. Whatever, therefore, in study or conversation, has no connexion with their divine contents, may be reckoned among the toys of literature, or the ciphers of discourse.

**Ther.** Here again the book of Scripture is somewhat like the magazine of nature. What can we desire for our accommodation and delight, which this storehouse of conveniences does not afford? What can we wish for our edification and improvement, which that fund of knowledge does not supply? Of these we may truly affirm, each in its respective kind is 'profitable unto all things'.

Are we admirers of antiquity?—Here we are led back beyond the universal deluge, and far beyond the date of any other annals. We are introduced among the earliest inhabitants of the earth. We take a view of mankind in their undisguised primitive plainness, when the days of their life were but little short of a thousand years. We are brought acquainted with the original of nations; with the creation of the world; and with the birth of time itself.

Are we delighted with vast achievements? Where is any thing comparable to the miracles in Egypt, and the wonders in the field of Zoan? to the memoirs of the Israelites, passing through the depths of the sea, sojourning amidst the inhospitable deserts, and conquering the kingdoms of Canaan? Where shall we meet with instances of martial bravery equal to the prodigious exploits of the Judges; or the adventurous deeds of Jesse's valiant son, and his matchless band of worthies? (2 Samuel 23:8, &c, 1 Chronicles 11:10 &c) Here we behold the fundamental laws of the universe, sometimes suspended, sometimes reversed; and not only the current of Jordan, but the course of nature controlled. In short, when we enter the field of Scripture, we tread—on enchanted, shall I say? rather on consecrated ground; where astonishment and awe are awakened at every turn; where is all more than all, the marvellous of romance, connected with all the precision and sanctity of truth.

If we want maxims of wisdom, or have a taste for the laconic style, how copiously may our wants be supplied, and how delicately our taste gratified! especially in the book of Proverbs, Ecclesiastes, and some of the minor prophets. Here are the most sage lessons of instruction, adapted to every circumstance of life, formed upon the experience of all preceding ages, and perfected by the unerring spirit of inspiration. These delivered with such remarkable conciseness, that one might venture to say, every word is a sentence; at least, every sentence may be called an apophthegm, sparkling with brightness of thoughts, or weighty with solidity of sense. The whole, like a profusion of pearls, each containing, in a very small compass, a value almost immense, all heaped up (as an ingenious critic speaks) with a confused magnificence, above the little niceties of order.

If we look for the strength of reasoning, and the warmth of exhortation; the insinuating arts of genteel address, or the manly boldness of impartial reproof; all the thunders of the orator, without any of his ostentation; all the politeness of the courtier, without any of the flattery—let us have recourse to the Acts of the Apostles, and to the Epistles of St. Paul. These are a specimen, or rather these are the standard, of them all.

I do not wonder, therefore, that a taste so refined, and a judgement so correct as Milton's, should discern higher attractives in the volume of inspiration, than in the most celebrated authors of Greece and Rome.

**Asp.** Another recommendation of the Scriptures is, that they afford the most awful and most amiable manifestations of the Godhead. His glory shines, and his goodness smiles, in those divine pages, with unparalleled lustre. Here we have a satisfactory explanation of our state. The origin of evil is traced; the cause of all our misery discovered; and the remedy, the infallible remedy, both clearly shown, and freely offered. The merits of the bleeding Jesus lay a firm foundation for all our hopes; while gratitude for his dying love suggests the most winning incitements to every duty. Morality, Theron, your (and let me add, my) admired morality, is delineated in all its branches, is placed upon its proper basis, and raised to its highest elevation. The Spirit of God is promised to enlighten the darkness of our understandings, and strengthen the imbecility of our wills. What an ample provision is made, by these blessed books, for all our spiritual wants! And, in this respect, how indisputable is their superiority to all other compositions!

## Witnessing to the 'polite world'

Hervey preached mainly to the poor and uneducated but he wrote with the chief aim of converting the educated rich whom he found far more closed to the gospel than the poor. Apart from Lady Huntingdon's circle, who were mostly far away in London, Hervey had little connection with the gentry and was shocked at the worldly manners of the high society who lived in the Northampton area. He was thus more than pleased, whenever he heard of an educated lady or gentleman who had been given grace to embrace the gospel and they could be assured of his eager support and good counsel. This assistance was, however, by no means one-sided. Those who had been privileged to be guided through the eye of a needle were soon sent Hervey's manuscripts with the request for corrections, alterations and improvements. Several of Hervey's one time worldly friends became ministers of the gospel. Then his joy was complete. The following two letters are illustrative of Hervey's correspondence with men of learning. The second letter also illustrates Hervey's humble view of himself though he was so successful in his ministry.

*Weston-Favell*, November 16, 1745.

Sir, It is not easy to express the satisfaction I received from your agreeable and useful conversation this afternoon. I rejoice to find that there are gentlemen of genius, learning, and politeness, who dare profess a supreme value for the Scriptures, and are not ashamed of the cross of Christ. I congratulate you, dear sir, on this occasion; and cannot but look on a mind so principled, and a heart so disposed, as a very choice and distinguishing part of your happiness. Was I to frame a wish for the dearest and most valued friend on earth, I would earnestly desire that he might grow daily in this grace, and increase in the knowledge of our Lord and Saviour Jesus Christ. And when my pen begs leave to assure you, that this is my unfeigned wish for ———, it only transcribes what is deeply written on my heart.

This brings the dedication and the preface, which are to introduce a little essay, entitled *Meditations among the Tombs*, and *Reflections on a Flower-Garden*, in two letters to a lady. I hope, sir, in consequence of your kind promise, you will please to peruse them with the file in your hand. The severity of the critic, and the kindness of the friend, in this case will be inseparable. The evangelical strain, I believe, must be preserved; because, otherwise, the introductory thoughts will not harmonise with the subsequent; the porch will be unsuitable to the building. But if you perceive any meanness of expression, any quaintness of sentiment, or any other impropriety and inelegance, I shall acknowledge it as a very singular favour, if you will be so good as to discover and correct such blemishes.

I hope, sir, my end in venturing to publish is an hearty desire to serve, in some little degree, the interests of Christianity, by endeavouring to set some of its most important truths in a light that may both entertain and edify. As I profess this view, I am certain your affectionate regard for the most excellent religion imaginable will incline you to be concerned for the issue of such an attempt, and therefore to contribute to its success, both by bestowing your animadversions upon these small parts, and by speaking of the whole (when it shall come abroad) with all that candour which is natural to the Christian, and will be so greatly needed by this new adventurer in letters, who is, &c.


*Weston-Favell,* August 30, 1749.

We have seen marvellous things today, said the people of old; and I may truly say, *I* have read marvellous tidings this evening. What! is —— become a serious and zealous preacher? He that so often fillled the scorner's chair, is he transformed into a strenuous advocate for the gospel, and a devoted champion of Christ? Never, surely, was the prophet's exclamation more seasonable, Grace! grace! Zechariah 4:7. How sovereign its power! How superabundant its riches!

I heartily congratulate you, my dear friend, my very dear brother I must call you now, on this change. And I thank Christ Jesus our Lord, that he hath counted you faithful, putting you into the ministry. I think the hand of Providence, in conducting this affair, is very visible, and much to be regarded; which must give you no small satisfaction, and tend to work, not the spirit of fear, but of love, and of faith, and of a sound mind.

How honourable is your new office! to be an envoy from the King of heaven. How delightful your province! to be continually conversant in the glorious truths of the gospel, and the unsearchable riches of Christ! How truly gainful your business! to win souls! this is, indeed, an everlasting possession. And how illustrious the reward promised to your faithful service—When the chief Shepherd shall appear, you shall receive a crown of glory that fadeth not away!

May we clearly discern, and never forget, what a Master we serve! so glorious, that all the angels of light adore him; so gracious, that he spilt his blood even for his enemies; so mighty, that he has all power in heaven and on earth; so faithful, that heaven and earth may pass away, much sooner than one jot or tittle of his word fail. And what is his word, what his engagement to his ministers? LO, I AM WITH YOU ALWAYS. I write it in capitals, because I wish it may be written in our hearts. Go forth, my dear friend, in the strength of this word; and, verily, you shall not be confounded. Plead with your great Lord, plead for the accomplishment of this word, and the gospel shall prosper in your hand. In every exercise of your ministerial duty, act in humble faith on this wonderful word, and the heart of stone shall feel, the powers of hell fall. Would to God I had health and strength, I would earnestly pray for grace, that I might join, vigorously join, in this good warfare. But you know, I am like a bleeding, disabled soldier, and only not slain. I hope, however, I shall rejoice to see my comrades routing the foe, and reaping their laurels; rejoice to see them go on, conquering and to conquer; though no longer able to share, either in the toils or the triumphs of the day.

I believe it will be no easy matter to procure a curate, such as you will like; at least, none such offers to my observation. I heartily wish your valuable friend, Mr. ———, that faith in the all-atoning blood of the Lamb, and that comfort in the communications of the Spirit, which may sweetly outbalance the weight of any sorrow, and enable him to rejoice in tribulation!

Remember, now you are a minister of God, that your tongue is to be a well of life: you are to believe in Christ, daily to cherish your faith in Jesus, that out of your heart may flow rivers of living waters; such tides of heavenly and healing truths, as may refresh the fainting soul, and animate its feeble graces.

Please to present my affectionate compliments to Mr. C—, and Mr. S—; engage their prayers to the Father of compassions in my behalf; and when you yourself draw near to the throne, through the blood of the everlasting covenant, fail not to remember, dear sir, yours sincerely, yours unalterably, &c.

### Letters to his flock from exile
When Hervey was whisked off to London for his health's sake by loving friends, he had no time to say goodbye or give his flock a last word of advice before departing from them. Hervey made ample amends for this negligence which was not his fault at all and many truly pastoral letters have been preserved from his pen to the flocks at Collingtree and Weston-Favell. The following two letters are examples:

*London*, Feb. 5. 1751

Dear Mrs. ———, I received your valuable letter, and thank you for it. I am exceeding glad, and bless the unspeakable goodness of God, if he has made my poor ministry in any degree serviceable or comfortable to your soul. I accompany my former labours (if such extremely feeble attempts may be called labours,) with my repeated prayers; and bear my little flock on my supplications and affectionate heart all the day long. Oh that the gracious God may fulfil in them all the good pleasure of his will, and the work of faith with power!

I rejoice to find that you know the truth. May you know it more and more; be established in it, and experience the efficacy of it. May the truth make you free! free from the prevalence of unbelief, the dominion of sin, and the oppression of sorrow! Give glory to God for opening the eyes of your mind, and bringing you to the riches of Christ. Take to yourself the comfort of this inestimable blessing, and by no means reject your own mercy. Pray do not harbour hard thoughts concerning the blessed God, nor cherish desponding apprehensions concerning yourself, though always frail, and in every respect imperfect. The great and good Father of our spirits knows whereof we are made; he remembers that we are but dust, and will not be extreme to mark what is done amiss. Extreme to mark! so far from it, that to those who seek him in sincerity, seek him through his dear Son, he is tender and compassionate beyond all imagination. 'As a father pitieth his own children, so is the Lord merciful unto them that fear him,' Psalm 103:13; and, 'as a mother comforteth her son, so will the Lord thy God comfort thee,' Isaiah 66:13. Since we want loving kindness and mercy to follow us all the days of our life, blessed, for ever blessed be the God of heaven, in these he delighteth, Jeremiah 9:24. 'cast thy burden upon the Lord,' says the Holy Spirit. Cast it upon the Lord Jesus Christ. This is an art which the Christian should be diligent to learn and watchful to practise. Christ is a Saviour, but we neglect to make use of him; we are come to him, but we forget to walk in him. When guilt accuses us, or guilt overtakes us, instantly let us fly to Christ, as the Israelites, when wounded, looked to the brazen serpent. There, let us say, there is the propitiation for this abominable sin. For this, and for all my other iniquities, his heart was pierced, and his blood spilt. The vials of wrath, due to my pro-vocations, were poured upon that spotless victim; and by his stripes I am healed. If our own obedience is deplorably defective, so that we are sometimes ready to cry out with the prophet, 'My leanness! my leanness! woe unto me!' let us turn our thoughts to the great Mediator's righteousness; this is consummate and divine; this was wrought out for us; this is imputed to us; in this all the seed of Israel shall be justified, and in this should they glory. If your prayers are dull and languid, remember the intercession of Christ. He ever appears in the presence of God for you; and how can your cause miscarry which has such an advocate? If the poor widow was heard, even by the unjust judge, shall not the dearly beloved Son of God prevail when he makes intercession to a most gracious Father? a Father who loves both him and his people. If you want repentance, want faith, want holiness, Christ is exalted to be a Prince and a Saviour, and to give all these desirable blessings. He has ascended up on high, has led captivity captive, and received gifts, spiritual gifts for men, yea, even for his enemies, for the rebellious. It is his office to bestow these precious graces on poor sinners; and he is as ready to execute this office as the mother is ready to administer the breast to a sucking child. Do you read the Scriptures? Still keep Christ in view. When dreadful threatenings occur, say, These I deserved; but Christ has bore them in my stead. When rich promises are made, say, of these I am unworthy; but my Redeemer's worthiness is my plea; he has purchased them for me by his merits. All the promises of God are yea and amen (sure and certain to the believing soul) in Christ Jesus.

To make such a perpetual application of Christ, is to eat his flesh, and drink his blood. Thus may you, may I, may all my dear people, be enabled to pass the time of our sojourning here below! deriving our whole spiritual life, our pardon and sanctification, our hope, and our joy, from that inexhaustible fountain of all good. Though I am not with you in person, I am often with you in spirit; and daily commit you to the great Shepherd and Bishop of souls; who is ten thousand thousand times more condescending, compassionate, and faithful, than your truly affectionate friend, &c.

*Undated.*
    Dear ———, I received your kind letter, and am glad to find that you, and Mrs. ———, and Mrs. ———, often meet together, and, like the people mentioned by the prophet, speak one to another of the things of God. O let us exhort one another to faith, to love, and to good works; and so much the more, as we see the day, the day of eternal judgment, approaching. Ere long we shall hear the shout of the archangel, and the trump of God. O let us imitate the wise virgins, and get oil in our lamps, true grace in our hearts; that we may be prepared for our Lord's second coming, and not dread, but love his appearing.

My departure from Northampton was sudden and unexpected. Could I have seen my people, and given them my parting advice, it should have been in the words of that good man Barnabas, who exhorted all the disciples, that with purpose of heart they would cleave unto the Lord.

Cleave, my dear friends, to the Lord Jesus Christ; cleave to his word; let the word of Christ dwell in you richly, and be your meditation all the day long. Let the Bible, that inestimable book, be often in your hands, and its precious truths be ever in your thoughts. Thus let us sit, with holy Mary, at the feet of Jesus; and, I hope we shall experience his word to drop as the rain, and distil as the dew.

Cleave to his merits. Fly to his divine blood for pardon; it is the fountain opened for sin, and for uncleanness. It purges from all guilt, takes away all sin, and, blessed be God, it is always open, always free of access. Fly to his righteousness. Let us renounce our own, and rely on his obedience. What unprofitable servants are we! how slothful in our whole life! how imperfect in every work! But as for Christ, his work is perfect; it is complete, and infinitely meritorious. In this shall all the seed of Israel, all true believers, be justified; and in this shall they glory.

Cleave to his Spirit. Seek for the divine Spirit; cry mightily to God for the divine Spirit. Let them that have it pray that they may have it more abundantly, and be ever filled with the Spirit. This blessed Spirit reveals Christ, strengthens faith, quickens love, and purifies the heart. Christ died to obtain this Spirit for us; he intercedes for us that we may receive it; and his heavenly Father, for his sake, has promised to give the Holy Spirit to those who ask it. He has promised (O glorious privilege!) to give it more readily than a parent gives bread to a hungry child.

Cleave to his example. Study his holy life, eye his unblameable conduct, observe his amiable tempers; look to this heavenly pattern, as those that learn to write look to their copy; and God grant that we all, beholding with open face the glory of the Lord, may be changed into the same image from glory to glory, even as by the Spirit of the Lord!

Thus let us cleave to Christ the Lord; cleave with full purpose of heart, incessantly, closely, inseparably. Let us say with our father Jacob, I will not let thee go. Let us imitate the Syrophoenician woman, whom no discouragements could divert from her purpose. Temptations, difficulties, all the assaults of our enemy, should make us hasten to, and abide in the stronghold, the city of refuge: And he has promised, 'I will never leave thee, nor forsake thee.' He will gather us with his arm, and lay us in his bosom. He will guide us by his grace, and receive us into his glory. There, in those happy, happy mansions, may we, and many, very many of my dear flock meet, and never be parted more! This is the hearts, and the daily prayer of their and your truly affectionate friend, &c.[1]

## Consoling and being consoled in his care for the sick
Hervey was always most diligent in caring for the sick and the dying. He never minced matters, however, and boldly broached the subject of death and thereafter with all with whom he came into contact. The following letters, written in 1751 are typical of the honest care Hervey took over the souls of those whose earthly lives were probably coming to a close.

Dear —, And are you very weak? is sickness in the chamber, and death at the door? Come, then let us both sit down with dissolution and eternity in view, and encourage one another from the word, the precious word of God. I have as much need of such consolation as you, my dear friend, and may, perhaps, have occasion to use them as soon.

What is there formidable in death, which our ever blessed Redeemer has not taken away? Do the pangs of dissolution alarm us? Should they be sharp, they cannot be very long; and our exalted Lord, with whom are the issues of death, knows what dying agonies mean. He has said, in the multitude of his tender mercies, 'Fear thou not, for I am with thee; be not dismayed, for I am thy God: I will strengthen thee, yea, I will help thee, yea, I will uphold thee with the right hand of my righteousness,' Isaiah 41:10. This promise authorises us to say boldly, 'Yea, though I walk through the valley of the shadow of death, I will fear no evil; for thou art with me, thy rod and thy staff comfort me,' Psalm 23:4.

Are we afraid to enter into a strange, invisible, unknown world? it is the world into which our divine Master is gone; where he has prepared everlasting mansions for his people, John 14:2. Luke 16:22. and has appointed his angels to conduct us thither. Having such a convoy, what should we dread? and, going to our eternal home, where our all-bountiful Redeemer is, why should we be reluctant?

Are we concerned on account of what we leave? We leave the worse to possess the better. If we leave our earthly friends, we shall find more loving and lovely companions. We shall be admitted among the 'innumerable company of angels, and to the general assembly and church of the first-born, that are written in heaven,' Hebrews 12:22,23. Do we leave the ordinances of religion, which

---

[1] Letter LXXX

we have attended with great delight? leave the word of God, which has been sweeter to our souls than honey to our mouths? We shall enter into the temple not made with hands, and join that happy choir, who rest not day nor night, saying, 'Holy, holy, holy, Lord God Almighty, which was, and is, and is to come,' Revelation 4:8. And if our Bible is no more, we shall have all that is promised, we shall behold all that is described therein. If we drop the map of our heavenly Canaan, it will be to take possession of its blissful territories. 'That city has no need of the sun, neither of the moon, to shine in it; for the glory of God does lighten it, and the Lamb is the light thereof,' Revelation 21:23. O, my friend! blessed, for ever blessed, be the grace of our God, and the merits of his Christ! We shall exchange the scanty stream for the boundless ocean; and if we no longer pick the first ripe grapes, we shall gather the copious, the abounding the never-ending vintage.

Do we fear the guilt of our innumerable sins? Adored be the inexpressible loving-kindness of God our Saviour! our sins have been punished in the blessed Jesus: 'The Lord laid on him the iniquity of us all,' Isaiah 53:6. 'He his own self bare our sins, in his own body, on the tree,' 1 Peter 2:24. So that there is 'no condemnation to them that are in Christ Jesus,' Romans 8:1. O that we may be enabled, with the apostle, to make our boast of this Saviour, and to triumph in this faith! 'Who shall lay any thing to the charge of God's elect? It is God that justifieth; who is he that condemneth? It is Christ that died, yea rather that is risen again, who is even at the right hand of God; who also maketh intercession for us.'

Is judgment the thing that we fear? To the pardoned sinner it has nothing terrible. The Lord Jesus, who keeps his servants from falling, 'presents them also faultless before the presence of his glory with exceeding joy,' Jude 24. Observe the sweet expressions, *presents faultless*, and *with exceeding joy*. Justly therefore does the apostle reckon it among the privileges of the Christians, that they are come to God the Judge of all, Hebrews 12:23; for the Judge is our friend, the Judge is our advocate, the Judge is our propitiation, the Judge is our righteousness. And is it not a privilege to come to such a judge as will not so much as mention our iniquities to us, but condescend to take notice of our poor unworthy services? who sits on the great tribunal, not to pass the sentence of damnation upon us, but to give us a reward, a reward of free grace, and of inconceivable richness?

Let me conclude with those charming words of the evangelical prophet, 'Comfort ye, comfort ye my people, saith your God. Speak you comfortably to Jerusalem, and unto her, that her warfare is accomplished, that her iniquity is pardoned; for her Redeemer, her all-gracious Redeemer, hath received of the Lord's hand double for all her sins,' Isaiah 40:1,2. May the God of our life and salvation make these Scriptures be unto us a staff in the traveller's hand, and as a cordial to this fainting heart, that we may be strong in the faith of our Lord Jesus Christ: that we may glorify him in death, and glorify him for death; because death will introduce us into his immediate presence, where we shall be sorrowful no more, sinful no more, at a distance no more; but be joyful, and be like our Lord; love him with all our souls, praise him to all eternity. Let us then be of good cheer, soon in our heavenly Jerusalem we shall meet again. Because God is faithful, inviolably faithful, and infinitely merciful, who both promised, promised to you, and promised to your affectionate friend, &c.

P. S.— My kindest respects to Mr. — and Mrs. —; bid them be of good courage, and go on their way rejoicing, for their Redeemer is mighty, his merits are unspeakable, and his love is unchangeable. My most respectful compliments wait upon Mr. — and Mrs. —.What a pleasure should I think it, was I able to execute the ministerial office, to bring home to their parlours the glad tidings of an all-sufficient Saviour, as well as to preach them in the pulpit. Polly, I hope, loves her Bible: may the word of Christ dwell in her richly; and may be with your father and mother now they are old and grey-headed.[1]

Dear ——, I hope this will find you a little better in your health; but if it should find you in a weak and languishing condition, I hope a gracious God will sanctify what it contains to the comfort of your soul.

Often consider, if you die, you will leave a world full of sin; a condition full of frailty, ignorance, and misery, a body that has long been a heavy burden, a sore clog, both to your services and to your comforts: and why should any one be greatly unwilling to leave such a state? If you die, you will go into an unknown world, but the comfort is, you have a kind and faithful friend gone thither before—Jesus Christ, your best friend, and the lover of your soul, is the Lord of that unseen world. Joseph's brethren were not afraid to go down into Egypt, when they knew that their dear brother was governor of the country. And since your most merciful Saviour is ruler of the invisible world, be not afraid to leave the body, and depart thither. It is said the spirit of old Jacob revived when he saw

---

[1] Letter LXXXI

the waggon sent to carry him to his beloved son; and the poor languishing believer may look upon death as the waggon sent by Jesus Christ to bring his soul home to heaven.

But after death comes judgment, and is terrible. Consider, who is the Judge. Was the father that begot you, was the mother that bare you, or the friend that is as your own soul; was any one of these to be the Judge, and to pass the sentence, you would not be apprehensive of rigorous proceedings, you would expect all possible clemency. Mercy, in this case, would rejoice against judgment. But, to our unspeakable comfort, we are informed by the Scriptures, that a glorious Person, far more merciful than a father, far more compassionate than a mother, far more affectionate than a friend, is to decide our doom—even the Lord Jesus Christ, who loved us with an everlasting love; who declares, that a woman may forget her sucking child much sooner than he forget to be merciful to those that put their trust in him; for thus it is written, 'God hath appointed a day, in which he will judge the world in righteousness, by that man whom he hath ordained, even Jesus Christ,' Acts 17:31.

The Judge calls himself our Husband, the Bridegroom of poor believing souls. And will the Bridegroom deliver to destruction his own bride, whom he has bought with his blood, and with whom he has made an everlasting covenant? Isaiah 54:5.

The Judge vouchsafes to be our Advocate. And will he condemn those for whom he has long interceded? will he condemn those for whom he poured out his prayers when he was on earth, and on whose behalf he has constantly pleaded in the presence of God? 1 John 2:1.

The Judge condescends to be our Head, and calls the weakest believers his members. And did ever any one hate his own body? Did ever any one delight to maim, or take pleasure to ruin his own flesh, and his bones? Colossians 1:18, 1 Corinthians 12:27.

The Judge has been our Victim, the sacrifice for our sins. And will he consign those to damnation, for whom be endured the agonies of crucifixion? If he has given himself for us, will he not with this gift freely give us all things? give us pardon at that awful day? give us the crown of glory, which fadeth not away? Hebrews 9:14, 26.

Farther, to confirm your faith, and establish your hope, it will be proper to consider what you have to plead. The proud Pharisee made his abstaining from gross iniquities, and his punctuality in some external performances, his plea. The blinded Jews went about to establish their own righteousness, and depended on this broken reed for acceptance. But we have a surer foundation whereon to build our comfortable expectations. If arraigned on the foot of guilt—great guilt—manifold guilt—aggravated guilt—long contracted guilt; we have an atonement to plead, a sacrifice of unknown value, a propitiation glorious and divine. We have the blood of the Lamb to plead; blood that taketh away not one sin, or a few sins, or a multitude of sins only; but (O delightful truth!) taketh away all, all, all sins. Yes it taketh away all sins from the believer, be they ever so numerous; all sins, be they ever so heinous; 1 John 1:7, Revelation 1:5.

Should the law take us by the throat, and a make that severe demand, Pay me that thou owest: It is paid, we reply, by our divine Surety. An incarnate God has been obedient in our stead. In the Lord, the Lord Redeemer, have we righteousness. And can the law insist on a more excellent satisfaction? Does not this magnify the law, and make it honourable? 'By the obedience of one, (that is, Christ) shall many be made righteous.' Isaiah 45:24, Romans 5:19.

Should it further be urged, Without holiness no man shall see the Lord: Is not holiness the thing that we have longed for? It is true, we have not attained to holiness; spotless and undefiled holiness, neither could we in the regions of temptation, and in a body of corruption. But has not our guilt been our sorrow, and our indwelling sin our heaviest cross? Have we not groaned under our remaining iniquities, and been burdened with a sense of our failings? And are not these groanings the first fruits of the Spirit? Are not these the work of thy own grace, blessed Lord! and wilt thou not consummate in heaven what thou hast thus begun upon earth? Do we not desire heaven, chiefly because in those blessed mansions we shall sin no more; we shall offend our God no more; be no more forgetful of a dying Saviour; no more disobedient to the motions of a sanctifying Spirit? And shall we be disappointed of this hope? It cannot, it cannot be. They that hunger and thirst after righteousness, are not filled while they abide in the flesh; therefore there remaineth the accomplishment of this promise—they will assuredly awake up after the likeness of their Lord at the great resurrection day, and in another world be fully, everlastingly satisfied with it.

I must now come to a conclusion: But I cannot conclude without wishing you all joy and peace in believing. Though your flesh and your heart fail, may God be the strength of your heart, and your portion for ever! I daily, I frequently make mention of you in my prayers; and, what is better than all, the dearly beloved of the Father remembers you now he is in his kingdom. I am your very affectionate friend, &c.[1]

---

[1]    Letter LXXXII

**Pastoring prisoners**

Here is a sample letter of how diligent Hervey was in taking the gospel to those who were doubly condemned by the justice of the country and the tribunal of God.

My POOR Fellow-Sinners, - I received a letter from you, and should have visited you; but my health is so much decayed, and my spirits are so exceedingly tender, that I could not well bear the sight of your confinement, your chains, and your miserable circumstances, as I can hardly bear the thoughts of your approaching execution, and your extreme danger of everlasting destruction. But, because I cannot come in person, I have sent you the following lines, which I hope you will consider, and which I beseech the God of all grace to accompany with his blessing.

You have been already condemned at an earthly tribunal; you are also condemned by the law of God, for thus it is written, 'Cursed is every one that continueth not in all things that are written in the book of the law to do them,' Galatians 3:10. If every violation of the divine law exposes you to a curse, what a multitude of curses are ready to fall upon your unhappy souls! And remember this is not the curse of a mortal man, but of the great, eternal, infinite God. If it was dismal to hear an earthly judge command you to be hanged by the neck till you are DEAD, how much more terrible to hear the Almighty Judge denounce that unalterable sentence, 'Depart from me, ye cursed, into everlasting fire, prepared for the devil and his angels!' Matthew 25:41. Had you committed but one sin, this would have been your deserved doom: 'The wages of sin,' of every sin, 'is death,' Romans 6:23. How much more of those manifold sins and multiplied transgressions of which your consciences must accuse you. You are soon to suffer the punishment of the gallows, and you are liable to the vengeance of the most high God; for thus saith the holy word, 'The wrath of God is revealed from heaven against all ungodliness and unrighteousness of men,' Romans 1:18. If against all and every instance of ungodliness, then how much more against your crimes, which have been of the most abominable and horrid kind! 'The wrath of God!' Tremendous word! who knoweth the weight and terror of his wrath! At his rebuke the rocks melt like wax, the earth is shaken out of its place, and the pillars of heaven tremble. How then can you endure the furiousness of his wrath, and the severity of his vengeance? and that not for a day, a month, or a year, but through all the ages of eternity! Yet this is the doom of them that know not God, and obey not the gospel of our Lord Jesus Christ. They shall be punished with everlasting destruction, from the presence of the Lord, and from the glory of his power.'

What can you do in this distressed condition? What, indeed! If you had a thousand years to live, you could not atone for one offence. How then can you make satisfaction for millions of provocations in the space of a few days? Alas! you are lost, utterly lost, in yourselves irrecoverably lost. May the God of all power make you sensible of your undone state! sensible that you are upon the brink, the very brink of an amazing, an unfathomable downfall. Perhaps you may say, Is there no hope then? is the door of heaven shut, and without any possibility of being opened to us? Must we sink into unquenchable burnings; and is there not so much as a twig for us to catch at? Yes, my poor fellow-sinners, there is not only a twig, but a tree, even the tree of life, a sure support, which if the Lord enables you to lay hold on, you may yet, even yet, be saved. Oh! beg of his wonderful goodness to accompany what you are going to read with his Holy Spirit.

Christ, the all-glorious Son of God, pitied the deplorable case of such sinners. He not only pitied, but resolved to succour and relieve them. For this purpose he came into the world, and was made man. Nay, more, he came into the place, and stood in the stead of sinners. Because we had broke the commandments of the law, he fulfilled them in all their perfection. Because we deserved the punishment of the law, he sustained it in its utmost extremity. He became poor, and had not where to lay his head, though heaven and earth were all his own. He submitted to scorn and reproach, though all the angels of God are bidden to worship him. Nay, he was condemned to death, the most shameful and tormenting death, far more shameful, and unspeakably, more tormenting, than the death which you must shortly undergo. He suffered unknown pangs in his body, and inconceivable anguish in his soul, from the indignation of God. In a word, he suffered all that shame, all that torment, all that vengeance, which the unnumbered sins of the whole world deserved. Here then is your door of hope. Sins are borne by Christ; and though there be much iniquity, there is no condemnation to them who are in Christ Jesus, Romans 8:1. Wrath is borne by Christ, so that sinners, who deserve eternal vengeance, are reconciled to God, and saved from wrath through him, Romans 5:9,10. A righteousness is wrought by Christ, a perfect and everlasting righteousness, such as brings in comparably greater honour to God's law, than all our transgressions bring dishonour. By all this, he has merited and obtained a full deliverance, and a complete redemption. Are you not ready to cry out, O blessed Saviour! O precious redemption! What a happiness, if we might be interested in this Saviour, and partake of this redemption! Millions of worlds for such a blessing! You need not give millions of worlds, no, nor any individual thing. These blessings are given freely, without money, and without price, without any deserving qualifications in us. All that are justified, are justified freely through the redemption that is in Christ Jesus. But we are sinners, vile sinners; we have not only nothing good, but much and grievous guilt. The Lord convince you of this more and more! Yet remember for whom Christ died; 'he died for the ungodly.' What says St. Paul? 'In due time Christ died for the ungodly' Romans 5:6. He died for the unjust. What says St. Peter? 'Christ hath once suffered for sins, the just for the unjust' 1 Peter 3:18. What says our Lord himself? 'The Son of man is come to save that which was lost.' Are you not ungodly men? Are you not unjust persons? Are you not lost creatures? For such, even for such, the divine Jesus died. Wonderful love! adorable compassion! The Lord enable you to lay hold on this hope set before you! Perhaps you may say, We are not only sinners, but the chief of sinners. O that you were convinced of this! To be the chief of sinners makes you unpardonable before men; but this is no difficulty with Christ, and should be no hindrance of your coming to Christ. Christ's merit and righteousness are infinite. They are as able to satisfy for a debt of ten thousand talents, as for a debt of a single farthing. Hear what the Scriptures saith upon this subject: 'This is a faithful saying, and worthy of all acceptation, that Christ Jesus came into the world to save sinners, of whom I am chief,' 1 Timothy 1:15. He came, not to save sinners only, but the very chief of sinners. And he is 'able to save them to the very uttermost.' But our sins are heinous, they have been often repeated, and long continued in. What says the apostle? 'The blood of Jesus Christ cleanseth from all sin.' Another apostle declares, 'By him,' by the divinely excellent Redeemer, 'all that believe are justified from all things'; from all accusations, be they ever so numerous; from all iniquities, be they ever so enormous. Nay, so wonderfully efficacious is the power of his death, that, through his great atonement, sins which are as crimson, are made white, white as snow, Isaiah 1:18. But will Christ vouchsafe his great salvation to us? Hear his own words, 'Him that cometh to me' for pardon and salvation, 'I will in no wise cast out.' Be his guilt ever so great, this shall be no bar. I will not on any consideration reject or deny his suit. Only let him come as a poor underdone creature, and he shall find me willing and mighty to save. Nay, he invites you to come. These are his gracious words, 'Come unto me, all ye that labour, and are heavy laden,' heavy laden with sin and misery, 'and I will give you rest,' Matthew 11:28. I will deliver you from going down into the pit; I will deliver you from the vengeance of eternal fire. All your sin shall be upon me, and all my righteousness shall be upon you. Go to a great man on earth, beg of him to use his interest in your behalf; he would scorn to take notice of you. But your dear, tender, compassionate, most condescending Saviour, invites you to Come to him, and assures you he will not abhor nor cast you out. Go to your earthly judge, entreat him on your bended knees to pardon you: He perhaps cannot, must not: the laws forbid him. But it is not so with Jesus Christ: he has made a full satisfaction for sin; he has made an infinite atonement for sin; and were your sins ten thousand thousand times greater than they are, before the power of his death they would all vanish away; by the washing of his blood they would all be as though they had never been.

This then should be the one desire of your souls, your incessant prayer to God, that you may come to Christ, that you may believe in Christ, that you may be found in Christ: then you will not perish, though you deserve it, but have everlasting life through his name; then you will have just the same foundation for your hope, as I must myself have when I depart this life. When I shall be summoned to the great tribunal, what will be my plea, what my dependence? Nothing but Christ! Christ, would I say, has been wounded for my sins, therefore they will not be punished in me. Christ has fulfilled all righteousness in my stead, therefore I trust to be justified when I am judged. I am a poor unworthy sinner; but worthy is the Lamb that was slain, worthy is the Lamb that was slain, for whose sake I shall receive both pardoning mercy, and everlasting glory. This is my only hope, and this is as free for you as it is for your friend and fellow-sinner, &c.

P. S. What I have written, I shall beg of God to bless; and will attend you with my prayers, though I cannot visit you in person.[1]

### Dealing with those who feel God has cast them off

Hervey's pastoral ministry extended far beyond the boundaries of his own parish. There are scores of letters extant which show how carefully he comforted afflicted souls, never showing false sympathy or encouraging false pride but always turning his correspondent's gaze back to the open arms of the Redeemer. Here is a letter to one who had been reproached, not undeservedly, by scoffers which led him to feel God had not only abandoned him but also cursed him.

DEAR Sir, — I should be glad to suggest any thing, either for your improvement or consolation. But what can I suggest while you entertain such hard thoughts of Christ, and will not be persuaded out of this strange notion, 'That the curse of God has lighted

---

[1]    Letter CXLI

on you, and will follow you to the grave?' Such a thought (and it must he taken up without any real foundation) not only renders you extremely miserable; but will blast all your future usefulness. Suppose you had rebelled against God, even in a more extraordinary degree than even your own imagination can paint; and suppose you were rejected by him at the present; yet what says the apostle St. James? chapter 4:10. 'Humble yourself in the sight of the Lord, and he will lift you up.'

As to the quotations from Mr. —'s letter to you, wherein he observes, with a kind of triumphant malignity, 'That the devil had taken an advantage of you, in relation to some imprudent management in the affair at ——, &c. &c. &c. and dragged you (as he expresses it) through a horse-pond dirtied and wet, to the great diversion of the spectators'; I ask, of what spectators? Of the worldly-minded only, and the envious, to whom your former flourishing estate, as a first-rate Christian, was a constant and visible reproach; yet Christ (though you are now thus depressed) is still your friend, and will break Satan's teeth; and though dirty, will cleanse you; though wet, will receive and warm you.

Now let me put a question to you: Would you reject your child, because, when dressed in its best clothes, he had met with a like misfortune? Or suppose he had rambled out in the snow, and scratched himself with briers, and come to you bleeding and cold, would you turn him out of doors, when he claimed your pity? We do not know Christ well enough. How kind! how good he is to us! What is my kindness and compassion for you (on which you seem to place so high a value) in comparison of Christ's? Have I been nailed to the cross for you? Oh pray earnestly to HIM; for

——        To Him. to Him, 'tis given,
Passion, and care, and anguish to destroy;
Through Him, soft peace and plenitude of joy
Perpetual o'er the world redeem'd shall flow.
                              Prior's Solomon.

He has satisfied God for all your sins; he is your advocate, and has procured for you the inestimable gift of the Holy Spirit to subdue your iniquities. Cultivate the love of God in your heart, and he will make your path of duty plain before you. I dare say, God will make you more abundantly useful than ever. Oh bring your mind off from this destructive notion, 'That the curse of God follows you.' This is a suggestion of Satan's to prevent your usefulness; but remember that text, 'The Lord knoweth how to deliver the godly out of temptation,' 2 Peter 2:9.; and he will certainly deliver you out of this, and restore you to his wonted favour.

Do not select such terrifying texts for your meditation, as in your letter you tell me you have done. It is as improper, as if you should eat the coldest melon, or choose the most slight covering, when shivering with an ague. Choose, the morning after you receive this letter, (by way of antidote to the texts of your own selecting,) the following for your meditation: 'His mercy is greater than the heavens,' Psalm 108:4. 'His mercy endureth for ever,' Psalm 118:1. Put together these two expressions and see whether they do not amount to more than either your imprudences or your distress. You have, to be sure, done amiss, and dealt foolishly in the matter of———. God forbid I should justify your conduct; but oh! let it not be said, let it not be once surmised, that it is beyond the reach of God's unmeasurable goodness to pardon, or of Christ's immensely rich merits to expiate. The Lord loves you with an everlasting love; and take, if you please, the latter part of Isaiah 30:18 for your contemplation: the words are, 'For the Lord is a God of judgment; blessed are they that wait for him.'

None can tell, none can think, what mercy there is with the Lord; with inconceivable tenderness his bowels yearn towards the weakest, frailest believer in his dear Son. We have dishonoured his holiness, and violated his law; but let us not, to accumulate our follies, derogate from the boundless riches of his mercy in Jesus Christ, to all those who seek and entreat it. There is a wide difference between humiliation and despair. Draw near to Christ with an humble boldness.

May you see many, many years on earth; and when the earth shall be no more, may you be received into the New Jerusalem; where dwelleth righteousness, consummate righteousness, and everlasting happiness. This, my dear sir, is my earnest wish and my fervent prayer for you, and for myself; who am, with great compassion and true regard, your obliged humble servant and friend.

P. S.— My favourite author Liborius Zimmermannus, whispers to me on this occasion the following passage: 'Said I not unto thee, If thou wouldst BELIEVE, thou shouldst SEE the glory of God, and experience his goodness, when least deserved, or rather notoriously forfeited?' Hence may we be convinced, that his loving kindness is unbounded, is unwearied, is infinite; as much surpassing all our follies and all our thoughts, as the world of waters exceeds the drop of a bucket. Oh for a spirit of steady faith, to live under the continual belief of this precious, precious truth.

## Hervey the theologian

Few preached justification, reconciliation and faith so fervently as Hervey who extolled them as being the gracious acts of God. These gifts of grace, in Hervey's preaching, were always shown to be anchored in the union of Christ's bride with her Husband and secured in the atonement. The following letter shows how useful Hervey's teaching can be today as, once again, Reformed men are denying the work of God in reconciliation and justification as being a finished work of Christ and even respectable and universally esteemed Reformed writers are denying that justification was a decree of God from eternity and that the believer was reconciled to God in that great work of redemption on the cross. For those brought up on Louis Berkof, it was a great shock to find John Murray in a 1976 Banner of Truth publication denying that justification was a decree of God in true Fullerite[1] style. What a shake-up to our evangelical faith to have Arthur Pink in a 1996 reprint of his 1930-31 *Studies in the Scriptures*[2] telling us that there was never an at-one-ment in the atonement and that reconciliation was not part of the work of Christ on the cross. Hervey comes back to these doctrines repeatedly and they prove a Balm of Gilead to the modern evangelical.

Dear Sir, — It is not the difficulty of answering Dr. —'s questions that makes me avoid it, but the disagreeable nature of the office; as it will oblige me to shew that he entirely mistakes both the nature of the Scriptures, and the nature of man. He would make Dr. — 's and Dr. —'s sentiment of things the touchstone of divine revelation. What is level to their apprehensions, must be right; what comports with their notions, must be true. At this rate, they are not doers of the law, but judges. On the contrary, if they do not understand the doctrine of union with Christ or the fitness of free justification to promote holiness, it is because their understandings are darkened; it is a sign, that they want the eye-salve; a proof that their senses are not exercised to discern between good and evil.

Dr. — has Roman virtue; but indeed he very much wants the eye-salve. He sees no glory and comeliness in Christ, but much in his own conformity to the commands of his Maker. While such sentiments possess the mind, people have no eyes to discern the beauty of free grace. Christ is just as insignificant as the physi-

[1]   *Collected Writings of John Murray*, 2. Systematic Theology, Justification p. 202 ff. Fuller teaches that individual justification is not 'in the mind of God' but is a free offer which becomes effective when the already-believer reaches out and grasps it. See Fuller's *The Gospel Worthy of All Acceptation* and his various articles on justification. See my *Law and Gospel in the Theology of Andrew Fuller*, Go Publications, 1996, pp. 109-129 for a detailed analysis of Fuller's theory of justification and reconciliation after the act of believing.

[2]   *The Satisfaction of Christ*, Truth for Today Publications, 1996, p. 58. Pink's view is far more Liberal than even Fuller's as Fuller taught that reconciliation was procured in the atonement but secured on the act of faith. Pink removes reconciliation completely from the atonement as not being a work of Christ at all.

cian's offering to prescribe for a person in perfect health. I am sure, my poor, lame, mangled conformity to my Maker's commands, fills me with shame, and would make me hang down my head as a bulrush. But my Lord's death, my Lord's obedience, my divine Lord's merit, encourages me, imboldens me, and enables me to say, Who shall condemn me? Be pleased, by the bye, to compare Dr.—'s foundation for comfort and confidence with St. Paul's, Romans 8:33,34. Who is in the right I leave you to determine. I will only venture to assert, that Paul of Tarsus had as much conformity to the commands of his Maker as our amiable friend. Oh that he was less amiable in his own eyes; and knew himself to be 'wretched, and miserable, and poor, and blind, and naked.' See Revelation 3:17.

1st, 'A persuasion of our reconciliation to God, previous to our performance of holy duties.' Dr. — asks, what is the foundation of such a persuasion? To which I answer, the doctrine delivered by St. Paul, Romans 5:10. 'When we were enemies we were reconciled to God by the death of his Son.' From this passage he will see, that reconciliation to God is previous to our performance of holy duties. It is a blessing procured for enemies; and to say, that enemies have performed holy duties, is to confound the difference between rebels and subjects; is to make rebellion and allegiance the same. Nay, more, this blessing has no manner of dependence on our performance of holy duties, because it is procured, not partially but wholly procured by the death of Christ. It is not said, when we, who were some time enemies, began to perform holy duties; but when we were enemies, while we were enemies; and considered only as enemies. Then, even then.—Wondrous grace! grace worthy of a God! Will not such grace incline the rebels to throw down their arms?

The Doctor, having laid down some premises, makes this inference: 'Hence the phrase of our reconciliation to God, when we have renounced our sins.' But does this inference tally with the apostle's declaration, or is it the proper consequence of his doctrine? Let not the acute disputant, but the wayfaring man, judge.

'Our blessed Saviour,' adds the Doctor, 'directly asserts, that the performance of religious duties is the sole evidence of reconciliation.' We are not inquiring about the evidences of reconciliation, but about the way to acquire them. To determine what are the evidences of a cure, is easy enough; but to prescribe the expeditious and certain method of working the cure, this is the thing we want, Here, according to my poor opinion, Mr. Marshall excels much in the spiritual, as Dr. — in the animal *Therapeutica*.

The Doctor urges our Lord's words, 'Ye are my friends, if ye do whatsoever I command you.' Wandering from the point again.

The question is, How we shall be animated, strengthened, and enabled to do them?

'Upon this subject reason tells us, that such a discharge of religious duties can alone convince a Christian of the sincerity of his profession.' It may be so: but pray, Madam Reason, do not be impertinent, we did not ask your opinion upon the point; if you would speak to the purpose, you must tell us, how we may be enabled to discharge these religious duties. Does your ladyship know, which is the first religious duty? tell us honestly and explicitly, how we can perform this duty? I question it; be content therefore, to receive information from Scripture: 'Thou shalt love the Lord thy God with all thy heart.' This is the first religious duty: now tell Dr. — and me, tell us honestly and explicitly, how we can perform this duty? Is it possible to love the Lord, to love him with all our heart, if we look upon him as incensed against us, unreconciled to us? Is it possible to love him, when we apprehend ourselves to be under his wrath, or suspect that he will prove an enemy to us at the last?

The Doctor having a higher opinion of reason than I, is a greater favourite with her; I would therefore beg to know of him, what reply she makes to this interrogatory; and I promise beforehand, that I will stand to her award, if she can point out any method of practising this duty, different from that proposed by Mr. Marshall; then my favourite author and myself will submit to the charge of enthusiasm.

2ndly, 'A persuasion of our future enjoyment of the heavenly happiness, previous to our performance of holy duties.' I ask Mr. Hervey, 'What is the foundation of such a persuasion?' Mr. Hervey answers, Our free justification through Jesus Christ, which we receive under the character of ungodly persons; consequently before the performance of good works, Romans 4:5. I answer again, The free promise of God: 'God hath given unto us eternal life,' 1 John 5:11. But is not this promise founded on our own duties and obedience? No; but on the duties and obedience of our great Mediator. 'This life is in his Son.'

In the first book of the sacred writings is this important interrogatory, made by God himself, 'If thou dost well, shalt thou not be accepted?' Here I beg leave to ask, in my turn, Which is the person who does well? Dr. —, who would persuade us to reject the gift of God, 1 John 5:11, and not believe his word? or Mr. Marshall, who would engage us to credit the divine declaration and receive the divine gift? The apostle says, by not believing this record 'we make God a liar,' 1 John 5:10. And shall we call this doing well? or is this the way to be accepted?

The Doctor farther urges, In the very last chapter of the same sacred volumes we are told, 'Blessed are they who do his commandments that they may have a right to the tree of life.' Let me ask again, Does the Doctor remember what the commandments of the Almighty are? He may see them reduced to two particulars and ranged in the exactest order, 1 John 3:23. The first of these commandments is, 'That we believe on the name of his Son Jesus Christ.' Let the Doctor only interpret this precept, tell me what is included in this injunction, and I am inclined to think, he will find each of Mr. Marshall's preliminary articles contained in its import. To believe in Christ, is to live under a persuasion that he has died to reconcile me to God; that he has obeyed to obtain eternal life for me and intercedes in heaven that I may receive the Holy Ghost the Comforter. Take away these ingredients from faith and its spirit evaporates; its very life expires; you have nothing left but a mere *caput mortuum.*

The Doctor charges us 'with spiritual pride.' But is it pride to confess ourselves ungodly wretches, and as such, to receive free justification from infinitely rich grace? 'With presumption and unwarrantable persuasions,' But is that a presumptuous claim, or that an unwarrantable persuasion, which is founded on the infallible promise of God, and implied in the very nature of faith? He bids us beware, lest we be the dupes of our own credulity. We thank him for the friendly admonition; and to show our gratitude, we would suggest a caution to our worthy friend, that before he argues on a religious subject he would gain clearer ideas of its nature. He talks of reconciliation, as implying concern and grief. Here he fights with a shadow, and a shadow of his own raising; no mortal ever affirmed or dreamed of any such thing.

Reconciliation is neither more nor less than a removal of offence and a restoration to favour. He mentions Mr. Marshall's three propositions as the requisite signals of faith; whereas they are the constituent parts, the very essence of faith. They differ as much from a signal as the florid blood and lively spirits differ from the bloom on the cheek, or the sparkle in the eye. He tells us, 'That the faith of the Jews was one thing; but after our Saviour's death, the faith of the Gentiles was another.'[1] St. Paul, who was a Jew by birth, and an apostle of the Gentiles by office, tells us the very reverse. There is one faith, of which Christ, the Lamb slain from the foundation of the world, was and is the invariable object. 'To him give

---

[1]    This, as seen in *Aspasio Vindicated*, was the doctrine of Wesley which thus makes it impossible for Abraham to be the father of all believers.

all the prophets,' as well as all the apostles, 'witness, that whosoever believeth in him shall receive remission of sins.' Believing in
Christ, we see, is the one, constant, unalterable way, in which both
Jews and Gentiles, the hearers of the prophets and the converts of
the apostles, obtained pardon, life, and glory.

Had Dr. — observed this caution, he would not have spent so
many needless and random words on the third proposition, which
proceed upon an absolute mistake of the point 'We advocate for
self sufficiency in man!' I wonder how the ingenious Doctor can
entertain such a suspicion, especially as he knows we have subscribed, we believe, and we maintain the tenth article of our Church.
He has blamed us for this belief; therefore he should, in all reason
blame himself for those extravagant excursions of his pen; which
are just as far from sobriety and fact, as the Antipodes are from the
latitude of London.

Our maxim and Mr. Marshall's meaning is, Though less than
nothing, though worse than nothing in ourselves we can do all things
through Christ's strengthening us.

I am, &c.

# Bibliography

**Hervey's Works**

Hervey, James, *Meditations and Contemplations* (with 'Life'), London, 1804.
Hervey, James, *A Series of Letters from the Late Rev. James Hervey, M. A. to the Rev. John Ryland, M. A. containing, Six Years' Correspondence before his Death which happened December 25, 1758. Never before printed* (appended to John Ryland's *The Character of the Rev. James Hervey, A. M.*, London, 1791).
Hervey, James, *The Works of the late Reverend James Hervey, A. M.* (with 'Life'), (6 vols.), 1771.
Hervey, James, *Meditations and Contemplations In Two Volumes* (with poems of appreciation), Edinburgh, 1774.
Hervey, James, *Letters to the Right Honourable Lady Francis Shirley*, eighteenth century but undated.
Hervey, James, *A Collection of the Letters of the late Reverend James Hervey* (Two vols. with 'Life'), Thomson, Benson, Bland et al, eighteenth century but undated.
Hervey, James, *The Works of the Rev. James Hervey, A. M.* (with 'Life'), Thomas Nelson, Edinburgh, 1837, including:
*Meditations among the Tombs*
*Reflections on a Flower Garden*
*A Descant upon Creation*
*Contemplations on the Night*
*Contemplations on the Starry Heavens*
*A Winter Piece*
*Theron and Aspasio*
*Aspasio Vindicated*
*Letters to Mr. Cudworth*
*Amendments Proposed in Theron and Aspasio*
*Marshall on Sanctification Recommended*
*Sermons on Several Important Subjects*
*Remarks on Lord Bolingbroke's Letters on the Study and Use of History*

*Considerations on the prevailing custom of visiting on Sundays*
*A Treatise on the Religious Education of Daughters*
*Preface to Burnham's Pious Memorials*
*Letter on Traill's Works*
*Promises to be pasted on Bibles*
*Letter to Richard Nash, Esq.*
*Rules and Orders of the Assembly for Christian Improvement*
*Hints for promoting Religion*
*Preface to Jenk's Meditations*
*General Collection of Letters* (Preface by Editor)
*Jacobi Hervey de libro Jobi epistola ad Carolum Thayer* (with translation)
See Periodicals for further works.

## Biographies other than those included in editions of collected works

Anonymous, *Some Account of the Life of the late Rev. Mr. James Hervey*, Gentleman's Magazine, 1760, vol. xxx, pp. 377-381.

Brown, John, *Memoirs of the Life and Character of the Late Rev. James Hervey, A. M.*, London, 1822.

Coxon, Francis, *Christian Worthies* (2 vols., 'James Hervey 1713-1758, one of the first of the 'Evangelicals' in vol.1), Zoar Publications, 1980.

Ella, G. M., *James Hervey: The Prose Poet*, Evangelical Times, Vol. XXVIII, No. 9, p. 15.

J. H. O. *Hervey, James (1714-1758)*, Dictionary of National Biography, vol. ix, OUP, pp. 733-735.

L., Michaud, *Biographie Universelle Ancienne et Moderne, Nouvelle Edition*, Tome Dix Neuvième, pp. 361-362.

Middleton, Erasmus, *Bibliographia Evangelica* (4 vols., *James Hervey* in vol. 4.), subscription, 1784.

Ryland, John, *The Character of the Rev. James Hervey, A. M.* (including a collection of Hervey's letters to Ryland), London, 1791.

Ryle, Bishop J. C., *James Hervey of Weston Favell, and his Ministry*, in *Christian Leaders of the Eighteenth Century*, Banner of Truth Trust,1978.

Tyerman, Luke, *The Oxford Methodists: Memoirs of the Rev. Messers. Clayton, Ingham, Gambold, Hervey, and Broughton*, New York, 1873.

## Works dealing with Hervey and background material

Abbey/Overton, Charles/John H., *The English Church in the Eighteenth Century*, Longmans, Green & Co., 1887.

Addison, William, *The English Country Parson*, Dent, London, 1948.

Andrews, J. R., *George Whitefield, A Light Rising in Obscurity*, Sovereign Grace Union, 1930.

Balleine, G. R., *A History of the Evangelical Party in the Church of England*, Longmans, Green & Co., London, 1911.

Balleine, G. R., *The Layman's History of the Church of England*, Longmans, Green & Co., London, 1923.

Bready, J. Wesley, *England: Before and After Wesley*, Hodder and Stoughton, 1939.

Bull, Josiah, *Memorials of the Rev. William Bull*, James Nisbet, London, 1864.

Carpenter, S. C., *Church and People 1789-1889* (3 vols), SPCK, London, 1933.

Carter, C. Sydney, *The English Church in the Eighteenth Century*, Church Bookroom Press, 1948.

Coleman, Thomas, *The Two Thousand Confessors of Sixteen Hundred and Sixty-Two*, John Snow, London, 1860.

Cornish, Warre F., *A History of the English Church in the Nineteenth Century*, (2 vols.), Macmillan, 1933.

Cudworth, William, *A Defence of Theron and Aspasio*, see 1837 edition of Hervey's *Works*.

Cragg, G. R., *The Church and the Age of Reason*, Penguin Books, 1960.

Dallimore, Arnold, *A Heart Set Free: The Life of Charles Wesley*, Evangelical Press, 1988.

Dallimore, Arnold, *George Whitefield* (2 vols.), Banner of Truth Trust, 1979.

Deacon, Malcolm, *Philip Doddridge of Northampton (1702-51)*, Northamptonshire Libraries, 1980.

Ella, G. M., *Law and Gospel in the Theology of Andrew Fuller*, Go Publications, 1996.

Ella, G. M., *William Cowper: Poet of Paradise*, Evangelical Press, 1993.

Ella, G. M., *Paradise and Poetry*, The Cowper and Newton Museum, Olney, 1989.

Ella, G. M., *William Huntington: Pastor of Providence*, Evangelical Press, 1994.

Ella, G. M., *John Gill and the Cause of God and Truth*, Go Publications, 1995.

Fairchild, Hoxie Neal, *Religious Trends in English Poetry*, Vol. II (1740-1780, New York, 1942.

Fisher, Edward, *The Marrow of Modern Divinity in Two Parts*, Philadelphia, undated.

Gill, Frederick C., *The Romantic Movement and Methodism*, Haskell House, New York, 1966.

Gillies, John, *Memoirs of the Life of the Reverend George Whitefield, M. A.*, T. Johnston, Falkirk, 1798.

Harrison, Archibald, W., *The Evangelical Revival and Christian Reunion*, Epworth Press, 1942.

Hart, A. Tindal, *The Curate's Lot*, John Baker, London, 1970.

Hart, A. Tyndal, *The Eighteenth Century Country Parson*, Wilding & Son Ltd, 1955.

Huang, Roderick, *William Cowper: Nature Poet* (Chapter 2, *James Hervey and Cowper's Literary Environment*), OUP, 1957.

King, James and Ryskamp, Charles, *The Letters and Prose Writings of William Cowper*, 5 vols, Clarendon Press, Oxford, 1979-1986.

Lecky, William E. H., *A History of England in the Eighteenth Century* (7 vols.), London, 1899.

Lecky, William E. H., *Rise and Influence of the Spirit of Rationalism*, Longmans, Green & Co., 1910.

Loan, Marcus, *Oxford and the Evangelical Succession*, Lutterworth Press, London, 1950.

Macaulay, Thomas B., *The History of England From the Accession of James II*, Everyman, 1917.

May, G. Lacey, *Some Eighteenth Century Churchmen; Glimpses of English Church Life in the Eighteenth Century*, SPCK, London, 1920.
Moorman, J. R. H., *A History of the Church in England*, Black, 1958.
Nichols, John Broadhurst, *Evangelical Belief*, Religious Tract Society, 1899.
Overton, J. H., *John Wesley*, Methuen & Co., London, 1905.
Overton, John H. / Relton, Frederic, *The English Church 1714-1800*, Macmillan, London, 1906.
Pickles, H. M., *Benjamin Ingham*, private and Huntingtonian Press, 1995.
Plummer, Alfred, *The Church of England in the 18th Century*, Methuen, London, 1910.
Poole-Conner, E. J., *Evangelicalism in England*, FIEC, London, 1951.
Reynolds, J. S., *The Evangelicals at Oxford 1735-1871*, Blackwell, Oxford, 1953.
Robertson, Sir Charles Grant, *England under the Hanoverians*, Methuen, London, 1938.
Quinlan, Maurice James, *Victorian Prelude: A History of English Manners (1700-1830)*, Columbia University, New York, 1951.
Romaine, William, *The Whole Works of the Late William Romaine, A. M.* (with 'Life'),
B. Blake, London, 1837.
Ryle, J. C., *Christian Leaders of the Eighteenth Century*, Banner of Truth Trust, 1978.
Schmidt, Kuno, *Das Verhalten der Romantiker zur Public School*, Bonn, 1935.
Schöffler, Herbert, *Protestantismus und Literatur*, Göttingen, 1958.
Scott, John, *The Life of the Rev. Thomas Scott*, Seeley and Sons, London, 1825.
Scott, Thomas, (ed. John Scott), *Letters and Papers*, Seeley and Sons, London, 1824.
Scott, Thomas, *The Force of Truth*, Banner of Truth Trust, 1984.
Shepherd, T.B., *Methodism and the Literature of the Eighteenth Century*, Haskell House, New York, 1966.
Sidney, Edwin, *The Life and Ministry of the Rev. Samuel Walker, B. A.*, Seeley and Burnside, 1838.
Simon, John S., Robert Culley, *The Revival of Religion in England in the Eighteenth Century*, London, undated.
Stanford, Dr. Charles, *Men Worth Remembering: Philip Doddridge*, Hodder & Stoughton, 1880.
Steadman, Thomas, Ed., *Letters to and from the Rev. Philip Doddridge, D.D.*, Shrewsbury, 1790.
Toplady, Augustus Montague, *The Works of Augustus Toplady*, Sprinkle Publications, 1987
Trevelyan, G. M., *English Social History*, Reprint Society, 1948.
Tyerman, Luke, *The Life of the Reverend George Whitefield* (2 vols.), Need of the Times Publishers, Hodder and Stoughton reprint, 1995.
Venn, Henry, *The Life and a Selection from the Letters of the Late Henry Venn, M. A.* (with 'life' by John Venn), John Hatchard, London, 1835.
Wakeman, Henry Offley, *An Introduction to the History of the Church of England*, Rivington's, 1914.
Wesley, John, *Works*, (16 vols), London, 1812.
Whitefield, George, *George Whitefield's Journals*, Banner of Truth Trust, 1960.

Whitefield, George, *Letters 1734-1742*, Banner of Truth Trust, Edinburgh, 1976.
Whitefield, George, *Letters, A Select Collection of Letters* (3 vols), London, 1772.
Whiteley, J. H., *Wesley's England*, Epworth Press, 1945.
Wood, A. Skevington, *The Inextinguishable Blaze*, Paternoster Press, London, 1960.
Wright, Thomas, *The Life of Augustus M. Toplady*, Farncombe, 1911.

**Periodicals**

(A number of the Hervey and Wesley letters listed below are available in other works included in the Bibliography.)
A.B.C., *To the Author of a Pamphlet called the Polyglot, On the Doctrine of Justification by Faith*, Gentleman's Magazine, 1761, vol. xxxi, p. 204.
Anonymous, *Further Anecdotes of the late Rev. Mr. Hervey*, Gentleman's Magazine, 1760, vol. xxx, pp. 553-554.
Anonymous, *Of Reconciliation with God (criticism of Hervey and Marshall)*, Gentleman's Magazine, 1760, vol. xxx, pp. 555-556.
Anonymous, *The Excellent of the Earth: James Hervey*, The Gospel Herald and Voice of Truth, Jan. 1, 1869, pp. 107-109.
Baker, Frank, *James Hervey: Prose Poet*, London Quarterly and Holborn Review, pp. 62-68 (copy undated).
Champion, L. G., *The Theology of John Ryland*, Baptist Quarterly, 28(1), 1979, pp. 17-29.
Clark, H. H., *A Study of Melancholy in Edward Young*, Modern Language Notes, XXXIX, pp. 129-136, 193-202.
Crito, *A Dialogue respecting the Works of the late Mr. Hervey*, Gentleman's Magazine, 1960, vol. xxx, pp. 468-469.
Cudworth, William, *Answer by the Author of the Polyglot to Crito's Remarks*, Gentleman's Magazine, 1761, vol. xxxi, pp. 251-252.
Ella, G. M., *Whose Righteousness Saves Us? (Hervey's doctrine of righteousness examined)*, Bible League Quarterly, No. 366, July-September, 1991, pp. 436-442.
Ella, G. M., *The Poor Man's Preacher (Risdon Darracott)*, Evangelical Times, Vol. XXVIII No. 12, December 1994, p. 16.
Ella, G. M., *Philip Doddridge's Rise and Progress of Religion in the Soul*, Evangelical Times, Vol. XXIX No. 02, February, 1995, p. 15.
Hervey, James, *Letter to Dr. Watts*, Evangelical Magazine, 1811, p. 338.
Hervey, James, *Letter to George Whitefield*, Evangelical Magazine, 1794, p. 373.
Hervey, James, *Letter to George Whitefield*, Evangelical Magazine, 1794, p. 503.
Hervey, James, *Letter to George Whitefield*, Evangelical Magazine, 1794, p. 295.
Hervey, James, *Letter to John Wesley dated Dec. 1, 1738*, Arminian Magazine, 1778, p. 132.
Hervey, James, *Letter to John Wesley dated Sept. 2, 1736*, Arminian Magazine, 1778, p. 132.
Hervey, James, *Letter to John Wesley*, Methodist Magazine, 1847, p. 965.
Hervey, James, *Letter to Mr. Pearsall*, Gospel Magazine, 1777, p. 298.
Hervey, James, *Letter to John Wesley*, Arminian Magazine, 1778, p. 34.
Hervey, James, *Letter*, Evangelical Magazine, 1777, p. 73.
Hervey, James, *Letter*, Evangelical Magazine, 1802, p. 393.

Hervey, James, *Letter*, Evangelical Magazine, 1806, p. 28.

Hervey, James, *Letter*, Gospel Magazine, 1771, p. 174.

Hervey, James, *Letter*, Gospel Magazine, 1771, p. 176.

Hervey, James, *Letter*, Gospel Magazine, 1771, p. 179.

Hervey, James, *Letter*, Gospel Magazine, 1775, p. 255.

Hervey, James, *Letter*, Gospel Magazine, 1777, p. 260.

Hervey, James, *Letter from the late Rev. Mr. Hervey to his Father, not published in his works*, Gentleman's Magazine, 1760, vol. xxx, pp. 75-76.

Hervey, James, *'Theron & Aspasio' on the Bible*, Bible League Quarterly, No. 366, July-September, 1991, p. 456.

Wesley, John, *Letter to Mr. Hervey*, Arminian Magazine, 1778, p. 136.

Oliver, R. W., *John Collet Ryland, Daniel Turner,* Baptist Quarterly, XXIX, 1981, pp. 77-79.

Porter, Laurence E., *James Hervey (1714-1758) A Bicentenary Appreciation,* The Evangelical Quarterly, 31, 1959, pp. 4-20.

Ryle, Bishop J. C., *James Hervey's End*, Bible League Quarterly, No. 366, July-September, 1991, pp. 442-443.

# Index of Persons and Places

# Index of Topics

# Index of Works Quoted

# Index of Scriptural References

*Other titles by* **George M. Ella**

# JOHN GILL

## AND THE CAUSE OF GOD AND TRUTH

'From the beginning men who obviously never read Gill warned me of what they called his "tendencies" toward Hyper-Calvinism and Antinomianism. Having read almost everything Gill wrote, I am still searching for even a hint of these "tendencies". Instead, I have found in all his writings the most faithful exposition of Holy Scripture, a consistent Christ-centred, Christ-exalting theology, and a constant, robust declaration of God's free and sovereign grace in Christ.'

*(extracted from Foreword by Pastor Don Fortner)*

**Large paperback, 368 pages, £9.95    ISBN 0 9527074 0 3**

---

# LAW AND GOSPEL

## IN THE THEOLOGY OF ANDREW FULLER

Andrew Fuller's theology changed the face of evangelicalism at a time when new lands were opening up to the gospel. Fuller was hailed as a teacher for a new era and his theological mark is evident still in the preaching of our day. What did Andrew Fuller teach and just how valuable has been his legacy to the Christian church?

Having written highly acclaimed works on William Cowper, William Huntington and Dr. John Gill, Dr. George M. Ella turns his able hand to exposing how one man's ideas, which pass for evangelical Calvinism, have little to do with true Biblical Christianity.

Dr. Ella deals with a subject of great importance to Bible-believing Christians; a widespread and popular system of theology which has blown a chill-wind over many ministries and blighted much faithful preaching of free grace. This book will be of great interest to all who long for the recovery of distinctive, Christ-centred gospel preaching in our churches today.

**Large paperback, 236 pages, £8.95   ISBN 0 9527074 1 1**

**Go Publications, The Cairn, Hill Top, Eggleston, Co. Durham  DL12 0AU**
*(send for list of publications)*